THE WHITE FENCE
ICONS AND LEGENDS IN A SMALL TOWN

Recollections of Eastern Long Island
before it became "The Hamptons"

By: Anton Prohaska

Copyright © 2014 by Anton Prohaska

All rights reserved. This book or any portion thereof
may not be reproduced or used in any manner whatsoever
without the express written permission of the publisher
except for the use of brief quotations in a book review.

Printed in the United States of America

First Printing, 2014

ISBN-13: 978-1502388544
ISBN-10: 1502388545

Library of Congress Control Number: 2014916736

GRATIA
BOOKS

TO MARTHA

Photographs courtesy of:

The History Project Inc.
The Prohaska Family
Louise Edwards
Frances Gardiner
East Hampton Library, Long Island Collection,
Harvey Ginsberg Postcard Collection

TABLE OF CONTENTS

PREFACE	1
PART I: FAMILY - FRIENDS - NEIGHBORS	3
EARLY DAYS	8
WALKING TO SCHOOL	12
GRADE SCHOOL	14
TOMMY	16
DRINKING BUDDY	20
MICKEY	21
CAROLYN'S STUDIO	26
THE OLD MAN	29
YAWN, WORK, FISH	35
RAY AT WORK	40
CAROLYN	45
EARLY CAROLYN	47
CAROLYN GOES TO WORK	55
CHESTER	60
MY PARENT'S: COURTSHIP AND MARRIAGE	66
KITTY, RUBE, AND THE '35 YUGO TRIP	70
JULIAN LEVI	75
THE EAST END	78
POST WAR AMAGANSETT	90
THE EX PATS	94
RAY JR. AND DOLLY	97
MOVING TO THE MAIN STREET HOUSE	99
ELENA	103
SONNY	106
NEIGHBORS	110
EDWARDS	119
THE FISHING VILLAGE	121
BUDD AND RUTH KING	122
LEONARD AND HERTER	128
JOHNNY ERICKSON	132
BOBBY "SCRATCH" BYRNES	139

> SCRATCH 141
> BOBBY AND MIM 144

SCRATCH, WAR AND AFTER 149
> HARRY STEELE 151
> BRUCE COLLINS 153
>> PINK GOLD 157
>> BRUCE HUNTING 158
> CARL, BILL, AND MARY ANNE 160
> JOHNNY MAXWELL 165
> SPORT WARD 167

COCKTAILS 168

BREAKDOWNS 170

SCUTTLE 172

ERICKSON BREAK-IN 174

RAY AND ABSTRACTION 176
> POLLOCK 178
> ARTSY KIDS 180

ADJUSTING AND COMPLAINING 181

DEATH OF ANASTASIA ILICH, 1955 182

ELSIE JOE AND THE BANTIES 183

SHAGWONG PICNIC 185

FISHING WITH RAY 187
> WRITERS AND FISHERMEN 191

LUCIA AND ROGER 194
> ROGER 196
> THE HOUSE ON ABRAHAM'S PATH 202

BRODOVITCH 206
> ALEXEY MEETS ROGER 209
> KLOON AND DE KLINING 213

JEFFREY POTTER 217
> PENNY 229
> JEFFREY'S BUSINESS 231
> JEFFREY THE WRITER 236
> JEFFREY'S ACCIDENT 238

    PATSY 239
BEACH HAMPTON 241
    TELEVISION 244

PART II: HORSE PEOPLE 252
    WOOLNOUGH'S 252
    FANNY 254
    DICKINSON FAMILY 258
    RODEOS 261
    THE DEEP HOLLOW RANCH 263
    THE HURRICANE OF 1938 268
    PARS AND JOSEPHINE 269
    WORLD WAR II 270
    PINCKNEY ISLAND 271
    POST WAR 274
    FRAN 275
    CHAMP 280
    ROY LESTER 282
        ED WELLES 289
        LIVERY STABLE 295
        DRIVING HORSES 301

PART III: COCA COLA, CIGARETTES & BEER 303
    BEATING 303
    CHRYSLER 306
    1956 307
    SICK DAYS 310
    HIGH SCHOOL 311
        HAIR 314
        MAIDSTONE CLUB DANCE 316
    SPRING FEVER 318
    THE FOX 322
        MOVIE BREAK 323
        DANCING, CARS, AND BEER 324
        CARTWRIGHT JUMBOS 327
        VIRGIN 329
        BARKER 330
        PEORIA 334
        GRADUATION 335

EPILOGUE 339
ABOUT THE AUTHOR 353

ANTON PROHASKA

The Prohaska House. Main Street. Amagansett, New York Ca. 1950

PREFACE

During WWII, Amagansett, New York was a sleepy village where it wasn't uncommon for a dog to fall asleep in the middle of Main Street. At the first hint of spring you could hear the chug-chug-chug of a John Deere tractor, and as the days grew warmer you could smell a perfume made up of a briny ocean breeze, freshly turned brown loam, limed seed potatoes and honeysuckle. Roosters crowed, cows mooed, and later in the season came the smell of DDT that was sprayed on the potatoes, and a peculiar and very potent fishy smell that came from the Smith Meal fish processing plant, a couple of miles to the northeast.

I was too young to remember my family's move from Manhattan to the little village on the eastern end of Long Island. My family became what in later years were known as year-round summer people. In my early grade school years I was the only child in that category. Although I remembered living nowhere else, I was considered to be "from away."

ANTON PROHASKA

PART I: FAMILY - FRIENDS - NEIGHBORS

I don't remember when I began the habit of sitting on the front fence. I suppose it was when I got big enough to climb up without a struggle. By stationing myself there on regular and frequent occasions I wasn't doing something purposeful, or if I was, the reasoning is long forgotten, but I could see all of Main Street. In retrospect it seems as if it was an almost instinctive move. Directly across the street was the post office, the place of arrival for the manuscripts and sketches that led to the illustrations that paid our bills and helped to keep the family calm. So the fence was kind of a look-out post, a place to exercise and tune up my hyper-vigilant way of observing things. I suppose I was also making a stand; being seen, and in a passive sort of way, being part of the action of the community. If I understood that to be an observer was to be part of the community, well then, I give myself credit for that.

    The fence was made of locust posts and three rows of one by four pine, with a top board lying flat on the top rail, which made it a good seat. I usually sat on the west end of the fence in front of a garden that had big clumps of Tiger Lilies and Irises, Lily of the Valley, and Bleeding Hearts and went back along the neighbor's property line. The garden was narrow, six feet wide and edged with railroad ties. A flagstone walkway went from a gate in a stockade fence that blocked the view of the patio to the front gate. Another run of stockade fencing followed the neighbor's large row of arborvitae back to our car garage and the beginning of the neighbor's extensive dog kennels.

    Along the front of our house, just behind the white fence, were several big Rose of Sharon, both white and pink, and a couple of round clipped privet bushes, and in front of my father's studio, a big Snowball Tree. I would usually drink a Coke while sitting on the fence. In those days it tasted so much better than it does today, and came in a nice green bottle made of hard glass. There was always plenty of Coke stored along with seltzer and tonic in the cool dirt-floored cellar; and when I finished one I'd flip the bottles into the big overgrown forsythia on the neighbor's property. At some point I would collect the bottles and take them to Toppings Store and trade them in for an Orange Crush and a Heath Bar, which I'd enjoy while sitting at the counter. At the same time I would function as a spy, all ears, gathering information about the village. Altogether, that pleasurable adventure cost fifteen cents. (Five Coke bottles and one Hoffman's Black Cherry quart bottle equaled fifteen cents.)

To my left across the street was the library, an old two storied shingled building that had been donated to be used as a library by a member of the Summer Colony. The librarian was Florence "Flossie" Eichorn, who gave off a scent of unbelievable rankness, possibly a result of her clothing and person having not been, for many a moon, too near a bar or a box containing soap. Stage left from there was a tiny real estate office, a small liquor store, a two-story brick fronted old-fashioned grocery store, Embro's, which had sawdust floors and a big wheel of store cheese on the counter, and next to that a newspaper store with a lunch counter; Toppings. After that there was a vacant lot, and then LaCarrubba's, a shoe repair shop, shoe store, and dry-goods store, all housed in an old Coast Guard building which had been moved from the beach at the turn of the century. Next to LaCarrubba's was The Amagansett Inn, a saloon with a good Italian restaurant run by Mrs. Catalano.

Having perused the dirty parts of adult novels like those my mother read, and *Saturday Evening Post* manuscripts that my father was sent, which were underlined for possible illustration ideas, and which were sometimes spicier or more sophisticated than one might expect considering *The Post's* square reputation, I was having adult sex fantasies precociously. I would sit on the front fence and watch the hot local housewives exit their cars and sashay into the post office, sometimes in tight jeans and bobby socks, and imagine, well, that they were mine.

The biggest event though, in terms of the post office surveillance, was seeing Patsy, who showed up daily, in bare feet during the summer, which my mother Carolyn seemed mildly offended by. Patsy was the beautiful young wife of a soon-to-be-famous writer. It seemed to me that not only I but my mother and father too kept a sharp eye for Patsy's appearance. It was an event. I was at my post, for instance, on the day she pulled up, it was diagonal parking in those days, and went inside leaving the car running. One of her two kids, Luke or Carey, both rug-rat stage, slipped the convertible into gear and allowed it to hop up and ram the west corner of the post office's brick-face. No one seemed to pay it any mind except Louis Nielson, the John Barrymore look alike postmaster, who briefly got to comfort Patsy before she drove off.

Before it was tarmacked sometime in the Sixties, Main Street was a mile of straight macadam facing more or less east and west. For geographical accuracy's sake, the East End is somewhat north of east, but for the sake of simplicity the citizenry tend to mentally align themselves with the beach, which runs northeast from someplace one hundred miles to the southwest along a straight line of sand aiming northeast in the general direction of Greenland. At ground level the eastern end is fifty feet higher than the west end. During hurricanes and northeasters the west end of Main Street became a lake rivaling the neighboring village's Town Pond, until, in the Sixties, a huge dry well was built just north of the highway.

Over the years the brick faced building with a stuccoed arch above, on my right-hand side next to the post office which had originally been built in the 1920s to house an A&P market went through a series of reincarnations. From the 1930s up until the early 1950s it was Joe's Restaurant, an ice cream parlor and family restaurant. Then it became a saloon, then another saloon, and another, and finally, in the late 1950s, it became a sort of Tea Room restaurant owned by a couple of middle aged homosexuals from Manhattan who kept an antique Rolls Royce parked right in front of the front door. They called the place Gordon's, my parents called it piss-elegant, and only went when someone else was buying. It remained Gordon's for the decade that "The Boys," as they were called, had it, and into an era when one of their cooks bought it, bringing us up past the time of the boy sitting on the fence and on into another century.

I made going to the post office into one of my family chores. Often there would be a big package, some returned sketches of a manuscript, that I could deliver to the studio. "Thanks, chum," the Old Man would say. Sometimes he'd come out of the studio to go to the post office himself, and I would follow him. I suppose I did it because that was where the action was, both good and bad; checks and bills.

When I was very little I would hold his hand until mostly across and then run ahead, and for one period during my growing up years, once in the building I would hook my hand around one of the steel columns in the middle of the front room and spin myself around it, making a squeaking sound with my palm as I did so. It was a nice ritual.

In those days the post office was the number one place in Amagansett for the whole village to congregate. The mail and freight came in on the night train, was sorted by Ira Baker, the Station Master at the Railroad Station, and delivered to the post office in the early a.m. Be there at seven in the morning and you would run into anybody you wanted to see.

There were two types of people in my life from the beginning. My parent's type, sophisticated and educated, and mostly residents of New York City, and the local type, a sub-category of what I began to think of early on for no well thought-out reason as real Americans. In dull, realistic terms, my parent's type of people were probably mostly politically left wing and either in the art or the magazine worlds.

Except for my parents, I became more bonded with the locals. Particularly the women. And that began with our two neighbors, the Milligans and the Ericksons. I'm sure my mother thought she was a modern and sophisticated mother. She was not the maternal type, I'm quite sure something she was aware of, but I don't think she thought it was a detriment. She was a friend-mother. From the time I could understand English, we were a co-dependent work-in-progress. But her deficit in the area of mother hen type nurturing left a vacuum which was easily filled by women who were close at hand.

I'm sure I would have been more comfortable had my father been a commercial fisherman, or a farmer, or a mechanic. There were many ways in which he was different from the other kid's fathers, all of which amounted to a cumulative sore point for me. He didn't recede into a proper place in the community; he stood out. He was a big man (by far the biggest father in my class.) He had been a little too young for the First World War, and a little too old for World War II.

Though he was raised in California from the age of eight, and spoke the clear unaccented English of a San Franciscan, he had been born in Eastern Europe in what was then the Austro-Hungarian Empire and the Kingdom of Yugoslavia. He was a magazine illustrator, at the top of his field, but as time went on it did begin to bother him that he didn't have more time for serious painting. He was a good "serious" painter.

Growing up, I came to believe, from the way they talked about their lives in Manhattan, and how much fun they seemed to have had there, that the most unusual, not to say perverse, thing that my parents ever did was to move to Amagansett full time and raise their kids there. My mother, who had been a busy and successful model and had studied acting before switching to painting, once told me by way of explanation when I asked, after a typical city people visit, "Where are the kids?" that their social group was "not big" on children.

One morning as we entered the post office, with me following close behind the Old Man (I think I was eight at the time), I dawdled, doing a figure eight between one support beam and the other, the squeaking of my hand on the pole blending with the ambient noise of the post office and the village outside, while my father worked the combination of the mailbox. And then the hypnotic morning routine was broken by the voice of a post office kibitzer who had his established place by the radiator under the bulletin board where the "Wanted!" signs and less important information was posted, next to the postmaster's window. The kibitzer made this snide remark; "Well, if it ain't the Artiste!" It was Ken Mulford, summer manager of the Amagansett Beach Club at Main Beach, performing for his two favorite idolaters, two little guys who were mechanics at Tucker's Garage, both of whom began snickering hysterically. I stopped spinning and hugged the round girder as my Old Man, in khaki shorts and leather sandals, a uniform that said "queer" in no uncertain terms to any local worth his salt in those days, walked up to Ken. About my father's size, Ken was considerably larger than his two sidekicks and was shocked into paralysis when he found himself lifted up by the front of his bib overalls and slammed against the wall hard enough so that his head made the whole building vibrate.

I rarely stayed around when the Old Man lost his temper. While he didn't often get into fights, if he hit you it wasn't theatrics. One of his favorite tricks was a quick, hard open-handed slap to the side of the head that made the recipient's ear pop and his head ring. Over the years I felt it myself more than once. Whether he popped this guy's ear or not I couldn't tell, as my view was blocked, but I distinctly remember hearing my father say, "From now on you'll say Good Morning, Mr. Prohaska, or nothing at all. Got that Buster?" After that the threesome shrank away.

In Grade School

EARLY DAYS

I grew up and went to the public schools on eastern Long Island from first grade through high school, at a time when city slickers, let alone artists' kids (both my parents were artists) didn't do that. Though we moved to the East End when I was less than two years old, my peers always considered me a city kid. Since being thought of as "from away" didn't bother my parents, they thought it shouldn't bother me. But it did. Up to my teen years I thought they, my parents, had sprung full grown from the party atmosphere of the magazine illustrator, artist, writer and radio personality crowd that they hung with in 1930s Manhattan, a time they remembered and kept alive with seasonal parties, filled with booze and lobster and visits by their collection of sophisticated city friends.

The kids in my grade school class were all from families where the parents went from childhood to parenthood with no in-between period of social singleness. Of the eleven kids who progressed together from first to eighth grade, four were from families whose male breadwinners worked in fishing related jobs, either through fishing or at the "Fish Factory," as we called it, a plant that made fertilizer out of menhaden, a fish commonly called bunker. The core class consisted of six boys and five girls. A few other children appeared for a year or two, kids from migrant farmer families or from the Air Force Base in Montauk, kids who would be gone when their father's jobs were done.

Geographically, East Hampton is located on one of two peninsulas, the North and South Forks, which stick out from the eastern end of Long Island like a fish's tail fin. East Hampton encompasses the eastern half of the bottom fin, Southampton Town the western half. On the northern side of East Hampton Town, north of the village of Amagansett, is an area called Springs, named for its abundant springs which drain into several harbors, the largest of which is Three Mile Harbor. On the east side of Springs is a small inlet called Accabonac, or by abbreviation, Bonac. Traditionally, people who live in the area around the inlet are called Bonackers, and until recent times they spoke a dialect called Bonac, a remnant of the Kentish dialect spoken by their forebears who came from that part of Southern England in the 17th and 18th centuries. The East Side refers to the area on the eastern side of the inlet where most Bonackers lived, and the main road through that little hamlet, the road from Springs to Amagansett, is called Old Stone Highway.

The word Bonacker, a term practically unknown outside the area of East Hampton, is a complex one, full of inconsistency and nuance. In the 20th century, in fact, the name became fluid, with some East Hamptoners calling themselves Bonackers no matter what part of the town they lived in. The Fire Department put the name Bonacker on its trucks. The name was alternately used as a proud appellation and as a derogatory slur (meaning poor and stricken with a backwoods accent.) Among high school kids, it was used to denote those born on the wrong side (literally) of the railroad tracks.
Not being an official local because of my citified parentage, and the fact of my birth in a New York City hospital, caused me no small amount of discomfort. From the time I remember having friends outside the family, I had difficulty explaining to my peers, and to myself, what exactly it was that was wrong with my parents. My world at school was old-fashioned, countrified, and square. Our home was a place of art, loud music, gourmet food, sophisticated talk, passionate beliefs and occasional violent temper tantrums.

Except for his fishing buddies and a few commercial fishermen, who told him where the fish were, my father Ray wasn't much interested in making local friends. He might have gone to two PTA meetings in his entire life, and that was like pulling teeth, for Carolyn, my mother, who shared his lack of interest in community bonding.

I never expected I could be like him; it seemed to me that he owned the magic in the studio, and that fishing, almost an obsession with him, was part of the alchemy. I didn't know it then, but I suppose I was looking for something, some sense of mastery, that I could call my own. He had put me in charge of yard work, mowing the lawn, bringing in firewood, and I had my Banty chickens; but the house was too much his; I was like a cartoon mouse, forever running into the little black hole in the wall that was my bedroom to avoid being swatted when he was trying to concentrate. I sensed, though, that while the Old Man was either in his studio or in the city, or beating a path straight to the ocean, the rest of the countryside was up for grabs. So I became a wanderer through the back lots of the village, through the potato fields and the woods. Maybe it was just being a kid, but the imprint that the countryside put on me was personal. My nose was finely tuned to all the different smells. I could have walked from my backyard to the beach blindfolded, and known where I was by the timothy hay in the apple orchard, the chocolaty loam in the potato fields, the potato blossoms and the honeysuckle and the shadbush on Bluff Road, and the wild grapes and beach plums and the swamp smells on the second dune. I was a nature lover.

Both my parents were brought up in cities, my mother in Newark and Jersey City, and my father in San Francisco. They had both studied art, both had successful careers in the city, and both had been married once before, to equally citified people. My father was a man of the world with a powerful personality and a powerful physique, not the effete Hollywood stereotype of an artist that was popular in the movies in those days. But to me the fact that he was an artist was itself a stigma. And, worse than that, though he had no accent, he was a foreigner. My mother was beautiful, rather short and busty for a former model, and somewhat of a smart-talking dame in the tradition of Dorothy Parker or Bette Davis.

Up until the early post-WWII period, the time of my earliest memories of my parent's world and the time when I first became aware of my surroundings, there was no clearly defined line of demarcation between Fine Art and Illustration. By the time I was a teenager, though, there was quite a wall being built between the two modes of expression. I was aware enough to understand the need for the separation. It was the result of a real revolution in painting, and the elevation of the importance of American fine art on the world stage. But, in my youthful identification with my father, I always felt caught in the middle, for two reasons, the first was that the local people whose kids made up my entire friend base were uniformly prejudiced against modern art, but showed respect and admiration for my father's illustration work. Reason number two was that my father was trying to do the impossible, which was to work both sides of that increasingly fortified line. As I was growing up, during the decade of the Fifties, I found it more and more difficult to answer that perennial childhood question, "What does your father do?" To the local kids, I emphasized his illustration. When they said, "What does he paint that shit for?" referring to the abstract works they would see when they came to the house, I was at a loss. I kept trying to explain it to them, the way he explained it to me, but I got nowhere. It was a language that I understood but couldn't translate.

In the summer there were a few extra kids around, and they were from two completely separate groups. The most visible group was the one from the old summer colony, which included Bluff Road and the group of large stuccoed mansions called Devon. I ran into these kids mostly at the Beach Club on Main Beach. Since they were children of successful business people, I emphasized his illustration, reasoning that commercial fame equals money. I made superficial friends with a few of these kids, who thought of me as a well-to-do "townie."

The other group of kids were children of art dealers and buyers, psychiatrists, writers, including almost any of those known as the New York Intellectuals, as well as people who were having romantic affairs with any or all of the above, and, after 1950, most of the existing television writers producers, actors, and directors in New York City.

I met most of these very adult seeming children when I tagged along with my parents to cocktail parties in Springs, or Mecox, or Beach Hampton, a privilege I enjoyed more than I let on. I was secretly and precociously attracted to alcohol and adult women, and these gatherings, which always included at least someone who counted as a star in the art world, were prime fodder for anyone with even the slightest of voyeuristic tendencies. The small population of kids belonging to this gang affected grown-up ways and went to bohemian left-wing schools like The Little Red School House and New Lincoln in New York. The girls smoked cigarettes by the time they were fourteen, and had deep whiskey voices. The boys seemed like little psychiatrists. When I came across these little monsters, who seemed to me like Charles Addams characters (he was often in the crowd), I tried to downplay what they called my father's "commercial" art (they said it with such disdain), in favor of his "serious" painting. I remember feeling like an outsider among the children of these New York City swells, and feeling mildly resentful about it.

As a complete population, the summer kids didn't double the small kid population and there was hardly any social mixing. There was nothing terribly advantageous in associating with them, other than for comparison of the us-versus-them kind.

WALKING TO SCHOOL

Walking to school on any given morning, Main Street, with its remaining elms, thinned but still stately, past the little green-roofed Catholic Church, and past Ayle's Garage, an old fashioned wooden storefront with an apartment to one side, where you could hear the household activity of George and his woman of the moment, the world seemed alive and benevolent. I hated school. It meant leaving my safe cave, my attic bedroom, in a house trembling with vitality. My father's studio hummed with its powerful hi-fi and his dynamic energy. Home seemed like a smarter place to be than school, which seemed like a demotion, a bogus sort of place; not any place Ray or Carolyn would have gone to. And the idea that one was supposed to learn something there, seemed like the basis of the bogusness. For some of the local boys at least, it was a place to hang out till you were old enough to quit and join one of the haulseining crews. (Haulseining is a form of commercial fishing with a long net taken from the beach through the surf by boat, then hauled back to the beach by hand or winch.)

No, I didn't like school. In my attic room I had my big globe and my *National Geographics*. I had the world at my fingertips. I found places on the globe, like Belem, Brazil, and constructed a fantasy life for myself and then carried that life around with me back to school, as ballast to counter my feeling of being a foreigner.

Coming from a house where the father had such an unorthodox way of making a living, where the parental way of life, so infused with the worlds of art and culture, was so glaringly different from that of the other adult parents in the village, made for a difficult job of self-presentation for me. It made for an asymmetrical environment, something that mightn't have bothered a boy of hardier stock, of which there was plenty on both sides of my immediate family. But instead of the necessary thick skin, I inherited oversensitivity and an unspecified mass of negative character traits.

From the Old Man there were the appetites. I inhaled food, money burned a hole in my pocket and, mostly at home, and in front of the two people I wasn't afraid of, my mother and sister, I often burst into rages. From Carolyn, I inherited the touchiness, the snobbery, the feeling of isolated specialness, the tendency to ruminate. From both parents, I no doubt inherited the pathological narcissism gene.

Our class in Amagansett Grade School was small. As I've said, there was a core group, and then there were a few kids who were there for a year or two before moving away. The core group was six boys: Tommy, Mickey, Billy, George, Jack, and me. There were five girls: Doris, Elaine, Josephine, Linda, and Lavinia.

Since most of us are still alive I'll say that some of us had experienced familial dysfunction; been beaten, seduced, betrayed, over-worked, and/or ignored. Even in such a tiny class, we had our leaders. They were Josephine and Tommy. Josephine was the best student. Her father was a truck farmer, a farmer of small acreage, and her mother was an immigrant from Poland, a no-nonsense farmer's wife who made a small farm stand into a very good business. Jojo, as she was called, was quiet but not shy and paid attention to the teacher, no matter how distracting the weather outside might be: snow, rain, or sea smell wafting on a spring breeze. None of our teachers seem to have been talented enough to extract from the homespun little group of War Babies that we represented, that fire-in-the-belly level of attention that is written about in books on education. But, in the eighth grade, in response to some urging that no one else in the class even seemed to hear, Jojo wrote a term paper on opera. It was like a book, with pictures, drawings, and synopses. She had read translations, borrowed records from somewhere, and listened to them. The teachers, and the kids, were impressed.

There were, except for me, no spawn of city slickers in my class, nor in the classes ahead of me, though there had to have been the odd duck over the years. Those few children that the art crowd produced in those times, didn't begin to appear as local school students, until after my War Baby class was in high school. My younger sister Elena's class had a couple of these kids, transfer students, who had the benefit of some New York City private or public school sophistication.

GRADE SCHOOL

First grade was also my teacher's first year. Mrs. Joyce, Peggy Joyce, was full of enthusiasm, and there were only a few kids in the class, maybe four, so we got lots of attention. We built a cardboard house big enough for a first grader to stand up in, and braided a rag rug for its floor. Because The War was just over and so few kids had been born during the last five years, the whole school was held back to increase its head count. So I joined a larger second grade. I didn't like the teacher, though, and I became self-conscious and bratty. By third grade my marks had mysteriously slid. I was having trouble learning cursive handwriting. The teacher tried to get me to use my right hand but I resisted. I still have sloppy handwriting. By fourth grade Alice Milligan, our neighbor and a retired teacher, was tutoring me in arithmetic.

My parents tried to con me into thinking that tutoring was a respectable part of the educational process, but I became convinced that I had a fatal flaw. Even the two kids who in sixth grade were still reading Dick and Jane could do the multiplication tables and solve the written problems concerning apples and oranges and trains and stations. By the seventh grade I would be in a cold sweat just thinking about being called on in class. I had full-blown Arithmaphobia. The eighth grade teacher wasn't above using ridicule as a tool either, or even corporal punishment. Because he was also the gym teacher, he brought physical discipline into the classroom. I could feel his impatience when I'd fumble and blush with nervousness over a simple arithmetic problem that most of the other kids could do in their heads. When my ignorance really began to wear on him he'd call me up to the desk, have me put my hands on the edge of the desk, and whack me with his yard stick. (He did it to a couple of the other boys, too, but not to girls.)

I was smart enough to know that as a grown-up I would be faced with the same problems that appeared at the end of each chapter in the text book. I knew it would get worse and worse ad infinitum. Arithmetic made me feel completely defeated. It became so obvious that the principal and seventh grade teacher, Harrison Schneider, searching for a cause, proclaimed on my report card that I suffered from a defeatist attitude. Nothing changed, and I continued to suffer, until the invention of the calculator.

Starting in fourth grade, Friday afternoon was for religious instruction. The kids were divided into Catholic and Protestant and sent to their respective churches. The Protestants went east to a handsome old parish hall in back of the Presbyterian Church. The Catholics went the other way to the cellar of the little green shingled chapel next to Ayles' Garage. I had rarely gone to Church, other than as an infant to be baptized, and neither of my parents had shown much interest in religion until this new activity was started.

My father told me that it's something he went through, and that "it's good for you." No more than that. No heavy pressure. "You don't have to believe all the hocus pocus," they both agreed, tentatively. I went through religious instruction from about fourth grade until my second year of high school, went through Communion and Confirmation and even tried out, with my friend Tommy, for altar boy. After one Mass we were both fired. We had, naturally, tried the wine, and broke into a fit of hystcrics during the Mass. My father had been an altar boy, but his career in the church had also been brief.

Tommy and I both lacked the fundamental ingredient: piety. Although we could both fake it, we couldn't manage to kill our sense of adventure. Not long after, we broke into the cellar after some sort of a Catholic stag party, and drank what was left of a keg of beer. We were consumers of sin.

When I had begun to do poorly in school (after first grade) my parents became concerned. "What are we going to do about him," they'd say; first Carolyn, then Ray. Report cards went from bad to worse. And I was also lousy at sports. In baseball, the fear of striking out would immobilize me to the point that I'd just flail helplessly at the ball. In the outfield I'd lose all sense of depth perception and watch as the ball fell fifty feet from me. Or else, after a few sprained fingers, I would dread making the catch; especially when the kid that hit the ball was the one who'd been helping his father pull nets since he was ten.

Occasionally they brought up the suggestion that I go away to a private school, which idea I thought of as a fate worse than death. For one thing, Ray would have to work harder to pay tuition and that would mean less fishing, which would make him unhappy. More than that, though, giving in to the idea that I didn't belong because I wasn't a local, that I truly was a city slicker, seemed like a death sentence. By then, I had my heart and soul invested in belonging.

When arguments proved ineffective, I played the beleaguered

lunatic. I had tantrums. These were screaming fits, in which I faced up to my parents about how little they seemed to be affected by my pre-adolescent angst, how they weaseled out of helping me with school work, and how snobbish they were about my friend's families. Somehow, I managed to explain to them that, what today I'd describe as The Art Religion, was distancing them too much from the community I lived in; but though they listened, obliquely, while going about their business, painting or doing the dishes, they didn't really give a rat's ass. In today's vernacular they would probably have said I should man up.

In retrospect, I think I was surprisingly clear in my berating of those two. But Ray and Carolyn had their own life blueprints; they had both managed to give themselves extraordinary self-educations, through reading, attending lectures, concerts, and visiting numerous museums, without receiving high school diplomas, so they didn't see why I felt so helpless. I had a mysterious problem that someone else would have to fix; or I'd have to fix it myself. And I would do that, but it would take longer than anyone expected.

TOMMY

From my earliest days in grade school I had two best friends: Tommy Scott and Mickey Miller. Tommy and I were friends and playmates in that fog of early childhood that is impossible to recall because you haven't come upon the need for memories; but a time when people can make deep impressions on you. Tommy's mother, Eileen, was our housekeeper, a position which I suppose today would be called a mother's helper. She had been a pastry chef on a private estate before coming to work for us in our first home on Hand Lane in Amagansett. She helped Carolyn with the cleaning and occasionally made lunch or dessert. She made the best rice pudding; it had a skin on it, like crème brûlée.

My mother, too, was busy keeping the house in order, but she had other chores. She was always busy, stripping and waxing woodwork, making curtains, making sets and costumes for Ray's illustrations, taking the three hour train trip into N.Y. see her analyst, and trying to squeeze in time to go out to her own studio, to keep up with her own painting. (She had studied painting at the Art Students League with Nicolaides and Kuniyoshi, and considered herself a good, serious, although sometimes blocked and frustrated painter.) Mostly, in her mind, she was blocked and frustrated by her obligations to my father and us kids.

Tommy was around so much that he was like an extra sibling. I remember riding double with him on my tricycle and having lunch with him, more often than not, kid food, peanut butter and jelly, grilled cheese or canned spaghetti. One item though, which I thought was unique to Eileen, was boiled potatoes in canned gravy. We loved it. Though he was six months older than me, we went through school from year one to year twelve in the same class. He was my big brother, protector, and when he felt like it, tormentor, which I suppose means whenever I annoyed him or attempted to thwart him.

He was always a beefy kid, average height, black hair, and like me, freckled. His mother, Eileen, was from Ireland, and had married Len Scott, part of a large local family. Len had been a local sandlot baseball star, but had broken his back falling off a ladder while building his own house. He had been left bent over at a ninety degree angle and wracked with arthritic pain. He worked as one of two janitors in the grade school.

The house Len built was a small, but neatly and cleverly built Carpenter Gothic with two shed-roof dormers. The whole house contained probably less than 800 sq. feet. In Tommy's day, it housed him, his parents and two sisters, and was heated with a coal stove. It was Tommy's job to keep the fire stoked by shoveling coal.

Tommy and Mickey each had two pretty older sisters who to some extent spoiled them. Partly because we were white males, I suppose, the three of us, in some ways, were all young princes. But unlike Mickey and me, Tommy didn't have a virile, healthy, paterfamilias at home, one that could turn into a fearful ogre.

Len Scott's period as a local baseball star happened at a time when competition between villages all over Eastern Long Island was fierce. His injuries, though, had made him a sidelined hero. While Mickey and I had powerful and threatening fathers, Tommy's father, although still a local hero, was resigned to sit back and admire his son's confidence. Tommy was a good ball player and tried extra hard to impress his father, who never failed to be parked in his car at the playground whenever Tommy played. They talked baseball constantly. Len monitored radio and later television to keep track of the Big League games and when television arrived in the local taverns it was a Godsend for him. From his earliest playground home-run, Tommy's whole family, father as well as mother and two sisters, and his uncle and cousins across the street, transferred their hopes and dreams for a heroic future on to the male heir.

With Len sidelined by his injury and his pain, for which he drank and took medication, Tommy was the family hero. He took to leadership easily, rising through the ranks of early boyhood hierarchy. I often felt that Tommy's quest to be Chief of Police began in the first grade and was quietly acceded to by the principal and the teachers and the students.

In grade school our small peer group didn't have another incipient strong-man. In school and out, Tommy was the boss. He ruled by intimidation, and well, charm isn't the right word, more like command presence. His aggressiveness was my cross to bear and I didn't question it. Besides, being my best friend, he was also, if I ever needed him to be, my protector. I accepted the way Tommy ruled the roost the way a boy accepts his stronger, older brother. He might punch you in the stomach, or just lean into you. I remember numerous times he got me down on the ground and twisted my arm until I said "uncle." When we played War, I was the Jap, and he was the American. When we played cowboys, I was the Indian. He did the same thing with Mickey. Carolyn said that she saw us as Krazy Kat and Ignatz the mouse, with me being Krazy, the one getting the brick on the head, and Tommy being Ignatz. Of course he was also Officer Pup, so the whole comparison didn't knit seamlessly. Carolyn also said she sometimes thought of herself as Krazy, and me as Ignatz, with Ray as Officer Pup, which, cleverly, made it about her.

From keeping the coal furnace in the cellar going, to shoveling the walk when it snowed, to starting and warming the car in the morning, Tommy was his father's hands and feet. To an extent, his mother and two sisters had made Tommy a surrogate husband and father, which no doubt assisted Tommy in becoming the tiny peer group's alpha male.

In his interactions with me though, Tommy must have felt some stress. In our early childhood, his mother's time was divided between his own home and mine, as she helped Carolyn with housework and with looking after me, my sister Elena and Ray, often cooking our lunch and helping with preparations for Ray's demanding dinner requests. He must have felt he was competing with us for his mother's love, something which in my childish selfishness, I was completely oblivious to. If it occurred to me, I swept it under the rug, and consequently must have oozed privilege and audacity. Adding insult to this, I lived in a relatively large house, full of objects of value, art and antiques, abundant and aromatic food, charming pets and intimidating adults, all of which must have been hard for a kid to compartmentalize, from the outside looking in; though I'm sure that unconsciously he was absorbing it like a sponge.

From my side, it was important for me to be accepted as a local, or as close to one as you could come if you were born "away." In fact, that hoped for acceptance was the single most important thing in my life. In my naive little head it seemed to determine my right to live.

Being an artist's son had no real status in the local community. The talent for producing art was seen as somewhat fluky and useless, at least in the communal mind, though some individuals might have been slightly more open minded. Being Tommy's best friend was my ticket to ride; my entree, as it were. It was like being a blood brother to the Indians. And of course I had the added support of having his cousin, Mickey, as my other best friend. When I thought about it, I might have thought I was lucky, considering that the gene pool was so small, that I had such well-qualified friends, except for the fact that, still, in one way or another, everyone in the small school was more local than me.

After we moved to our Main Street house, when I was still too small to do yard work, Ray often hired a guy named Indian Jim. What sort of Indian he was I never knew, but to Tommy and me he seemed mysterious. On one occasion, when he had neatly raked up a pile of leaves, we jumped into the pile and kicked it around, thinking that was too tempting to bypass. He chased us away with his rake, swearing, which scared hell out of us and caused us without further ado to demonize him into an evil goblin. He looked like "one of those coconut Indian heads that people bring back from Florida," we decided. That began a recurring dream, the first recurring one I can remember; that Indian Jim lived in my mother's studio. I would dream that I'd walk by the studio and see his face staring out the window.

DRINKING BUDDY

I first became aware of the actual effect of alcohol the way many European immigrant's children do, by being served wine mixed with water at the dinner table. This was done when we were small children, at what age I don't remember. I liked it though, that watered-down wine, better than the straight stuff, of which I occasionally had a sip. It went down easy and left a fresh, grapy numbness in my back nasal passages. I felt an immediate and considerable easing of the tension at the familial table; and a slight buzz. But that small amount of wine at the table wasn't a nightly ritual, just an occasional thing, when the Old Man was into his peasant persona.

Sometimes at the end of the school day after Tommy and I had carried the waste paper down to the incinerator in the school cellar, his father would send us across the street to the General Store to buy a quart or two of beer for him and his colleague, fellow custodian Mr. Griffing, brother-in-law of our sixth grade teacher. Mr. Ryan, who owned the store, never questioned us. He and Len were old sandlot baseball buddies. So when the time came, I guess we were about twelve, we began to buy for ourselves, two quarts of Ballantine and a pack of Luckys. Money was never a problem; there was always the change to be swept off my father's dresser.

Next to the Catholic Church was a two acre property with two houses on it. In front was a big white Victorian that was unoccupied in my day for all but a couple of weeks in the summer, when the children and grandchildren of the late Mrs. Pleasant, would appear. In back was a tiny house that was rented by a series of sad single men. Behind the Pleasant property was the same potato field that our yard backed up on. Along three sides was a hedgerow. Only in spring and summer, when young Bart Hadel went back and forth on his tractor, would an adult eye be on the particular part of the hedgerow that was our first drinking spot. It was a corner where someone years ago had left several small granite boulders, probably leftovers from the building of a cellar. There was also, a very large maple tree marking that rear corner lot. There were initials carved in the tree from the previous generation (maple trees don't live that long.) Every kid had a jackknife in those days and every jackknife had a bottle opener, so there was no problem there. The hard part was getting the Ballantine down; it had the flavor of sour Coca Cola. The spot was close enough to my house that at least once in our early drinking career we made it back to my house just in time for both of us to puke all over my bedroom.

MICKEY

Mickey Miller, my other best friend besides Tommy, was a sensitive and observant kid, the kind who would collect rocks for their colors and shapes. He was prone to spontaneous unprovoked happiness. He called his father the Old Man, something I picked up from him and which Ray thought was funny. His old man, whom he referenced with gruff admiration, was a well-respected fisherman.

Mickey's full name was Milton L. Miller Jr, the middle initial standing for Louamina, a name neither of us could figure out. We never did. Milton Sr., called Milt by some, was a handsome man, well built, medium height, with a George Jones crew cut, a tan, wrinkled neck, strong working man's hands, and forearms like Popeye. He was a hard working entrepreneurial sort who had at one time or other done construction, hauled seine, and started a small cement block plant, but never gave up fishing.

Mickey's mother, Etta, was from a North Carolina Eastern Shore fishing family, the Midgetts, that had moved up to Amagansett to work for the Edwards Brothers Fish Company. In our grammar school days, Milton Sr. owned a dragger, the *Liloetta,* named after his wife Etta and his two daughters Lila and Lois.

The Millers lived on Hedges Lane, the first lane to the west of our house, half way between Main Street and The Bluff. There were six lanes in all which ran perpendicular off Main Street heading southeast to the Bluff Road, and the lane at each end of Main Street had a beach at the end of it. Hedges Lane, as well as Miankoma and Hand Lane, were about half empty with vacant lots which were often planted with secondary crops like cabbage or strawberries. The western beach, at the end of Indian Wells Highway was called Main Beach. To the east at the end of Atlantic Avenue, was the Coast Guard Beach.

There was a potato field behind our house which was called the Hadel lot, because Bart Hadel farmed it. It wasn't much more than ten acres, between the building lots on the two lanes that went to the Bluff Road from the middle of Main Street. I always walked to Mickey's house along the edge of the potato field in the furrow that bordered the backyards of Hedges Lane. His was the third backyard, and his house was the only two-story bungalow on Hedges.

Milt was a great story teller. Among the most far-fetched and probably ancient stories that he told to Mickey and me was one he told us when we were quite young. It was about how the sea became salty. It was an elaborate yarn that ended when a man took his magic salt making machine, which other people were envious of, and put it on a boat to bring it someplace where he'd have it all to himself. On his way to wherever he was headed, the boat sank. End of story. We didn't believe it, but we enjoyed listening to "The Old Man," as Mickey called him. (He was probably in his early thirties then, in the neighborhood of 1950.) A few years earlier, he had been in in WWII, in the Coast Guard as a Chief Boatswain's Mate, piloting landing craft at places like Iwo Jima. Mickey and I went into his old foot locker one day, down in the cellar, and found Japanese money, a bayonet, and a pack of Japanese cigarettes which were so dry they went up in flames when we tried to smoke them.

One of Milt's sisters, Mickey's aunt Florence, who was often around, occasionally babysitting for my sister and me, was fond of correcting or even trashing her brother. Milt liked to say that the shack he was born in had been built out of fish boxes and that he had been raised by the fishermen on the beach. These were not literal truths and annoyed Flo. But it was true that the house hadn't been much more than a shack, and it was also true that from the time he was a little boy he'd been mascot to the fishermen on the ocean beach, and as soon as he was able, he'd become one of them.

Tommy, Mickey and I were a Three Musketeers gang, the way boys often do team up. But when we were on the outs with Tommy, Mickey and I would hang together, often just wandering through the countryside. Both of our fathers encouraged us, in words and deeds, to develop a romance with nature. With Spike, Mickey's dog, even before we were old enough to have guns, we spent our time covering the entire village tracking deer and game birds. On several occasions we conspired to beat Tommy up, but we always chickened out on account of what we perceived as his hypnotic personality, which we thought would paralyze us into defeat. During those times we tended to think of ourselves as Tommy's victims. He was stronger than either of us, so at one point we spent a few days in Mickey's cellar, weightlifting with old antique hand irons that his mother had collected.

Without Tommy, we created a triangulation (it makes relationships more stable, they say), by making Spike, Mickey's dog, human. This wasn't hard because, like Border Collies everywhere, he was brilliant. To illustrate:

In the fall of the year when we were in seventh grade Mickey was laid up with a very bad case of poison ivy from walking through poison ivy smoke while his father was in the back yard burning brush. Mickey's eyes were almost swollen shut and his mouth opened only enough for a straw, so that he had to live on milk shakes. He was in misery. I brought him a *Donald Duck* comic from Topping's Store, and we sat in the sun porch while I read him his favorite part, the "Beagle Boys" section. I didn't know then and so couldn't tell Mickey until fifty years or so later, that the inventor of Donald Duck was a contemporary and friend of my father's. His mother left the house to go shopping. She was just getting into her Studebaker when Mickey, spying a little gray kitten sitting directly under the near back wheel of the car, jumped up from the couch and opened the door telling Spike, "Quick! Get the kitten Spike!" And within a few seconds, Spike brought the little critter in and deposited it in Mickey's lap. True story.

Although the three of us branched out somewhat in high school, the triangle bond was still there. Even before we went to high school, Mickey, Tommy and I had talked quite a bit about hunting. We heard hunting stories from the older guys and occasionally ate duck and pheasant that our parents were given by hunters. Neither Milton nor Ray did much hunting.

In our second year of high school Tommy, Mickey and I and most of the boys in town, came into the possession of shotguns, and were given a short course in gun handling by an adult member of the local gun club. (The gun clubs, each East End town had one, raised pheasant and sometimes quail, for the members and anyone with a license to shoot.) Tommy got a 16 gauge Remington pump, I got a 12 gauge pump also a Remington, and Mickey a single shot 12 gauge Winchester. We would follow Spike, or we would comb any brush or woods within walking distance of the village, but sometimes my mother or Mickey's mother, would drop us off near our chosen spot and wait for us.

Today the dunes west of Amagansett Main Beach are sealed off from development and have been turned into a Green Belt, which acts as a buffer between the beach and the houses of the rich and famous denizens of the *New York Times* society pages. They are no longer grassland, but are tick infested, grown over with tall shadbush trees and beach plum bushes. But, in "our day," as the locals say, there was periodic controlled burning and the dunes were a mixture of beach grass, other tall wild grasses, and a few shrubs, and were alive with pheasants. And as an added bonus, if you flushed one and missed it, it would fly up into the Summer Colony estates, where we would be forced to follow. There, a pleasant English park-like environment existed, something ideal for the ancestral right of poaching. It was a nice feeling, flushing a big cock pheasant out of an overgrown garden of sun-dried mums; or taking a shot that might end up peppering the side of a big grey-shingled mansion.

My 12 gauge Remington pump was a present for Christmas 1957, and was accompanied by six plastic Black Duck decoys. On a cold, cloudy morning that winter, with the occasional snow flake swirling in the light breeze, Carolyn drove Tommy, Mickey, and me to Montauk, to a place called Stepping Stones Pond, to do some gunning. (We were probably the first generation of East End hunters who felt fond enough of creature comforts to do a fair amount of our hunting in the warmth of an automobile. True, the older fellows had their hunting camps, which were quite comfortable, but that camp style of hunting was dying out by the late 50's.) We didn't realize that the pond, being connected to Lake Montauk inlet by a culvert under a road, was affected by the tides; so we were surprised when, after we put out my six decoys and Mickey started quacking with his new duck call, the tide lifted the decoys up off their weights and floated them into the middle of the pond. We didn't have Spike with us, so I had to do the retrieving. At least I was able to learn the depth of the pond, up to my rib cage, when I went in after them. But, without waders, I was soaked, so we had to make a day of it and take me home for dry clothes and a hot shower. Carolyn agreed not to tell anybody, especially the Old Man.

The fall we entered high school, Mickey's father ran off with the mother of one of our school chums, leaving Mickey alone with his mother, who was pregnant. Mickey had two older sisters who were out of the house, one in college, and another a very young bride. With no way to pay the rent and nowhere to go, Mrs. Miller moved into a small trailer in the back yard of her brother's house. Mickey, now a 14 year old high school freshman, was stuck in that tiny trailer with his mother and a wailing, diapered, newborn.

I would come by often before school and walk to the bus with him. We would comb our oily pompadours facing a small mirror on the inside of the front door of the tiny trailer. We'd walk to the bus. We'd talk about Tommy, who remained a friend-adversary, a protector-bully, depending on the state of our complex relationship, or about girls, of which we knew little, and occasionally he would refer to his anger about his father, anger which neither of us understood well, though there was no doubt his father had broken his heart.

Mickey survived the abandonment by his father, but he was wounded. Years later he would sometimes refer to those times in a way as to suggest that he'd had a breakdown. I don't doubt that he did, but he suffered through it quietly. Fortunately, his father came back. Torn by guilt and faced with tough going in Florida with low wages and stiff competition for jobs, and being homesick for the special ambiance that is Bonac, Milton and his girlfriend each went back to their spouses and began to pick up the pieces. Milton went back to fishing, the trade he knew best. He moved into his mother's little house, not much bigger than the trailer, with his wife, the baby, Mickey, and his grandmother Nettie Mariah. It was the same house he'd grown up in down on the beach, that had been moved during The War over to the East Side, on property his grandfather had owned, and next door to his brother, Mickey's Uncle Russ, who owned a dragger he fished on out of Three Mile Harbor.

When not in school, Mickey began fishing with his father. How much of that awful winter they spent hashing their feelings out I don't know, but from talking to both of them over the years, I don't think it amounted to much. Their relationship always seemed to me to be one in which Milton talked and Mickey listened. A Filibuster!

Though an uneducated man, Milton had an ego not unlike that of his famous artist and writer friends. And he could use it to spin a shield of words. He did know a lot about fishing and the sea, though, and Mickey has learned it all. From the old fishermen that taught Milt on the Amagansett Beach, he learned hundreds of years of fishermen's wisdom, about how and where and when to catch fish. He didn't stop there, though. He had opinions on everything and sundry, especially Town politics.

From his exposure to the gaggle of left-leaning intellectuals that he'd gotten to know through Peter Matthiessen and Pete Scott, Milt developed a line of thinking that put just about any politician in any office as the bad guy, and he and his fellow fishermen as the exploited party. He was emboldened in this reasoning by a legend, either passed down from someone in his family or created out of the whole cloth of Milton's mind, that, long ago, back in England, the Miller family had been swindled out of a fortune.

One day after he was settled in over on the East Side I rode my bike over to Mickey's house for a visit. We were sitting on the couch in the tiny living room smoking cigarettes when his Miller grandmother, Nettie Mariah, came in with a male admirer, Bill Bassett, well-known local ladies' man.

I don't know how that little house fit three people and a baby but it did, and everyone except the baby smoked. In those days most people started smoking in their teens and as far as I can remember few parents ever said anything. I remember how compact that little house was. It probably wasn't five hundred square feet. The living room, smaller than most small bedrooms, had two tiny couches, a small book case with a small black and white TV on top of it, and an old radio along-side. The bookcase was filled mostly with books about fishing and books by Peter and a few of the other writer friends that Milton had picked up through Peter, and a pile of *National Fisherman* magazines. Each couch took up a whole wall. Bill Bassett and Nettie Mariah sat down, lit up a cigarette and said hello to Etta who was in the kitchen just a few feet away, and engaged in some small talk. Then, with little advance notice and both of them toothless, they began ferociously making out!

Mickey was, to put it mildly, embarrassed. He never quite said it, but when we were out hunting a few days later he allowed as how he thought it was disgusting and kind of an affront to his dignity, not in so many words; he was sensitive but not wordy.

CAROLYN'S STUDIO

With two kids and with assistant duty required in Ray's studio, scenes to be photographed for later use in painting illustrations, with occasional dresses to make or alter (sometimes with the help of Betty Bunker, a seamstress and the wife of the radio and TV repairman), and models and sets to put together, Carolyn had too much to do in the house to get out to her studio often. When she did, her painting could at any time be called to a halt by the Old Man's needs. He might need help in the studio, or a sandwich, or he might come down with an attack of bursitis or a cold and need a hot water bottle or an aspirin.

Not having time to paint was a thorn in her side which was not hard to interpret. She had a capacity for stoicism that came no doubt from her wasp ancestry, but her Irish side could break through on occasions when she would swear at my father that "Goddamit I need time to paint!" She was an artist too, don't forget. During those occasional quiet times, though, when she would go to her studio and work, she painted crockery, flowers, driftwood, children and, on occasion, a landscape.

When I was eleven she painted me in a blue-grey parka holding an orange and called it "Local Boy." I remember being determined not to look happy, as if that way I'd make my statement for posterity. I suppose the statement, if I'd put it into words, would have been something about what was wrong with my mother's thinking, for instance, "Why the stupid orange? Why must my hood be up? Why doesn't she work faster, like Ray?" She wanted me to hold the orange in my hand the way Queen Elizabeth, at her Coronation, had been holding a jeweled orb, in a picture torn from a magazine and tacked to her studio wall.

I remember coming home from school for lunch, I was still in the grade school, and she had twenty minutes to work on the painting, for which I would earn fifty cents. I tried to concentrate on the money and not on the fact that someone eventually was going to look at this picture with me holding an orange in a way no self-respecting twelve year old would ever hold a piece of fruit. As instructed, I was wearing my blue parka with the hood up and with the coat hanging over my shoulders like some affected city-person. If I took a break or scratched an itch, she would be frustrated because it wasted so much time getting "Local Boy" back into the right position. But I'd had lots of practice posing for Ray, so I was good at standing still. I would stare off in the distance, and tune in to some short-script daydream. "Are you going to smile or frown," my mother would ask, and I would frown again.

"Are you doing my head, Ma?" I remember asking in a pained whine, and she said no, she was working on my hands. My mother's style of painting was mannered and delicate; she was careful, and progress was slow. I scratched my nose and let my eyes wander around the studio to the old dented bird-in-a-gilded-cage that hung from a rafter. When wound up, this half molted bird, a family heirloom (though eventually I found out that everybody and his brother had one) would chirp its mechanical but still eerily lifelike song and give me a nostalgia for my fast receding childhood.

On a stool in a corner she had placed an ironstone dish and a matching pitcher and in the pitcher was a bunch of dried oregano with a yet another stuffed bird perched in the twigs, which she was using as a prop in a painting of a neighbor's daughter. The painting was stacked above a pile of window screens behind me. I looked up in the rafters at an antique cradle balanced there and tried to remember being in it. My mother shifted her feet quietly. To keep her feet warm she was standing on my father's old raccoon coat that he had worn to Princeton football games with his friends and Princeton graduates the Rankin brothers. She freshened her palette. The itch on the tip of my nose began to burn. I put the orange down on the window sill and scratched the itch with my parka sleeve. "I'm done," I said, defiantly. "OK, its twelve thirty, I have to make Dad his lunch," she said, giving up.

When my mother was painting, she seemed happy enough, and gave the impression of someone who was always on an even keel. Though I don't think she liked being interrupted, she enjoyed, at a time of her choosing, leaving a painting unfinished. She was big on Process.

But a fight with the Old Man over an unbalanced checkbook, or some thoughtless criticism from him, or from one of us kids, could cause her to blow up like a brush fire and when she was in a rage she was fearless and could match the Old Man with her fury. She might threaten to leave him, or us, to stop being our "scullery maid," and drive out of the driveway spraying gravel against the studio wall, leaving the household alone for an hour or so, to think, to notice her absence, while she drove the back roads, pulling up at a beach after having calmed herself, to watch the windswept waves and the sea ducks. Periodically she would run into Manhattan on the train for a tune-up with her analyst, Dr. Ribble.

I have no doubt that the decision to move to Amagansett helped my parents to remain together and to become a family, and I feel that with all the bumps in the road, "The Hostilities," as Carolyn referred to the family fights as well as Ray's rages, that my sister and I were better off than if they had gotten divorced. This thinking on my part, though, is after decades of thoughtful consideration. I also think, though, that the aforementioned idea is a reactionary one, from the point of view of mid-20th century enlightenment.

The idea that someone other than Carolyn might have raised my sister and me brings forth interesting ideas; perhaps I would have been pacified, if more warmly nurtured by an earth-mother type. Or, on another tack, perhaps someone with a stronger hand towards Ray could have better defended herself and me, and even kept him in harness better; less fishing, more working, more attention to the books. Or, with a different father, Carolyn might have been less neurotic and complained less about not having time to paint. But, for better or for worse, in the house on Main Street, what had started as a love affair turned into a family, no matter how flawed.

Father and son ca. 1944

THE OLD MAN

He was a magazine illustrator who also painted "Fine Art." Among my earliest memories of him was sitting on his lap in his studio while he drew. On a work table, stacked in piles, and tacked on the walls, and lying around on the floor, were stacks of photographs and sketches. There was a big storage rack for paintings, behind which was a workbench for framing, two big wooden filing cabinets for "scrap" (mostly torn pages from magazines to use for reference), a bookcase full of over-sized art books and an old *Encyclopedia Britannica*, and behind the bookcase, a darkroom which included a red, painted toilet seat.

I particularly remember a photo of my mother modeling a Lilly Daché hat; and another of my father looking a little like a young Jack

Dempsey, almost naked, doing the hula with a scarf wrapped around his waist and a flower in his ear. There was another picture of my mother looking tenderly at an infant, me, in her arms. I also remember from early on, riding his shoulders along a broad, white, sandy beach. I remember his warm skin and the smell of his hair and the dizzying height and marvelous view from on high.

Raised in California from the age of seven, he had been born in what was then the Kingdom of Yugoslavia, part of the Austro-Hungarian Empire, on February 5, 1901, in a small stone house on the water's edge, beside a bay called Boka Kotorska, in a village called Muo. Muo is a tiny hamlet on the Dalmatian Coast a mile outside the walled town of Kotor (Cattaro in Italian), about thirty miles south of Dubrovnik. My father was the first surviving child of a mother who had had numerous miscarriages. At birth he was named Gratia, after Saint Gratia, the patron saint of the area around Muo. (His name was changed to Raymond when he came to America, at the suggestion of his first school teacher.) Both children, Gratia and Graciella, were named after St. Gratia, patron saint of Muo.

House in Muo where Ray was born

He had few clear memories of his childhood in Montenegro, but there was one childhood story (whether remembered or handed down to him by his mother) that was important to my father, and probably helped shape his ideas about himself: He had been a small child taking part in a religious procession at a little chapel (Sveti Gratia, named after the saint), high on the mountainside above the family's waterfront home. The ceremony included his mother and Godmother, many older people from the village, several priests, and the area's Roman Catholic Bishop. When someone rang the chapel bell too hard, it fell down from the tower and just missed both the

Bishop and my father, then named Gratia, who was holding up the Prelate's trailing gown. To his mother and the other women in the village, the event was considered a miracle, a belief they must have imparted to the child, because, for the next eight decades, until the day he died, he carried with him a feeling that he had been touched by the hand of God. He always felt lucky, privileged, and, perhaps through God and his mother both, entitled to a certain degree of freedom.

It was my father's Uncle Sam (Sam Ilich, my grandmother's brother) who came to California in the 1890s, who helped the family immigrate. Sam was by then a fairly well-off man. He had started out buying and selling cattle in the East Bay, in Oakland and Berkley, and then opened a restaurant. He liked the start-up phase of restaurant owning best, and would sell as soon as business was going well. Over the years he owned more than 20 restaurants, usually luncheonettes or blue plate special places. He was a more understanding man than his sister's husband and became something of a substitute father for Ray, whose own father was ever-present but emotionally absent.

Sam helped his brother-in-law's family immigrate. First came my grandfather Sima (Simon in English) six months before the 1906 earthquake, followed a year later by my father and his mother Anastasia and his sister Grace. A year after settling into their new home at 9th and Irving in the Sunset District of San Francisco they had another daughter, Antoinette.

Ray professed to love both sisters but thought the younger one, Antoinette, was "a bit simple," possibly from having become comatose after drinking a bottle of wine as a toddler. He did, though, pay for her to go to secretarial school, and she managed to hold down a secretarial job until she retired.

Throughout her life Antoinette was an avid though somewhat infantile letter writer, repeating a litany of the boring details of her life in a San Francisco suburb and her job at Schlage Lock factory and my mother was the only family member who cared enough to answer her letters. Neither of the sisters was much interested in Ray's career, so he was somewhat dismissive of them. Though having grown up in America, the two sisters were both forced into arranged marriages and both eventually divorced and remarried. Grace, the older of the two, married three times. Neither sister had children.

Simon was a shoe and boot maker and presumably a good one, because with help from introductions by Sam, within a year he had established a good business. According to my father, "the Old Man" worked in his shop all day, eating little, drinking Turkish coffee laced with brandy and smoking Cue-Bab cigarettes. He was a gruff, burly man with a handlebar mustache, the son of an Austro-Hungarian Army officer. Though he lived in Kotor when he married my grandmother and referred to himself as a Croat, his family, probably in his father's time, had been moved from Bohemia in what is now the Czech Republic by the Austro-Hungarian Army.

Their new home in America was at the outer reaches of the developed city of San Francisco, in the Sunset District, an area that had escaped the worst damage from the 1906 Earthquake. To the west toward the ocean were only sand dunes. The building included an apartment upstairs and, on the ground floor facing Irving Street, his shop and eventually a shoe store. He must have been a resourceful man and talented in his trade because with the help of samples of his work brought from Europe he quickly acquired a contract with Federated Hospitals of San Francisco and began making all their orthopedic shoes.

Ray was supposed to inherit the shop. He learned the trade quickly, seemed to have a talent for it, and especially enjoyed the Ghirardelli Chocolates he would buy on his frequent trips downtown, with the small change he stole from the cash drawer. When my father announced that he wanted to go to art school, though, his father took him into the cellar and beat him with a homemade cat o'nine tails. That beating erased any admiration he might have had for the Old Man.

As a small child, he had begun drawing religious pictures for his mother. She encouraged him, and with the help of her brother Sam, overcame Simon's insistence that he continue in the shop. After one year of high school, where he was a good student and won a medal in the broad jump, he transferred to the California School of Fine Arts, where, early on, he became a favorite student and protégé of Lee Randolph, the new Director. He studied Art History and learned anatomy by drawing from plaster casts and dissecting cadavers before being allowed to see the live model. He learned about color by grinding his own pigments.

By the end of his second year, Randolph secured Ray membership in The Bohemian Club, which gave honorary membership to local artists. While still going to school and with encouragement from

Randolph and Bohemian Club members, he began to do newspaper drawings.

For those who don't know about the Club's annual Power Orgy, The Bohemian Grove, just Google Conspiracy Theory, and you'll discover all you need to know. The Club and my father's school, the California School of Fine Arts, were intimately connected, having both been started by many of the same people, and having shared a floor of rooms in the same building in their early days, though the School went through many name changes over the years, and a few more moves, and didn't evolve into the global power center that The Bohemian Club did. Ray kept some of his Bohemian connections for most of his life, though he eased out of the Club orbit as he gravitated towards the East Coast.

At age 16 his studies were interrupted when he came down with a mysterious illness which doctors diagnosed as a "nervous heart." At his doctor's suggestion he spent six months working as a cook in a logging camp in the Sierras, where he developed a love of fishing and a belief that spending time outdoors was the answer to most psychic and bodily ills. He left the mountains fully recuperated and the mysterious heart ailment never came back.

His first job was a black and white drawing, an advertisement for the White Lunch chain, a group of restaurants in the San Francisco area. As he got busier, he rented a studio downtown and took on more and more advertising work and got so busy that he hired an assistant. He switched to night school and attended for a couple more years. Before long he was doing work for the J. Walter Thompson Company, an advertising agency which had a branch in San Francisco, and they assigned him a series of illustrations, paintings on canvas, for the Sun Maid Raisin Growers.

He continued to get more skilled and more successful. His studio became Prohaska's Art Service, a commercial art studio that included a full time lettering man, Louis Traviso, "who taught me everything I know about lettering, a brilliant guy, very talented," and several assistants, including a "steward," Albert Sperisen, who got coffee and food for clients and sharpened pencils and eventually rose to be a senior V.P. at Foote, Cone & Belding.

In 1926 J. Walter Thomson sent Ray to Dallas to work directly with the owners of Dr. Pepper on a new advertising campaign. The company offered him stock instead of pay, but he thought that was too risky. "I was so stupid! We coulda been rich, kiddo," was how he expressed it to me. I heard him say several times that he was "just a kid" when he married Dolly (Dorothy Ashcroft.) It was while he was in Dallas, which coincided with the time when J. Walter Thompson suggested he move his base of operations to Chicago so that he'd be nearer to many of their clients. They were giving him more and more work and he was going to need a bigger studio anyway; but the idea of leaving San Francisco was unsettling. He sent for his girlfriend Dolly, married her in Dallas, and a year later, after Ray Jr. was born, they moved to Chicago.

What I know about his days in Chicago is my father's official explanation, from which he must have redacted tons of jobs cranking out boring but lucrative commercial art, and lots of drinking at speakeasies. "I made more money than I ever did in my life! I had a whole floor in the Blankity Blank building in downtown Chicago." (I used to remember the name of the building, and its street number.) He mentioned names of important men in business and advertising, names I wish I could remember. He had another steward, or studio assistant, a young kid named Warren Brandt, who, with the help of Grace Borgenicht, his gallery owner wife, became a famous painter in New York. Dolly spent most of her energy trying to keep up with Ray's after hours partying, and Ray Jr. was sent to one boarding school after another, laying down a bone-crushing loneliness and resentment that in his adult years he spent a fortune trying to exorcise with individual and group therapy, to what effect no one will ever know.

During the three or more years that he was in Chicago, Ray made frequent trips home to see friends and clients and his mother and sisters. He traveled in style on the very plush and modern cross-country trains of those days, the Santa Fe Chief and the Union Pacific's California Limited. Both trains were the only mode of travel for Hollywood stars and movie executives, as well as Bohemian Club members and everyone else who was in on the boom of the Roaring Twenties.

What I thought was reticence concerning talking about Dolly was probably more just a lack of empathy for her. My father, anyway, was always willing to take the mute approach; he was not analytical or verbose. And my mother was more than willing, it seemed, to make Dolly into a two dimensional character and the marriage into a slapstick comedy. Whether there was any love or hurt feelings, I would never know. Though admittedly an attractive woman, with naturally blond hair and a "lovely," aquiline nose, she was describable thoroughly enough for my mother, through a few humorous anecdotes depicting her ditsy-ness and her alcoholism. "She was a pyromaniac!" Or, at least she allegedly set fire to two houses. I would think of it, when I heard this, as a woman going around half lit, smoking cigarettes and throwing a still lighted cigarette into the trash, or falling asleep smoking in bed. "She wore lots of jewelry. Lots of bracelets, everyone called her Bangles," my mother said.

When the crash came, Ray found he had lost several hundred thousand dollars in the market, not to mention a bundle that he'd invested in bathtub gin through Bugs Moran, a friend whom he said liked to discuss painting. So, as he succinctly put it, though I can't really pinpoint the exact month or even year, he took what cash he had left, packed up his Pierce Arrow, and went fishing for a month. And then, with wife and child, he moved to New York.

Ray's father died way before I was born, probably around 1917. His mother still lived in San Francisco, where she remained close to her two daughters. He visited his mother once a year until she died sometime around 1955. Each sister came to visit us once over the span of my childhood. Ray was rhapsodic about his mother's character and about her cooking, but my mother never got to meet her and neither did I. My mother thought it was because "Mama" was illiterate and spoke poor English, and Ray didn't want to tarnish his idealized image of her.

YAWN, WORK, FISH

He would wake up in the morning and yawn, a high-pitched, playful yawn like a baby elephant. He always took his time. He had no boss to report to. Reaching across to the window adjacent to his bed he would pull up the Venetian blinds with a yank that made a loud clatter and look out across the yard with its outbuildings, barn-red garage, Carolyn's studio, my horse barn, and further on to the fruit trees and the potato fields, a brown line of cross-hatching all the way to the bluff, topped with a thin horizon band of blue Atlantic.

More often than not Carolyn would have squeezed fresh orange juice for him, even though she hated the sticky mess and sweet smell it made all over the kitchen. Often as not he would fry his own bacon which he liked cut thick. I remember the way he towered over

Carolyn while he stood there laying down the strips of bacon with the same graceful hand motion he used to place a wet watercolor down on his work table or a bluefish filet onto the drain board of the sink.

   He always had to have toast, which had to be burnt and crunchy, and soft scrambled eggs and coffee to get him going. Though he didn't smoke as a habit, some mornings he'd have a cigarette from a pack of stale Camels he left sitting on the window sill in the studio. The cigarette, after coffee, gave him an adrenaline kick, and would make him sneeze. That was the signal that work could begin. The sneeze would rattle the windows. Sometimes he'd sneeze three or four times. Occasionally the sneezing would begin over coffee and go on intermittently until late morning, when the sound would be almost drowned out by the music from the hi-fi.

Saturday Evening Post, 1943, 1949
For more see: rayprohaska.com

When he was working on a fiction illustration, something romantic or dramatic, he might listen to "Don Juan," or "Tosca," or Bach's "Toccata and Fugue," but if he was painting for himself it was usually something like the Dorsey Brothers, or Harry James, or Stephane Grappelli, but, only when everything was going very well would he play Benny Goodman. There were moments in the house when all was right with the world. When the Old Man was in his zone; with the hi-fi blaring and a job (illustration) or a painting (usually abstract) was in the works. With brushes and paint rag in hand and the smell of turpentine in the air, he would shuffle about and you could feel and hear throughout the house the old studio floor bouncing as he moved about the studio half dancing. There was a palpable feeling that the house itself, built of hand-hewn beams that creaked in a heavy wind like a ship, was some sort of instrument and Ray's being at work meant the ship was under way.

When he needed money, he drove to New York City, all the way west on the dark two-lane macadam of Route 25 in the days before the Expressway, and beat the bushes for illustration jobs. He did work for the *Saturday Evening Post, Redbook, McCall's* and similar magazines. Manuscripts, sketches and final illustrations came and went from the post office across the street and, during down time he did what he saw as part of one continuous creative process, he fished, and he "easel" painted.

At The Society, as he called his club, The Society of Illustrators, 128 E. 63rd, NYC, he was the romantic poet-artist, a Hemingway among illustrators. The other members were jealous. They assumed he was semi-retired and wealthy. He'd talk about fishing and painting and forget the scenes he caused at home. He would play the big shot. At home, if any magazine art director called, we, Carolyn, Tony, and Elena, were under orders what to say; that Ray was busy and would call back. Art directors were never to be told he was fishing, let alone sick or broke. "They'll kill you off if they think you aren't busy," he'd say.

He was torn between two worlds. One was the art of illustration; a world in which he was established and well thought of, where he was a member of a fraternity of gentlemen. In the other, which referred to itself as a Fine Art, he was eyed with suspicion because of his success in what was called Commercial Art.

Always, though, when there was a new check deposited in the bank, he would fish. He'd fish in the surf according to the tides, sometimes during the day, sometimes in the moonlight, sometimes in the pitch dark with a miner's lamp on his forehead. Soon after we moved from Hand Lane into the house on Main Street, he had decided he needed to expand his fishing reach to include the long stretches of sandy beach that were too far to go on foot. For that he needed a beach-buggy; so he bought an old Model A and outfitted it with over-sized tires, which, when left with low air pressure allowed the light old Ford Coupe to glide across the sand without getting stuck. He named it the "Gut-Bucket," and with it, he began chasing the haulseiners. Ray became friends with Ted Lester, one of the best haulseiners, and friendly enough that Ted let him paint, draw, and photograph himself and his crew many times over a period of years. Sometimes the fish were easy to spot, splashing right behind the breaking surf, with birds working over them, sea-gulls, gannets, fish hawks, or all three. At other times you just had to find one of the seining crews; they went on instincts honed by generations of experience, and, like their dragger captain brothers and cousins, they knew where all the wrecks were and how to get close without fouling their gear.

Ted Lester: Photo and Painting by Ray Prohaska

In between tides or when the fish weren't hitting, he'd come home and paint. Water and rocks, pebbles, skate eggs, driftwood, foam, the sky, the beach; gulls, bones, shells, the wind and the rain, the rosy dawn, the haulseiners and their nets; all went into these pictures, whether they were small sometimes realistic watercolors or large powerful abstracts. He allowed himself to be influenced by many other painters; by the Abstract Expressionists; and by Cezanne and Matisse; and artists as diverse as Piero della Francesca and John Marin. But he never detached himself from a fascination with the sea.

Everyone thought we were rich. And we might have been, possibly, if Ray's Fine Art painting had ever grown to something approaching the market value of what the major abstract expressionists were getting, or if he were getting paid for his time spent fishing, but that wasn't going to happen. The truth is he was snobbish as an illustrator, too. He only wanted to illustrate interesting stories; he wanted to show his versatility and talent. He was in the top tier of illustrators and accepted as such by his peers, which is why he remained close, throughout his career, with the best in the field. They were the guys and in a few cases the women, who could draw and paint exceptionally well; that weren't dependent on gimmicks and gadgets and technique.

Ray never worried about money until it was all gone. When a check came in we lived high on the hog, everyone in the family following Ray's lead by becoming money drunk. That meant lots of guests and food; fish, of course, and steak, and lobster, or paella, or spaghetti with clam sauce, and for hors d'oeuvres or snacks, or last minute guests, clams casino, fried blowfish, or snapper blues, home-smoked fish (striped bass or bluefish or sturgeon), or almost anything smoked, with black pepper and lemon juice, squid fried in bacon fat, and on rare occasions, striped bass liver, sautéed in butter. All of which went well with whiskey, which during that period was usually a top shelf bourbon on the rocks. Scotch came later.

Steaks would be broiled on the outdoor fireplace (which Ray had designed, made of old brick with little wooden-doored cabinets on each side that were topped with big flag stones that got greasy from the meat) with corn on the cob and beefsteak tomatoes from my classmate Josephine's parent's farm stand. Guests from the city would appear, like illustrator Robert Fawcett and his gorgeous former model wife Aggie, later the wife of illustrator Austin Briggs, and art director and Society of Illustrators member Howard Munce, or Yasuo Kuniyoshi's widow, Sara, who worked at MoMA , or Don Phillips, the top male model for The Ford Agency, and his model wife Bobbi.

After a few days, or a few weeks, of good fishing, we would quickly be down to our last dime and parental panic would set in and spread to my sister and me. Ray, after fruitlessly trying to balance the checkbook with graceful strokes from his Parker pen, would bellow from the studio, "Jesus Christ, where did all the money go?" And Carolyn would scream back defensively, "We have mouths to feed," throwing a Goddamit in there somewhere. It always seemed that we were the guilty party, Tony, Elena, and Carolyn. His family was the cause of this latest bout with destitution. My sister and I would stop fighting and sometimes we'd hide upstairs in my attic bedroom. Now he'd have to "prostitute" himself again. (Suddenly the big shot at the Society of Illustrators was a prostitute.) We were driving him out into the world of bloodthirsty competition, forcing him back into the cruel city to find work.

Given his success as an illustrator, Ray couldn't expect to be a contender among the accepted group of leaders and up-and-comers in the new world of fine art, the abstractionist school. That would have been true no matter how good his painting was. At least, that's what we felt, the family and his small but enthusiastic group of friend-collectors. This would have been true even if he hadn't also been too old, too much aligned with the earlier well known American artists like Gladys Davis, Alex Brook and Abraham Rattiner. (Brook and Rattiner lived in Sag Harbor.) Nevertheless he painted, and was accepted into some important shows, and gained some small level of acceptance.

At his clubs in the city though, The Society of Illustrators and The Dutch Treat Club, he'd be back to being Hemingway again. Some of his friends in illustration thought Ray was being a snob, that he preferred fishing and artistic experimentation to what they saw as their dignified craft. And to an extent, he was. But there were illustrators who were willing to talk about serious painting, whether abstract or not, and he exempted them, and he went on, with one foot in each world.

Ray Prohaska in his Amagansett Studio 1946

RAY AT WORK

Our house, our home, was a cottage industry. It was where we lived, and where my father worked; where he performed his function as the lone breadwinner. The studio was separate, of course, and off limits much of the time, but its function was intimately tied to the order in the home part.

When Ray was "cookin," that is focused and happy with his progress, engaged in a burst of energy during which he would "knock out a job," or satisfy himself concerning some progress on a "serious" painting, there was a feeling in the house which caused my mother, sister and I to shift gears; we would go about our business in a guarded way, expectant, hopeful, but careful not to make too much noise.

My father's hand eye coordination seemed to be part of his personality, part of the way he moved and the way he went about his life. He was never clumsy, rarely faltering in his movements. He could draw so well that even many of his contemporaries enjoyed going to the chalk-talks on drawing that he occasionally gave at his club or at schools like Pratt Institute. His drawing, though, as accurate and realistic as it could be, was never formulaic, he had no system, he just drew from inside out, as if by feel. His studio too was arranged to fit his movements, and had very good north light, a high ceiling, white walls, a big stand-up easel, an old, sturdy drawing board with a wheel crank, and a taboret with four drawers full of paints, inks, charcoal, pencils and erasers, and, on top, a large milk glass palette.

If he was working in oil there would be turpentine in a beaker on the taboret, or if watercolor or gouache, a beaker of water. Sometimes, usually when he was working in oil, he asked me to clean his brushes. I did that in the darkroom, in an old sink high enough so that I had to use the toilet seat as a stool to reach the water. After rinsing in them turps I would scrub the brushes, three or four at a time depending on size, against a big bar of Ivory soap while running warm water over them.

Over the years he immortalized dozens of local people by using them as models. One year he did illustrations for a series of Western stories in *The Saturday Evening Post* using several of the local men who owned horses and dressed in western garb. In one these, a man had been shot and was being operated on by a frontier Doc. The men stepped into their parts as if the pose was only a flicker away from their true lives. They acted it out. To make it bloody, Ray put red paint in a basin full of water that the Doc was using to rinse his tools. That wasn't necessary for the shot, since the pictures were only to be drawn from, but it seemed to help the ambiance. The sheriff had a real gun in his holster. The atmosphere was like that on a movie sound stage. Since everyone in town knew everyone else in those days, the female interests, always local beauties, were well known to their male counterparts.

Many of the stories he illustrated were about family scenes in which I was the little boy. It wasn't unusual for me to walk in the door just home from school, and have him call my name in an ominous, all-too-cheery way. "Just a quick shot that's all!" is what he'd say when I'd groan from his saying, "I need you in the studio!" Sometimes the picture would be a stop-action shot of me holding a baseball bat or throwing a ball. Or, I would be sitting on the lap of a woman I hardly knew, or I'd be being hugged by eager housewife-model, or I'd have to pretend I was running, one foot to the rear held up by three telephone books, hand resting on an easel, looking up over my shoulder directly into the big old theatrical spotlight. "Look into the camera and smile," he'd say. The spotlight, usually right over his shoulder, brought tears to my eyes. My muscles would start to burn. "Just one more, kiddo," he'd say, while he ran through another roll of twelve exposures, click and rewind, click and rewind, repeating "just one more," while he kept winding his old Rollei. Then my heart would sink when I'd hear the camera pop open for another reload of film.

If it was a group pose, I might be needed as a sort of stage hand, to hold a light or a reflector or to hold a skirt out so it seemed to be swaying in the breeze. If he was shooting a sexy pose, a clinch, or a "boy-girl," as he called them (a shot that didn't require me), he might lock the door to the studio to "keep down the traffic," which meant to keep me out. At that point I'd be suddenly desirous of being in on the action, and, silent as a cat burglar, I'd climb onto the roof and peek through the skylight.

Saturday Evening Post 1955
All local people except blonde professional model

From the time I was ten years old, he would ask me to help him find models. If he needed a character for an illustration, he'd ask me to help find him a certain type, "a rugged type," he'd say, or, "a dame with good drawing," by which he meant a woman with a well-proportioned, somewhat angular face. Though he did occasionally hire professional models in the city, more often he found his cowboys, mothers, mechanics, glamour girls, and freckle-faced kids all quite close to home.

It wasn't called a photo shoot, it was, "shooting a few pictures," and after the fun was over (everyone but me thought it was fun) he would fix all the models a drink and give them a check for ten bucks, which some people wanted to refuse because it didn't seem like work. For me, though, and my sister, it always seemed like work and we could never be paid enough.

One Christmas, we posed for a realistic charcoal sketch that my father donated to the *New York Times* for its *100 Neediest Cases* fund drive. We were pictured standing forlornly, arms around each other, me clutching a teddy bear, both dressed in ragged clothes.

We were the children in most of his illustrations, sometimes accompanied by one or more of our playmates, sometimes with different colored hair or looking slightly older or younger. Ray had several cameras and one was always loaded and ready, so we were the most photographed kids within a hundred miles. He would take pictures just for candid family history's sake or, often, to use as "scrap," which meant for possible help in doing some future illustration. One candid shot he took of my sister asleep at the dining room table hung in our living room for years. It shows her, shirtless, about six years old, bathed in sunlight, her hand resting on a white porcelain sugar bowl. It brings me back to the days when she was my dynamic, gutsy little pal.

Our lives were well documented in photography and illustration. There were piles and piles of photographs of the two of us from infancy. One, that I always wanted to destroy but didn't dare because my mother seemed to think it was cute, was of me having my newly circumcised penis swabbed. Another, that I still have, is of my sister swaddled in a cotton blanket as she is held by a beautiful dark haired woman in corduroy skirt and Mexican blouse; Carolyn at thirty-nine.

Sometimes in the evening after dinner he would work in the darkroom developing film and making prints to draw from, and he might call me in to be his assistant; really just to keep him company. I'd stand on a stool and look over his shoulder in the red light and never fail to be amazed when my own face appeared out of the blank matte surface. I wanted to consider myself his assistant, but I was thwarted by arithmetic. The developer and stop needed to be diluted using some sort of calculations, which though simple, triggered my arithmaphobia.

If an art director sent a job back for changes, he would fume and slam things around and make everyone miserable until the job was finished and accepted. Sometimes he would threaten to give up illustration, to just go fishing and paint, and we could all just go and starve to death. At times like this, no part of the house was free of the vibrating tension. My mother would be sick with anxiety. She would try to control my sister and me with desperate threats. If, by our fighting or sniping at each other, we pushed her too far and she would start screaming at us, he would come barreling out of the studio and chase us into our respective rooms. Then he'd yell at her for not being able to control the kids.

If Carolyn got mad enough, she would threaten to "wrap herself around a telephone pole," and then get in the car and spray gravel spinning the wheels out the driveway, while Elena and I wondered what we'd do without a mother.

But when the pressure was off, when an illustration went well and one of his own large abstracts could be rolled on its big easel out to the center of the studio and be worked on, and progress was being made, you could feel the stillness in the air, a peaceful quiet, hear the soft click of a couple of brushes wrapped in a piece of paint-rag being placed on a milk glass palette, hear the studio door being unlocked. I would amble into the studio in stocking feet and watch him study his work and even dance around on the Masonite floor, slipping and sliding to Benny Goodman.

CAROLYN

I had been led, mostly by Carolyn, but also by conversations I had overheard, to believe that all artists were neurotic and that most drank too much. Her drinking though, was a source of great annoyance to me. It was scary sometimes to have my beautiful, charming, wise mother turn into someone else, a stranger obsessed with some distant world. Her facial expression would change. (She later told me her face became numb when she drank.) Often she would go on about various things in an unending monologue, like some wind-up doll; about her childhood; her first marriage, her early days as a model. Mostly though, it had to do with the early days of her marriage to Ray, in Manhattan and in Amagansett during The War.

    She would mention names; some of whom, like Becky Jones, a fellow League student, and Sara Kuniyoshi, Yas's wife, my sister and I got to know when they came out for visits. Some, like Yas Kuniyoshi, and "Vit" Vytlacil, well known artists in their day, were dead. Others had gone into different social circles.

    She loved all kinds of gossip, too, from stuff about local people, to the tabloids. Wallis Simpson's exploits were a favorite. The Duchess was background material for The Life of Carolyn. When she worked the switchboard for Seaboard Airline (her first job as a teenager), it was Simpson's maternal uncle who was president of that company. As Mrs. Simpson's notoriety grew (she was, perhaps, a Nazi or a sympathizer, or at least a spy by some accounts), Carolyn kept track of all the scuttlebutt about the wife of the Duke who was a former King.

Sometimes after a cocktail party or a night of having visitors she would come into my room and, while I pretended to sleep, lie next to me with her arm around me, her body pressed close to mine, and breathe her whiskey breath into my face. I was frightened by it. It would take me minutes, which seemed like hours, to un-paralyze myself long enough to turn around in feigned sleep and curl up in a fetal position, face to the wall. Then, when she'd start to doze, I would pretend to kick in my sleep until she got up and went to bed.

A frustrated writer, Carolyn had a great memory and loved to tell stories. She had tried acting; had become a good, but unacknowledged painter; took some writing classes at Columbia, but all her stories were still in her head. Perhaps the most important work of art for her was this unending monologue; but if that's the case, she didn't know it. She believed her most important work was painting, and she was absorbed in what she called "the act of painting." She loved the process of it. I believe that was her meditation; and it might have also been an outlet for her religious impulses.

She kept track of the art world and the world of intellectuals, in a way that Ray couldn't be bothered with. She would refer to chance encounters she had with people who were friends of friends; Irving Berlin, Dorothy Parker, Flannery O'Connor, and with the help second hand material, make these tales seem like something she had eavesdropped on yesterday. And as time went by (though she felt more and more that she was "stuck" on the East End), without having to leave East Hampton she and Ray increasingly met stimulating people, people who could not only talk painting but literature too. In the late 1950s they became friends with newlyweds A.J. Liebling and Jean Stafford who lived nearby in Springs. Liebling died on my birthday in 1963. They continued to see Stafford until her death in 1979.

Starting during The War she got into the local gossip too, beginning with a fellow telephone party line member, Alice Kelsey, wife of the head of the vegetable department at East Hampton's A&P, Vernon Kelsey, an important guy for Carolyn to know because of

Ray's fussiness about salad. Party lines continued until the late Fifties, with several homes being able to listen in on each other's calls and some houses sharing the same number but with different alphabetical designations.

In the early post-war days, the gossip was often about the Summer Colony, the handful of people who lived up on Bluff Road overlooking the ocean, along with those in the Devon Colony; wealthy people who belonged to Devon Yacht Club, on the bay. One favorite topic concerned which of those ladies, officer's wives during The War, had affairs with local men or members of The Coast Guard contingent stationed on Bluff Road.

Sometimes, perhaps outdoors on a warm summer day, Ray and Carolyn would have a little cocktail party by themselves, with a pitcher of martinis, or perhaps mint juleps, made with bourbon and sugar with ice crushed inside a special canvas bag and hammered with a big wooden mallet. (The mallet was also used for crushing giant lobster claws.) At times like that my sister and I would hover around like yellow jackets and be rewarded with an occasional sip.

If it was really hot out, they might shower (together, nude), in the outdoor shower and then have drinks on the patio still in the nude. (While Main Street, on the other side of the stockade fence, went on about its business.) They talked about the old days; the radio dominated, Art Deco cultural period in New York City of fifteen or twenty years earlier. They would bring up the old familiar names, Kitty and Rube, Ted Behr, a popular model; and illustrators; Johnny Maxwell, Ben Stahl, Gladys Davis, Al Dorn, Austin "Bud" Briggs, Bob Fawcett, and the rest of their old crowd.

EARLY CAROLYN

My mother could remember back to when she was three years old. She could remember the wooden floor boards in the kitchen and the early morning *clump, clump, clump* of the rubber shoes on the milk wagon's horse. Borden's delivered milk by horse and wagon continually into the Forties; Hoffman Beverages, a soda company, held onto their Percherons for years because it was good advertising. She could recall her Aunt Mary and husband coming to visit in a horse and buggy. One of her clearest memories (this would have been at age seven or eight) was of two old ladies in an electric car, driving by on the boulevard every afternoon precisely at two-o'clock.

She was born on the 12th of March, 1908, in an apartment in Bayonne, New Jersey, on Linden Avenue, in a section called Greenville, where, in those days, there were still open fields and an unobstructed view of the Statue of Liberty. Her maternal grandmother acted as midwife. I have a photograph of little Carolyn at about age five, standing on the boardwalk in Atlantic City with her mother and her two aunts all in white lace dresses and little Carolyn dressed in a white laced pinafore.

Mae Bradley Pierson, my mother's mother, could have been the model for Gustav Klimt's Golden Woman or, perhaps, a very thin Gibson girl. Her husband Edgar, a salesman who was called Ned, had three married brothers, Joshua, who was called "Dod" for what reason I don't know, Jim, and Malcolm, called Mal, and two sisters, Laura and Ella who lived with their mother, my maternal grandmother, Inez Decker Pierson, at the family house in Bayonne. (My great-grandfather, Civil War veteran James Malcolm Pierson, died in 1905.) Grandma Pierson was a member of the Grand Army of the Republic and a soap box orator. When she died in 1910, Laura and Ella moved in with Ned, Mae, and Mae's mother (Carolyn's Grandma Bradley.)

Mae and both her sisters-in-law, Laura and Ella, shared Wilsonian Democrat Suffragette political sympathies. (The three young women were shocked when it was revealed that Wilson had been having an affair.) All three girls were attractive and always dressed well in corseted Edwardian finery. Laura was considered the great beauty of the Pierson clan. She had the big bust, and long, straight, light brown hair popular at that time, and wore a bustle. Mae was pale, lightly freckled, wasp-waisted, charming and bright and, for those times well-read for a middle class girl.

Ned was a handsome man, Carolyn referred to him as "a John Barrymore type," thin, of medium height, with a pencil mustache. He was accustomed to being around smart older women and didn't seem to object that his home had become a bastion of Suffragette thinking. As a young man he excelled in sports, played touch football and baseball, and at one time was a pitcher for a minor league team out of Newark. He and his friends, who called themselves "The Bayonne Bunch," were part of an ice boating team that raced when the bay was frozen over. Among the group was a fellow named Gene Tumulty, who later became President Wilson's personal secretary. It was Tumulty who introduced Ned to his future bride, Mary Irene "Mae" Bradley.

Mae, over thirty when they married, was several years older than Ned. She had been in school with and been friends with his older sister Laura. She had gone to Rutgers long enough to get a teaching certificate, taught for a while, designed children's dresses and, for a short time, had been a secretary. She and her mother, Carolyn's Grandma Bradley, had an ongoing testiness between them. Mae was a non-religious Catholic and had married a non-religious Episcopalian. Grandma Bradley, born Julia Casey in a Catholic section of Northern Ireland, had married a Protestant Ulsterman, a teamster (carriage driver), who abandoned her in America with five children, and, at least as far as we know, was shortly thereafter killed while driving a team of horses.

In tough Irish tradition, the mother and five children held things together, with mother at the helm working as a seamstress. She put up a good Catholic front, but whenever she began to moralize, Mae would say, often in front of Carolyn, "You're just a sanctimonious old Irish hypocrite!" (Even as a little girl, Carolyn knew that Grandma kept her church fliers and some religious literature in the top left-hand corner of her writing desk on top her secret copy of Balzac's *Droll Stories.*)

The mother-daughter sniping continued. The year that Carolyn was to have gone off to school, Grandma Bradley went off in a huff and was gone several months. She was staying with cousins. She might have stayed gone, too, but Carolyn became sick with typhoid and then, shortly after that, Mae came down with TB, so Grandma B. returned and became Mae's nurse. Carolyn, when she recovered from typhoid, helped her grandmother by fetching tissues and being a tempering influence between mother and daughter.

On Sundays, before Mae became too sick, Ned would rent a Stanley Steamer and the women would get dressed up in dusters and scarves and go motoring over to Hackensack to see Aunt Mary, Mae's sister, who was still living in the old farmhouse where she and Mae had been born. A year or two later, Ned bought his own Model T Ford with brass radiator and headlights and they would take their Sunday drive up to the Bronx to visit relatives who lived on the Grand Concourse near the Edgar Allen Poe House and then down into Manhattan to the Library and Bryant Park, and past the Spaulding's Sporting Goods Store on 42nd St. where he was then floor manager.

The big excitement in Carolyn's early days, though, was the birth of the Motion Picture business, right there in that northeast corner of New Jersey. "Once," she told me, "I remember they were shooting a big extravaganza, almost next door to us in a big field. They put together a battle scene with lots of horses and explosions going off. Those were the same fields that in winter would get flooded and my father and mother and the neighbors would go ice skating; on the cliffs, right across from 103rd Street in Manhattan."

One day her mother, grandmother, aunts and friends, dragging along camp stools to sit on, brought her along to watch a movie being filmed. She remembered her Grandmother Bradley saying afterward, "Did you see that actress, Pearl White, sitting there with her legs crossed, smoking? And then when the director said something to her, she said 'I don't give a damn.'" Even though for their time they were liberated women, smoking and swearing were unacceptably risqué for these ladies.

When Mae was dying in 1917, she allowed a priest to visit. That might have been partly to appease Grandma Bradley, but she did ask Ned to marry her in the Catholic Church. He was okay with it, too, but by then she was too sick and died before it could be done.

I once asked my mother about the day her mother died. "You must have been very upset," I offered. She answered that she had "toughed it out." Her father broke the news to her, she said, and he held her, and "we both cried and cried, and then we didn't," she said. I thought it was telling the way she said that. She didn't seem to realize what she was saying, but what I presumed was that, after a brief cry, they shut down their feelings. It was a Victorian world and the stiff upper lip still applied.

The next day Ned took Carolyn, who was now nine, to his brother Dod's house to live. He might have stayed on, he told her years later, and raised her with his mother-in-law's help, but he used Julia Bradley's disposition, what he called her cold-heartedness, as his excuse.

When she was a teenager Ned told Carolyn, concerning his mother-in-law, "She outlived all of her children and never shed a tear!" So Grandma Bradley went to live at a cousin's, where she'd gone when she had her "huff." Ned visited Dod's every day for a week and then, when Carolyn seemed to be settled in, he vanished. Her grandmother, who had packed her things, took her battered little

Teddy Bear out of her arms. "Oh, you don't need that old thing, you're too old for that now," she said. Carolyn recalled this exchange with a matter-of-fact tone, leaving me wondering, "Where did the feelings go?"

Both Ned and his brother Dod (Joshua), two errant Episcopalians, had married Catholic women. Dod's wife was a Czech Catholic named Mona. Mona and Dod had two little boys, William and an infant, Milton. But Mona had always wanted a girl. So, though they were not well off and could hardly afford another mouth to feed, they were happy to have Carolyn. Mona, though born in Czechoslovakia, had been in this country since she was a child and was well assimilated. Dod was a salesman who made less money than Ned, but they were frugal and they were kind-hearted people.

Now nine years old, for the first time in her life Carolyn began to attend school full time. By the end of that first year she had caught up and was able to graduate grammar school in 1921 at the normal age of thirteen. And she always went off to school well dressed. Mona, who loved making clothes, made nice things for Carolyn. At one time she made a sailor suit for Willy to go with his Buster Brown haircut and out of the same material a lovely little pinafore for Carolyn.

I asked Carolyn if she felt like an orphan living at Uncle Dod's. "No," she said, "The only time I felt out of place was about a month after my mother died. Mona and Dod's little baby, Linley (Milton Linley Pierson) died. He was six months old." [The child may have died from what is today called crib death.] "Mona and Dod and Willy were all three crying together, so I had a good cry by myself. But I was left out of it." Years later when she told me about that time, I was puzzled by her matter of fact tone.

I met Ned, full name Edgar Tremaine McGreavy Pierson, and Carolyn's step-mother Flo, only a few times. (Neither Ray nor my mother seemed to value highly the idea of keeping relatives close at hand.) The first time was when Carolyn brought my sister and me to visit them in Newark. I was about seven and all I remember was that Ned had a cute little dog, a sort of Jack Russell type, that danced around on its hind legs, and that he brought up from the cellar a life-size cardboard picture which had been a display in a movie theater lobby, of Carolyn in a bathing suit with the words Miss Newark emblazoned on a ribbon across her chest. It embarrassed my mother.

Carolyn's stepmother, not much older than Carolyn (she lied about her age so there is no record of her real age), had a gravelly voice and a heavy New York accent. On another visit they had moved to Trenton because Flo had gotten a job as a housemother at Trenton's Reformatory for Girls. My sister and I both remembered for years that one of the girls had yelled obscenities out the window at her; as in "fuck you Mrs. Pierson!"

In 1918 both Carolyn and William were stricken with Spanish Influenza, but by November 11th, Armistice Day, the end of the First World War, they were well enough that Carolyn could lead a small band of kids up Ocean Avenue in a parade. She remembered having a patriotic feeling in her breast. Willy and Carolyn were two survivors of an epidemic that killed tens of millions of people around the world. An older boy, Harold Yoakum, whose brother would now be returning from the front, carried the flag and another kid had a drum. They got their picture in two papers, the *Jersey Journal* and the *Hudson Observer*. Sadly, Harold died of the Spanish Flu before he could welcome his brother home.

By January 1919, Ned with his new girlfriend, Florence, began bi-monthly visits to Dod and Mona's home. Other relatives visited too: Mal's brood (brother Malcolm and his family), Uncle Jim and Aunt Pauline; and on special holidays, such as Thanksgiving and the New Year, a group from the New York Dutch side of the family, Grandmother Pierson's sister's brood, the Van Diens, would arrive unannounced, having come by jalopy all the way from Chicago, hungry and lovable and willing to sleep on the floor. Carolyn and Willy were allowed to stay up after dinner and sit at the kitchen table listening to the adults, kicking each other when someone said something they thought was funny.

Carolyn's father was from the ninth generation of Piersons descended from Henry. Henry Pierson, a Yorkshire man and a weaver, was a founding settler of Southampton, Long Island, circa 1640. My mother's grandfather was Civil War veteran James Malcolm Pierson. When I was fifteen, my mother gave me his Meerschaum pipe, darkly tanned from years of use, broken in to perfection, which I was meant to treasure, and did, for a few years. (In my teens it wasn't unusual for a teenager to take up pipe smoking as an occasional hobby; pipes were especially proper when duck hunting, because you could warm your trigger finger hand with it.)

James Malcolm, who was called Pop by his immediate family and The Captain by everyone else, had raised a company of volunteers who fought in the battle of Fredericksburg. After the war he had worked at numerous jobs including one as a guard at Sing-Sing Prison before retiring to his porch on an old farmhouse in Bayonne, New Jersey, surrounded by his loving brood. He died in 1905.

Captain Jim was the son of a man who was born in Southampton, New York, but was referred to by my mother's family as William of Cairo on account of his having moved west, a sometimes necessary move for an Eastern Long Islander if you wanted to own your own land, or if you wanted to avoid marrying a cousin. William Pierson had "removed to Greene County," as it says on Aunt Laura's one page genealogy. He settled in Cairo, New York, a small village on the Hudson, south of Albany, where he married a woman named Eleanor Carbine and raised his family. One son of William, Charles, was thought to have been "killed by a whale" somewhere in the South Pacific. In 2001 I discovered, by searching on a genealogy website that, in fact, he had died on dry land. After entering some of Carolyn's genealogical notes that she'd received from Aunt Laura onto the website, within a few days I received this message:

"I too am a descendant of Henry Pierson from England, Joseph 1649, Henry 1678, Samuel 1721, Timothy ?, James ?, and William 1789, of Cairo N.Y. Charles Anson Crocker Herrick Philetus Pierson was born in 1837, son of William and Eleanor Pierson of Cairo, New York. I think that he was the youngest child of 8 and that your ancestor was James Malcolm, his older brother, no. 6. Charles, my great-grandfather, migrated to New Zealand in 1860 and there are a large number of his descendants here in New Zealand. Am keen to make contact with family members and to find out more about the Piersons."

Four generations of Piersons did not know of their relatives in the Southern Hemisphere, and for William of Cairo it must have been especially hard because another son, his oldest, William Jr., had also been lost at sea. (There are many Henrys and many Williams in the genealogy.) But my New Zealand relative knew how to get my attention, make me realize her claim was legitimate, by listing the names in that order; Henry, Joseph, Henry, Samuel, Timothy, James, and William of Cairo.

The new relative was Mrs. Diane Lay, and in the intervening years she has done more research. Aunt Laura's notes on William of Cairo have him fathering only four children, including James Malcolm, a daughter Mary who married Sen. Joshua M. Fiero, and the son Charles of "killed by whale" fame. In fact, William sired nine children by Eleanor, the ninth having been an infant that died at birth. Charles of New Zealand, born in 1838, was number eight. He and his New Zealand wife Hannah also had eight children.

The two Pierson men who first hit American soil in the 1600s at Lynn, Massachusetts, were either brothers or, more likely, cousins. (In those days, cousins called each other brother.) They also brought along a third "cousin" about whom little seems to be known other than his name, Thomas. Of the two men Aunt Laura referred to as cousins, Abraham and Henry, only Abraham left an impression on posterity outside of Eastern Long Island. Though they were both good breeders, as was Thomas the mysterious third, Henry's most noted accomplishment was to become the first Southampton Town Clerk, a position he held for many years. One descendant of Thomas, Wilson Pierson, a teacher at Yale, wrote what many consider the best book ever written about Alexis de Tocqueville.

Abraham was a Puritan preacher who came to Southampton after being hired in absentia to be the new settlement's first Rector. After leading the town for a few years, he was involved in a dispute over whether the town should join either the Connecticut or New Haven colonies, and he came down against the majority which voted for Connecticut, and so in 1664 he took a few parishioners to Branford in the New Haven colony, where he established a new church. While there, he translated the Catechism into the dialect of the Quiripi Indians spoken in that area.

 The following year he pitched another fit. The laws of colonies of New Haven and Connecticut were not strict enough to satisfy Abraham, who followed the most severe of the Mosaic laws on blasphemy, heresy, profaning the Lord's Day, cursing, and smiting of rebellious children. This time he left for New Jersey, where he established the town of New Ark, later Newark, bringing most of Branford and its town and church records with him. Though he never carried out the severest punishments to which these sinners were liable (i.e. death), he was nevertheless not a soft-hearted man.

 Henry's descendants stayed in Southampton Town and environs for generations, wandering a few miles east or west. Occasionally, a son would travel off to New Jersey or Connecticut to find a wife, sometimes only a more distant relative than they could find at home (someone you could trust, who was not a total stranger), but few pulled up roots before James Malcolm's father migrated up the Hudson.

James Malcolm Pierson learned the carpentry trade and married a woman from the then plentiful New York Dutch community, Inez Decker (her mother was a Schermerhorn). They moved often, first to Kingston and then to various parts of New York City. Along the way they had seven children: William, Laura (Aunt Laura), Eleanor (Aunt Ella), Malcolm, Joshua (Dod), James, and Edgar. Before the Civil War James M. was a sergeant in the New York Militia.

In the Vedder Library near Kingston NY is a file of letters he wrote to various doctors over the years following The War of the Rebellion, in which he pled his case for a disability pension. In one signed affidavit, very meticulously, he lists every doctor's name and, when appropriate, mentions that they are "now dead." He goes over his entire Civil War history, including his time as a soldier in a company of infantry attached to the 120th Infantry Regiment of New York Volunteers, where he "took sick" after drinking stagnant water while on the march to Manassas, Bristol, and Warrenton Station.

My mother resting during a photo shoot ca. 1930

CAROLYN GOES TO WORK

Ned and Florence got married in 1921 and set their sights on giving Carolyn a real family, an idea she met with skepticism. She started high school at Lincoln High in Jersey City but within two months the newlyweds decided "all that academic stuff" was a waste of time. She should be taking a business course. They insisted she enroll at a commercially oriented school, the big, impersonal Central High in Newark. She hated Central and hated her father's newly found sense of "too little, too late" parental responsibility. She began cutting classes; gym, and anything else she didn't like, and when Flo and Ned found out she was given the ultimate punishment, being sent off to a Catholic girls' school, St. Vincent's Academy.

In fact St. Vincent's would have been her mother's wish. She immediately felt comfortable there. Two teachers especially impressed her and made her stay there enjoyable. They were Sister Depulta, her homeroom teacher, and Sister Pascal, who was French but taught Spanish with a French accent. When Carolyn was bold enough to correct her accent, the Sister would call her "incorrigible." "By then I was getting fresh," she said.

She made a friend of a girl named Eileen and the two ate lunch together. Near the sacristy, the dressing room where the priests dressed for Mass, the two girls found a secret place under the chapel staircase, where two big plaster angels with broken heads were stored, and where there was just enough room for them to eat their homemade lunch in private, away from the lunch room. The sacristy and the headless angels became a secret that the girls bonded over. But when she finished out the year at St. Vincent's and Flo and Dad asked if she was looking forward to going back, she said no, she was finished with that. She had decided she wanted out from under their thumbs. It would be a more involved process than she imagined.

Her first job was in Manhattan with the Telephone Company, where she learned to operate a switchboard. She would take a streetcar from home to Manhattan Transfer Station in Secaucus, "in the middle of the pig farms and the Newark Dump, where on a steamy hot summer morning the stench was so thick you could watch it waft across the meadows." There she would buy a newspaper and perhaps a magazine, have her shoes shined, and board the train for the trip through the tunnel to Manhattan. It was at Manhattan Transfer that she bought her first *New Yorker*. Being gone all day, her time spent with Ned and Flo was down to almost none. Never mind that she was still living at home, she had her own railroad pass, was reading the *New Yorker*, and the New York papers and other magazines. She was beginning to feel all grown up.

Shortly after she started working, she went on a religious kick. She began going to Mass every morning at St. Francis of Assisi Church, right across from Penn Station. For several months she became "Almost pious. That really set them on their ears too!" she said, referring to Ned and Flo who did not consider this excess piety, especially its Roman theme, to be good for her marriage prospects. (In those days, only white Protestants were completely first class citizens.)

She kept the Penn Station job for about a year, and then went to work in the same building making Pullman reservations at Seaboard Airline, so named not because it was an airline, that concept hadn't been invented yet, but because it traveled the coast to Florida and was, theoretically, like floating on a cloud. She occupied her spare moments at the switchboard making drawings of a model and actress, Ina Claire, who appeared on posters and calendars gracing all the walls of the switchboard office. Claire was the girlfriend of the President and Chairman of the Board of Seaboard, S. Davies Warfield, who would soon become better known as the uncle of the Duchess of Windsor.

Then, in the autumn of 1926, when a hurricane caused the bottom to fall out of the Florida real estate market and Seaboard's business took a radical dive, she was laid off, and she took a job at Corn Exchange Bank in the women's department (a special *women only* part of the bank.) At the bank she was making $22.00 per week, but got no railroad pass, so her commuter fare made her take-home less. She quit and went to work at Westinghouse in Bloomfield, New Jersey, a nightmare job, she said, "for a real slave wage." It involved typing on a billing machine which had a huge roll with five carbons. One mistake necessitated starting everything over from scratch.

Around this time, with her religious kick having dissipated, she met a young man on the train and they began dating. He was a local Newark boy, Al Hoffman, whose family owned the Hoffman Beverage Company, they of the horse-drawn delivery wagons. Hoffman's was a soda brand that was popular up into the Fifties all over the East.

Al called her for weeks, but she was shy of dating and kept putting him off, sometimes pretending she wasn't home, until New Year's Eve, 1926, when she came downstairs from her room to find all sorts of little packages waiting for her, scarves and trinkets and things. She relented. Their first date was to a very good and quite famous restaurant, Simonson's, a fish place in Newark. Ned and Flo, nervous, one supposes, that Al would lead her astray and trying to be good parents, followed them, closely, like Sherlock and Watson. After all, Al was an older man of 26, almost as old as Flo! (It irked Flo that Al called her Mrs. Pierson.)

Through Al, Carolyn met a young woman named Helen Corcoran, who was dating Al's brother. Helen had been Miss Newark two years before, and convinced Carolyn, desperate to get away from the billing machine, to try her luck with a beauty contest. Her first attempt was at a food show, which had a contest called Prettiest Girl in Newark. She came in second. Next she went to a Miss Universe contest where she was a runner-up and met two of the judges, both former actors. The two former actors were John Robert Powers, owner of a modeling agency, and Chester Beecroft, a film production manager for William Randolph Hearst. Through them she began to work as an extra at Cosmopolitan Studios.

Next, she tried out for and won the Miss Newark contest. The jury was made up of some of the most famous illustrators of the day, including; McClelland Barclay, Franklin Booth, Arthur William Brown, Haskel Coffin and Howard Chandler Christy, all of whom asked her to model. Although the Miss Newark position didn't pay anything, it did supply a wardrobe, some publicity, and some test-shot photographs, and she began getting all the modeling work she could handle.

Being Miss Newark meant she had to be in the Miss America contest in Atlantic City, where she came in as a semi-finalist. Another must-do as part of the Miss Newark job was to be a judge at the Miss New York contest held in Yankee Stadium. The illustrator Franklin Booth was there and asked her to do some modeling for him. On the day she went to Booth's studio, her father came along as a chaperon. Booth did some charcoal sketches of her, but was really more interested in her father, whom he thought looked a lot like John Barrymore. Ned politely declined, not wanting anything to do with such a sissy business, but that did succeed in cooling him on chaperoning.

Soon she would say goodbye to all those beauty contests, because all the illustrators were calling her. For Haskel Coffin she became the new look for his illustrations of women. Being unusually short for a model, only 5'2", Mac Barclay gave her the nickname vest-pocket Miss America, after the new, small paperback books that were then popular.

Being a model doesn't require a high intellect but it does have some standards that applied then as well as now. Dependability is crucial. Nowhere does the truism "time is money" apply more aptly. A certain amount of acting ability is helpful too and, in that regard, an ability to take directions. Being able to stand still is important, as is (and was more so in those days) an ability to smile while hot spotlights are burning your eyes.

Carolyn enjoyed the work and, as she would begin to realize over time, she liked being around artists. Though she had no real interest in being famous, she liked being busy, making money, having fun, and most of all being independent. She no longer had a curfew and didn't have to report everywhere she went. Living with Ned and Flo, however, became more and more irritating. They treated her like a child.

During her modeling years she made friends with two women with whom she stayed in touch for the rest of her life. One was Jeannette, a favorite model of the photographer Steichen, the other was a girl named Van, who became Johnny Power's secretary after first having held that job for Chamberlain Brown, another modeling agency across the hall.

Still living at home, and wanting only to sleep there, Carolyn often went to lunch or dinner with Van and occasionally helped out at the office. She invented the idea of using a clipboard system for jobs (each individual assignment was called a "job"), with clipboards for each model hung on a wall so that they could come in and see their job and sign up and go without Van having to fish through files. It was a system they used for years.

"The guy to work for," Carolyn said, "was the photographer Anton Bruehl. He would book you for the whole day, no matter what. You would come in at ten o'clock in the morning and never mind when you were finished, maybe it was eleven and maybe it was five in the afternoon, you would get twenty-five bucks for the day." The standard rate was five dollars an hour.

There were, of course, exceptions to the rule. That standard rate didn't apply to the superstars of their times. One of those stars was Marion Morehouse, who married E. E. Cummings. She was a tall, willowy high-fashion model who worked for Steichen and for Anton Bruehl. Morehouse was one of the highest paid models in those days, making twenty-five dollars an hour. That was the absolute tops.

The most used, though, was Betty Mar who, according to Carolyn, "It was in the newspapers that she made thirty-five thousand dollars one year." Another was Betty, Betty Russell, who was Rosalind Russell's sister-in-law. (She was married to Rosalind Russell's brother, a film cutter.) "Russell was, a beautiful dame, you could almost compare her to Michelle Pfeiffer, and she had heavy, naturally blond hair she could roll up and hold with one hair pin. She was always the bride in all the fashion shows."

CHESTER

I was twelve years old when at breakfast one morning, Carolyn, while reading the *Times* obituaries, exclaimed, "Oh my God, Chester died!" "Who's Chester?" I asked. Chester was her first husband. I had heard bits and pieces of this story before, eavesdropping on adult conversations, but hadn't paid much attention. She read me his obituary and then matter-of-factly began the story.

He had appeared at the beginning of her modeling career. She was dating her first boyfriend, Al Hoffman. They had a standing date on Saturday, Sunday, and Wednesday. They routinely went to the movies and out to dinner at a restaurant in Washington Park, in Westville, New Jersey, where they'd have their usual chicken salad or turkey dinner, and Nesselrode pudding (the Tiramisu of those times) for dessert.

It was 1927, the year the Holland Tunnel opened. Chester later said that he must have paid off the Tunnel driving over to Newark in his new Marmon to pick her up. In retrospect, she felt she may have been nudged more in Chester's direction when Al, claiming he was playing second fiddle to Chester, had gotten angry with her. But for whatever reason, when Chester Beecroft began courting her, it was the beginning of the end for Al.

Chester had made a name for himself in a number of ways. At the turn of the century a Greenland Eskimo boy had captured the attention of the New York area press when he was abandoned in the city by arctic explorer Robert Peary, after being "given" to the Museum of Natural History, as a human artifact. After hearing about the case, Chester, then an actor on Broadway, became famous for lobbying President Theodore Roosevelt on behalf of the boy, whose name was Minik. He went on to be the boy's advocate and one of his surrogate fathers until the boy's death in 1918.

While Al was just a few years older than her, and could look forward to an affluent life in his family business, Beecroft was sixteen years older than Carolyn and a widower. He had been a War Correspondent during WWI, and an actor on Broadway in the 1920s, and had worked in the motion picture industry for some years. "He was just more interesting than Al," Carolyn said, "And he was very handsome!"

A complex man who presented himself to the world as full of joie de vivre, Chester nevertheless carried emotional wounds that must have resonated with Carolyn, who had with such determination tucked the death of her mother and her orphaned life with Aunt Mona into the back of her mind and gone forward into the world.

Several years before meeting Carolyn, Chester had been married and living in a beautiful home in New Canaan, CT. He and his wife, Eleanor, had a child with multiple birth defects, including Down syndrome. While being bathed by a nurse, the baby went into convulsions and died. Not long after, Eleanor also died of a botched abortion.

Chester proposed to Carolyn after a lunch date on April Fool's Day, 1928. "You're not serious!" Carolyn said. He insisted he was. At twenty years old she wasn't serious about much, other than being alive, but with a "What the hell, we're having fun," attitude, she said yes.

They sent a telegram to Ned and Flo, and Carolyn told them, "Please don't tell Al! Tell him I'm at Montauk Point, on location." She'd never been to Montauk, and all she knew about it was that her Uncle Will died there while in the Army. She picked The Point, she said, because she thought the distance would discourage them from coming after her. That night they stayed at the Roosevelt Hotel and the next day they went out to Hart's Island near City Island, NY to an Inn called Carey's Point. The Inn was owned by Harry Carey, a friend of Chester's, who was, and remained for many years, a big star in Westerns.

The following day in Rye, NY, a Justice of the Peace performed the marriage ceremony with Chester's good friend Gustav Tacot, called Tee, and his wife as witnesses. Meanwhile the Piersons, along with Al Hoffman, were hot on the trail with enough cops to make a *Keystone Cops* movie. Carolyn and Chester made it to Lanes Beach in Pelham and rowed over to Rat Island, their final destination. They had escaped the pursuers. Fait accompli!

While married to Chester, Carolyn lived either on "The Boat," a 70' sailing yacht which Chester shared with his friend Tee, or in a little cottage on Rat Island, off of Pelham Manor, NY, or, if the weather was bad and they were in town, in a secret apartment at Hearst's studios in Astoria. This apartment was one of his many secret hideaways, a little love nest where Hearst could stay with his mistress, Marion Davies, when he was in New York.

Entrance to the apartment required pushing a button in Chester's office, which caused a panel to slid open revealing an elevator. The elevator took you straight to a penthouse on top of the studio building, a complete apartment with paneled walls, bedroom, kitchen, dining room - the works. Chester was a favored employee; he'd been production manager for some of Hearst's big extravaganzas, including *Little Old New York* and *Little Lord Fauntleroy*. "The Old Man" had just recently given him a big cash bonus.

For years I knew little about "The Boat," as my mother called it. She had forgotten its name. In 2007, searching the Internet, I eventually found Tee's grandson and then the son. Both were named Charles and lived in Tallahassee, Florida. The elder Charles, who was in his seventies, filled me in on his father, Gustav "Tee" Tacot:

He had been born in France in 1877 and been in the French Cavalry before moving to Canada, where he became a lieutenant in the Canadian Cavalry and also took training in artillery. After entering civilian life he became a trainer for racing thoroughbreds, first in western Canada and then the western U.S. and eventually down into Mexico. While in Mexico he worked with Pancho Villa training his army in both cavalry and artillery. At the same time, his sister, who lived in Rye NY, was lead to understand through a New York newspaper, that Tee had been hung by the anti-Villa forces, information that she soon learned, to her relief, was false. In 1913 or 1914, possibly to assure his sister that he was still alive, he traveled to Rye. It was there that he met Chester.

Tee and Chester were two handsome and available bachelors. Tee had taken a job at the Westchester Biltmore as the manager of the hotel's stables and carriage rental. The Biltmore was a center of social activities for the wealthy and prominent. Chester met many beautiful women when he hired them as extras and walk-ons for Hearst's movies. Before too long Chester, looking for a good horseman for a film, was introduced to Tacot and they became fast friends. Being handsome and eligible bachelors, they were soon making the rounds together, hobnobbing with the wealthy and prominent at the Biltmore and double-dating beautiful young women who flocked to them both.

The Boat, from what Chester implied to Carolyn, was owned by him and Tee together. They'd bought it very cheaply, little more than a hull, and restored it themselves. When I talked with Tee's son, however, I heard a different story. According to him, Tee owned the boat, plain and simple. Chester, according to Charles Tacot, liked to embellish, especially for the benefit of women. From what I have since learned, I tend to believe that. But, coming from a seafaring town, having grown up with many fisherman and boat aficionados of varied types, I know that it is quite common for men to go in on boats in a casual way, starting as partners in what initially costs little or nothing, and ending up pouring small fortunes into what is sometimes referred to as "a hole in the water into which you pour money." I don't think it's unfair, therefore, to suppose that Chester had some kind of informal "piece" of the boat. Boats are females that men are not disinclined to share. (As far as I can tell, there was never any argument about ownership.)

They had found the stripped-down hull in a City Island boatyard and, while refitting it, also changed it from a sloop into a yawl. It needed new sails, new hardware, new everything. It had never had an engine, so it needed that, and adding a driveshaft on to a big wooden hull like that must have been no easy task. The boat's name was *Irondequoit*, the name of a town and a river on the shore of Lake Ontario adjoining Rochester. It had started its career in the 1800s racing on the Great Lakes, and had also raced in the Atlantic, winning The King's Cup twice. By this description alone, it was the kind of boat that men of a certain type fall in love with.

Carolyn and Chester had been married for a few months when a former girlfriend wrote that she was coming for a visit. Tee and his newlywed wife Mary were near hysteria. "My God, what's going to happen? Should we tell Carolyn?" was how they expressed it. Naturally, they told her, and Carolyn, having grown into the broad-minded and casual young *New Yorker* reader that she was, said, "Alright. What the hell!" Graciously, when this girl named Jill arrived, Carolyn invited her to spend a weekend at the Island. And, not so graciously, Jill spent the weekend, then spent two weeks, and then three weeks. More luggage arrived. It appeared she had moved into the cabin and wasn't going anywhere.

Chester gave all of his girlfriends nicknames. Jill, whose real name was Ethyl, got her name because he thought she saw the world through a children's book mentality, as in Jack and Jill. He called Carolyn Tinker Bell, because she was short, and seemed to be everywhere at once. Another of his love interests, Beryl Cummings, was named Starlight. (Beryl had another nickname, "The Phenomenon of the Foothills," given to her by Marion Davies, because she had the power to thwart the will of William Randolph Hearst.) When Chester met her, she was married. Her husband was the son of future Attorney General of the U.S., Homer S. Cummings.

The affair with Beryl happened while both were married and fell apart when Beryl met an illustrator named Carl Mueller, who Carolyn would, coincidentally, become friends with at a later date. Ray and Carolyn eventually met at Carl's apartment.

On a hot, sticky, and dull end-of-summer weekend, with no wind, they were moored off the north fork of Eastern Long Island near Greenport. It was morning. My twenty year old future mother lounged on the bowsprit. Jill sat on deck reading *The Rime of the Ancient Mariner* to Chester, who she referred to as "Doll." Carolyn was quietly annoyed. She felt that she might as well have been invisible. Invisibility has its costs and its freedoms. She removed her wedding ring and tossed it over the side and watched it go down, down, down, into the muddy Greenport bottom. No one had seen her do it and she didn't say anything, she just bided her time. In early fall, she went back to work. She got a week's work from Haskell Coffin and at night stayed at Johnny Power's apartment. On Friday she headed for Rat Island. Better let Carolyn tell it from here:

"So, I guess I stopped at Charles' Market and bought a thick steak and some good butter and made my way up to City Island. But I must have been a little ahead of time, or Chester and Jill had spent a little more time than they planned to. I looked across from Lanes Beach and saw Beecroft rowing the boat toward Hart's Island and I thought, bastard. You know, I could see the girl in the boat. I knew it was Jill. Chester was rowing from the island towards another landing, not the one that we usually went to, Lanes Beach, which had bath houses and showers and which was where we changed our clothes. He'd been trying to duck me. So, I high-tailed it up to the landing and she got off and I gave her an earful and then she sputtered something or other, some lame excuse and I beat her up."

I was forty-six-years old at the time and thought I knew my mother well, but this stopped me in my tracks. Calmly, Carolyn added, "Well, I gave her a good shaking and she may have been clawed. And I would think maybe she carried the scars the rest of her life. But, she didn't come back." *May have been clawed.* I remembered being just a little bit shocked on hearing that. I might have heard this story before but it must have been in an edited version because I hadn't remembered the clawing. Or the calm "carried the scars for the rest of her life." In other words, she most definitely had been clawed. That action would be felonious assault if it happened today. And Jill was gone, and she never came back, ever.

After the wedding ring went to the muddy bottom off Greenport and after Chester found out about it, and after Carolyn's attack on Jill a week or so later, there was some arguing and discussion and a reassessment of plans. In just a matter of a few months, the honeymoon was over and divorce was in the air. She had never been madly in love with him, but she liked him. In fact, up to that time, she'd never been entirely serious about anything. Chester had this act of being a free spirit, and he was charming. "He was fun, and he was full of shit," she added, as an afterthought. Maybe, she mused, she was just tired of being married to a 45-year-old when she was still only 21.

The Carolyn-Chester divorce used the most common method available in those days, the mock-adultery charade. It was either that or go to Reno, and they both decided they could not afford the waste of time or money for that. The play-acting took place at Van's new apartment on 51st Street. Carolyn paid for the detective, who doubled as a photographer. Isabel Jewell, a Broadway actress and another of Chester's old girlfriends, played the adulteress, appearing with Chester before the assembled group in a state of mild disarray. She called Chester "Chet" and was crazy about him.

That same year, 1930, Jewell was a big hit with a starring role in *Up Pops the Devil* on Broadway. Then she appeared in the play *Blessed Event*. *Blessed Event* was turned into a film and she moved to Hollywood to recreate her roll in it. She stayed in Hollywood and over the years appeared in over 100 films. Most remembered for her role as the prostitute Gloria Stone in "Lost Horizon" in 1937, she continued to act in small but often juicy roles, such as the white-trash hooker in "Gone with the Wind." "She was a darling ham. Very sweet," Carolyn said. After the performance everyone, including Captain Tee and his wife Mary, went out for dinner.

Carolyn divorced Chester in 1931. After the divorce she moved into the Barbizon because "well, that's just what you did," is how she put it. It was the posh thing to have a room with your own bath, and for that she paid all of $18 a week. Then for a while she moved into a new building at 310 East 44th Street with a two year lease and two months free rent, for which she paid $37 per month. She asked Van, who had been commuting from her family's place in Ridgefield Park, to move in with her. But Van drove Carolyn a little loony most of the time, frequently wanting to chat, while Carolyn needed solitude for reading. (After having read Stanislavski, she became interested in the creative process in general and began reading about art and painting.) Before long she moved back to the Barbizon. The magazine business continued to do well during the Depression, and therefore so did modeling. Around that time, Carolyn was signed to do Thom McAn Shoes, an on-the-road fashion show, dressed as and portraying Little Annie McAn.

MY PARENT'S: COURTSHIP AND MARRIAGE

They first met each other at a cocktail party one night in the mid-1930s at the apartment of Carl Mueller, a famous illustrator and elder statesman of his field. It was fall, and Carolyn had gone to bed early because of a headache or something, when Carl Mueller called. He was a couple of sheets to the wind and wanted her to "put on your drawers" and come over. They were having a party. James Montgomery Flagg was there; he had spoken on the radio that night. Flagg was another very famous painter and illustrator; a man about town, a ladies' man, a friend and fellow bon vivant of John Barrymore. Today he is remembered mostly for his recruiting poster of Uncle Sam, in which he used himself as a model with his finger pointing at the viewer, and the caption reading "I Want You."

    Flagg was a new friend of Ray's, and someone Ray looked up to as a mentor. Several other illustrators were at this party, as well as members of the press, both radio and print. Most of the revelers, including Ray, belonged to one if not all of the following clubs; The Society of Illustrators, Artists and Writers, The Dutch Treat Club. Carl's apartment was nearby at 59th Street and First Avenue by the bridge, so Carolyn walked up the hill, took the elevator to his penthouse and, as she emerged from the elevator, a garlicky plate full of salad was shoved in her face. "Have some of this!" Carl said. "They were all way ahead of me in the booze department," she remembered.

Carolyn knew many of the revelers. There was a guy named Jimmy Stranahan, who was always in the picture. He had a girlfriend, and they were draped over a sofa. The place was jumping, with everybody high on red wine. Ray was in the kitchen doing the cooking and when he was introduced to Carolyn he emerged from his labors. A tall man with black wavy hair and blue eyes, at six feet two inches tall he was a full foot taller than Carolyn. He said to her, out of the blue, "What are you, the intellectual type?" She wasn't going to be put on the defensive. Instead, she countered with, "Yeah, read any good books lately?" And Ray enthusiastically launched into a description of a new book, *The Native's Return,* written by his friend Louis Adamic, a famous left-wing writer of the time. Adamic was a Yugoslav and a critic of American culture. Carolyn said, "Well, I've read *The Return of the Native,*" but Ray brushed that aside. "I am a peasant! I'm going back!" he exclaimed. He was planning a trip back to his birthplace, Yugoslavia.

The rest of the party they both remembered as boring. Carolyn later remembered Carl's girlfriend Ruth complaining because Merrill Mueller, Carl's son, who was all of eighteen then, had run up a $15 dollar a month dry cleaning bill! She would recall that remark every time when, years later, she watched Merrill on the TV news. (By the time of J.F.K.'s presidency, he had become an anchor for NBC News.)

After a while Ray said, "Come on, let's get out of here," and they went down to Billy's, a popular steak joint on the corner of 56th and First where they sat drinking until 3 a.m. And then he wanted her to come up and see his paintings. "You know," he said, "I don't just do that shit you saw," referring to the double-page spread illustration he'd just done for American Magazine which had been on display at the party. It was the most important job he'd done since moving from Chicago. The Art Director of *American Magazine*, Al Lefcourt, had come with Ray to Carl Mueller's party, so Ray could rightly think he had made it in the Big City. But he was letting Carolyn know that he thought illustration was of lesser import than "serious" painting, an attitude which as time went on would not win him any friends in his chosen field. In fact, it was around that time when a few illustrators, like J.M. Flagg, began to be vocally dismissive of Modern Art.

Ray began a campaign to have Carolyn see his things, his non-illustrations, what were often called in those days "easel paintings." Carolyn said "Well, some other time, not now, it's a little late." That was in or around October, and he called her for a long time, but Carolyn was always busy. Then came the Christmas holidays and her roommate Van was really sick with the flu complicated by asthma. Over the Christmas weekend she abandoned Van for a few hours to go out to Little Neck with Freddy Siensen, an advertising executive and art director. Siensen's father was Danish and his mother was Japanese and he had grown up in China. By Carolyn's account he was an interesting and nice fellow. She got home around one o'clock in the morning. Freddy left Carolyn at the door. As she entered the apartment, there was her invalid roommate sitting up with a bottle of bourbon and this guy Prohaska. Carolyn said to Van, "You made a rapid recovery, didn't you?" With that, as she remembered it, "And this was typical Prohaska; he picked Van up, gave her a kiss, carried her into the bedroom and dumped her on the bed and said, "Okay now, let's talk. You're the one I wanted to see." Love was in bloom.

Before he put Van to bed, there had been a conversation about what was going to take place New Year's Eve, only a few days away. Carolyn, who was feeling jolly, said, "Well, my buddy here, and I, we're going to a friend's place, he's an Art Director, for roast suckling pig, and I'm sure you're invited."

The words Art Director and suckling pig both got Ray's attention. He confessed he had a date with Winnie Strickland, a model they both knew, to go and hear Ozzie and Harriet sing. But it would be no trouble breaking that. So, they had a date. They ushered in the New Year of 1935 at the party at Freddy Siensen's. Ray brought along two of his friends, the brothers Ham and Bob Place, Princeton boys he had met through Rube Rankin of the Rankin Agency. They arrived when the party was in full swing, the aroma of roast pig wafting into the hall; three guys with instruments, saxophone, mandolin and guitar (Ray on sax), singing *"Put on Your Old Gray Bonnet."* Everyone began dancing and the party was a big hit.

When they began dating, Carolyn had been divorced for four years. She was 27. Ray was 34 and had been separated from his first wife for about six months. He was staying in his studio on 44th Street and his wife Dolly was living in their apartment on 38th Street. It would be several years before Ray and Carolyn got married, and another several years before they had their first child together. Ray's son with Dolly was conveniently away at boarding school most of the time. Ray had been instantly successful as a fiction illustrator from the moment he hit New York and Carolyn continued to make money as a model. Prohibition was over and the cocktail party was now an accepted part of the culture. They were a couple and they were having fun.

The Artists and Writers Club had quarterly meetings which were mostly social. In the winter they went to Palm Beach, while in spring, summer and fall they often met on eastern Long Island, either at the Montauk Manor or in Southampton at The Mansard. Among those who attended the A&W meetings were Al Dorn and Neysa McMein, illustrators; Grantland Rice, sports writer; Russell Paterson, Rube Goldberg and Otto Soglow, cartoonists; and magazine fiction writers such as Clarence Budington Kelland and Pearl Buck. As soon as they began dating Ray and Carolyn became part of that social set as well as that of the Society of Illustrators. (Ray by then had also become a member of the Dutch Treat Club, founded by Rube Goldberg, but that was for men only.)

The first beach they went to when they started dating was Barnegat. They went there for the weekend. But when they started going out to eastern Long Island, they found that they both liked it better than the Jersey Shore. At first they only went for the Artists and Writers Meetings (they were not actually meetings, but excuses to eat, drink and play golf) and stayed either in Southampton at The Mansard or Burnett's, or in Montauk at the Montauk Manor. The Manor was a Rankin Advertising Agency client, and Ray and Carolyn stayed there gratis because they were friends with the two Rankin brothers and their wives.

Carolyn remembered in particular one weekend spent in a posh apartment at The Manor with Kitty Rankin. It was a bleak gray day and Kitty laughed and said, "Accept for the quiet, and the fog horn, we might as well be in Manhattan!" But Ray was enjoying it, driving around looking at the rocky shoreline and discovering surfcasting. So, before long they were going out on their own, often bringing along Ray's friend and father figure, the illustrator Wallace Morgan.

Curiosity had led Carolyn to visit East Hampton in the early 1930s when she became friends with fellow Power's model Elise Gay, who was born and raised there. She was curious because her Uncle Will had died at Montauk, part of East Hampton Town and because she was a direct descendant of one of Southampton's first English families.

Uncle Will was James Malcolm Pierson's son, named after his grandfather William of Cairo. Will had been in the Spanish American War, serving as a Sgt. Major with the 71st National Guard Regiment of N.Y. when it was attached to Teddy Roosevelt's Rough Riders in Cuba. He died of a tropical disease while recuperating at Camp Wikoff at Montauk, N.Y.

Elise Gay's father was a builder and house mover who had worked on the East Hampton houses of Grantland Rice and Ring Lardner. Her parents were divorced and she and her mother had an apartment in Manhattan on Sutton Place. It was through Elise that Carolyn and Ray learned about a rooming house, what would today be called a bed and breakfast, in the home of Mr. and Mrs. Ned Dayton. Mr. Dayton, who would become one of Ray's most frequent models, was a descendant of an East Hampton founding family.

KITTY, RUBE, AND THE '35 YUGO TRIP

Sometimes after dinner, or on returning home from a party, my mother would sit with a brandy and a cigarette and talk to me about her life before me, a subject which began to fascinate me as I entered adolescence. It was then that she talked about Van, and Rube, and Kitty, and Yas [prn. Yash] and Sarah, and enough characters to fill a novel. In my pre-adolescent days my listening had been peripheral and sporadic. Her drinking annoyed me. She seemed like a different person when she was buzzed; sort of numb; sort of strange. But when I began to smoke cigarettes and have a glass of wine openly and with parental approval, at about fifteen, listening to her rambling became something I looked forward to.

I would question her about Ray's history, about which he was either too vague or fragmented when I tried to pry him open. Carolyn, during their courting days, had gotten to know some of his Chicago and San Francisco friends when they came to New York to visit. She would talk to me about Rube and Kitty as if it had all happened yesterday.

From what she said I gathered that the Rankin brothers had been the core of Ray's social life from the day he arrived in New York. When he and Carolyn became a couple, Kitty Rankin had become one of her best friends (and, later, my Godmother; my "Aunt Kitty.") Rube

Rankin and his brother Chuckles, who of course had another name which I never learned, had inherited an advertising agency from their parents that had offices in Chicago and New York. Rube had run the Chicago office and had moved to New York around the same time that Ray did. The Rankins did the advertising for the White and Red Star Steamship Lines. It was through them that Ray, on several occasions, wrangled free passage to Europe. He would do sketches of passengers while sitting at the Captain's table. During the Thirties, he made four trips to Europe that way, traveling around with his sketch book and watercolors. One year he went to the Brussels World's Fair.

In 1935, shortly after meeting Carolyn, he went for his most important trip, back to his roots, to Yugoslavia. Before leaving for Europe, Ray left money for his wife and son and gave Carolyn and Kitty an assignment: to find an apartment for him that would be ready when he got back. In those days, apartments were going cheap. It was still the Depression and people moved often, so perhaps that wasn't quite such an imposition as it would be today.

It was summertime. Carolyn was taking plenty of time off for herself, going to Rockport, Maine, and on several occasions to Block Island, traveling via steamship. She would stay in a boarding house, sketch and read. But she didn't forget Ray's imperious demand. "Find a place for me to live and work!" he had said. Kitty and Carolyn, who knew the neighborhood pretty well (Kitty's mother lived at 32 Beekman Place), went apartment hunting for him.

They found a place they liked at 18 Beekman. The price was $55 a month. It was a "delightful place," both Kitty and Carolyn agreed, with two windows looking out on Beekman Place and a bay window looking out on 51st Street. There was a beautiful parquet floor, which Carolyn scrubbed by hand. At one point though, she told me, she did ask herself, "Why am I doing this?"

Both Carolyn and Kitty were "Mad!" for Ray. They really wanted him to like it. They were worried that he'd come back and look at it and say, "Boy I'm not gonna live in this dump!" He'd told Carolyn, "You're not going to be some spoiled dame, I'm not going to open doors for you," and she had accepted that. She said, "I guess I thought it was part of his native charm." He'd figured out to his own satisfaction that Al Hoffman and another of her boyfriends, Gene Suter, had made fools of themselves over her, and he damn sure wasn't going to do that.

It was to be his first trip back to Yugoslavia since he had left as a child. He planned to spend most of the summer there, long enough to reconnect with his roots. He had been inspired by Louis Adamic, whom he'd gotten to know and planned to meet up with in Dubrovnik.

All he had to do on board the cruise ship was be polite to the customers and make drawings. The first night out he saw this gorgeous gal and decided he was going to dance with her and be her "friend." After all, you know, five or six days across the Atlantic could be a long time. (This is the story he gave to Carolyn which she took with a grain of salt.)

A German fellow came up to him while he and the gal were dancing. The man was mad. He wanted to dance with the lady. So he punched Ray, and Ray punched him, and they brawled every night on the dance floor, until the captain had to put them both in the brig. Germans weren't too popular in those days, so in spite of the fact that the guy was an executive for a big company that did its shipping through the Red Star Line, he became the villain. Ray had been protecting the lady's honor.

Carolyn knew about the brawling before Ray's return. It seems a Capt. Dwyer, a board member of the Red Star Line, had had dinner at Kitty and Rube's and Carolyn was there and the Captain relayed the story as a humorous anecdote. When the ship docked in Southampton, England, the German was met by his wife and children, so there was no official documentation of the fight over the dame, who of course belonged with a third party.

Throughout the summer Carolyn got cables and radiograms from Ray, such as, "Dear Putsie, I need a place to live and work! Love Ray." And toward the end of August she got a cable that said, "Arriving so and so date, meet me at Pier so and so." Carolyn had to cable back that she wouldn't be able to meet him because she'd heard through the grapevine that Dolly and Sonny (Ray Jr.) would be meeting the boat. According to Carolyn, Dolly was going to make a big scene, she would, "Pull the broken hearted wife crap. She would say that Ray left them to starve in New York." Carolyn's roommate Van, having gotten married (to a Norwegian fisherman in New Jersey), there was a new roommate, named Rose Walker. Rose was dating a doctor named O'Brian, a resident at St. Vincent's who happened to be a friend of Al Hoffman's, with whom Carolyn was still friends. O'Brian was an Irishman from Brooklyn and what Carolyn referred to as a "fixer." He knew everybody. He made a couple of calls and said it was all taken care of. Carolyn would meet the ship on a Dallwell Towing tugboat which would be escorting Ray's ship up The Narrows. The tugboat was the *SS Carey Messick*, which was good luck, because Carey was her nickname. She bought a new black skirt for the occasion, and it fluttered in the breeze as she climbed the rope ladder onto the ship with everybody on the boat hanging over one side waving to the Statue of Liberty and watching Prohaska's girlfriend coming aboard.

As Carolyn remembered, "It was all kissy kissy, and Putsy that and Putsy this, and introductions all around," and when the ship docked she was ushered through a special exit "around back" and made her way to the new apartment where Ray, after pacifying Dolly and Sonny with some leftover cash, joined her.

As soon as he had settled into the new apartment he called Mama and Carolyn experienced the initial shock of hearing him speak Serbo-Croatian. He stayed on the phone for a long time and Mama cried when he told about the feast that was prepared for him in Muo, his home village in Yugoslavia. He promised to send her photographs. Carolyn got to say hello, the first of only a few conversations she ever had with Mama. She was surprised to discover that Mama could barely speak English.

Mama in fact was mostly illiterate; her daughters and niece were still trying to teach her to read and write in English when she was an old lady. She communicated by mail with letters written by Ray's younger sister, Antoinette, who had been sent to business school by Ray, and could take dictation and type. Carolyn never got more out of Ray about his mother than that she was an Icon; the source of all wonder, knowledge and intuition, and the greatest cook in the world. Whether she herself could ever live up to that kind of comparison when she became wife and mother was left definitively unanswered.

He loved the apartment. Of course, it needed painting, so he ordered painters and the bedrooms were painted dark brown, "beautiful, elephant ass brown," Carolyn called it. The living room was white-white, and the bathroom was a deep blue. He closed off the window in the bathroom so it could double as a dark room. He lived there until they got married in 1939.

Dolly and Ray had split in 1934 and were divorced in 1937. They had a son, Ray Jr., who had early on become an overly chubby and somewhat sulky child; a disappointment to his father. Ray, Carolyn's Ray, had been unhappy. In fact, he was so miserable, he told Carolyn, he wanted to jump in front of a train. But, he was making lots of money in Chicago, more than he ever made in his life. He had a trunk line to J. Walter Thompson and was doing tons of work for them. It wasn't until he lost all his savings in the 1929 Crash, that he was motivated to try something new.

When he got to New York, Ray quickly established himself as a fiction illustrator, which, no matter how much money you might make in the advertising world, was a world apart, and a step up, from being the owner of an art service. In the 1930s, illustrators were artists, and artists were frequently illustrators, and though the chasm between the two would begin to grow in a few years, it hadn't happened yet.

Carolyn & Ray on their honeymoon

Ray and Carolyn were married in the spring of 1939. They had intended to sail for Europe on a Red Star Line ship, but the North Atlantic was by then thick with U-boats, which worked out well for Ray since his second choice for a honeymoon was to go fishing on the Miramichi River, a river that flows from New Brunswick, Canada, northeast into the Gulf of St. Lawrence. They hopped into Ray's Pierce Arrow and headed north, stopping in a small town somewhere in New Hampshire to be married by a Justice of The Peace.

Aside from having to fight off black flies by chain smoking,

Carolyn enjoyed herself; she was married to a guy she really loved and she loved seeing him enjoy himself. They were gone for almost a month, stopping to fish at several places on the way north. Ray caught enough trout and Atlantic salmon to keep himself happy for some time.

When they returned to Manhattan they moved into a larger place at 32 Beekman Place, a second-floor apartment that was, at $65 a month, quite expensive. It had a huge kitchen which had once been a conservatory. They were still at 32 Beekman when it came time to vote in November of 1940, because Carolyn remembered that they voted uptown. They were, both of them, waffling between Willkie and F.D.R., but decided they shouldn't "change horses in midstream," as F.D.R. was warning against.

Then, a studio at the famous 10th Street Studios building in Greenwich Village became available and Ray snatched it up. He had long wanted one of these studios, and was soon taking the bus downtown every morning to work. That arrangement worked out well until Carolyn became pregnant. They were warned that the tenants at 32 Beekman didn't like babies, so when an apartment became available across the street from the 10th Street Studios, it was too much good luck to be discounted, and they moved again.

JULIAN LEVI

Though he was a dedicated fine arts painter who had no interest in doing illustrations, Julian Levi would occasionally, for a small fee, do layouts for his friend Al Lefcourt. Lefcourt was Art Director for *American Magazine*, for whom Ray had done his well-received, first nationally published illustration. With one of Levi's layouts, Lefcourt had won an Art Directors award. Julian and Ray met shortly after the party at Karl Muellers. Lefcourt and Levi, along with Julian's cousin, Bob Wertheimer, had rented a small bungalow on Barnegat, and Ray and Carolyn became occasional visitors. Wertheimer owned a small sailboat and Carolyn loved sailing. By this time, they had already met Gladys and Floyd Davis at the Society of Illustrators, and with the addition of Julian they were welcomed into the circle of the more established of the "easel painting" crowd in New York at that time. (The most important really modern painter they met in those days was Stuart Davis, whom they met through Julian.)

Julian, about the same age as Ray, was born in Yorkville in New York City, in 1900 and studied at the Pennsylvania Academy of Fine Arts. He had been in Paris during most of the decade of the 1920s where he became friends with many of the better known painters of the period and was particularly friendly with and probably influenced by Jules Pascin.

When he returned to New York from Paris he established himself in an art world that was a mixture of the more purely American styles of painting and that which was being influenced by the European Modernists. He painted romantic, lyrical landscapes and portraits and still lifes that were American in feeling and yet revealed the influence of both Pascin and Picasso. Julian Levi came of age and went on into middle age, as a known and respected fine artist during the time before New York was a center of the Art World. He had gone to school with Abraham Rattiner and Adolph Gottlieb, and remained friends with them throughout their lives, though he never had the kind of success to equal either of them. He was also good friends in those years with Alex Brook, who in the pre-abstraction years was very successful.

In a more forgiving world, one that didn't throw out all but the pick of the litter every time the Goddess of Art whelped, Alexander Brook would probably be known today as one of the great artists of his time. He was certainly highly respected by his peers, including Ray and Carolyn, who enjoyed visiting him in Sag Harbor (just a few miles from Amagansett), in spite of his usually alcohol inflamed bitterness about the world of abstraction.

Born in 1898 in Brooklyn to Russian immigrants, Alex contracted polio at the age of twelve and during that time developed an interest in painting. When he recovered, though permanently crippled, he continued his education by reading at the New York Public Library and spending time at the Metropolitan Museum of Art in Manhattan. He enrolled at the Art Students League in 1915 and married the artist Peggy Bacon, whom he had met at the League in 1920. Both Peggy Bacon's parents were successful artists, who also met at The League during its early years.

Peggy Bacon might be considered one of the most striking examples of an easel painter who was also an illustrator and was equally successful and respected in both fields. She was also a cartoonist and on occasion a writer. She worked for the most successful magazines of her day including *Vanity Fair* and *The New*

Yorker. Alex and Peggy were married for twenty years and had two children, Belinda and Alexander, known as Sandy.

Alex had become part of The Whitney Studio Club, organized by Gertrude Vanderbilt Whitney, and soon became an important part of that group of emerging artists. In 1931 that club evolved into The Whitney Museum of American Art. In 1938 he went to Savannah and did a series of paintings and drawings using the people and the landscape of an impoverished African American neighborhood as his subject. These remain among his most successful and best known works.

Brook served as an army correspondent in Panama during WWII, providing sketches for the military. When released from this assignment, *Life* magazine commissioned him to continue his war effort as an illustrator of the same subject; and after The War to produce a series of portraits of Hollywood actresses. These were done in his own style and while they were sold as illustration, it had no negative effect on his career. After a brief marriage in Georgia, Alex married his third wife, artist Gina Knee, in 1944, and in 1948 they moved to Sag Harbor full time where they lived for the rest of their lives. Alex died in 1980.

After several summers spent staying in boarding houses in East Hampton or Amagansett, in 1947 Julian and his wife Jean bought a house in Springs just up the street from Jackson Pollock. The house Julian bought had been owned by Belle Kahn, an older Jewish lady who owned a variety store on Main Street in Amagansett. A variety store sold "notions," anything you might get a notion to buy, such as thread, a towel, a door stopper, small toys, cards, hair curlers, bubble gum and candy.

The first time Carolyn and Ray heard of Jackson Pollock was in the fall of 1944, when they were living on Hand Lane in Amagansett. Julian called and said a friend of theirs was coming to Springs, the daughter of Arthur B. Carles, a former teacher of Julian's at Pennsylvania Academy. Julian's friend was a fashion artist who worked for *Harper's Bazaar*. She was looking for a house. She said that her friend Jackson Pollock was renting in the area and that his wife knew of some houses, so she wanted to get in touch with them. Ray and Carolyn hadn't a clue. Julian, being closer to the contemporary scene, knew about Pollock, and in fact knew some of the group around the Art of This Century Gallery; the Guggenheim crowd. He was able to find the Pollocks by asking his neighbor Ed

Cook, a real estate broker.

THE EAST END

Ray and Carolyn rented in East Hampton in the summers of 1941, '42, and '43. Starting with the first summer, they often invited Wallace Morgan to stay with them. Morgan (1875-1948) was an older man, ancient in fact to the young couple, but a dear friend. He had been a sketch artist for the *Herald Tribune* for some years and a celebrated combat artist with the Army in WWI, before becoming an illustrator. He was probably then in his late sixties. He was a great and highly esteemed illustrator, a master at charcoal drawing, and an icon at the Society of Illustrators. Carolyn had begun her modeling career when she was eighteen years old as a result of meeting Morgan and illustrator Arthur William Brown when they were judges and she was a contestant at the Miss America pageant in Atlantic City in 1926. Because he was a friend of May and Jimmy Preston, they often had cocktails and dinner at the Preston house on Baiting Hollow Road.

In those days, illustrators often drew straight from the model rather than using photographs. Carolyn, in fact, had posed for May Preston in that way just weeks before the Wall Street Crash. She remembered being impressed that May had an entire closet filled with nothing but shoes; at least 300 pairs.

Jimmy Preston, though less famous, was a successful designer of books and book jackets. May and Jimmy had both been part of the Glackens/Ernest Lawson group, early Twentieth Century painters. May had studied with Robert Henri, who was a part of that group. Both Ray and Carolyn were impressed that May and Jimmy owned many Ernest Lawson paintings and that they referred to Glackens as "Glack." During this pre-war period the Preston's house was an important East End hub for the New Yorkers who represented their era's version of The Art Crowd. It was at the Preston's that Carolyn and Ray first met Warren and Enez Whipple, another young couple who would come to be year-round residents of East Hampton. Warren Whipple was an illustrator, and his wife Enez would become Director of East Hampton's Guild Hall Museum.

Another member of that informal group had been McClelland

Barclay, one of the most well-known illustrators of the 1930s. Both Ray and Carolyn knew Barclay from Artists and Writers; and Carolyn had done a fair amount of work for him over the years. In the mid-Thirties, Barclay had built a house in the Beach Hampton development, east of the village of Amagansett. His house survived the 1938 Hurricane with only a scratch, while a nearby large and brand new beach club with cabanas was reduced to matchsticks.

By 1941 though, Barclay was absent. He had become Lieutenant Commander Mac Barclay and had been on active duty since a year before (he had been in the Naval Reserve since 1935), and was sending back portraits of all the big brass from the Pacific Naval Front, as well as full color action illustrations of fighting ships at sea. He distinguished himself by inventing new patterns for camouflage and became the most famous illustrator associated with WWII in the Pacific.

Leonard Lester, a local East Hampton man who was also an artist and also in the Navy, met up with Barclay in Brisbane, Australia. Leonard was the son of a local man who had been a chauffeur for a wealthy East Hampton summer person. He had grown up on the Upper East Side of Manhattan and gone to parochial school. He spent every summer living with his aunt in Springs. He had attended The Art Students League and then, with a partner, he opened a photographer's studio on East Hampton's Main Street.

By the mid-1930s, Leonard was offered a job as an apprentice-assistant to Albert Herter, an artist well-known as an illustrator, fine artist and fabric designer, as well as for his murals. Herter had created the great estate in East Hampton called The Creeks, today owned by billionaire investor Ron Perelman. (Herter's son, Christian, was a Governor of Massachusetts and became Secretary of State during the Eisenhower Administration.) Through Herter, Leonard met and became friends with Mac Barclay, and when he, Leonard, married his wife Theo, she became one of Barclay's models.

Shortly before he died McClelland Barclay
dedicated this photo to Leonard Lester, 1943

In Brisbane, Leonard was making scale models of places the Navy had plans to attack. (This entailed doing aerial photography so he'd know what the places looked like.) Barclay had just arrived in Brisbane, found out that Leonard was there, and gave him a call. As Leonard recalled it: "Leonard, this is Mac. I'm gonna paint a portrait of MacArthur. I want you to give me a hand. I want you to take some photographs of MacArthur that I can use to paint from." Leonard and Mac went to see MacArthur and took some pictures, and when Mac realized that Leonard was the same size as MacArthur, he borrowed his hat and jacket and had Leonard do some live modeling for him, this being the way illustrators then worked, going back and forth between photographs and live models. "I put on the famous hat, and it fit me perfectly. And the leather jacket that he wore. Fit me perfect. I was exactly the same size as MacArthur." Mac did the portrait quickly, and then did a charcoal sketch of Leonard to show his appreciation for his help, and the next day he got on a ship headed for the Solomon Islands. His mission was to make sketches while the ship transported ammunition and supplies from Guadalcanal to Rendova, New Georgia, in the Solomons. At 1:30 a.m. on the 18th of July, 1943, the ship was hit by a torpedo which struck the aft portion where all the officers were berthed. Barclay and most of the crew perished. He left his Beach Hampton house to his mistress, Marty Hoff, the daughter of illustrator Guy Hoff. She lived there until the mid-Fifties when she moved to Southampton, selling the house to Robert Q. Lewis, a famed television game show host.

When she became pregnant with her first child, Carolyn decided to seek help with parenting. She was anxious. She realized she was clueless on the subject of motherhood. She had the good luck, however, through word of mouth, to be teamed up with the well-known psychoanalyst Dr. Margaret Ribble, author of a new and well-received book, *The Rights of Infants*. Ribble's office was on the 12th floor of a building on 12th Street, right around the corner from their new apartment on 10th Street.

Even while they were still living at 32 Beekman, with Ray taking the bus down to 10th St. to work, Carolyn began to notice that he often came home when dinner was cold, or called and said "Cancel dinner and join us at Peter's Backyard," a steak and booze place in the neighborhood of 51. At a certain time of day, not every day necessarily, 10th Street Studios, at 51 W. 10th, would cease to be a work place and become a floating studio party. Someone would bring a bottle and a guitar or a concertina into someone else's studio, an artist would begin dancing with a model, perhaps nude, or a nude would sit on an artist's lap. It was not the life of the average hardworking Joe in America in the early 40s. Having Carolyn and the baby me across the street must have, to some extent, cramped Ray's style, but she was in love and she was a liberated woman, raised, remember, by Suffragettes and a part of the work force since she was a teenager, so she tried to be a good sport about the loose morals of life on 10th Street.

After getting married and moving into 32 Beekman, Carolyn had set up her easel in the middle of the apartment and begun to paint there. Daily, she would move Ray's prize possession, an antique cherry chest highboy with a brass screen front that he had been schlepping around for years, so that she could paint by window light. (While I was growing up, it stood in our elegant little front parlor.)

One day in the late summer of 1942, while pregnant with her first child, me, and working on a still life, she shoved the chest out of the way of her arrangement and her back went "*Krrrk!*" From then on she suffered from terrible sciatica. On consulting an orthopedist, she was told that someday she'd probably do something as simple as step off a curb and that would be the end of it. She wouldn't be able to walk.

So, when I was three months old, after having gotten several opinions, she entrusted herself to a Dr. Smith who had done successful surgery on someone who was a member of the Society of

Illustrators. Dr. Smith, working as part of a team with a neurosurgeon who removed material from her spinal canal, did the spinal fusion, a procedure that was still in its infancy.

We were living on West Tenth when I was born. It was a privilege to spend my infanthood in a Greenwich Village building that formerly housed Mark Twain. A plaque still exists on the front of the building at 14 W. 10th St. to inform passersby of his one-time brief residency. On the other side of the coin though, and to my future horror, the same building was at a later date the home of the infamous child murderer, Dr. Joel Steinberg and his lover, Hedda Nussbaum, a creepy story.

While she recovered from her spinal fusion, the plan was for Ray to take care of the then three month old baby. An artist friend of Ray's, a fellow Yugoslav named Yanni Dobrova, had a mother who was, like Ray's mother, a peasant. Mama Dobrova lived in the neighborhood. Always dressed in black and full of peasant wisdom, she was by all reports another Saint. So the boys decided that Mama should come and stay and help with the baby.

Ray could see how this would work out well, since by all accounts Yanni's mother was a good cook, just like Ray's mama. (He could almost taste the roast lamb.) She was going to be housekeeper and babysitter. But Yanni's mama became offended when Ray brought in his new best friends John Alan Maxwell, Bill Irwin and Kip Saver, the whole gang, all from across the street, and when she found out she was expected to clean up after parties. She seems to have thought there was stuff going on that wasn't appropriate for somebody with a baby in the home. Then, too, she had a fit when the doctor came in to give the baby his shots, "putting poison in the baby." That was all the excuse Ray needed to get rid of "that goddamned old gypsy."

After the operation, Carolyn chose not to have a private room. Instead, she had a roommate, a "beautiful dame" by the name of Nan Taylor, who was married to an editor at the publishing company Raynal & Hitchcock (publishers, in 1947, of Malcolm Lowry's *Under the Volcano*.) They had two kids. Nan was there being treated for osteomyelitis, which she'd had since she was a child. The treatment, which was experimental (and which in her case was successful) involved the use of penicillin. A week after the operation, Ray, against regulations, sweet-talked (or bribed with cigarettes) the nurses into letting him onto the ward with the baby. He also brought in Nan's husband, who brought their kids.

Taking care of the baby full time made it impossible for Ray to work. When he became desperate, his close friends art director Eddy Eberman and his wife said they would just love it, and the girls would just love it (they had two little girls) if the baby were parked with them for a couple of weeks. The Ebermans ran a pheasant farm as a hobby, had a lovely house and grounds, and a Dalmatian dog. Ray and Kitty drove the baby, now called "Beanie," up to the Eberman's in New Canaan for the remainder of Carolyn's stay in the hospital.

A nurse named Callahan came home with Carolyn to work as a nanny. She promised to stay with them for a year. To avoid the crowd of mothers and nannies, she went at off-hours when she took the baby in the carriage to Washington Square Park, just a few blocks away. After one such trip she reported, "There's the most beautiful woman with two kids. The kids play in the sandbox, and the mother speaks French to them all the time." Thinking the two kids might interest Tony, Carolyn started going out to the park, found the woman, Carol de Havenon, and her two kids Andre and Michael, and introduced herself. Andre was a little older than Tony, and Michael a little younger. By what seemed to Carolyn an astonishing coincidence, Carol was the wife of Gaston de Havenon, a great friend and former bachelor roommate of Ray's buddy, Julian Levi. Carol was a Philadelphia Main Line Wasp, with pale white skin, black eyes and black hair. Gaston was a French Jew who was a wealthy perfume importer. Before Julian had paired off with his own wife, *Women's Wear Daily* staffer Jean Laurent, he and Gaston and art director Ken Stuart had shared an apartment in the village. Stuart became Art Director of the "Saturday Evening Post" in 1943 and remained there for 18 years.

When Callahan left unexpectedly after just a few weeks, having gotten an unexpected proposal from her high school sweetheart in Worcester Mass., they found a replacement for her by the name of Northy. Northy had been taking care of newborn twins for the writer Willard Espy. (One of the twins, Freddy, grew up to become the first Mrs. George Plimpton.) When Ray and Carolyn rented a place on Baiting Hollow Road in East Hampton in the summer of 1943, Northy stayed with Carolyn during the week while Ray went back to work at 10th Street.

After Labor Day, with no traffic on the roads, Northy began taking the baby carriage out to Montauk Highway and a half mile up the road to a filling station and back. Carolyn thought, why, with all of God's green earth, did she have to take a baby carriage out onto a major highway? When criticized for that, Northy's "nose went out of joint, she got huffy," according to Carolyn. Suspicions aroused, Carolyn noticed that on Northy's dresser was a bottle of pills, barbiturates. Conferring with Ray, they decided she might be a junkie. When, a few days later, Northy began complaining that her blood pressure was too high and that she was going to have a stroke, Carolyn called Dr. Edwards, one of two doctors in the area. "How old is she?" he asked, and when told fifty-five or sixty, he said, "Pay her off and put her on the train back to the city. She's just giving you a hard time." Armed with Dr. Edwards' advice, and with no train that night, Carolyn told her she could leave the next morning and barricaded herself and the baby in her bedroom, locking the door and pushing a chest of drawers against the door. In the morning she called a cab, put her on the Cannonball (the New York train), and that was the end of Northy.

In the summer of 1944 they rented a tiny house in Amagansett belonging to Elbert "Shorty" Parsons and his wife Emma. With Shorty off in The War in North Africa, Emma was living with her in-laws. She decided she could use some cash and offered the house for sale for a good price, around $3000. Ray had decided they should move to Amagansett full time. He didn't want his kid growing up in the city. More importantly, perhaps, he was hooked on surfcasting. So, they bought the house, and, soon after, they let go of the 14 West 10th Street apartment. From then on, when Ray went into the city he would leave Carolyn in Amagansett and sleep on a cot in the studio at 51W.10th Street. If Carolyn came with him, they would get a room at The Beekman Tower Hotel.

 The house was on Hand Lane, one of six lanes that begin at Main Street and go toward the ocean, ending at Bluff Road, which follows the ocean parallel with Main Street. Bluff Road also sits atop the very edge of a geological formation called the Bridgehampton Loam,* where the sand dunes begin. The houses on the northwest side of the road are on two feet of dark brown topsoil, while across the narrow tar road, at the beginning of the dunes, is white sand. Scrub growth like chokecherry, shadbush, and honeysuckle sprouts from the berm on the dune side where topsoil was built up when the road was graded, before it was tarred, probably around the turn of the 19th century.

This thick, fertile soil is so named because it was scraped off the surface of Connecticut by the last Ice Age glacier and deposited on the south side of Eastern Long Island, where its widest point is in Bridgehampton.

My earliest memories encompass a world circumscribed by Hand Lane and Main Street as far as Bunker's Radio Shop. I vaguely remember an adventurous tricycle ride up Main Street with my first friend, Tommy, he pedaling and I standing up in back, before being captured by Harry Steele, the ubiquitous Chief of Police. Another snapshot memory is of Mrs. Petty's backyard next to the Hand Lane house, with clothes flapping on the line and chickens scratching the grass. Mrs. Petty's backyard touched corners, conveniently, with that of the Gardell property, which was a rooming house with a horse barn in back. Conveniently, because one of Mr. Gardell's two grown sons was "keeping house" with Mrs. Petty, whose husband was off in The War. Keeping house was the genteel word in those days for having sex.

Mr. Gardell Sr. was a teamster. He made his living with his two horses, mostly by plowing gardens and cutting hay. In winter when it snowed, he also used a single horse hitch to plow the sidewalks on both sides of Amagansett Main Street, up to the East Hampton Village border. In summer he also ran an old-fashioned horse drawn lawnmower on several large estates and, on occasion, took groups of children and/or adults on hayrides. His horses were well fed and hard worked, as he never seemed to take time off, even during blizzards.

Probably the first artist friend the Prohaskas made in Amagansett was a painter named Stanley William Hayter, who had been a visiting teacher at Hilton Leech's Amagansett Art School. A Brit who for many years traveled frequently between Europe and The States, in 1927, in Paris, he founded the legendary print-making studio Atelier 17. That year (1944), he taught a print making class in New York and took a year's lease on a house near Ray and Carolyn. He and his wife, a sculptor from California, had a son a year older than me. The Hayters were charming and articulate, and became fast friends with Ray and Carolyn. Credited with influencing everyone from Picasso to Pollock in the art of print making, he was also a respected painter. During The War he collaborated with British artists Roland Penrose (uncle of the physicist Roger Penrose) and others in setting up a camouflage unit for the British Military. After The War he continued going back and forth between Europe and the U.S.

With few cars on the road and so many people away in the military or working in defense plants, Amagansett was quiet during The War Years. The ambient noise of the village consisted of an occasional rooster's crow, cow's moo, or a neighbor's sneeze combined with the dull rumble of waves slapping the sand along the ocean beach, and now and then the sound of a car going by, its heavy six-cylinder engine grinding away and its old rubber tires thumping loudly over each asphalt seam that joined the macadam slabs of Route 25, Main Street. So quiet was it that in the evening and early morning, you could often hear the diesel engine sound of a fishing boat dragging its nets just outside the sandbar on the ocean beach.

During Carolyn's first winter in Amagansett, whenever she heard that sound she thought it might be a German submarine. German U-2s had been attacking merchant ships up and down the Atlantic Coast since 1940, and had landed four spies on the Amagansett beach in June of 1942. The four men were intercepted by a Coast Guard man on patrol, who then alerted his superiors, who in turn had contacted the FBI. The saboteurs were apprehended before they could accomplish their mission but the brazen incident left eastern Long Island in a state of tense readiness.

The Hand Lane house had painted gray shingles with white trim. It was new and well built, but tiny, a shotgun shack with ranch house pretensions, not much bigger than the two car garage behind it. It had a bluestone driveway down the right side of the small, third of an acre plot. It was one story with an attic and a cellar, one bedroom, a kitchen, a small dining room, and a small living room in front with a fireplace. Ray hung his portrait of Carolyn over the fireplace; in it, she is curled up in a wing back chair wearing riding breeches and a leather vest and her hair is bobbed in the style of the Thirties. She is small and the chair overwhelms her.

The previous summer, while they were still renting in East Hampton Village on Baiting Hollow Road, Ray had begun renting a studio on Main Street in Amagansett. It was Ray's great luck that the studio, which had housed the Amagansett Art School, the summer school run by the Hilton Leech, had gone empty when Leech and his wife had gone off to Buffalo to work in a war plant and McClelland Barclay, a partner in the school and also a teacher there, had gone on active duty in the Navy. Ray, already in his forties, was too old for military service. It was also a stroke of luck that the post office was directly across the street so that he could send his illustrations directly to New York. The mail went out twice a day on The Cannonball, the steam engine train that went to Penn Station in Manhattan.

The studio was a large addition connected to an old house that was part of a two acre Main Street plot. The main part of the old house, a simple two-story colonial style building, uninsulated, unheated, and with no plumbing other than a well, but with an outhouse in back, served to house some of the poorer Art School students who attended in summer. The others stayed in rooming houses. A small outbuilding, formerly a bicycle shop,* had been moved behind the studio for use as the art supply store. Ray's rental agreement gave him year-round use of the studio. During the winter, the main part of the house, wreck that it was, with little or no plumbing or electricity, ancient seaweed for insulation, and heated by fireplace and wood stove, was rented by service people from the Coast Guard station. In the summer, after The War began, although the school was closed, artists continued to rent the house part.

The Bike Shop had been the business of a precocious teenage boy named Ralph Monroe Parsons, uncle of Shorty. Ralph Parsons invested the money he made fixing bikes and built, along with his father, a large cement block machine shop, which later became Tucker's Garage. The building still stands and is now a shopping mall on the south end of Main Street. When he went off to Pratt Institute and later to WWI, Ralph passed the building on to his brother Viv, Elbert Vivian Parsons, who sold it when he and son Elbert "Shorty" Gosman Parsons inherited the Amagansett Lumber Company from their father. After the War, Ralph moved to Los Angeles, where his business, The Ralph M. Parsons Co., rapidly expanded into one of the largest engineering and construction companies in the world, a precursor to Halliburton.

The Art School property was owned by William E. Cartwright, who lived in a newer house next door to the east, that he had built himself. Cartwright, called Will or "Pop" by his friends, had been born in the older house. He had been on some of the last off-shore whaling ventures, and for many years was Amagansett's postmaster. He was a charter member of the local order of the Masons. (According to local legend, when he filled out his personal history for his application, underneath the description for occupation he had written: "Gentleman.") When Ray met him he had been retired for years.

This older Cartwright house had been built in 1834 by Col. Samuel T. King, a local militia officer, mason bricklayer and member of a whaling crew. His son, a doctor, inherited the house and later sold it to William L. Cartwright (1851 - 1921), Pop's father, who owned a blacksmith and carriage-making shop on an adjacent property. The blacksmith shop building had been sold to the fire department for use as their first firehouse, and moved several hundred yards to the east. The building still exists, but was moved another time, and is now a flower shop, a mile in the other direction.

Pop Cartwright's daughter Alice, her husband Charlie Milligan, and their two children Bill and Mary Anne, all lived together with Pop. Ray, in his expansive and enthusiastic way, when he first began using the studio, said to Carolyn, "You should see Pop Cartwright's granddaughter, what a beautiful kid! She'll make a terrific model!" She was tall, tan and blond, with incredible high cheekbones. She became my babysitter and the first love of my life. When we met, I was two and she was sixteen.

Main Street in the 1940s was a self-sustaining little village. A hundred yards to the northeast, across from the new grade school, built in 1937, was a general store, formerly part of a chain called Roulston's, now a privately owned market; the building had two apartments upstairs. Across from Ray's studio was a barber shop, Cavagnaro's Restaurant, the post office, a library, a liquor store, another market, and another general store (this one with an impressive comic book rack.) Then, past a vacant lot that led to fields in back, there was a shoe repair and clothing store, The Amagansett Inn, and a 5&10 which, before World War II ended, moved north past the barber shop to make room for a radio repair shop.

Above the post office were several small apartments. One was used as a studio by Charlie LaSalle, an illustrator, and another was fitted out as Agnes's Hair Salon, run by the very same Agnes. LaSalle did mostly Western illustration, that is to say he illustrated cowboy stories, which remained popular in many magazines that produced fiction right up until television reached the mainstream and took over that genre. After living in Amagansett for a few years, LaSalle removed to Arizona and got rich supplementing his illustration work with painting expensive Quarter Horses.

Ray had been volunteering for the USO* in New York, going to events and doing sketches of service men. As soon as they moved out to Amagansett, he notified the USO, and was given the phone numbers of the local volunteers. The USO's most active branch on the East End was at Camp Upton in Yaphank,** though there were also occasionally smaller events in Southampton and Montauk. Ray and Carolyn began going to Montauk with a group of locals who, because both gas and automobiles were in short supply during the war, traveled in car pools. Ray, who had a nice pre-war Lincoln Zephyr, often drove. A landscaper named Joe Hren and his wife Bette, were part of the group; Hren quickly picked up some business from the Prohaskas and landscaped their small, third of an acre Hand Lane property. Joe was a good amateur actor (after The War he joined the best local acting group, the Guild Hall Players) and also played the accordion. Several of the local "good-looking dames," as both Ray and Carolyn referred to them, came along. Two women sang in the fashion of the Andrews Sisters, and most everybody, including Carolyn and Ray, pitched in by acting in skits. Those women who didn't perform handed out cookies and danced with the G.I.s.

---

*Beginning in 1940, with many U.S. and British Merchant Marine sailors in U.S. hospitals having been saved from drowning after their ships were torpedoed by German submarines, Ray, through the USO, had been visiting various N.Y. hospitals and doing charcoal sketches of the men. Doctors had found that many of these men could be brought back from unresponsiveness by having their portraits drawn. Seeing their own likeness constructed before their eyes often gave them just a moment of recognition, time enough for a communication with a psychiatrist or doctor to begin. Ray was great at doing these quick charcoal sketches, creating perfect likenesses, and saved photographic copies of many of them in a scrapbook, with companion letters of thanks from parents and spouses.

**During the 1930s Yaphank was also one of the main headquarters of the German-American Bund (or Federation) organized to promote the German Nazi Party. The location, called Camp Siegfried, was closed down in 1939 when its liquor license came up for renewal and was rejected.

POST WAR AMAGANSETT

In the early post-WWII period Amagansett's population grew slowly. It wasn't until the 1960s, when the whole East End became popular with middle class tourists, that the population began to grow more rapidly. In the 40s, summer visitors were limited to what was known as the Summer Colony, most of whom lived in the not quite mansion sized turn of the century shingled cottages along Bluff Road, and further on west toward East Hampton. And there was one other colony, more grouped together and isolated, on a big hill overlooking both the ocean and the bay, which was called Devon. It consisted of several families, banking and manufacturing people from Cincinnati. They lived in large brick and stucco mansions with their own water and electric plant and yacht club.

When my mother talked about the Summer People she usually meant the Bluff Road people and in particular Mrs. Austin and her daughters, especially the daughter named Ellie Sutherland, wife of a high-ranking Army officer who stayed in the Army after The War. The Austins had moved out from Bellport at the same time as the Prestons, with whom they were friends. The Austin girls called May Preston "Auntie May." Ellie was a pretty redhead who was not afraid of a good party and was popular at Main Street's Amagansett Inn where there was a good jukebox and plenty of young Coast Guard boys to dance with. Carolyn's attitude toward Ellie seemed to alternate between a little bitchy and a little envious; the latter having to do with Ellie's unfettered existence.

Ray and Carolyn met their first East End friends through nurseryman Joe Hren, while they were all involved with the U.S.O. shows, which the Prohaskas joined while they were still renting. Joe, who did the landscaping on Hand Lane and later on the Main Street property was a rough-hewn renaissance man of Hungarian ancestry who had broken off from the family nursery business (owned by his father, Anton Hren) in Huntington, Long Island. During The War he bought land in Amagansett and East Hampton and got into farming on the East End by leasing extra land to farm potatoes in Montauk and Amagansett.

When the Prohaskas first met Joe he was still renting a home but he soon designed and built his own ranch style house on a corner plot of his new 100 acre nursery. The house had hot water heated flagstone floors, an attached greenhouse with a Koi pond, a potting shed at the far end, and beyond that a stable for the plow horse used to cultivate between rows of trees. As his family grew to eight children, he added bedrooms to the house.

Joe flew an airplane (good for finding real estate), did his own architectural drafting as well as landscape design, played the accordion and got involved in the local theater group. In addition, he was a subsistence farmer, growing his own vegetables and raising poultry, and hogs. He made the best bacon I've ever tasted.

As soon as he was settled into his home on the nursery property, he took a few lessons in painting from Ray and Julian, built his own studio, and began painting. He painted in a kind of Kuniyoshi, Ash Can School 1940s style and was talented and for a regretfully few short years, prolific. Around this time Joe let his curly reddish brown hair grow down past his collar and over his ears and began to wear a frayed bandana around his neck, either pink or blue, with the added affectation of a long green jade cigarette holder for his Chesterfields.

In his landscaping work, Hren collaborated with Albert Scheffer, a local architect, who in turn collaborated with Kay Perkins, an interior decorator. The combination Scheffer, Perkins and Hren style was a real local genre during the first decade or two of the post-War period on eastern Long Island. The style incorporated Cape Code roof lines, old colonial buildings or converted barns, as well as toned-down ranch-style buildings sheltered into dunes, lots of grey Cabot stain, soft, dark interiors incorporating driftwood as sculpture and grass wallpaper, and, near the ocean, lots of beach grass terraced with railroad ties, and Joe Hren's specialty, Japanese Black Pines (a long-leafed conifer.) Whether the style would be considered dated or not I can't be sure, but that hardly matters because it has mostly been erased today, to make room for the McMansion style (modeled after Batman's house, stately Wayne Manor), which is much more saleable in today's market, and rendering moot the question of architectural style.

Though he was new in town, and possessed an artist's sensibility, Joe Hren was also a man of the soil. Through his business, he became locally connected very quickly. For the Prohaskas and friends he became the go to guy, who let you know where to get a plumber, an electrician, or, while The War was still on, some black market meat.

Not that any of these folks were unpatriotic, but as Carolyn was always fond of saying, "Once in a while you just need a good piece of meat."

Through Hren's gregariousness, artist-illustrator Jan Balet was brought into this new circle of friends. Balet was a reclusive artist who lived in a saltbox house perched on a dune in the no man's land between Amagansett and Montauk. There was not a house near his at that time, only the Mackay radio transmission towers that were placed in the wetlands on the bay side of this narrow strip of land that almost made Montauk into an island. Besides providing him with a few friends, Hren was able to sell Balet a handful of black pines, some topsoil and a few yards of sod, which helped to convince people further east that improvements could be made to those properties hanging to the edge of Montauk's cliffs. Shortly after The War was over Balet returned to his native Switzerland.

Jim Perkins was an illustrator's agent who was known for his high integrity, a quality virtually unknown in the world of agents in any field. His illustrious stable included many well-known artists of those times, including Melbourne Brindle, Robert Fawcett, Everett Henry and Noel Sickles. He and his interior decorator wife Kay, a very aristocratic southern lady, bought a house on the ocean around the time that the Prohaskas moved into Hand Lane, and a few years later, when Jim retired, sold that house and bought the largest house on Main Street (known as the Old Rackett House, for the family who built it), with several acres of land and out buildings. Kay opened a gallery which displayed her decorating skills (she had a successful decorating business in Manhattan before they retired), Jim's crafts, and a few paintings by one or another of the handful of artists then living in the area. (There were no lines at the door.)

The Perkins were a somewhat stuffy couple. Carolyn secretly referred to Jim as "Grim Jim" because he rarely smiled, and Kay had an accent that was very upper class Southern and somewhat British sounding. But, as Carolyn said, "After a few drinks Jim loved to cut loose and have fun, especially if there was a good looking dame around, and that just made Kay depressed."

The decor of our house was influenced by Kay, who, wanting in on the act, was insistent and didn't charge. (Carolyn damned Kay for years every time she had to reach up to a high shelf in the kitchen for a plate, for letting Kay locate the shelves to her own height. Kay was five ten and Carolyn was five two.)

It was Kay who discovered Worthington, the first house painter I ever knew (and our only house painter for many years), and it was she who initiated his being called by his last name. (His first name was Elwood.) He was an old school craftsman, coming to work in a jacket and tie and donning overalls when he worked. Both Ray and Carolyn treated him with great respect; he was skilled, neat, and a gentleman. He came to the house and did small projects: one room, a few doors, or he might wallpaper a room. He had an air of quiet calm.

Two other illustrators lived in Amagansett during The War and the early post-War years. They were Everett Henry and the aforementioned Charles LaSalle, both of whom, with their wives, helped make a quorum for cocktail parties. The Henrys had one child and the LaSalles had two.

And another non-artist member of the war time social set was Bill Campbell, an Episcopal Bishop who was known both for being a regular guy who liked a stiff drink now and then, and for his handiness at butchering poached or road killed deer. The Campbell's two acre property joined corners with the two acre lot of the Prohaskas on their southwestern corner, with their northern property line fenced in with Hren's signature black pines. Hren was the one person who profited in dollars and cents from all these relationships. His black pines became a symbol of the era, and eventually extended the length of the New York State Thruway.

Charlie LaSalle moved to Amagansett about a year after the Prohaskas. The year that Ray and Carolyn bought the Hand Lane house, Gaston and Carol de Havenon rented a house on Bluff Road, which they retained for several summers, and Julian and Jean Levi came out frequently and stayed at rooming houses.

Ray and Carolyn were at a party "Chez Gaston" the night before Carolyn went into labor with my sister Elena. Her memory of the party centered on Jim Perkins dancing up a storm with a gorgeous house guest friend of Gaston's. While my mother sat between Julian and Kay Perkins, she eavesdropped on Kay saying to Julian, referring to being back in Manhattan during the week, "I'm going to a new therapist on Monday." "It was like a *New Yorker* cartoon," Carolyn said.

THE EX PATS

In 1941, ahead of the Nazi invasion of France, and leaving behind numerous lovers, Peggy Guggenheim, along with her estranged husband Laurence Vail, their two teen aged children, Sinbad and Pegeen, Vail's other significant other Kay Boyle and her four children, Bobby (fathered by poet Ernest Walsh), Apple, Kath, and her new baby Clover, sired by Mr. Vail (they seemed to have had a naming impulse similar to the later Hippie generation), along with Pegeen's school friend Jacqueline Ventadour, and Peggy's soon to be, however briefly, husband Max Ernst, departed Lisbon, having plied their way through the red tape of Nazi occupied Southern France. Their escape vehicle was a Boeing B-314 Flying Boat, which took them on an almost two day trip, stopping to refuel first in the Azores and then Bermuda before finally landing in the East River of New York City.

After checking into the Great Northern Hotel and recovering from the grueling odyssey, the whole crew embarked on a whirlwind tour of the U.S., spending enough time in California to give full consideration to whether or not to make it their home for "The Duration," but eventually headed back to New York, where after another spate of camping out at the Great Northern the crew found a suitable pad, The Hale House, almost a castle, in the Beekman Place area. The many roomed mansion, named for the American Revolutionary War spy Nathan Hale who, though he never lived there, was executed nearby in 1776, had a giant drawing room, large gallery, tall, mullioned windows, and "a master bedroom with a room next to it converted into a studio for Max,* the star of the show, due partly to his esteem in the eyes of Ms. Guggenheim, but also because of his superior charisma.

See "Art Lover," a biography of Peggy Guggenheim, by Anton Gill, Harper Collins U.K., 2001

The Beekman Hill neighborhood, to which Beekman Place was Main Street, was where Ray and Carolyn had lived from the time they met, up until my own felicitous birth in that glamorous part of New York City. The Beekman Tower Hotel, where our family often stayed when

I was growing up, located on the corner of 49th and First Ave. at #3 Mitchell Place, one block from where Beekman Place junctions at Mitchell Place, was erected in the late Twenties. Originally called the Pan Hellenic Tower, it was designed by John Mead Howells, with Art Deco ornamentation by architectural sculptor Rene Chambellan. Chambellan had also worked on the Russell Sage Foundation Building and many of the Art Deco influenced buildings of the era. Parenthetically speaking, Russell Sage was married to a Pierson, from the same Henry of Southampton line as was Carolyn.

In the spring of 1944, Lionel Abel, of *The Partisan Review* rented the living part of the house on Main Street in which Ray had his studio. Abel invited Jean Helion and Lawrence Vail, technically still Peggy Guggenheim's husband, to share the rent. Vail brought with him his two children Sinbad and Pegeen and Pegeen's friend, Jacqueline. Pegeen was nineteen, Sinbad was 21. (Max Ernst, their soon to be stepfather, was staying a mile up the street, in a small cottage rented by Jane Bowles.) Helion, an early European abstractionist, had lived in the U.S. during the 1930s and been married to an American citizen. He returned to France during The War, was captured by the Germans, escaped, and wrote a book, called, *They Shall Not Have Me*. In 1946 he married Pegeen. They were married ten years and had three boys. Sinbad married Jacqueline eventually and had two children, and then had two children by a second wife. Helion divorced Pegeen after 13 years, and married Jacqueline. (In the meantime, like their fearless leader Peggy, they all slept with practically everybody.)

Among the visitors of what my mother referred to as the Guggenheim contingent, were Isamu Noguchi, Robert Motherwell, Ernst, Bowles, Henry Miller and Abraham Rattiner. It was Jean Levi, during a conversation we had in the Sixties, who pointed out to me that Henry Miller had visited the house I grew up in. By then I had become a huge Miller fan, particularly of *Tropic of Capricorn,* which I read three times in that decade. Jean and Julian had met Miller in Paris, through Abraham Rattiner. In 1944, Miller had just finished *The Air Conditioned Nightmare*, a non-fiction account of his travels with Rattiner around the U.S. In a few years, my childhood proximity to the path of my hero gave my beatnik ambitions a great boost.

Ray had an encounter with Noguchi which, much later, became problematic for me. Early one morning he had gone to Main Beach for a quick dip in the ocean to fix a hangover and he saw Noguchi, out past the breakers, with Lionel Abel's girlfriend, both caught in a sea puss. A sea puss, also called a seapoose, from the Long Island Algonquin dialect Unquachog, is usually caused by tide water flow through a channel in the outer sandbar. Every year to this day on Long Island, swimmers are dragged off to their death by these strong currents. During the years of my childhood, I saw several lifeguards save people from them. Ray pulled out several people, including me, more than once. All you see of a sea puss is a bit of a swirl on the top of the water; if you don't know what they are, they can seem invisible.

Noguchi seemed to be a competent swimmer, but had lost control of the girl, who had panicked. Ray swam out and saved her. Since there was no one around, I suppose, there was no record of the event; Ray only mentioned it once, to Carolyn, when he got home. Years later, though, after Ray died and I was interviewing my mother for my Oral History of East Hampton,* she mentioned it. I blabbed to a young woman I knew who was friends with Noguchi, and of course she went right back to him, and he was highly indignant. "I am a great swimmer," he said. To which I suppose I should say, for the good of art history, "Of course he was!"

*From 1997 until 2004, Martha Kalser and I conducted 176 interviews with older residents of East Hampton. The interviews were transcribed and are now in the East Hampton Library, Long Island Collection, along with over 1000 pictures given to us by our interview subjects. The collection is called The History Project, Inc.

The big question I've always had, though, about the Bohemians of Amagansett during The War years is, what did the locals, particularly the local kids, think of them? For the most part, my intuition tells me, they didn't think much about them. They were "from away," a definitive appellation in those days, queers, in the sense used colloquially to mean either "queer" or "from away" and they were childlike, which to a population of hard working country folk who faced the elements head on as a matter of course, meant foolish.

RAY JR. AND DOLLY

At one point during that summer while Ray was in the city working, Carolyn, while taking care of two year old me had to wait on both Wallace Morgan, elder statesman of American illustrators, and Junior. Junior kept playing the phonograph too loud, with some uproarious music blasting away, and the elderly Morgan would meekly complain to Junior's stepmother Carolyn. Finally, he said, "Do you think he'd explode if I turned it down?" He went ballistic.

Ray Jr. had by this time become an angry teenager, but one who kept himself occupied with an impressive assortment of gadgets. He had a trunk full of magic tricks and considered himself an amateur magician. He had several crystal sets and dismantled radios. He spent a great deal of time out in the garage building and taking things apart. At one point he came out from the garage into the backyard and announced he had constructed a flame gun, and then proceeded to blast the side of the house almost setting it on fire. "Flames shot out of the damn thing, scorching shingles on the house and then the garage," my mother told me. I was too young to remember.

After that, he took it down to Cavagnaro's and showed it to the Railroad Station Agent's daughter and Mary Anne Milligan, two of the regulars at the soda fountain. Miraculously, he didn't set fire to the restaurant or the house across the street. At seventeen, that was his approach to fair young womanhood. A few weeks later, toward the end of The War, Ray Jr. joined the Navy. After Boot Camp at the Great Lakes Training Center, he was stationed in Hawaii, where he began learning Navy applications for electronics.

Before he left though, Carolyn and Ray Jr. and the oblivious baby sat through the 1944 hurricane. With the electricity off, Sonny took the time to sit by candlelight and write to his mother, while Carolyn sat with me in the bedroom waiting for the house to collapse. It blew so hard that one of the chairs from The Amagansett Beach Club half a mile away, came flying across the potato fields and landed in the back yard. But just as it had in the '38 hurricane, the house held fast to its moorings.

In the spring of 1945 Dolly and her husband Pete, an executive for Kraft Cheese, came to Manhattan. They were staying at the Art Moderne style Beaux Arts Apartments, across the street from Beaux Arts Institute of Design on East 44th St. The Institute, a professional organization composed of former students of the prestigious Parisian Ecole des Beaux-Arts, had been formed to serve as the national headquarters for architectural instruction based on the curriculum of the Parisian Ecole. Raymond Hood and Kenneth Murchison, influential members of The Institute, had designed the apartments. The apartment which Pete and Dolly were borrowing had just been newly decorated and furnished for another tenant who would soon be moving in. As soon as she arrived Dolly telephoned Ray and Carolyn. She wanted to get together. "You know, and say hello and everything?" was how she put it to Ray. (Dolly was an early precursor to the Valley Girl, San Francisco version.) Ray told Carolyn, "You'll love her, everybody loves her!" So Carolyn agreed to the meeting, and when they met they did in fact hit it off well. Years later, she would refer to Dolly as "a kind of a Flapper." "The Rube" and Kitty (the Rankins) were happy to see her, and so a few other couples were invited and they had a great all-things-forgiven "Reunion" party.

A few days later, just about Christmas time, Pete went out to dinner with a client friend and left Dolly and one of her old friends at the borrowed apartment. They were to meet up later. At length the girls left and when they all returned later there had been a fire. The apartment had been burned out. Gutted. Dolly had left a cigarette burning on the Murphy bed, put the bed back into the wall, and then took off, leaving the fire to destroy not just the apartment but all of her own clothes and all her friend's clothes. They had no choice but to return immediately to San Francisco. Fire seemed to follow Dolly everywhere she went. When she was married to Ray she had set fire both to their apartment on 38th Street and to a house they had in Westport, Connecticut.

One of Carolyn's favorite stories, one that I heard several times, was of Kitty Rankin at a party on 10th Street the following New Year's Eve, coming out of the kitchen and saying, "Carrie, come here quick! There's a fire in the garbage can! Dolly must be here!" Carolyn loved delivering that punch line with a hearty laugh and an exhale of cigarette smoke through her nostrils, looking like a cigarette ad from the period. She had successfully demonized poor Dolly. Ray and Carolyn never saw Dolly and Pete again but, for years after, they received gift packages of Kraft cheese every Christmas. Dolly died in 1950 of cirrhosis, she was 45.

It was also around this time that the Ebermans, the New Canaan people who had taken care of me during Carolyn's spinal fusion, came to Amagansett to visit. They brought along a six month old housebroken Dalmatian puppy, registered under the name Suzy Sequins. The dog was for me, and as boys and dogs do, we bonded immediately. I was not quite two. Suzy was six months. Within a limited spectrum of dog-boy growth, we grew up together. I remember her being spayed, and having a pink shaved place from the operation, and feeling some sympathy for her about that, which contributed to the bond; that and of course that she slept with me, so I really never slept alone as a child until she died when I was thirteen.

MOVING TO THE MAIN STREET HOUSE

The Prohaskas had owned the Hand Lane house for two years when on a spring morning in 1946 Pop Cartwright's daughter Alice called and said her father wanted to speak to Ray. Pop had decided to sell the old house and studio property. He wanted $3500 down and would hold the mortgage, which would be something like $97 a month.

At around the same time, a fellow whose wife was the daughter of a wealthy Bluff Road summer person offered to buy the Hand Lane house and pay cash. Ray lost no time deciding to make the deal. He even made a little money on it. The move made sense. It would be perfect, having a house attached to the studio in which he already felt at home.

Though technically they would now own the house, the main part of the house had already been rented for the summer. Ray would continue using the studio that summer and pay the down payment on the property, but we couldn't move in until after Labor Day because Pop had to honor his summer rental agreement with Hugh Tyson. Hugh Tyson was the less well-off brother-in-law of Carolyn Tyson, an important benefactor both locally and in the art world at large. She had a large estate in Amagansett and another one in Carmel, California.

The renovation started the same day we moved in. Mr. Guthrie and Mr. Coleman did most of the carpentry. Eventually, Mr. Coleman would become known as Burt, but Mr. Guthrie would always be Mister Guthrie.

The original part of the house, where the Tysons had been living, was built on a stone foundation with a small dirt floor cellar under its southeast corner. This part of the house had a footprint of about 30x30 feet, and included two stories and an attic. The attic had a window (without glass) on the roof which was hinged and opened up like a cellar door. Called a scuttle, this window, like many others in the village, faced south, and had been put there for spotting whales.

Since the house had no heat or indoor plumbing, a kitchen and bathroom were added, along with cast iron radiators and an oil burning hot water heater (by Alice Milligan's cousin, Fillmore Miller) and were ready in time for the worst part of the winter. The wiring was very primitive and had to be redone. Where the house had been insulated with seaweed, new seaweed was added to what had dried up and shrunken. New insulation was added where needed.

The main living area of the house had a chimney that serviced four fireplaces: one in the kitchen, which faced out the back; one in the front parlor; and one in each bedroom on the main second floor. The two south facing fireplaces, one downstairs in the kitchen and one upstairs in what became Ray's room, were walled off. The remaining two were in Carolyn's room upstairs and in the downstairs front room, called the parlor. The parlor, which in olden days had been kept shut except for special occasions, would become our small living room, but would still be called the parlor.

There was a problem with the fireplace though. It didn't draw well and tended to back up. Phil O'Brien, the mason who was doing the plastering, stuck his arm up the flue feeling for something. O'Brien knew there was often a small shelf in the flue of these old houses, the result of a bend in the chimney stack, and on this one someone had put a whiskey jug, no doubt to keep it away from prying eyes. Phil tried carefully dislodge it, but it crumbled to pieces and fell into the grate, after which the fireplace drew beautifully. Carolyn spent weeks stripping and sanding and waxing the mantel until it had the patina of a museum piece.

The floorboards in the living room, dining room and the upstairs hallway were exceptionally wide. They were sanded down to a raw pumpkin color and varnished. Like the fireplace mantel, the floorboards had been milled from the giant White Pine trees that grew northwest of East Hampton Village in early 19th century.

Upstairs, Ray had the back bedroom. He liked sleeping by himself. He was a foot taller than Carolyn and one hundred pounds heavier and he needed room to stretch. His room was smaller than Carolyn's, but Misters Coleman and Guthrie made him a big, 6' 7" custom made bed and custom made pine closet and chest of drawers. Above his head was a small built in two-shelved bookshelf and beside his bed was a tall, solid brass standing gooseneck lamp for reading.

While the main part of the house had a stone foundation with a small stone walled, earthen floor cellar, the studio was footed only with locust posts. The posts, though in fine shape (no telling how old they were), were replaced by three courses of cement block and during that process the floor was somewhat leveled, though it retained a slight slope toward the south in its back half. Coleman and Guthrie covered the rough sub-flooring with Masonite, which was still in good shape twenty years later. The interior roof and walls were insulated and covered with a kind of particle board used in those days, something akin to sheet rock.

The skylight had been built for the art school and was probably the only part of the building that was up to date. It was eight feet in length and six feet high, made of individually fitted large glass panes, probably 10" x 14" lapped over each other by a half inch, higher over lower, with vertical mullions made of 1" x 2" hardwood. It was solidly built and well flashed, and survived many hurricanes and northeasters, requiring only the replacement of an occasional pane of glass. It faced north onto Main Street and through it, north light filled every corner of the forty by forty foot square room. The trim of the skylight was white to match the trim of the house. Though few people other than wood craftsmen buffs would think of building something like it today, it was for its time, a thing of beauty. Outside, the clapboard siding was painted Ray's beloved gray-green, or what Carolyn called Elephant Ass Green, a variation on Elephant Ass Brown.

A windowless darkroom was built, with cabinets and its own indoor ceiling, above which was more storage space; and Fillmore Miller added a sink and a toilet. The sink was needed for developing, but the toilet was so that, at least when the studio wasn't off limits, the whole family could have a downstairs bathroom.

Carolyn told everybody the following story about the toilet in the darkroom; "We put in a john upstairs, and Dad wanted one in his studio. He painted the toilet seat red and Sylvester (Robert Sylvester, columnist for the New York Daily News and Ray's fishing buddy) called it the Red John. Red John came from Sylvester's name for John Chapman, the drama critic on the Daily News, for some defense Chapman had made, vis a vis a wrangle with Harry Truman or something, about a crack Truman had made about a red herring, and ah, I guess Chapman got teased about his so-called Red leanings, his defending the faith so to speak. So Sylvester called him Red John and when he came in to the studio and saw that Dad had painted the toilet, "Aha, the Red John!" It was thereafter called either the Dark Room or The Red John, depending on the context.

The front wall of the darkroom was completely made up of giant bookshelves for art books and the *Encyclopedia Britannica*. The rest of the rear of the studio was taken up by a large painting storage rack which enclosed a small workbench area for making frames and other projects. There was additional space above the painting rack and the darkroom which was used for more storage. Above the rack there was a small collection of driftwood and above the darkroom were several large specimens of fan coral. The pièce de résistance though, was a beautiful Colman and Guthrie 4' x 8' paper storage cabinet with six drawers and some sort of black glassine counter top.

In the spring of 1947, Coleman and Guthrie built a one car garage with a peaked roof which allowed for storage space for the storm windows and screens which were exchanged and painted seasonally. Joe Hren landscaped the property. He placed stockade fencing along both sides of the yard behind the house as far as the garage and stained the fencing gray. He covered the driveway with gravel from the sidewalk to the garage. At the bend in the driveway where it turned toward the garage, he made a small rock garden and planted a weeping willow at its center. Along the inside edge of the eastern fence in the now enclosed back yard, Joe planted perennials like violets and bleeding hearts. He pruned the big black maple in the middle of the yard and the big Greening apple tree that stood on the west side of the yard in the corner between the fence and the garage. The maple was cabled together to make it more storm-worthy and more climbable for kids.

Elena leaning against the Black Maple

ELENA

I'd been living the life of a provincial prince, well entertained with action, loud music, and visitors, and then came the arrival of my half-brother, whom I hadn't seen since I was pre-verbal and, even more traumatizing, the birth of my sister. I remember, vaguely, on that fateful day in the fall of '46 (I was three years and eight months old), milling around Ray's studio, wondering aloud where my mother was, and receiving an indiscreet answer from my preoccupied father who was busy working on a big semi-abstract canvas. My response when told that Ma was off at the hospital having a baby, was one of horror. "Jesus Christ," I reportedly said, imitating my father's booming voice, "I'm getting the hell out of here." I ran next door to Mary Anne's house, past Alice standing at the sink and past Sharpie, Pop's Chesapeake dog. Pop was sitting in the living room and I ran upstairs to where Mary Anne was sitting on her bed painting her toenails. I jumped on the bed and spilled the nail polish and got my first rejection from a girl. "Good God, Sweetie, be careful," was all she said when she pushed me off the bed.

    On Sept. 2nd, 1946, as Carolyn remembered it, she was upstairs and not feeling very well. Eileen Scott had been about to leave for home but was afraid to leave her alone. Carolyn convinced her she was not in labor and that she'd be alright, but Eileen said she would come back later to check up on her. I having removed to the neighbors, Ray decided to vacate too and went off fishing. Carolyn remembered it this way:

She was lying on the couch in the living room and Ray, having returned from fishing after a couple of hours, helped her upstairs. The bed was brand new, having just come by truck from Macy's in Manhattan. She was about to lie down on the unmade bed when she realized she was in labor. Ray called the doctor, then realized they didn't have a car because Sonny, just out of the Navy and a fast worker, had borrowed it for a date with a young a model he'd met on the beach, a girl named Pat Donovan.

Patricia Donovan Sr., the girl's mother, was a big, handsome gal, and a shrink: Dr. Donovan. She was in fact Kay Perkins' new analyst. Pat Junior, beautiful Patricia Donovan, was a top-flight model. She and her mother were staying at the Perkins house. Sonny's short military career, spent mostly driving around in a Jeep in Honolulu, had cured his shyness and he was out in the car with the girl and was in fact wearing a pair of his father's best shoes.

Ray called Jim Perkins who gave them a ride to Dr. Nugent's house in East Hampton. Dr. Paul, as he was called, came down from bed needing a shave and Carolyn said, "Oh God, I hope I don't have the baby in Perkins' car." Nugent said, "Don't worry about that, just send Perkins and your old man home, I'll drive you to the hospital." Ray and Jim left and Dr. Paul went out to the garage to find that his son, Paul Jr., who also had a date, had taken his father's car, forcing them to take Mrs. Nugent's car. Carolyn noted, as she was inclined to do, that it was exactly like a slapstick comedy.

In a wild unexpected thunderstorm they drove to Southampton to Dr. Nugent's very own private hospital. The trip took about twelve minutes (with today's traffic it would take about 45 minutes.) In the hospital room Carolyn said she didn't want to be knocked out because she didn't want an ether hangover, to which Dr. Paul said, "Don't worry, we don't boast of an anesthesiologist."

At seven in the morning (September 3rd) Dr. Nugent, who had been napping, began singing to himself a popular song of the day, *"Doin' What Comes Naturally."* Carolyn gave a couple of yelps (they had given her some nitrous oxide, dentist's gas) and the next thing she knew a little girl appeared. Carolyn said, "Oh look, she's got beautiful hands, like her father." To which Dr. Nugent said, "Ah, another artist!" and an indignant Carolyn countered, "Hey, look here, I'm an artist too!" (Not the last time she would say that.)

The baby was named Elena Anastasia, Anastasia after her beloved grandmother whom she would never meet. As soon as Ray saw her she was given the nickname "Baba," a Yugoslav name for grandmother or baby.

She had fine blonde hair that had to be shaved when she was three when she got ringworm. Before too long she had adopted a security blanket, a worn faded pink baby blanket she called "Mine." She carried "Mine" over her shoulder, chewing on the end of it, occasionally stuffing a small piece up her nose, which habit eventually caused her to have repetitive nosebleeds. One very clear memory I have of those times was when we were milling around in the studio getting underfoot, about to be kicked out, and I, for no good reason, cuffed her on the ear. Blood started gushing out of her nose like a faucet, threatening to get on something important like the illustration my father was working on. The Old Man cuffed me one but good, and sent me whimpering to my room, and Baba was administered to with towels and ice packs. It would happen more than once. All I had to do, it seemed, was raise my voice and her nose would start to bleed.

Because it got filthy as she dragged it around like the *Peanuts* kid Linus, they tried taking "Mine" away from her, but her reaction was a fierce anger which no one could stand up to. Carolyn got the idea to tear the dirty old blanket in half so that while one part was in the wash the other half could still be doing its job hanging over Baba's shoulder. Years later, long after she'd given up "Mine," she still had occasional nosebleeds, and eventually, when she was eleven, she had to have her nose cauterized.

When she was still an infant, I once hid Baba under her bed and caused a panic. Another time, when she had gotten to the toddling stage, I threw her big life-sized doll down the stairs and called to my mother to come see, nearly causing both Carolyn and Eileen to have heart attacks. Alternately, I would drag her around, hugging her like a rag doll.

Soon she became a tomboy who liked to wear overalls or jeans with suspenders. She became very assertive. Once, I remember, the toilet in the upstairs John, as we called it, was stopped up. Ray said to her, "Baba, did you stuff something in the toilet?" She looked up at him with her hands on her hips and said, "Did you see me?"

Ray Jr. in our father's studio ca. 1946

SONNY

In his high school years, Ray Jr. boarded at Northampton Prep in Massachusetts. In the summer he would first go to his mother in San Francisco where she lived with her, Pete Humphreys. Then he would come and stay with Carolyn and Ray for a month or more, in New York and East Hampton. Ray's attempts to entertain Sonny were half-hearted. He expected a child to be problem free; to just join the party. He would take him along to an Artists and Writers shindig at 21, or The Stork Club, and then not understand why the kid just sulked. He took him off fishing in Canada and when they came back Sonny said his father had hit him over the head with a fishing rod. Sonny just didn't appreciate the great adventure of traipsing through the woods and portaging with a canoe. He wasn't an outdoorsman.

On September 1st, 1946, two days before his half-sister was born, he arrived in Amagansett. After being discharged from the Navy in late August, he had spent a few days visiting his mother and stepfather in San Francisco. He told Ray and Carolyn that Dolly and Pete were terrible alcoholics and that Pete had beat him up. He never saw either of them again. For several months I would be his full time roommate.

Our newborn sister Elena, aka Baba, was sleeping in a cradle in Carolyn's room, according to the precepts of Dr. Ribble. It was an antique, though, and after a few months, she was given a crib and the cradle was stored up in the attic. Ray Jr. and I shared the room which would eventually belong to our sister, the little room above the living room. It was fine for one child, but had a low ceiling which made it cramped for six foot two inch Junior. There was a cot and a little iron bed and a window which faced east. I slept in the iron bed, which loomed high above Ray Jr.'s bed. I would be four on the 28th of that December, and I remember clearly not being crazy about this little bedroom off the stairs, partly because it was never really completely mine, but also because the rear wall of its big closet had a trap door which hid the eaves connecting the main house with the studio, a small attic space, and I'd sometimes get the feeling there might be something or someone spooky hiding in there; nothing that I remember clearly; perhaps Indian Joe or some undefinable monster.

The new male member of the household immediately got a job working for Clay Bunker, whose radio repair shop was just a few doors down and across the street. With his father's permission, he began putting together a high-fidelity record player in the studio, which he continued to beef up over the next few years. He installed a woofer, a huge speaker, into the painting rack at its east wall end and a tweeter on the roof of the rack, which was the same height as the darkroom (above the rack as with the darkroom was more storage.)

Along the front and east sidewalls, Coleman and Guthrie had built custom cabinets (painted the same gray-green as the exterior clapboard siding) which extended along the walls with wooden slats similar to grillwork, which allowed ventilation for the baseboard heaters. There was a space among the cabinets for the record changer, amplifier and FM radio. On the roof of the studio was a tall aerial which pulled in WQXR in N.Y.

On warm days, with the windows open, music from his substantial collection of old wax 78s would be blasting from Ray's studio and could be heard up and down Main Street; Beethoven, Benny Goodman, Boogie Woogie, and a favorite of mine, drummer Warren "Baby" Dodds. The music drowned out the sound from the jukebox at Cavagnaro's across the street, but as far as I know, nobody ever complained.

As winter set in, though, Ray Jr. got bored and decided he should move into the city and start going to the Arts Students League. He thought he'd try his hand at becoming an artist. It was Julian Levi's first year of teaching at The League. Julian was happy to have not only Ray in his class, but another child of his contemporaries, Gladys Davis' son Tuffy. Tuffy remained an artist and eventually became known as Noel Rockmore Davis.

After spending a week or two sleeping on a cot at his father's studio at 51 W. 10th, the Old Man decided he was using up too much space, and Julian was able to talk Gaston de Havenon into taking him on as a roommate. Gaston had moved his wife and children to Bucks County and spent weekdays at a bachelor pad in the village while he ran his perfume importing business. Gaston was never comfortable with the arrangement. Ray Jr. was a hi-fi geek, with spare social skills and no interest in neatness. They lasted out the winter together though, and by that time Junior was familiar enough with the village that he easily found himself a cheap apartment. The following spring, 1947, with the approval of Ray and Carolyn, who thought he deserved a summer at the beach, he resumed bunking with me.

He was still focused on becoming an artist, so he rented a small work space across the street on the second floor of the post office, where the illustrator Charlie LaSalle had a studio, as did Kay Perkins for her interior decorating business. Again he worked part-time at Bunker's shop repairing radios. Bunker was glad to have him.

In Julian's class he had done a portrait of me from memory. The portrait, unaccountably, was in black-face; burnt umber skin and startling blue eyes. From family and friends, unanimous praise. Carolyn thought it was "brash." In his studio over the post office, he used a model he discovered at Joe's Restaurant, one of my babysitters who worked behind the counter. According to Carolyn, he entered the painting of me in a show, "I guess it was at Andover, Andover or Dartmouth. Young American Artists sort of thing. We had that funny little painting for years," she recalled later. Carolyn's later critique of his work was that it was "good student work."

The War ended just in time for him to collect the G.I. Bill, and owing to the government's largess, he now had a complete life. The summer went well. He became friends with all the local kids that hung out at Joe's, including our neighbors Mary Anne, Little Carl and Bill. Then, summer being over, all the kids, Mary Anne, Little Carl, Bill, and the small group of Summer Colony kids, went off to college or moved away or got married and went to work.

No one could blame him if, after being short-changed in the fall of '46 by missing the best of summer being processed out of the Navy, he wanted a full summer at the beach. And by the time summer was over he'd decided on a goal which he would pursue successfully, starting immediately. He would spend another semester at The

League and then transfer to Pratt, where he would study industrial design. Before he finished a year at Pratt he would begin working for an important designer of hi-fi equipment, Bogen.

As I was growing up my half-brother would occasionally come out weekends, often with one or another scruffy bohemian girl he had met in group therapy. He stayed in "Group" for decades, bouncing from one to another, using it to vent about the loneliness and emotional abandonment of his childhood and as the basis of his social life. Into the late Sixties, he lived in the same apartment on Bank Street in Greenwich Village, an apartment full of electronic equipment, including ham radio paraphernalia and the detritus of a sloppy bachelor. In my teens I described him as a gear-loose type. He was successful enough in the days of hi-fi to win several awards for design, including a Venice Biennale.

The thing that stood out for him that summer though, was not, as Carolyn had incorrectly surmised, that Mary Anne, in love with her boyfriend Bobby, was not available to him. What he'd never forget was the beach party he organized one night during that summer, when, in spite of the best advice against it, he cooked spaghetti in ocean water boiled on the bonfire. Bill and Carl and Mary Anne and several other local kids were there, including some from East Hampton Village, and a few summer kids from the Bluff Road Colony. The spaghetti was full of sand, inedible, something everyone told him would happen, but to which he wouldn't listen. He was, he told me years later, almost suicidal with embarrassment.

In the fall Coleman and Guthrie made the attic into a new bedroom for me. It had a chimney coming through the floor and out the ceiling, sort of off-center, about two thirds toward the west side of the house, which went up through the peak. They portioned the one-third space past the chimney with a wall and a small door made of wainscoting slats to be used for storage. The larger space, on the north east side of the house, encompassed the small steep stairwell and had a small window that looked up Main Street and from which, at night, George Ayle's Shell gas station sign looked like a scalloped shaped moon. The small staircase had real stairs, not a ladder, and at the bottom a simple door made out of planks and closed with a latch and for further privacy, a hook and eye.

My bedroom-office-studio-hideout was insulated and covered with that same wallboard, it might have been called Beaverboard, which Worthington painted a nice warm white according to my specifications. I was happy to be a big kid with his own room.

I went off to school. They didn't have kindergarten yet in Amagansett, so Carolyn elected to send me to East Hampton. I was four. "Dad was in New York and I didn't have a car, so Julian drove us in his car. We had gone for an interview the week before. The interview was with the teacher, Dotty Vollmer. "She was Mrs. Jones then. She was very sweet. She knew us from the camp shows, you know, the U.S.O. I remember letting you out of the car. And you got out and walked up, no protest, no nothing, just walked up the pavement. Julian laughed and said, 'God, doesn't that just break your heart?'"

NEIGHBORS

Next door on our northeast side, in Pop Cartwright's house, except on days when a good spring cleaning necessitated all the windows being open, there was a strong doggy odor. The aroma was the result of Pop Cartwright's Chesapeake, Sharpie, who after a swim in the ocean or the bay, or a mud puddle, would lie on the radiator grate drying off, steaming up the house. The house had its own special sounds, too, with its creaky staircase, the "*crick*" sound of Pop's old rocking chair, the deep, hollow metallic stroke of the Grandfather Clock, Sharpie's yawning and scratching and his heavy Chesapeake toe nails clanking on the floor radiator grate. I remember the kitchen and its sweet, warm smell, its two stoves, one a gas range and another an old wood-burner; its coziness, Alice's African Violets on the east window facing our yard, and, on several occasions I remember watching Alice, standing at the sink, fixing a Bromo-Seltzer.

In the cellar, which was deep and cold, they had a new oil furnace, installed and maintained by Alice's cousin, Fillmore Miller, who was our plumbing and heating man too, even though my Dalmatian, Suzy, never ceased trying to take his leg off. Young Bill and his friend Little Carl went clamming often and would store a full bushel basket of hard clams in the coldest corner of the cellar where they'd keep for a month. Clam chowder, called clam chowder soup by Little Carl, and clam pie, were Amagansett staples.

Charlie, the father of Mary Anne and Bill, was rarely around even in my earliest memories, and eventually, never. Most of the time, he was living in one or another of several asylums up-island, there for an undetermined mental problem, most commonly thought, in his relative's memories today, to have been depression combined with some form of epilepsy.

Babe and Carl Erickson, Sr.

On the other side of our house lived the Ericksons, parents of Little Carl. The father was Big Carl, and the mother was Babe. Babe was born in January 1910, Carl in 1908. They both came of age in the era of Prohibition (1920-1933), and their social lives were influenced by it. The underground economy resulting from it was bigger on the East End than in most parts of the country, and fishermen were in a good position to make money in the illegal booze trade.

Babe and Carl were both born on Main Street, Babe in the house in which she still lived. She was the daughter of Harry Conklin and Stella B. Canfield Conklin. Stella was also born in the house and was the daughter of Charles Canfield, a fisherman and amateur easel-painter, who built the house. Anna Barnes Canfield, Babe's grandmother, was born next door in the house on the corner of Hedges Lane owned by her father Benjamin Hedges Barnes. Carl was born across the street and a few doors east, in the oldest house in the village, built in 1600 and called by historians the Baker House after its builder Nathaniel Baker, but in Carl's day called the Maude Erickson house because his mother lived there.

Aside from being a good commercial and a good charter fisherman who had been written up in books about big game fishing, Carl had also, as a younger man, been active in the rum-running trade. From Ray and Carolyn's point of view, Babe and Carl were

"Waspy" types, though local. They drank rye whiskey highballs in glasses with pheasants on them and ate salad with Mandarin oranges and little marshmallows. They played Bridge and Canasta. Babe was a handsome, athletic, outdoors woman. Her given name was Lillian, but nobody (including Little Carl) ever called her anything but Babe.

My mother's memory of those days was highlighted by an occasion when Carl Erickson dropped a giant lobster over the stockade fence as a gift. The lobster was big enough to defy belief in today's world, where lobsters get caught before they have a chance to grow that big. Later that day, after a pot was found big enough to steam it, Ray made a sketch from memory of Suzy barking at the Dalmatian-sized crustacean.

Though Carl was only two years older than Babe, he seemed like an older man. His father had drowned in 1924, forcing Carl at the age of fourteen to quit school and go to work fishing to support his mother. Babe had gotten pregnant while still a senior in high school in the spring of 1928. The only down side of pregnancy for Babe was having to quit basketball. She had been a star player for East Hampton High. Good fathering for Harry Conklin was making sure she got off that basketball team in a hurry. Babe and Carl were married while she was still in school and life went on merrily. Babe Erickson had an aggressive, dominant personality, and was the center of gravity in the Erickson home, but Carl, in his Gary Cooper strong silent way, was a match for her.

Carl Jr. was born in December of 1927. When he was a small child the Erickson home housed six people: Babe and Carl, Babe's father and mother, and Babe's maternal grandmother. In his growing-up years Little Carl's Grandfather Conklin with daughter Babe as partner raised and trained Chesapeake Bay Retrievers. Behind the house was a barn with a two-car garage, and a grooming room for dogs connected to a group of dog runs which butted up against the fence bordering the Prohaska property. There were eight dog runs, each with a small dog house, stretching back to an open field of more than an acre, which made an L out of the property. The field reached to the edge of Hedges Lane to the west, wrapping around the rear boundary of the Benjamin Hedges house.

Harry Conklin with two of his Chesapeakes

Harry Conklin ran and won just about every field trial he was ever in. He was considered one of the best trainers of retrievers in the country. He was good enough as a trainer to work with dogs for people like R. N. Carpenter, a Delaware man who made movie shorts shown throughout the country, films on different outdoor sports including duck and goose hunting. R. N. Carpenter eventually bought the Philadelphia Phillies baseball team. Wealthy people invested in these dogs and claimed ownership, but the animals rarely left the hands of trainers like Harry and Babe. (During her tenure as co-trainer of his dogs, Carpenter gave Babe several gold and diamond watches to celebrate field trial victories.) Their most famous dog was Skipper Bob, National Champion Field Trial Dog of his day who garnered a stud fee of $500 in pre-WWII dollars.

Hobnobbing with her Chesapeake owners and Carl's charter fishing customers, Babe had been exposed to upper-class chic. She kept her hourglass figure even up into her eighties and bought most of her clothes at Saks Fifth Avenue in Southampton or in New York City, She had a housekeeper, Mary, the wife of another fisherman, who did all the cooking and cleaning.

Babe was an enthusiastic hunter. Like her father Harry, she liked all kinds of gunning; upland, duck, and deer, and was a great shot. Her favorite place for deer was Hither Hills in Montauk where she usually hunted with her friend and cousin, Charles "Hooker" Hand, who drove the laundry truck for Banister's Laundry in East Hampton Village. Occasionally when Hooker was on his route and heading to

Montauk, Babe would hop in and go along with her rifle. They always brought back a deer, but it was never Hooker that shot, always Babe. Hooker was the spotter. Big Carl did the skinning and butchering in back of the garage.

There weren't that many deer around in those days when they were a viable food source. Today, with animal rights people over-running the population, the whole East End is suffering from a Lyme disease epidemic, a direct result of the tick-spreading deer.

Unlike the subdued quiet of the Milligan house, the Erickson house was always alive with activity. During the day, especially when Carl was out fishing, the big console radio in the living room crackled with ship-to-shore transmission, so that Babe always knew exactly where on the ocean Carl was. In the summer, if his boat was working near home, "on the back side," as the fishermen called it, she would drive to Main Beach, swim through the surf out past the sand bar, and climb onto the boat for a visit.

"Little Carl," though an only child, grew up with Mary Anne Milligan and her brother Bill as constant companions. He and Mary Anne were both born in '27, and Bill was only a year older. Until they went off on the bus to East Hampton High School, they walked to school together every day.

Grandpa Harry bought Little Carl a pony, which they kept in the garage. The pony was used under saddle or with a cart but mostly with the cart because it held up to three kids. With the pony cart it was easy for the three kids to visit friends, go to the beach, or to meet at several of the makeshift baseball diamonds around the village. The Pony, so-called for so often that his name got lost to history, lived mostly on grass and went to his small stall in the garage on occasion but more often wandered loose in the village.

All three were good students, but from first grade on Mary Anne was at the top of the class. (There were about twelve kids in each class, with a total of 75 kids in the school, the same as when I began attending a few years later.) Mary Anne's mother, Alice Milligan, was one of their teachers. She taught second grade. To Little Carl, having Alice as both his teacher and the mother of his two best friends was like having a second mother.

Ray always referred to Mary Anne as "his favorite model." It was, plain and simple, and by the grace of God, a scandal that never happened. She was the golden child of the village and any impropriety would have been, given the openness, the freedom of motion, the sense of being on a well-lit stage that was our little Main

Street, unthinkable. And my imperfect father wasn't that much of a damned fool. He sublimated. Carolyn became a second mother to Mary Anne. She made her lunch. She made dresses for her. She bought clothes for her. As Carolyn once said, "We smartened her up a bit!" She remained a family friend for the rest of her life.

Ray had begun using the three kids as models as soon as he began renting the studio, before he bought the house. But he drew and painted Mary Anne many times for his own pleasure, in addition to using her in illustrations. He did charcoal sketches of her first, and then pastels, and then a carefully done, life-size pencil drawing. He painted her portrait, again life-sized. I think she was about fourteen at the time, with straight blond hair, against a blue background, which he framed with an elegant white-stained frame and hung in his studio for several years. One of the last times she modeled for Ray was for a cigarette ad. After she graduated from high school she posed as a glamour girl at the beach, getting a light for her Camel cigarette.

To my mind, the first five years for a child are comparable in adult consciousness to an Age, such as the Romantic Age or the Middle Ages. Mary Anne was in the eighth grade the year I was born, and by the time I was five years old she was a senior in high school. My memories of being with these three almost-grown kids, when Mary Anne would babysit me by bringing me along with them to the beach, to the soda counter at Cavagnaro's across the street, and to friend's houses, are fuzzy and vague from age three and a half to five, and then became more clear just in time to watch the three of them go off into the world.

There was a day in that age that I mark as an early moment of recognition to not trust grown-ups. I was probably four years old by then, because Mary Anne, Bill, and Little Carl had come into focus for me as individuals. They took me hunting just off Main Street, down a small overgrown street called Deep Lane, with Bill and Carl carrying shotguns and me with a salt shaker which they had instructed me to sprinkle on the tail of a pheasant in order to capture the bird. I clearly remember a eureka moment when, with one foot in a puddle of mud, I realized I'd been had.

Every school day, from our living room window, by standing on a chair, I could see the kids getting off the school bus coming home from East Hampton High School, and see them go into Joe Cavagnaro's restaurant next to the post office. Joe's was right across the street so it was a great hangout for The Three. They went there often for sodas and ice cream and to listen to the jukebox. The song I associate best with Joe's came out a year after Mary Anne's graduation, when I was beginning to develop my individual taste; it was Kay Kyser's *The Woody Woodpecker Song*.

The popular times to go to Joe's were after school or around post office time, which was sometime between 6 and 7 in the evening after the mail train came in. A great congregation would appear at the post office, a meeting of the elders and the not so elder, and some of them, especially the kids, would spill over into Cavagnaro's. Several of the boys in the village were "philatelists," that is, stamp collectors, and would meet at Joe's to negotiate the trading of stamps.

The Cavagnaros had a daughter named Elaine who was about the same age as Bill, Carl and Mary Anne. Elaine made all the sodas, working both behind the counter and as a waitress for the restaurant. She was very competent. Old man Joe Cavagnaro had "sugar diabetes" as it was called then and eventually had to have his foot amputated.

Whenever they went out for the evening, Babe and Carl would give Little Carl four dollars to take Bill and Mary Ann to Cavagnaro's for dinner. Four dollars bought the three of them a complete meal. It was good "home-cooked" food. They had a menu that included hot roast beef or hot turkey sandwiches, stew, grilled cheese and select Italian fare, ravioli, spaghetti, and such. Besides the soda fountain, they had tables in back and for a nickel per selection the jukebox played all the most popular records, including the Mills Brothers, The Ink Spots, and Hoagy Carmichael singing *Ole Buttermilk Sky*.

Or, sometimes Little Carl would eat at the Milligan's, which he enjoyed because Alice was a good cook and he loved listening to the radio with Uncle Will (Pop Cartwright), to baseball games and to the news commentator Gabriel Heatter.

During her high school years, Mary Anne played the organ at the First Presbyterian Church, which she, her brother and Little Carl attended every Sunday. She was, according the parishioners of the time who remember, a very good (and very pretty) organ player. This was in the days of the Reverend Scoville's tenure, when a large meeting hall and an auditorium were built, and where for many years an energetic series of local theater productions were put on. The Meeting Hall, later named Scoville Hall after the beloved Reverend, was the social center of Amagansett, where many different club and society meetings happened and where frequent bake sales and covered dish suppers were held. There were two other churches in the village, a small Catholic Chapel built in 1928 and an Episcopal Church built in 1907, open only during the summer and used primarily by the summer colony. (There had been a tiny Methodist Church, built in the 1840s, but by the turn of the century it had closed its doors and eventually was turned into a private home.)

I remember one day in particular watching the kids get off the bus, when they were especially jubilant. I learned later that it had been something called Senior Day. It must have been 1947 when Mary Anne and Carl graduated. The girls were all wearing ribbons in their hair and some of them carried Teddy Bears. I was just beginning school and they were coming to the end. I seem to remember something in my chest which meant that I realized a separation was pending.

To my child's mind, Mary Anne, Bill, and Little Carl, were the magical kids of Main Street, two clever boys led by a blond angel-goddess with a long golden mane and pink nail polish. They were my perfect models for what being an older kid meant: a romantic still-picture; my own *Summer of '42*.

Population growth on the East End during the mid-Twentieth century was more organic than boom. One way to look at that growth during my childhood days would be to say it was a time of expansion of the local gentry beyond the original old families. The region was non-industrial, resource rich, low in population, and had a spirit unique from New England and the rest of New York State. More upbeat, I would say. Because of the good topsoil, the abundance of bays and creeks full of fish, eels, scallops and clams, the ocean with its whales, cod, bass, and its sandbars which collected shipwrecks full of salvage, and its access to Rum, there had always been abundance. Among the old families there was no rigid hierarchy. Over the years, since the 1600s, the original gentry had moved upward, downward and outward. For instance, the Daytons moved west and south, putting their stamp on Dayton, Ohio, Dayton, Wyoming and Daytona Beach, Florida. Even into the mid-Twentieth century, if you were a Dayton, Mulford or Osborne, you were East Hampton Main Street gentry, and if you were a resident of the East Side, you were a true Bonacker. But, the post-War baby boom did require more doctors, more teachers and more purveyors of baby food and kid's clothes.

Amagansett, though younger historically than East Hampton, and really just a hamlet on the road to Montauk, was more fluid socially, and Carl and Babe rose easily up the social ladder. Through Harry Conklin's dog business, the Ericksons had become friends with Morgan Belmont, the grandson of August Belmont who had been one of the powerful bankers of the Gilded Age. Morgan's mother, Caroline Slidell Belmont, was the daughter of Admiral Perry, who opened Japan to the West in 1854. Morgan Belmont and his wife Margaret Andrews Belmont loved fishing, hunting, hunting dogs, and going to field trials. A few years after Margaret died in 1945, Morgan married a widowed cousin of Babe's, Helen Hildreth of Southampton.

The local well-off on the East End traditionally built summer camps. Many from the village of East Hampton built their summer camps on the cliffs above Three Mile Harbor. Those included two couples that were friends of Babe and Carl, the Tillinghasts and the Ed Osborne family. (Both were also owners of Conklin-Erickson Chesapeakes.) A group of East Hampton businessmen had a camp near Montauk Point that was a clubhouse and resting place for duck hunters. Among the notables who used that facility were Gary Cooper and Jock Whitney. There were several other camps for hunting, including several in the area around the west side of Three Mile Harbor and near the next small inlet to the west, Northwest Harbor.

Harry Conklin and Morgan Belmont had a camp at Napeague Inlet that they used for duck hunting. It had an outhouse in back and inside, in the kitchen, Belmont had outfitted the place with dishes Commodore Perry had brought from Japan. As Little Carl told me once, "Anybody could have walked in there, it was always open, that camp. Could've stole that stuff out of there anytime. But nobody ever did." The Napeague camp was on the west side of the inlet at the edge of a little pond that emptied through a stream, what locals called a dreen, near a small community called Lazy Point. Years later, someone moved the building, leaving the fireplace and chimney standing in the tall meadow grass.

When I was growing up most of my friends had never been to New York City, in fact, many had never traveled further west than the Shinnecock Canal. Not so with Little Carl, who by age twelve had learned how to use the 7th Avenue Subway. In fact, on that day in 1942 when Nazis landed on the beach in Amagansett, Little Carl, who had just graduated from eighth grade that June, was staying for the week in Greenwich Village, getting an education in city life. His hostess was Lydia Hess Allen, whose father had been a musician with the Boston Symphony and who had married an executive with the I.R.S. in N.Y. Mr. Hess loved fishing and for years took charters with Harry Conklin and Carl Erickson. Lydia hated fishing, so while her husband went off-shore, Lydia was entertained by Babe, with whom she became fast friends, often coming out to visit on her own; and Babe made return visits into New York to see her.

Carl said, "I learned the City like you wouldn't believe. I can still ride a subway anywhere in New York City or any place else. I love going to the City. Used to go to Yankee Stadium and the Polo Grounds all the time."

In high school Little Carl was both a good athlete and a good student. He was a member of the first string basketball team for four years and captain for two. He played on the baseball team every year and football for one year. He was on the track team and he was an All-Suffolk County ping-pong player.

Dragger *Mary A. Edwards*
Edwards Brothers Dock at Promised Land, Winter 1936

EDWARDS

Northeast of Amagansett Main Street, from late nineteenth century on, on a cove of the Bay in a general area called Promised Land, there were several small plants that processed a sardine-type fish called menhaden, or bunker, into oil and fertilizer. The plant that was extant during my childhood was the biggest, and included a large dock area, the largest on the East End at the time. Most of the complex was owned by the Smith Meal Company, whose Promised

Land plant was one of several they owned along the Atlantic Coast from New Jersey down into the Carolinas. The processed fish was used in a variety of ways, both industrial and agricultural. (Smith Meal had originally been called Triton Company and was then owned by a man named Sickler, who had commissioned the building of the original steamships that worked out of Promised Land.)

When the situation called for it, rum-runner Budd King would let Big Carl and his father-in-law Harry Conklin know about some rum boat that had dumped its cargo during a Coast Guard chase, and Carl and Harry would go out in a dragger and retrieve the stuff in their net. On one occasion they had several hundred cases piled up on the Promised Land dock and had Babe sitting on it while they arranged for a truck to come pick it up.

Part of the dock area was owned by the Edwards Brother's Fish Company, a family corporation of fisherman who owned several large fishing draggers, which they ran or farmed out to other captains. Each brother also, at various periods, captained one or another of the big bunker steamers, for Smith Meal. The bunker steamers were large boats, over one hundred feet. One was named Amagansett, one named *Herbert Edwards*, another named *East Hampton*. Smith Meal owned all the bunker boats. The brothers owned most of the land in the vicinity of the plant, more than Smith Meal owned, and they had their own separate dock, an ice plant, and a provisions store. Before refrigeration, they got their ice from Cranberry Pond, on property they owned to the west of the plant, harvesting and transporting it by horse-drawn vehicles. For some years Big Carl captained the 116 foot dragger *Mary A. Edwards* for Capt. Bert Edwards of the Edwards Company.

Lib Davis' Namesake the Bunker Steamer *Elizabeth Edwards*
at the Edward Brothers dock at Promised Land

In the early part of the 20th century the Edwards brothers kept big fish traps off the ocean beach, and had to travel all the way east, around Montauk Point and then back west, to Amagansett and further west, to get at the traps. For this work they had two big fishing boats, the *Elizabeth* and the *Ocean View*, almost the size of bunker steamers. To signal how many trucks they would need for the fish, they would hoist baskets up the mast after they emptied the traps, as a signal to someone on land in Amagansett. The trucks would then rendezvous with them back at the dock.

Elizabeth "Lib" Davis, a daughter of Bert Edwards and a neighbor of the Prohaskas when they lived on Hand Lane, remembered as a little girl often being the one to climb into the attic and, with the help of a telescope, spy from the scuttle the two ships and count the hoisted baskets. She would then call the dock to tell them how many fish trucks to order for shipment to New York.

THE FISHING VILLAGE

In a number of places the East End is nearly cut in half by a combination of inlets, ponds and streams. Those places include Mecox and Seven Ponds; Kellis Pond; Sag Swamp, Sag Pond, Poxabogue, Crooked and Long Ponds; Georgica Pond, and in Montauk, Fort Pond, which extends from a stone's throw of the ocean to a stone's throw of the bay; and further on to Lake Montauk and a series of little ponds called Stepping Stones. Montauk is an isthmus, a place where the potential schism is connected to Amagansett by a narrow land-bridge of low sand dunes several miles long, called Napeague.

From the turn of the century on into the Thirties, many of East Hampton and Amagansett's fishermen moved in summer to the Montauk Fishing Village. The Village, on Fort Pond Bay, was made up of small houses built on posts, with streets of sand and, for the most part, outdoor plumbing. The little village thrived from the time the Long Island Railroad extended from Amagansett to Montauk in 1895 until 1938, when it was completely destroyed by the infamous Hurricane of that year. The present village is on the other side of Montauk, just behind the ocean dunes on the original Montauk Highway, which still connects the East End with the West End. Like the rest of the town, up till Repeal, on December 5th, 1933, the fishing village thrived through both its fishing and its illegal booze trade.

In 1895, railroad tracks were laid across the sand dunes of the Napeague isthmus through its scrub pine, shadbush and berries (blackberries, beach plums, cranberries, high bush blueberries, bearberries) and through the woods on the north side of Montauk to the sandy beach between Fort Pond and the bay, a sheltered cove in the lee of Culloden Point. Fishing boats moored in the bay, using the docks only for loading and off-loading. There were four loading docks in Fort Pond Bay: Jake Wells and Duryea's both sold provisions; a big dock called the Railroad Dock was used by trap fishermen and draggers who loaded their fish onto freight cars backed down onto it; and then there was the Union News Company dock down the beach to the west installed by the Long Island Railroad, then in the recreational fishing business, to dispatch party boats out from the bay. The L.I.R.R. ran a special train from New York to Montauk called the Fisherman's Special, which let its customers off right at the dock.

Budd King

BUDD AND RUTH KING

Budd Nelson King, a native of Springs, was a Bonacker and a friend and associate of Babe and Carl's. He was a top dog in the Prohibition booze trade, possibly the biggest rum-runner on eastern Long Island. He was involved in the design and operation of some of the fast boats that delivered booze from offshore freighters to beaches or docks on the East End. Sometimes, to avoid detection, his operations ranged further to the west, as far afield as Jones Beach and New Jersey. There is no proof, nothing written down, about whether the relationship between Budd and Big Carl included the booze business. No investigator would ever get more than a wink and a nod to go on, but it's probably fair to say, yes, they were running rum. (Rum, at that time, was another word for booze.) Although exactly who was involved was very hush-hush, much was implied and many have been implicated through word-of-mouth history. Almost certainly, Carl captained one or more of the sleek, souped-up, wooden rum-running boats of varying design, that paved the way for P.T. 109 and its sister ships - the torpedo boats of World War II.

Budd got into the booze business as a young man of 19 or 20, as a result of having worked on Gardiner's Island, a privately owned island in the bay off East Hampton. Like many East Enders, he loved Gardiner's Island and felt privileged to work there. He loved the isolation, the romance, the beauty of the place. (Captain Kidd buried some of his treasure there.) Budd owned a little Jersey Boat with which he shuttled the wealthy and prominent to and from the Island where they had bought shares in a club that leased the Island for hunting. Being a charming and knowledgeable guy, Budd made friends with all of these Dukes and Whitneys and assorted swells. These folks were used to having their scotch and their brandies and felt that they shouldn't be deprived of a drink now and then, especially by some damned politicians.

Sometime in the early 1920s, someone of this group introduced Budd to someone who brought booze down from Nova Scotia in a big boat. Budd got involved with this fellow whose name will forever be secret (though it may well have been McCoy, who may well have been working for someone named Kennedy.) Budd's clients were not just ordinary people who'd buy a bottle of booze. They bought the very best. In fact, when Budd went to Quebec to pick up his first order, he had orders from some of the world's wealthiest people who happened to have homes in East Hampton and Southampton. Business boomed.

After it landed on the East End, the booze had to be put in a safe place. Budd had people on the payroll the whole length of Long Island, including many in law enforcement, who would protect each shipment all along the way. Many homes had false cellars, which were used for booze storage. The basement in Carl and Babe's house had one which could hold 400 cases of whiskey.

During the years that I performed my own version of community surveillance by sitting on our front fence, Hazel Morford was a regular member of the cast of characters. She was a handsome grey-haired woman who lived in a room in the Maude Erickson house and came to the post office every day dressed in fine contemporary style, often an expensive looking tweed woman's suit, with sensible heels. She was a friend of Carl and Babe and was a regular at their Canasta parties. She was something of a mystery to me, as was the late Mr. Morford. I never did find out what happened to him.

I eventually did find out that Ned Morford had at one time owned the Baker Brother's Dairy which, though it went through several owners, was always called Baker Brother's. (When I was a child it was owned by Clem Eichorn, a former railroad man.) The dairy, right behind Maude Erickson's house, had twelve cows, but between the silo and milking parlor was a middle barn built to hold hay that was somewhat larger than needed. Behind a false wall was a hidden room which could hold hundreds of cases of whiskey. During Prohibition, whiskey came and went down the cinder driveway past Maude's house, riding in an innocent looking milk truck. Ned Morford was more into whiskey than he was milk.

Budd King built up his business until he had over a hundred people working for him. He had built a nice home of his own on a cliff overlooking Three Mile Harbor, which of course had a big hidden cellar. On occasion, boats were brought up practically to his doorstep. He had his own yacht, *The Nor'west*, moored out in the Harbor. He was one of those men who were talked about in those days, who would be in a speakeasy in New York and light a cigar with a hundred dollar bill. And as the old-timers are fond of saying, "That was when a hundred dollar bill was worth something!"

One of Budd's customers was a well-known artist and illustrator Albert Herter, the owner of perhaps the most palatial estate in East Hampton, The Creeks on Georgica Pond. Herter in those days was busy with mural commissions. He had a high, 14 foot wall in his studio on which he hung huge rolls of canvas, which would then be lowered into a long trough on the floor as he and his assistant painted the higher parts. On one of his visits, Budd told Herter, "I bet I could stash quit a few cases in there!" "Bring it on over!" Herter said. Herter was just another customer anxious to help and nobody was ever the wiser.

Carl and Babe often accompanied Budd on his frequent trips to

New York, where they would combine business with pleasure. For Babe, New York meant shopping and visiting with friends. (On the East End in those days there were few places for a young woman to get nice clothes.) Often Budd would stop in to see his friend Len Lester. A chauffeur for a wealthy East Hampton summer person, Len lived with his family, five girls and a boy, in New York in winter and in East Hampton in summer. This made the Lester children both city folks and full-fledged locals, in those days a rarity beyond measure. One of the girls, Ruth, about Babe's age, would often go shopping with Babe, and they became friends.

The Lesters had five girls: Mary, Ruth, Ann, Margaret, Rita and an older son Leonard Jr., from a different mother. Leonard Jr.'s mother had died when the boy was two years old and Leonard Sr. had taken the child home to the East Side to live with his sister Kitty Belle until he remarried. His second wife, the mother of the girls, was an Irish woman named Hannah McCauley, whom Leonard Sr. met while she working in East Hampton as a domestic at the home of the famous actor John Drew.

 Rita, the youngest daughter married Doctor Francis Cooper. I remember on several occasions while being sick with flu or tonsillitis, hearing the doctor come to the door downstairs. Doctors still made house calls then, when we, my sister and I, were growing up. In earlier years it was always Dr. Nugent and a few years later Dr. Cooper became the main house call Doc in our area. I particularly remember the sort of combination of fear and excitement that accompanied the sound of the doctor's voice. (Both doctors had warm, pleasant voices.) I associated the coming penicillin shot with relief, and so it was with some good expectations, along with the needle fear, that the doctor's voice was elevated to almost God-like.

 My sister's favorite doctor was Dr. Cooper, who had joined Dr. Nugent in Southampton and later helped him start a group clinic in East Hampton on Pantigo Lane. Handsome, with an elegant manner, he joined Paul Nugent in delivering most of the human beings born on the East End after the Second World War. Coop, as he was called, had married Rita Lester in Salinas, California, and before going overseas he assisted in Rita's delivery of twins, Robert and Leonard. With Coop off in the Pacific, Rita traveled cross-country with the twins to spend The Duration with Budd and Ruth.

 Leonard Lester Sr.'s sister, Aunt Kitty Belle, was married to Ezra Bennett. They lived on the East Side in an old Lester homestead, where she and Leonard Sr. and the whole family of Fred Lester had been raised. That was home base for Leonard Lester's family when they were in "Bonac." The small house and several acres had been the Lester children's grandfather's property, and their great, great grandfather's. (Great grandfather Lester was a whaler and after fathering his family he left on a ship out of Sag Harbor for the South Pacific, and, like so many East End antecedents, was never seen again.)

Kitty Belle worked as a maid in a mansion situated on the edge of a cliff overlooking Gardiner's Bay and Gardiner's Island, which was surrounded by a hundred acres or more of woods. The mansion was part of the Bell Estate and was owned by Dr. D.M. Bell, inventor of Bell/Ans Tablets, the Tums of their day. Ezra and Kitty Belle's house, the Lester homestead, was situated on the edge of the Estate. The childless couple were grateful to be entrusted with the care of Leonard Jr. during the child's period between his father's marriages, but when the new Irish Catholic wife came on the scene she insisted on taking the baby back so that she could raise him in the Church. By that time, almost two years had gone by and Kitty Belle had grown to feel that the child was her own. It broke her heart, but she gave the child back to her brother.

Twenty years later, when he was a young artist working in New York, Aunt Kitty Belle came into the city and Leonard Jr. took her shopping. When a clerk who was helping Leonard's aunt try on shoes asked her if the young man was her son, she replied, "No, he's not my son, but he almost was." She then told the shoe salesman all about her period of mothering her brother's son, a story that Leonard had never been told and had no memory of.

Ruth, the second oldest Lester girl, had gone to St. Catherine's Catholic girls' school and to Julia Richman High School, and after taking a business course had done a short stint as a secretary on Wall Street. She then landed a job more to her liking working at International House, a residence house for diplomats, scholars and graduate students. This job, more diplomatic than business, included arranging teas and dances for representatives of different countries having hostilities toward each other. She was, she said, sort of a peacemaker.

She had begun dating Budd King at seventeen and they dated for two years. (Ruth may have been a Bonacker by virtue of family ties, but she was also a Catholic and a New Yorker, so the courtship would not be a repeat of Babe and Carl.) Budd would come up to her office on Riverside Drive and they would have lunch in the dining room, and the residents, students and diplomats would come over to the table to say hello to Miss Lester. They were mostly foreigners and it was common for Bonackers to refer to foreigners as "queers." Budd was beginning to have qualms and second thoughts about who his girl was associating with. He found himself running back and forth to New York more than he needed to just for business, and so in June of 1930 they married. Ruth was 19, and Budd was 28.

Budd and Ruth settled down in his house on the cliff above Three Mile Harbor. Since he was still bootlegging (Repeal wasn't until 1933 and bootlegging continued till the last minute), he let his bride in on some of his business secrets. Although in later years Ruth spoke openly about those times, there were some things she never revealed, such as, "What was the name of that fellow who got Budd into the business?" All she would say was that he was a very, very notorious and wonderful man "not connected to any mob or anything," just an individual who knew all the right people. He trusted Budd completely and Budd never let him down.

One night early on in their marriage, Budd decided to bring Ruth along on one of his operations. He took her to a hiding spot he had on the north side of Montauk, less than a mile west of the busy fishing port of Fort Pond Bay. There, an old Indian trail followed the northern coast of the island as far as Napeague Inlet, in Amagansett. A friend of Budd's had a shack there in a little hollow called Rod's Valley, out of sight of the inhabitants of Montauk's fishing village. Budd had taken an old barn and moved it on to his friend's property and camouflaged it. He left Ruth there with his friend who monitored a ship-to-shore radio, and went off in "a pretty good-sized boat, to pick up a good-sized load." When he returned, a few good men appeared out of nowhere to help Budd and his small crew unload the cases of whiskey from the rum-runner onto the beach and up and over a small cliff to the hideout. That night there were no Coast Guard boats and no gunfire, but it was frightening enough so that Ruth decided never to go again.

When prohibition ended in 1933, Budd converted his yacht into a party boat and began fishing out of Fort Pond. By 1938, still on the *Nor'west*, he moved the boat to the Montauk Yacht Club. Soon after moving there, he got a call from a man in Boston named Charles Campbell, the retired head of E.E. Badgers, a big chemical company.

According to Budd's wife Ruth, "The next morning, before dawn, Budd began fuming because he was all ready to go fishing and the guy was late. He'd already decided to double his price when guy finally arrived, drunk as a skunk, in a chauffeur-driven car. And this guy Campbell says, 'What's the matter Budd? What are you upset about?' And Budd says, 'I'm supposed to be earning a living here and you're not even ready to go out fishing.' 'Don't worry about it,' Campbell said, 'Whether I'm fishing or not, you're gonna get your pay.' After that, it was smooth sailing with Campbell."

Budd King and Charles Campbell on the *Wee-Gon*

When he began fishing regularly with Budd, Campbell soon decided he needed both his own boat and an exclusive deal with Budd. So he said, "I'm gonna build a boat and hire you and then you can't take any more parties. So you have to just go with me." That boat was the *Wee- Gon*. Budd designed it. Then Campbell said, "And if I come down here and I want to play golf, you're gonna play golf with me."

LEONARD AND HERTER

Leonard Jr. had quit St. Vincent's Catholic High School for boys in Manhattan at 16 (in 1920), after deciding he wanted to become an artist. He began studying at the Art Students League. At the same time he bought a camera and began learning how to use it. After several years as a student and as an assistant to various fashion illustrators and photographers, while continuing to go out to Aunt Kitty Belle's in the summer, he and a friend, a young East Hampton man named Charlie Lynch, decided to open up a photography studio in East Hampton, with Charlie doing the darkroom work and

Leonard handling the camera. They quickly began getting work from the local paper, the *East Hampton Star*, and doing portraits for local people and members of the local country club, the Maidstone Club.

This was during the height of Prohibition and Leonard was part of his sister Ruth's social world, the world of Budd King and Babe and Carl and a small crowd of locals still benefiting from bootlegging; investing in boats, hunting dogs, small businesses, and real estate; so Leonard had good connections. Aside from his photography, during Prohibition Leonard started another business in East Hampton, a business in which he was backed by another bootlegger friend, a friend of Budd's named Emerson Taber. The business, a gift shop, was in the Edwards Movie Theater building. The idea was that aside from gifts, they would sell booze under the table. That business flourished until Prohibition ended, when they sold it to someone who continued it as a completely legitimate gift shop.

In 1932 Leonard was hired to be an assistant to Albert Herter, whom he had met through Budd King. Herter, the well known muralist, illustrator, painter and designer, was heir to a small fortune from his parent's furniture and decorating business in Manhattan, and owned The Creeks, the famous estate in East Hampton on Georgica Pond, built by famed architect Grosvenor Atterbury, and completed in 1899. Born in 1871, Herter and his wife, Adele McGinnis Herter, had two sons, one killed during WWI (Everett Albert, an artist like his father, had been part of a camouflage unit when he was killed. East Hampton's V.F.W. Post 550 is named after him), and another, Christian Herter, who went into politics, became Governor of Massachusetts, and after a long legislative career became Secretary of State under Eisenhower.

Herter put Leonard to work on a big mural he was doing for a hotel in San Francisco. Herter's method was to do small sketches and then complete illustrations and, with assistance, transfer them to very large canvases which could then be fastened to the intended wall. Leonard worked along with him, drawing in the larger versions with charcoal secured with fixative, and then painting in the colors. They worked in the same studio, on the same 14' tall wall underneath which Herter had often hidden Budd's whiskey. The trough, which had been an opportune whiskey closet, was used to lower the canvas so that the artists could paint the higher parts without using scaffolding. When the canvas was nearly completed, Herter took Leonard with him to San Francisco to install and fine-tune the work.

The exhibition space for the new mural was a wall of the main restaurant of the then new St. Francis Hotel. The grand opening for the hotel and the restaurant happened to occur while they were still working on it, and Leonard was enough of a showman to enjoy being up on the scaffolding, or as he called it, "staging," while people below were eating their meals. Once the mural was hung on the wall, they would stand back and study it, deciding what needed touching up.

When they finished the San Francisco job, Herter had another mural to work on at his studio in Santa Barbara and brought Leonard with him to his Santa Barbara estate, El Mirasol, and got him a studio apartment at The Hotel El Paseo. Leonard worked on that project for about a year and a half, during which time he became friendly with Christian Herter and his wife, Mary Caroline Pratt, granddaughter of Standard Oil magnate Charles Pratt. Mary's nickname was Mac. It was also during this stay that Herter introduced him to the daughter of an employee-friend who worked at their estate. Her name was Theodora Cobb. Leonard and Theo fell instantly in love. During the 1933 social season in Santa Barbara, after a small dinner party at The Paseo, Theo and Lester were married. He did one more job for Herter, working on a mural for the Four Arts Society in Palm Beach.

The Society of the Four Arts mural was commissioned by Mrs. Lorenzo Aston Woodhouse (the second Mrs. Woodhouse), one of the great cultural benefactors of East Hampton. The first Mrs. Woodhouse, along with her husband, had created a great East Hampton estate called Greycroft, surrounded by a magnificent garden. The first Woodhouses were also among the founders of the Maidstone Club and were benefactors of the Library. The second Mrs. Woodhouse commissioned the architect Aymar Embury II to build, as a gift to the village, the village's cultural center, Guild Hall. She also had the Clinton Academy restored. The Four Arts, something to keep her busy when in Florida in the winter I suppose, was and still is a small cultural center, though growing, that has periodic painting exhibitions, musicals, and theatrical performances.

In East Hampton, the Herters had a lovely little house that was the gatehouse to The Creeks, and they offered it to Leonard and Theo to live in. Theo though, was afraid she'd feel "held captive" behind the gate, and she didn't want to be beholden. They politely declined, and instead set up housekeeping in the second floor apartment of the saltbox cottage which housed Leonard's Photo Shop.

Herter had no more work for him at the time, so Leonard reopened his Main Street studio and went back to doing photos for *The Star*, as well as portraits for the local gentry and summer folks, and glamour photos of the rich and famous who were even then in abundance and which he sold to New York papers and magazines. It was during this period that John Bouvier III, known as "Black Jack" called him to take a picture of his daughter Jacqueline, with her pony. It was 1934 and Jackie was five years old.

The Main Street place was their East Hampton residence until the Hurricane of '38 came along and knocked one of the street's big elms onto its roof. The tree fell through the middle of the house, destroying the center chimney and all three fireplaces.

Leonard's life belies the idea, common among visitors from New York in my growing up years, that there was no cultural interaction between the art world and the life of locals on the East End prior to the coming of the Abstract Expressionists. Leonard was a citizen of both worlds. Through his earlier contacts in N.Y. and his society contacts in East Hampton, he began picking up jobs in fashion photography in New York City, and by the time of the years leading up to WWII he began working full time in Manhattan.

When I interviewed him at his retirement home in Fort Myers in 1999, he was ninety-five, spry, dapper (he wore an ascot), and very much "with it." He showed me prints he had saved from his days in New York in the Thirties. These included photos, some taken when he was a staff photographer for *Harper's Bazaar*, of Somerset Maugham, Robert Eichelberger, Ted Williams, General Kenny (head of the Army Air Corps when Leonard in the service), Cecil Beaton, Vivian Leigh, Katharine Hepburn, a young and beautiful Hedda Hopper, a picture of Joan Crawford in a full length leopard skin coat, and Madeline Carroll. Some of the shots were of people who were his personal friends, including Bob Adams, who did cartoons for early *Life Magazine*, a photographer named George Platt Lynes, and another photographer named Barrett Gallagher.

"I want to tell you something about her," Leonard said, speaking of Crawford. "The day that photograph was taken, she was due at 3 o'clock in the afternoon and I was getting ready for her. I had put a 9 foot, no-seam paper up on the wall. She arrived early, at quarter to 3. I heard a knock on the door and I walked to the door and it's her. And I said, 'You know, you are a little early, aren't you?' And she says, 'Yes, I am, I didn't have anything to do.' She had just flown in from

California. And I said, 'Well alright, come on in.' She said, 'What are you doing?' I said, 'I'm getting ready for you.' And she looked all around and said, 'Is there anything I can do?' 'No,' I said, 'not really.' And I took a broom in my hand and I was about to sweep the floor, because those no-seam papers are expensive and I didn't want to dirty them, see. She said, 'Wait a minute. Give me that.' And she swept the floor for me." She had arrived, fresh from California, and was perfectly made up, with perfect hair. The prints Leonard showed me were all that he had, and there were no negatives. He had destroyed them all.

JOHNNY ERICKSON

I learned from my father: Ray understood, as illustrators tend to, that there really were these beautiful movie star looking girls in small towns all over the nation. It wasn't just wishful thinking, but almost every small to middle sized hick town or village, had its drop-dead gorgeous women and movie star looking men.

Now, if someone from a movie star magazine, of the type there were in those days, such as *Modern Screen* or *Confidential,* had come out to Amagansett and wanted a picture of a woman who could pass for a movie star, they might even have passed up Mary Anne Milligan (God forbid) for another local girl, who just happened to be the wife of a local legend, fisherman Johnny Erickson.

Dorothy, the daughter of Mrs. Petty, she who notoriously "kept house" with Emil Gardell Jr., had wavy white blond hair, perfect teeth, a straight nose and a drop-dead body. She was right out of a Movie Magazine. And wouldn't you know, she was a handful.

When I was in grade school the Johnny Ericksons lived on Miankoma Lane, the lane just to the east of my house. Like the Miller's house on Hedges, it was the only two-story on the lane. (Both lanes in those days were mostly empty lots.) Johnny owned a dragger named the *Brucenda*, named after his two kids Bruce and Brenda. Bruce was a year or two older than me and Brenda a year younger. I remember, as a kid, thinking the combining of the two names for Johnny's boat and Milton Miller's *LiLoEtta*, his boat's name after his two daughters and his wife, were incredibly clever. I guess I still do.

Johnny was born in Amagansett in 1918. His father and Carl Erickson's father were brothers, sons of a Swedish fisherman who in the 19th century settled into a small Scandinavian community in Montauk, close to the Fishing Village, in a little hollow behind Duryea's Dock called, for reasons lost to time, Murder Valley.

The two sons moved to Amagansett, and Johnny's father, John Erickson, married Gertrude Lester, sister of Ted, Theodore Roosevelt Lester. That branch of the Lester family, who were, more formally called the West Amagansett Lesters, were often called the Posey Lesters due to Ted's father's habit of perpetually wearing a posey in his lapel. Gertrude and Ted were from a large family of eleven children of whom Ted, born in 1908, was the youngest. The area around Cross Highway, at one time populated almost exclusively by the Posey family, was called Poseyville.

According to Johnny, during his childhood, they were, "far from rich, but we never went hungry. Everything was inexpensive, and there was a lot of bartering going on. Most people had a pig or chickens and things. Every year when Bart Hadel dug his potatoes, he'd pick the best ones, some lots had better ones than others, and he'd bring up my father 4 or 5 bushel, and he'd put them in the cellar. And then whenever Bart wanted a fish my father would give him one. My mother canned vegetables and we lived all year long on that stuff. It was good! And every Sunday, of course, we had meat of some kind. Some kind of a roast or something. Every morning we had bacon, liver, pork chops. We had pancakes pretty nearly every morning. Every supper we always had potatoes. It wasn't a meal without potatoes. And my mother, she used to make bread, she'd work on it in the afternoon, put it in this big kettle about 2 foot across. One big lot. She'd knead it down, keep on working it, then overnight she'd put a cloth over top of it and next morning she'd get up she'd do the same thing again and a little later on she'd put it in the baking pan. That loaf was a little bit of a thing, but gee it would swell up so it would go right over the top of the pan. Everybody wanted it. When I went to school, once in a while I'd get a quarter to buy lunch. A ham and cheese sandwich and a coke for a quarter, from Stavropolous. Of course, most of the time I'd take my lunch. A sandwich. The kids always wanted to trade."

I last visited Johnny in November of 1997, shortly before he died. He used to get visitors all the time. The younger fishermen would come, the fellows who run the big million dollar plus boats out of Montauk today. Every local fisherman, and lots of other people, held Johnny in high esteem. His name was synonymous with swordfishing.

He wasn't in good shape physically, but he was happy and content. He was confined to the house, almost living on his sofa, hooked up to various tubes and things. He was living with his third wife in a house he had built on property near where he was born, on Schellinger Road in Amagansett. They owned the house free and clear and were living on Social Security. (They had money left over at the end of every month.) He'd been paying into it since he'd worked for the WPA in 1938, when he got $3 a day for sawing up the trees felled by the Hurricane. (That was the only job he ever had outside of commercial fishing.) "It's good to reminisce," he said. I have a whole lot of friends and I know when they're coming. If one don't come in a month or two I'll call and see if he's sick. Mostly they're a little bit younger than I am. They come and we sit here three, four hours, talking about everything."

We were talking about the WPA job; "You had two-man saws, they were six or seven foot long, one man on each side. Those trees in front of your house down there (the Prohaska house), I remember how big they were, six foot through, a man couldn't reach around them. We sawed them up. We had no electric saws or chain saws. Imagine having to do that, you couldn't get anybody to do that in this day and time, for all the money in the world. Main St. was full of them. After we worked down in Amagansett, they moved us to Wainscott. Up there, some guy name of Clinton was the boss. They had a lot of pheasants up there at that time, so I'd take a gun with me every morning. I'd drop the other fellows off; Mr. Tucker and Bill

Schellinger. I'd drop them off and go look for a pheasant. They wouldn't miss me if I wasn't gone long. And come back with a pheasant more often than not."

Johnny harpooned his first swordfish when he was 14. That would have been 1932. He had begun steering the boat for his father when he was ten. "Every year, I'd get out of school about the 20th of June, and we'd put the pulpit on right away. The next day my father and I, we'd go. And as a rule we got one or two the first couple of times we'd go out. Some days you'd go four or five days you wouldn't see one. A calm day you'd go out and you'd see two or three or more, then the next day you'd go out and the weather's good you can see them better, and you'd see just as many, but then if you had two or three calm days in a row, the first calm day they'd show and the next couple of days they wouldn't show again. It was just, I don't know what it was, happened that way.

"One day, we had eight fish on board, it was gettin' late. In the afternoon we see another one. My father, he wasn't doing very good harpooning them. The last one he harpooned he hit alongside the dorsal fin and it just bounced right up because it's just bone there. So then they got talking and they said let Johnny try. So next time we went out I struck one and I kept striking them right on. The old man, he'd sort of lost his touch. He never did much of it, never really got good at it, because he was always with Captain Gabe Edwards, and since Cap'n Gabe owned the pulpit, he let him do it, and old John didn't wanna do it anyway. I practiced a lot. When we was out fishing, draggin' for fluke, flounders, whatever, and we had the pulpit on, I was always out there just throwing the bare pole."

Johnny's father's boat was the *Ondine*. It means crest of the wave. It was 38 feet long; the pilot house just about big enough for three men to stand up in. If they got 12 or 15 swordfish a season, that was considered pretty good, some days they'd get three or four. Later, when Johnny had his own boat, they caught as many as 38 in a season. "But," he added, "we weren't swordfishing all the time, we just went out once in a while when the weather was good. We'd go draggin' you know, and if it turned out to look like a good swordfish day, light breeze to the north, say, we'd go."

They didn't make a lot of money. Money wasn't that important to them. They woke up in the morning wanting to go fishing. "When you go out, you make $100, you get a lot of money by a cut of three of four fellows. Ted Lester fished with me one winter and Elmer

Fenelon he fished with me quite a few years and every week we used to share up $25 apiece. Elmer had a big family, three kids I think. I had two, Ted had four or five and every week we'd take out $25, then, end of the month, we'd square up, you know, we'd share up anything left."

He fished with his father until he got married. "And then I had to make a little bit more than that so I went on the *Magdalene* out of Promised Land with Capt. Sam Edwards. There was Jack Edwards, Norman Edwards, Kenneth Edwards, Red Cantwell and myself. It was yellowtailing mostly. Then The War come on and of course Norman, he was the young one and he had to go to The War, and we was exempt. I was always exempt because I guess I had a couple of children and fish were pretty important. Feeding the Home Front. And Red, he went to war and Jack he went bunker fishing.

"Then we went fishing butterfish and swordfish. The swordfish would be where the butterfish are 'cause they like to eat them. We'd drag for the butterfish and if the weather'd get good, then we'd go look for the swordfish. We lost money by going swordfishing 'cause the butterfish was the same price as swordfish, but we went anyway because we enjoyed it. The big butterfish was 50 cents a pound, the swordfish was 50 cents. Anyway, one day Ken's wife came along with us; Louise. There was Louise and her son, little Kenneth, he was adopted you know. We fished for two days; stayed overnight on the boat. We came in with nine swordfish and 4,000 lb. of butterfish. Now, when we got to the dock, Capt. Sam was there. He didn't believe in having any women on the boat. Kenneth and Sam, oh they had some argument! You could hear them 500 feet away. As far as the little store they had there. So that was the end of that. Kenneth he didn't go no more. Red Cantwell and I went, so, then there was three of us on the boat.

"Sam was very good, he paid us good because he didn't take much out for the boat. He took a third out, for all the running and expenses, the fuel oil and the ice, whatever the boat expenses was, he took them out and then we whacked it up. The boat took a third out and the fellows got the other two thirds. Didn't matter how many men were on the boat. Three men, of course, each got a third. A few years after that they wanted 50%. Sam's wife would cook pigs for us to bring on the boat, or a roast, or a chicken or we bought stuff too, cold cuts, but, she would see we didn't starve. She was a wonderful lady.

"Winter times we went yellowtailing. During The War there was so many yellowtails and small flounders. We went on the outside hole mostly. What they call the Butterfish Hole. There'd be a dozen, maybe fifteen boats out there, scattered around; east of the Montauk Lighthouse. We'd tow for probably an hour and a half, then we'd have to sit there and pick a few bushel up before we put the net over. Probably fill her up, probably 100 boxes. Wooden boxes. They was 125 lb. boxes in them days. We'd probably get 90-100 boxes, come in, ship every night. After a while, I guess two thirds were yellowtails, the other third were flounders. I was making good money then, about $1000 a month, I mean that was about an average."

It was during the period that he lived near us, on the east side of the potato field on Miankoma Lane, that Johnny and a partner had the *Brucenda* built. It was built up in Waterboro, Maine. Way Down East. His marriage at this time was a tempestuous one, a point well noted by neighbors, including my family, yelling carried far in those quiet times, and by the people (the tenants fluctuated), who rented the downstairs apartment.

Waterboro was up a little river from the coast. It was a dry town, so they had to take beer along. They drove up several times to see how the boat was coming along and when the boat was finished, Johnny brought the boat back and his partner drove the car. Johnny remembered that as he climbed aboard he dropped a wrench between his boat and another, bigger boat laying at the dock, a big 70, to 80 footer. "I thought, 'by God I'll never retrieve that, it's sunk down in the water,' but when the tide was out, I went and picked it up off the mud. There must have been a 15 or 20 foot tide there.

"Every summer we'd put a pulpit on the *Brucenda*, and we'd go down to Noman's, (a point on the southern side of Martha's Vineyard) and different guys would come with us. Bill Lusty went with us sometimes when he had a month's vacation. He worked for Eli Lilly Drug Co. He'd take a month and just go swordfishing with us. Never got paid. One trip he'd take one boy with him and another trip he'd take the other boy. Bruce went pretty regular. Down there, we'd stay about a week. Down underneath Noman's there. That's where the swordfish went when they left here.

"Well anyway, we were out this one day. It was a beautiful day. We got maybe eight anyway. We harpooned eight, got them aboard, we were sitting there nice, Bill says 'If we see another one why don't you let Bruce try it?' He was 14 then, I think it was. I'm pretty sure he was. So I said, 'gee I never thought of that.' So, darned if we didn't see another one, you don't know when you're going to see one, you know. It's just like gambling or anything. We did see another one, the biggest one of the whole day. I said, 'Okay, Bruce go ahead,' and so he went out and damned if he didn't strike him and hit him in the backbone. You hit them in the backbone, it stiffens them out. They just lay there. In about five minutes they come to, they go like a streak of greased lightning. He'd stunned him. He just laid there like bloated. So I come down out of the mast, I got halfway down, I jumped the other half and landed on the pilot house, it was probably about ten foot, maybe more, sprained my ankle, but we got him in 'fore he come to life. So, you get them up there and you cut their throats and make them bleed. If you put him aboard the boat and he come to, he tears everything apart. 'Cause, I don't know how much he weighed. He probably dressed 300. He was the biggest one for the day, anyway. So that was Bruce's first fish."

Johnny sold the *Brucenda* when his wife left him. He sold the boat because he was mad at the world, and he never owned another boat after that. Dorothy had run off with Frank Tillotson, his partner in the boat. (In Amagansett in those days you didn't get divorced, you "ran off".) Johnny had decided to wipe the slate clean. That and drink a lot. He said he stayed mad for, "A year or two, but not longer. Because I couldn't do anything about it, and, well, life is too good!"

Frank and Dorothy opened up a fish market on Sagaponack Main Street, near Bridgehampton. That didn't last too long, and after a few years, she got tired of Frank too. Then she got tangled up with a mailman.

By 1970, Johnny had gone out to California with his second wife, Mary Higgins. They were staying with Mary's daughter and thinking about retiring out there. Mary was a smart woman who was a real estate salesperson in East Hampton and a friend of many of the New York set. She had bought and sold a nursing home in East Hampton, turning it over for a small profit. She met Johnny while they were both on a spree and it was a minor scandal among the locals that they married so soon after meeting, but they did have a short happy life together until she died in July of 1973. In California though, Johnny had had a heart attack. California didn't agree with him. He might have been homesick. So they came home and rented a place in Montauk.

When he got back, Johnny didn't do a whole helluva lot, as he put it, other than spend a lot of time in Fitzgerald's Bar on the Docks, drinking. Mary got a job selling real estate. Johnny would fish off the dock in front of Fitzgerald's with a rod and reel and catch flounders. "There were plenty of flounders then," he said. Sometimes he gave them away and sometimes he gave them to the bartender in return for free drinks.

Then Elisha Ammon asked him to come fishing with him. "He says 'you'll be all right, you don't have to do nothing, just steer. Just go with us.' So I went with him and stayed with him for quite a few years. We was always friendly and good company, you know. And the funny part about it was yellowtail was eight cents a pound, which was good. Fish all day get, get 15,000 to 20,000 lb. no trouble, they were so thick you know. We went to Stonington to take em out."

"And that would be it for the day?" I asked him. "Yeah. Well, you had enough by the time you got to Stonington and iced up and come back here probably dark or maybe later. The next morning you'd start all over again. They must have been that deep (gestures a couple of feet) on the bottom. They're like a flounder. You can't pick 'em up fast enough. That was with Elisha. He had the *Nianza* then. Christ, he's had a lot'a boats; the *Rhode Island*, the *Big Dipper*, the *Golden Dawn*, the *Russell S.*, a lot'a boats."

BOBBY "SCRATCH" BYRNES

In 1998, for the Oral History I was doing of the town of East Hampton, NY, I interviewed Robert "Scratch" Byrnes and his wife Miriam "Mim" at their home in Montauk. I told him how I happened to be there the day his partner Sy died, twenty-eight years previous. I had been sitting on the dock, waiting for a friend (Sy's nephew) who was going to help me frame a small addition on a house. As they nosed into the dock, Sy collapsed. Scratch caught him as he fell and let him gently down on the deck. He had died instantly. The Coast Guard building is right there, and so he was laid out on a stretcher and left on the lawn, covered with a sheet, while the coroner made his way from up-island. It was a solemn but peaceful and quiet half hour or so.

The friend I was waiting for, Einar Handrup, was at that time living on his Nova Scotia lobster boat which was tied up in the slip next door. Scratch knew I was part of a crowd that included Einar and a handful of other guys in that age group, most of whom were fisherman, all of whom drank and "partied." Einar and I had gone to high school with Scratch's daughter Eileen. Scratch hadn't known that my friend was at that time engaged in informal litigation with the Town of East Hampton, over whether or not he had to pay rent for the slip his "Novy Boat" (Nova Scotia Boat) was docked in. Einar claimed that he had inherited the boat slip from his father and that it was therefore his real estate. Over time this became an issue with the Town Board, but was settled, at least to Einar's satisfaction, when he pulled the plug on his boat and let it sink right there at the slip. With that he washed his hands of the matter.

The boat Scratch and Sy had come in on that day was the *Marion H.* "In fact," as he reminded me during our conversation, "That boat was Einar's father's, originally." The boat had been built before The War over in Stonington Connecticut, by Einar Sr. and his father during a time when they were working there. She was named after Einar Sr.'s sister, whose husband, Sy, became Einar Sr.'s, and later Scratch's partner. She was fifty feet long and drew seven feet of water, and was of a typical Stonington Dragger design, a smaller version of the New England Trawler but about half size, or around fifty feet, and like the larger boat using the Otter Trawl, a net that scrapes along the bottom. She held 25,000 pounds of fish. After the War, Einar Sr. fished it a little bit and then decided he wanted out, wanted to go charter fishing, so Scratch bought him out, and since Marion had inherited her father's half, her husband, Sy, and Scratch became partners.

They had started out sailing out of what had been Charlie Bonner's marine gas station, now part of Gosman's Dock, a large tourist complex. As that area became more and more crowded, with several more independent commercial docks, the *Marion H.* moved over on to Star Island, to the # 3 Dock, the town-owned dock adjacent to the Coast Guard Station. Scratch worked the boat from there for thirty years; twenty with Sy till that day when he died, and then alone for ten years after that. "So ya see, Marion and I became partners, the boat was in her name and mine." I had been a silent witness in that change in Scratch's life.

SCRATCH

Bobby Byrnes was born in 1920 in a section of lower Manhattan called The Gas House District, a mostly Irish neighborhood. Budd King gave him his nickname, Scratch, either because of his high level of baseball playing, or because of his high pitched, scratchy voice, or both. He had an uncle who was the Assemblyman for the District and later became Chief Justice of the City Courts of the City of New York.

Sometime around 1930, Bobby's father, Peter Byrnes, who worked for the phone company, was transferred out to the fishing town of Freeport, Long Island, where he met and became friends with Budd King, who was doing some of his bootlegging business out of that harbor. When Bobby's mother died in 1930, Peter, a.k.a. Petey, married Budd's wife's sister, Mary, part of the Leonard Lester brood. Whether Petey met Budd through fishing or through rum is another fact lost to history.

Once Petey and Mary were married, they spent much of their time out in Bonac, and Bobby, now Mary's stepson, was welcomed into the bosom of the Lester clan and fell in love with the East End. During the school year, they lived here and there in western Long Island as his father was transferred around, and every summer he spent out East with his new relatives. Sandlot baseball was big on the East End in those days, even down at the old fishing village, and Bobby made fast friends through that sport. With his father's approval, after he finished high school in Valley Stream he began living full time with Budd and Ruth.

Being a relative of Budd King, even through marriage, was a high level transfer, making Scratch a dyed-in-the-wool, full time local. If it hadn't been for the fateful timing of the end of Prohibition, he'd have probably gone on to work for Budd in the rum trade. As it was, though, when the end came for Prohibition in '33, Budd took his yacht *Nor'west* and made a party boat out of it, and Scratch, only thirteen at the time, began working on it as a summer job. They fished out of the Fishing Village. For Scratch, it was fun, not work.

"Down on the beach," as he referred to life at the Fishing Village, Scratch, with Budd and Ruth, lived next door to Harry Conklin and Babe and Carl and Little Carl. The Conklin-Erickson family all lived in the same house, a slightly bigger and nicer house than most of the others. Harry Conklin's sister (another) Ruth was married to Sheldon Miller, and they lived on the other side, in another house owned by Harry, Babe, and Carl. Later, when Scratch got married, he and his wife rented a house next door to Ruth and Sheldon, another Conklin-Erikson house.

There were a couple of small grocery stores in the Village, and Jake Wells and Duryea's carried some canned goods and stuff, but to save money most folks would drive once a week into East Hampton to get groceries.

Though they were only a few feet above sea level, a pump and holding tank near the railroad station brought clean, fresh water through a pipe running the short distance to the village with connections to most of the houses. Most folks had outhouses, but a few, like the Harry Conklin clan, were "more high-class" and had inside toilets with a sewer pipe that ran down to the bay. You had to step over the pipes when you were swimming. Scratch's wife Mim recalled, in answer to the implied health question, "We never saw a doctor, we were all healthy." From what I knew of the people who lived down there, she must have been right.

Scratch had an excellent memory. He remembered everyone that was there; Hooker Hand coming by to pick up laundry and say hello to Babe and Carl, just like he would do when they were in "Gansett." Not everybody in the little village sent their laundry out, of course, but Babe did. "If people ran out of coal during cooking time, the kids would go down to the railroad tracks and pick some," Scratch told me. "The engineers used to throw us some coal along the tracks down at the end of the line near the beach. We was primitive, let's put it that way!"

A fishing village isn't a commune. If you are a captain, you are an independent contractor; the same goes if you are a captain running someone else's boat, or even if you are just a crew member. At any time you are free to get up and go with another boat; no hard feelings. Whichever way, everything depends on catching fish, so there is strong team spirit as well as strong competition. Some are better fishermen than others. A few are good, all around entrepreneurs, good at catching fish, running boats, and holding on to money.

There were three restaurants in the fishing village. One was The Roadside, Alma Handrup's place; another was The Trail's End, owned by Ann Fallon and run by her sister, Mrs. Ecker; and a third, Willard's, owned by, well, a guy named Willard. Everybody just called him Willard, according to Mim. All three restaurants were big enough to hold forty or fifty people in a pinch, and all three had a bar. A fisherman could run up a tab at one place and then go on to the next. The owner's insurance was simple. No one was going anywhere, and there'd always be another trip, another load of fish. In the meantime, the bars were so close you could fall out of one and into the next.

The restaurants were fraternized mostly by locals, fishing village people, with visitors including the occasional boat that came in from the North Fork, Shelter Island, or Connecticut, and people from East Hampton and points west who might feel like taking a drive all the way out to the wilds of Montauk. Then there was the Montauk Manor, a large hotel whose customers enjoyed roughing it at the rustic saloons. The village saloons got plenty of customers from "up on the hill," as they referred to the Manor, and many connections between fishermen and the rich, famous, or in-between, were formed by that literal trickle-down.

Johnny Erickson, Big Carl's cousin, once told me, "I even got to know a fellow named Dr. Baruch, Bernard Baruch, he was a pretty famous statesman years ago, he had a boat named the *Monsoon*." Baruch had discovered it was more convenient to leave his boat at Jake Well's dock, rather than the Yacht Club. He could take the train right to his boat. Every weekend he'd come down, this large man with a goatee wearing his knickers and sporting a cane, and, every weekend he had a different nurse. Instead of hiring a taxi, he'd have Johnny take him up to the Manor, "And anywhere else he wanted to go. He had a good looking niece too, who used to come along sometimes. I liked her a little bit," Johnny added, "I didn't really date her. We just hung around the docks there. Everybody got together, all the kids down there, we had a lot of beach parties. Didn't have much fancy food. We had hot dogs sometimes, but we always had potatoes, we were great with potatoes, you ever eat burnt potatoes? (That was still a tradition with local kids in my day, potatoes cooked on a stick in the bonfire.) It was whatever we could get ahold of. One thing, there was plenty of driftwood in those days."

BOBBY AND MIM

Scratch met Miriam Ammon when they were both "On the Beach," as they used to call living at the Fishing Village. Bobby was at Budd King's, and Mim, as she was called, was with her family, the Elisha and Annie Ammon family. In fact, they had something in common, because they'd both been to The Big City. Mim had spent a year or so in New York City working as a babysitter for an Irish couple to whom she had been introduced at Sunday school, which in those days was held in a barroom in the fishing village.

The Fishing Village had no church. They'd had one, a tiny chapel, but it had been torn down for being unsafe. For church they traveled to East Hampton and most went to the Episcopal Church. (That's where most of the Fishing Village kids were baptized in those days.)

Mim, four years older than Scratch, was born at the Fishing Village, in 1916, and delivered by the Amagansett doctor and historian, Dr. Frederick Finch. Dr. Finch, after traveling to Montauk, had stopped at the Trails End and had too much to drink and registered her as William; which was why when she went looking for her birth certificate, she couldn't find it.

She lived most of her life on Montauk. (Most old timers in East Hampton Town, including Mim, pronounced Montauk with the accent on the second syllable.) Of course she knew the "Gansett people," as she called them, because so many of them came down to Montauk. "I knew the two Erickson families, John, his family, and the Carl Erickson family, and Babe, I mean, she was The Queen of Amagansett. Everybody knew her."

Scratch said of Mim, "Well, on account of her being older than me, she knows a little more about the bootleggin', cuz her brothers were older than her and they used to unload the rum boats. And Mim knew the older kids, "like the Edwards', they came down too. Nat and Sam Edwards' crew, they all lived down here in the summer. They did trap fishing. And they had homes here and then went back to Amagansett in the late fall."

The Edwards brothers were the most successful East End fishing family, and, like most of the other local families, they too were interrelated with everybody. Mim is related to the Edwards by marriage, through her brother, Elisha, who was married to Dottie (Ammon), who was a King, from East Hampton. Emma King. Emma's aunt was the mother of Kenneth and Jack Edwards. (Their mother and Dottie's father were brother and sister.)

I'd never been too clear on the local Edwards lineage, so I asked Scratch what was the relation of Dick Edwards of Amagansett, who was a friend and contemporary of Mary Anne Milligan and Carl Erickson, to the men of the Edwards Brothers Fishing Company of Promised Land. "Well, see, I guess it goes like this," said Scratch. "Dickie Edwards' father was Nat Edwards (Nathaniel Talmage Edwards #10) and he was the big trap fisherman. And Nat's kids were Dickie, Ale (Mary Ellen), Emma and young Nat. Emma, she married Shorty Parsons, and young Nat, Dickie's older brother, he drowned cod fishin' with Kenneth. (Feb. 19, 1937.) The four of them, they grew up on Atlantic Avenue there, just across from where Norman lived. Now, that's how they're related.

"Then there was Kenneth and that bunch, Kenneth, Joshua, Iantha, Norman, they were Capt. Sam's kids, and there was Dr. Dave Edwards, he was Capt. Sam's brother, he had the two sons James and Dick, who was called Old Dick, to distinguish him from Dick Edwards of Amagansett, who was younger, the former born in 1904, the latter in 1926. James "Jim" Edwards, used to be a salesman at the Buick dealership in East Hampton. Doctor Dave also had a daughter, Katherine. Whether she's alive or not, I don't know, but she was a nurse, for the Doc.

"Then Captain Sam and Doctor Edwards had two other brothers, Everett J., called E.J., and Herbert, or Capt. Bert, was another brother, and who the hell else? Geez, I don't know, I can't, guess I can't keep track (he laughs) of 'em all."

Everett J. had a daughter Jeannette who wrote *East Hampton History and Genealogies*, and several other books about East Hampton Town. With her husband, Arnold Rattray, she began the small publishing dynasty that still owns the *East Hampton Star*, the local newspaper of East Hampton Town.

There are probably thousands if not millions of Edwards, all over the U.S., and an appreciable amount of them come from this Amagansett family, starting with the first William Edwards, who came to East Hampton from Maidstone, Kent, in England, sometime in the mid-1600s.

Though she lived most of the time in Montauk, Mim's family homestead was on the East Side, on Barnes Landing Road, a road that connects with Old Stone Highway after that road heads south from Bonac Creek toward Amagansett and ends up at the beach on Gardiner's Bay. (Her mother, Annie Scott, who was born on the East Side, had worked for the Prohaskas for a short time when they first moved into Hand Lane.) The Ammon's house was next door to the Bell Estate's private chicken farm and across the street from Elsie and Joe Bennett. (Elsie, who was locally famous for her thick Bonac accent, worked for Carolyn as housekeeper after Eileen Scott, the wife of Annie's brother.) Elsie's husband Joe worked at Bell's poultry farm and raised his own chickens as well. Joe gave me my first little flock of Bantams.

By the time she came along, Mim's family included five other siblings, two brothers and three sisters, and the family were staying most of the year at the Fishing Village, where her father, Elisha Sr., had gotten very good at finding lobsters in Fort Pond Bay. Mim's brother, Elisha Jr., a fisherman of Scratch's generation, had a son Edward, who was in my high school class, and is a cousin of both of my best friends from grade school. Mim grew up in the old Fishing Village and was friends with Little Carl. "He must have liked me, cuz he used to throw rocks at me all the time!" She told me laughing. She went to the old Montauk School, first in a building which later became the firehouse and then, when it opened, to the new, red brick school. She is very proud of her Montauk grade school class. "We never lost a basketball a game in four years. We tied one. It was fabulous. That was my game."

Mim goes on, "We had our own fun. We sewed clothes for our dolls by hand and, being so athletic, we had a telephone pole that had ropes on it that we used like a merry-go-round. It had an old mattress wrapped around it. We'd take cattails and we'd light them up and pretend we were smoking. And, the funniest thing, we always had goldfish. And some mornings on our way to school we'd be late because we had to stop and have a funeral for a little goldfish! We were happier than these kids today, I think."

Every summer, when the Ericksons came from Amagansett to Montauk they would bring the pony and his cart and all the kids would get rides. The Pony (with no name) was solid brown in color and ran wild at Montauk the same as he did in Amagansett. When the Excursion train pulled in, he would go to the parlor cars and beg lumps of sugar from the tourists. (During the '38 hurricane he holed up in the woods on the high ground behind The Manor.) When Little

Carl was grown, Babe and Carl gave the pony to their friends the Tillinghasts, who had young children and owned a dairy farm in East Hampton. One of the Tillinghast sons told me he was "pretty sure" the pony's name was Major. When Carl would go to his high school class reunions, those he'd gone to school with would never fail to ask him about that pony.

Scratch worked summers on the *Nor'west* until he graduated from high school and then he also graduated from party boat to commercial fishing. "With commercial fishing", he said, "if you don't get any fish, you ain't happy, but you don't have to listen to people complain about it. So I was lucky, I got that party fishing out of my system young."

NOTE: In my younger days, I worked a summer on a party boat and to me, the worst of them came every day. Beer swilling guys from the city who belonged to so-called fishing clubs, actually drinking clubs, who stumbled around on the deck getting lines fouled, smoking, drinking, coughing and complaining, while you tried to keep their hooks baited.

Scratch's first job on a dragger was on the *Dorothy*, a boat owned by the Duryea Company. After a few trips on that boat right around the start of WWII, he became part of a five man crew that fished the winter out of Promised Land on the *Magdalene*, one of the Edwards Brother's boats, with three Edwards men, Kenneth, Norman, and Jack, and Johnny Erickson. Johnny, who had two children, stayed on all through the War with Kenneth, but The War Effort nailed Norman toward the end. He got called up to work as a civilian, supervising construction of boats at Norfolk.

Norman ended up coming home with a boat. "He bought the boat down there, in Norfolk?" I asked Scratch. "Yeah. The *Edith Hudgens*, you remember her? She was a hundred and ten footer. Another sub-chaser." I did remember her. A boy I grew up with, Jim Fenelon, went to work on her in the Sixties.

The Edwards brothers already had several converted WWI sub-chasers, the *Robert E.*, the *Magdalene* and the *Mary A*. This new boat, the *Edith Hudgens,* was a similar boat, whether a WWI sub-chaser or not, not sure, but Norman saw her in the Navy Yard in Norfolk, and bought her, along with half dozen spare engines and dozens of batteries and other odds and ends. He sailed her home himself.

The Fishing Village, which had been built on land leased from the railroad, was almost completely destroyed by the '38 Hurricane. Right after that, with war approaching, the government, recognizing the value of this property which was adjacent to a railroad terminal and a dock, requisitioned all the land that encompassed the Fishing Village for use in the war effort to build plants for the manufacture of airplane parts, and for whatever other military purposes fit their needs. Mim was the last person living in the old fishing village when Scratch went into the service. Theirs was one of the few houses left. When I talked to her, she recalled the day their house had been dragged up to Shepherd's Neck, a plot of land on a hill to the west of Fort Pond, a distance of about a half mile, and was sitting up there on skids. She couldn't get in it because it was all boarded up. She can remember that day because it was the 7th of March, 1943, the day their daughter Eileen was born.

They had paid for the move themselves. "I don't know where it came from, that money," says Bobby, though, he adds, "After the war, the government did give us two hundred dollars for Mim's father's house (a very similar building), which they had demolished." That was what the moving had cost, so you could say, they got their money back.

Marion H., the 50' Montauk Dragger that Bobby Byrnes fished on for 30 years. Seen here coming into Lake Montauk in the 1960's.

SCRATCH, WAR AND AFTER

During The War Scratch was in The Coast Guard Picket Patrol, a flotilla made up mostly of requisitioned or privately turned over sailing yachts. Though some were quite small, the one Scratch was on, the *Thistle*, was one hundred and three feet, drew fourteen feet of water, and was made of bronze. (Not just the keel, but the whole hull was bronze; stainless steel framing and bronze hull.)

I asked him where they went when they went off shore. "They had these different grids. We would go off to the fifty fathom line. Pretty near all along that whole fifty fathom, all up and down the northeast, every so many miles they had a location, it was called a station, and that's where you'd go. And we'd just go there and sit. The little boats smaller than the *Thistle* was fine because if it blew, they'd call in to seek shelter, and they'd be close enough inshore somewhere where they could go to. But every time the *Thistle* got a call to seek shelter, we'd just head her out into the southeast and we'd be further off shore so we hardly ever did get to go in. The object was to stay in more or less the same area. The main mission was to keep the German subs hiding. If the subs surfaced, even if they destroyed a picket boat, that meant they had been spotted and become vulnerable; it was a long way back to Germany." When Scratch saw the A&E documentary on the Picket Boats, he said, "I saw the Thistle sail right by. Old 30-85."

When he first got out of the service Scratch ran the *Fan and Mary*, the sister ship to the *Alwa*. The *Alwa* and the *Fan and Mary* were at that time owned by two guys named Charlie Walker and Red Alfred, alleged bookies from Southampton. They had had both boats built for them so they could have a legal income. The two boats were Stonington draggers. Scratch's brother-in-law Elisha had run the *Fan and Mary* for a while and he was set to buy his own boat, so Scratch ran the *Fan and Mary* for about two years and then worked on a little boat he was planning to buy but didn't, the *Anna Esther*.

Then, after running another boat that he didn't like, "She was an Eastern rig and I didn't care for that too much. She was sixty-five foot, which was good, but it just wasn't what I liked in a boat, you know? So, I told the owner if he could get his money back, he should sell it, which he did. And then I ran the *William B.*, for Willie Parsons. And Willie'd stay home sometimes, especially in the winter so, mostly, I was the one running her for a couple a years. And when I was runnin' her, Ted Lester came on during the winters. And it was Ted and I and Mel Curlew. Did you remember Mel? And then I bought into the *Marion H*." Ted Lester was the haulseiner that my father was friends with. He figures heavily in Peter Matthiessen's book about haulseiners, *Men's Lives*.

When Scratch mentioned Mel Curlew, I had to ask him if he had a son. When I was about ten, there was an older kid, who had a driver's license, who lived on Oak Lane near my friend Tommy's house. This kid was quite short, so when he'd drive by, you could see that he was keeping himself propped up with his left arm hooked over the door window sill so he could see over the steering wheel. The kids name was Jay Curlew, and rumor was he was somehow related to Bette Davis. We, Tommy and I, thought that it was Jay's brother or father, who had been married to her. So, when Scratch mentioned Mel Curlew, I asked him about the Bette Davis connection. "Well," Scratch said, "Mel had three kids. Jay, Ronnie, and Gary. Jay was the youngest."

With assistance from Mim, Scratch began to sort it out. "Let's see. Mim was an Ammon. Her father was Elisha Sr. Her mother was Annie Scott Ammon (who, remember, cleaned for the Prohaskas when they first moved to Hand Lane.) Annie was a daughter of Granny Scott, whose maiden name was Phoebe Loper. Now, Phoebe, she first married a Payne and had eight children, including Nettie, Mickey Miller's grandmother. Then, when Phoebe's first husband died, she married James Scott, and with him she had eight more children including Mim's mother, Annie."

Annie had another brother, Thomas Scott, who was a real estate broker in Amagansett and was my friend Tommy Scott's great uncle. Tommy's father Leonard was the son of another sibling from the second Granny brood, James.

Granny (born in 1853; died 1938), was the daughter of Daniel Loper, a whaler, born in 1811, and died in 1888. (It was a Loper who first taught the Nantucketers how to whale off the beach.) Granny had a brother named Abraham, born 1835, who was the father of E. Grant Loper, born 1865, who was the father of Marian and of Madeline, Granny's nieces.

Madeline married Mel Curlew and Jay was her son. Marian married William Sherry Sr. a Broadway set designer who moved out to East Hampton, went local, and fell in love with Marian an Amagansett girl. Marian was the mother of Bill Sherry, the same William Grant Sherry Jr. who married Bette Davis. This explains the Curlew connection to Bette Davis.

Marian's mother, Effie Bennett Loper, a woman with a thick Bonac accent and a sharp tongue, lived for a time in Hollywood with Miss Davis herself, with whom she was said to have gotten along better than her son did. Effie was also the great aunt of Josephine Bennett, the smartest girl in our class.

Mim is also a cousin of Tommy Scott's father Len, and Mickey Miller's grandfather, Russ Miller Sr., Coast Guardsman and keeper of the Montauk Lighthouse, was her uncle. So, of course, Mickey's father (and therefore Mickey) was her cousin too. But she had uncountable cousins, many that lived, or still live, up-island, so that she never got to know them. It may be, she told me, that she remembered the fishing families more. "It's very surprising," she said, "I had an aunt in Patchogue that had twelve children and I wouldn't know any one of 'em. With my grandmother, Granny Scott, having had sixteen children, you can imagine the cousins I'm countin."

HARRY STEELE

Every child in East Hampton Town, it seemed, had a Harry Steele story. Harry was the Chief of Police from 1923 to 1957. He was a big man with a big belly and he wore a pearl-handled revolver, slung low like a cowboy. The first time Little Carl Erickson met The Chief, "I was going to first grade. I will never forget it. Harry Steele had stopped with his motorcycle and he was directing traffic, 'cause there were kids crossing the street, and he was out there holding up traffic or waving them on, what few cars there were. And Harry grouped about ten of us kids together and he said, 'All right, kids. I want everybody to hold hands.' So we all hold hands, all ten of us, and I was at the end. And when he started the motorcycle he put his finger on the spark plug or whatever it was, and it went right through all the kids out to me and I was the one that got the shock! I'll never forget that, you know? It took me right off my feet! And he laughed! Oh, he thought that was the best thing that ever happened! Now, he must have pulled that probably a hundred times with different kids, you know? I was a first grader. Just started. But that was Harry Steele. He was great. Really nice. Grown-ups were tougher in those days."

He was still pulling that one when I went to grade school but I don't remember getting shocked by Harry. I did, though, learn about electricity from Ray Jr. who zapped me a couple of times with a little wind-up generator, and from the wire fence around the dairy pasture which was right behind the post office, and which boys loved to grab to prove how tough we were, and if that wasn't enough, Mr. Ryan, who ran the general store across from the grade school had several coins, dimes and nickels, embedded in the floor, and if he saw someone trying to pick one up, he'd flick the switch and shock you that way. (In those days, jokes had to have a real kick.)

There was only one black family in the village at the time, though it was a big one. The father, Girly Hayes, worked at Toby Griffing's dairy, and the whole family lived in a house on the property. James Hayes was in Mary Anne and Carl's class, and Lee Hayes was ahead in Bill's class. Girly's daughter Jane Hayes was in my class, and Bobby Hayes was in my sister's class. Harry Steele, the Police Chief, liked Lee and often took him to school on his police motorcycle. It was just a short ride, a few blocks, from the little farm to the school. Lee Hayes went on to become a bomber pilot with the Tuskegee Airmen.

The *Malolo*, owned by Carl Erickson of Amagansett.
Aug. 1948 in Boat Basin of Edwards Bros. Dock, Promised Land.
Left to Right: George Payne, Bruce Collins, Capt. Carl Erickson, David S. Miller.

BRUCE COLLINS

In the same way my father had a glorified, if hazy, memory of his childhood in Yugoslavia and retained a longing for the little hamlet of Muo, I still carry a sentimental feeling for my early childhood with Mary Anne, Bill and Little Carl. It was all over by the fall of 1947 when I was five.

By then I was a big schoolboy going off to East Hampton for kindergarten. Amagansett didn't yet have a kindergarten, in fact barely had a first grade since few kids were born during The War. Now that both of her children were out of the house, Alice Milligan had begun entertaining a boyfriend. Bill was at Farmingdale College, up-island, studying construction, and Mary Anne was working as a floor model at Saks in Manhattan. Little Carl was at New Paltz State Teachers College, upstate. To celebrate a new phase in our lives I suppose, Babe invited me to lunch.

We sat in her kitchen at her calico covered table next to the window with the African Violets, perhaps they were related to the ones on Alice's window sill, and we each had a tomato stuffed with tuna fish. Delicious. I'd never had one. I don't remember what we talked about but I do remember that I felt very grown up and privileged to have The Queen of Amagansett all to myself. I hope we talked about being sad that Mary Anne and Carl and Bill were all grown up and how difficult it must be for me to have a sister and how nice it would be when Ray Junior went back to New York. I was probably in need of some context.

On the 1st of August, 1948, just out of high school, Bruce Collins, a slightly younger friend of Little Carl and Bill and Mary Anne, went to work for Big Carl. The complete crew was Big Carl and Bruce and George Payne and Dave Miller. They fished out of Promised Land that summer.

A tall, handsome blond haired boy who had been good in both sports and academics, Bruce could have gone to college, but had made the decision not to. His grandfather, William H. Collins, had a farm on the northeast side of East Hampton Village, in a little hollow near the Hook Windmill. Though a farmer, his grandfather fished in the winter, at least in his younger days. "He was in the Lifesaving Service and he was one of the farmer-fishermen that made up the core of the East Hampton population going back to the Seventeenth century," according to Bruce.

Bruce's mother, a Hulse, was also from a fishing family and her mother was a King, and as Bruce says, "They have all been baymen for as long as anybody can remember." Though Bruce's father, William Payne Collins, wasn't a fisherman but instead became a fuel oil dealer, and had been in business in East Hampton since 1910, Bruce always wanted to be part of the fishing tradition. I interviewed him for my Oral History;

"My mother's name was Florence Jane Hulse, from Springs. Her mother was a King. She was Wesley's aunt. (Wesley, a friend of mine, had been the groundskeeper of the local country club, The Maidstone Club.) There were 11 children. Nina Federico was my aunt, my mother's sister. She was Jungle Pete's wife (Jungle Pete's was the bar made famous by steady customer Jackson Pollock.) There were several that married into the Card family and spread around. There are a lot of King connections, too. Dorothy King was for years the curator of the Long Island Pennypacker Collection of the East Hampton Library. Her great-grandfather and my grandmother were brother and sister. So we go back, in that tribe, too."

Bruce had started lobstering as a summer job just as The War was ending. He first went with Bill Petty, whose other trade was plumber. Petty was Emerson Taber's brother-in-law, and the father of the beautiful Dot Petty, the Dorothy who was Johnny Erickson's first wife. Taber had a thriving lobster business at his place on the Three Mile Harbor Commercial Dock. Bill Petty brought his lobsters to Taber's. Bruce worked with Petty for one summer and the following summer, when he was fifteen, went to work for Harold Kip.

Mrs. Kip was more well-known than Harold. She owned a hat shop next to the popular soda shop The Marmador, in the store that had been Emerson Taber and Leonard Lester's Card and Booze shop, next to the Movie Theater. Her name was Mildred Kip. (The shop was named The Kip Shop and was still there when I was in high school.)

"You rarely saw Harold. He was a lobster fisherman. He lived in Montauk on his boat all summer long. I went with him in the summer of '46. He was a very unique person. For instance, he wouldn't wear a shirt. (That was unusual in those days.) His skin was the color of deep dark mahogany. And he had only one eye. He had a pair of binoculars on the *Aloha,* his boat, which he always kept setting right out in the weather and everything. They were terrible, all scratched up. You couldn't see a thing through them.

"Well, there was a fellow by the name of Otto Scherer who had a little boat called the *Pumpkin Seed.* Ted Lester ran it for him. Otto and Ted went bass fishing and things of that nature; out of Montauk. So Scherer came down to the dock one day and, because he had seen Harold's old binoculars out in the weather and everything, Scherer had brought him a brand new pair of 7x50 Zeiss glasses. Real nice glasses. And gave them to Harold, who promptly picked up a hammer and bashed the lens out of one side. Scherer was appalled. He said, 'What did you do that for? They cost of a lot of money!' And Kip said, 'Well, I've only got one eye.' Yeah, he was a little eccentric."

When Bruce worked for Harold Kip, he drove every morning to Montauk in a 1929 Ford Model A Roadster that he bought from Little Carl. "And then in the summer of 1947 I went with Taber. I ran the *Rey-Del* for him. Emerson had another lobster boat called the *Libby*, and Dave Howard ran that. And then in the fall of...let's see... '45 Petty, '46 Kip, '47 and '48, I was with Taber till I went with Carl. Those were summer jobs."

After the '48-'49 season with Carl, the following winter they went to Morehead City, N.C., as an experiment more than anything, and fished out of there for the whole winter, coming home in the spring. They made out well, so they did it the following year, fishing all the way from Cape Lookout and Cape Hatteras, up the Virginia Capes as far as Cape Charles. They were on Carl's new boat, the *Malolo*, which Carl had built at the Brigham Shipyard in Greenport, in 1947. She was sixty feet, had a fish hold of 33 tons net, and drew ten feet of water. Budd King went too, fishing alongside on his new boat, the *Bonacker*, sister ship to the *Malolo*, which was built at the same place and time. Both ships were built out of surplus war materials. A third boat also traveled with them, the *Capt. Mel*, out of Freeport, Long Island.

"Trawling off the bight at Cape Lookout, we caught a lot of bottlefish. Also round trout, as they call 'em down there, what we call weakfish. And a big run of croakers would come ashore there, at Chicamacomico Coast Guard station around the 25th of March every year. And we caught drum, red drum, black drum, and a lot of kingfish, a lot of fluke, flounder, and codfish. All that type of stuff. The fishing down there in the winter was very good and the weather a little milder than up here. Not that you couldn't get bad weather. On occasion you got some very bad blows there at Hatteras and up along the Virginia Capes, up around Wimble Shoals and places like that. It got rough down there, let me tell you. And there's times when you needed that stay-sail."

In 1950 they had gone down to Morehead City for the winter, and Bruce was due to get married in February. Carl had gone on a vacation to Florida. That was when Babe bought her pink Cadillac convertible that made a big hit on Main Street when she pulled into the driveway in Amagansett that spring. Bruce was planning to go home to marry his fiancée Jane, and bring her back to a house he'd rented in Morehead City. Then he got a phone call from Florida, from Carl. 'Tell the broker to get rid of your house for you. Call Jane up and tell her you can't get married 'til next month, and bring the *Malolo* down.' He said, 'Bring her on down here to Fernandina Beach. I'll meet you on the dock by the fisherman supply place. We're gonna put on new net and we're gonna go shrimp fishing. You can't believe what's going on down here!'"

It was the beginning of a boom in shrimp fishing. Bruce went on, "So I went and got the *Malolo* and brought her down and we put on new doors (net spreaders), and got some new twine, and went around the Dry Tortugas, picked up a trip (caught some shrimp), and flipped a coin to see where we were gonna dock. We decided it was gonna be Ft. Myers, so we docked at the South Fish Company, owned by a fellow by the name of Tom Smoot. And, so, that's where we settled in. Jane and I had postponed our marriage for a month, and so I flew up in March and we got married. I bought a brand new Hudson Hornet from Dan Tucker in Amagansett for $1500 and we drove it back to Florida."

The *Capt. Mel*, companion boat to Carl Erickson Sr.'s *Malolo*. Bruce Collins shrimped on both boats during the mid to late 1940s out of Ft. Myers, Florida and off the Campeche Banks near Mexico

PINK GOLD

The group actually pioneered the Mexican grounds for the Florida fleet. No Florida shrimp boat had ever been to the Campeche Banks in Mexico. They were four boats that generally fished together, especially in the fall or the winter of the year, the *Captain Mel*, Ben Eldred's boat; the *Cherokee*, owned and operated by Fred King, out of Atlantic City New Jersey; the *Malolo;* and Budd King on the *Bonacker*.

"The Banks were anywhere from right within sight of the beach, to 50 or 60 miles off shore. It was 80 hours, three days and three nights from Ft. Myers to the Campeche Banks. The first trip, we got there in a hurricane and we had to ride it out. The white shrimp, of course, or the blue shrimp or green shrimp, all the same breed of cat, have very little iodine. Pink shrimp have more iodine, which you can tell, because they're pinker. And then as the iodine content goes up, then they become the brown shrimp. There were certain times of the year when you would get both white and pink shrimp down there. And if you went up the coast to the 19.10 line, up around Vera Cruz and places like that, you would get into the big brown shrimp, you know. The really big shrimp. But the brown shrimp are not as valuable as the pink shrimp."

Bruce worked for Carl for a year, and then captained boats for a couple of other shrimp companies. One was the Endeavor Shrimp Company. He ran the trawler *Endeavor* for them. "And then, one summer, Carl took the *Malolo* back to East Hampton one last time, and when he did, I came up with him and Jane's father went down and got her and they drove back. Carl was gonna come back to see if he wanted to return from Florida to up here in the summer and he decided that they didn't and they went back and stayed. And I stayed up here. I didn't really know what I was gonna do at that time so, I got back with Emerson Taber for a short while, and then I worked for a very short time for the old Frank B. Smith Lumber Yard up here. (A stop-gap job for many East Hampton men over the years.)
   "And then, in 1954, very early in the year, around January or February, Jack Edwards came to see me. He wanted to know if I would go with him as Coast and Harbor pilot on the steamer *Shinnecock*, out of Amagansett, which I did. I stayed with Jack for 6 years until 1960. You've got to understand, by this time we also owned the oil business and Jane was running that. But in the summer, of course, the oil business dropped off dramatically, so it allowed me to go fishing. Then, so's I wasn't fishing in the hard winters, I'd come off the boat in the fall and go back into the oil business."

In 1960 the bunkers dropped off dramatically and Bruce stopped fishing and got into politics. Before that, he'd had no political affiliations, so he got into politics cold. He ran for Councilman on the Town Board, successfully. For many years afterward, he remained in politics and in the oil business, and became one of the most important and trusted leaders in the Town.

BRUCE HUNTING

Bruce loves to hunt and to cook wild game. "One year Bob Gardiner invited me over to The Island to help thin the herd out. I shot seven deer. I love venison. But most of my hunting has been ducks and upland birds. All the Collins men cook. Tom Collins; an excellent cook. Dave Collins, who's dead now, used to be a partner with Rudy

DeSanti in Dreesen's Market. He was an excellent cook. I do all the cooking at my house, just about."

He got his first lessons in how to shoot from a neighbor by the name of Dave Gilbride who lived next door to his family home on Cedar St. "Dave was a pickpocket and second-story man. And he was bad to the point that finally to get him straightened out they made him a turnkey in the Riverhead Jail, because he was in there so much that they figured he ought to work there. He became a Deputy Sheriff. He taught me to shoot. And then Elmer Rost (father of Barry, one of my high school classmates), who lived right next door and was my cousin, taught me some. You could shoot everywhere in those days. We used to shoot at Cedar Point, Sammy's Beach, and of course we did a lot of shooting at Napeague. Almost anywhere. All of this property up here (around his house) was vacant land, just about. There were only a few houses.

"On Sundays I would get together with some of those Round Swampers (the neighborhood near Three Mile Harbor.) Charlie Elley and Randolph Lester and Uncle Fred Lester and Albert Lester and the whole bunch of them, along with Dutchie Baker, we'd go fox hunting, run the foxes. Dutchie Baker, I think his real name was Charles, had a little place up on Baiting Hollow Road in Georgica. He was a gardener and caretaker. Anyway, there was quite a gang; 20 to 25 people on Sundays that would go down and turn the dogs loose and run the foxes through Northwest and Springs. And, more often than not, we'd get one.

"We used hounds. Blue Ticks, Americans and Walkers, and ran them all over Northwest Woods. That was before there were houses in Lion Head Beach and Clearwater Beach. Nothing. It was just woodland. Pars Funion (his real name was Charles Ellsworth Fournier), would go with us sometimes. He hated that name, you know, Ellsworth, nobody would dare call him Ellsworth Fournier, or he'd get all riled up. He liked the name Pars Funion better.

"And I hunted with Babe, too. I was friends with Little Carl, he was a year and a half older than me, but we were great friends from the time I was fifteen or so. Babe was just great to be around. We used to go out to Goff Point and jump shoot for Sheldrake."

At the time I interviewed Bruce he hadn't been gunning in a couple of years. With land getting scarcer and the town getting busier, like many other local men, he put off getting his hunting license. "The last gunning I did was with a club, a rather exclusive club, with only 12 members, that I got involved with through Kip Farrington. (A well-known outdoorsman and writer of books on big game fishing.) We rented Turkey Point and Havens Point and Tuthill's Point and Swan Island, up in Great South Bay. When Kip passed away, and with the rest of the club, people like Brinkley Smithers, being much older than I am, well, I just sort of gave it up. And besides that, you know, hunting's gotten difficult around here with all the crowding."

CARL, BILL, AND MARY ANNE

Bill Milligan graduated from East Hampton High School in '46 and moved fifty miles west to study carpentry and building at the State Agricultural and Technical School in Farmingdale, Long Island and then began working in the building trade on the west end of the Island. He married and raised a family, and I remembered him coming by once or twice with his wife Helene as I was growing up. When he retired, in the 1980's, he moved back east, bought an old Stonington dragger, and began fishing out of Lake Montauk.

Mary Anne graduated from high school with Carl in '47, and after spending the summer working as a model at Saks Fifth Avenue in Southampton, in the fall she went to work at Saks in New York. Soon after she married Larry Rogers, a young man on the fast track with management at Saks. Larry was Jewish, or, as Hooker Hand put it, "very Jewish."

Then, after having three children with Larry, she divorced him. According to Little Carl, "Larry could not control Mary Anne. She was too dominant a personality. She married again, to another Jewish guy, Mort Aronson, in Pittsburgh. Mort was a psychiatrist and she married him and they were very happy. Mort, he could control her, like Larry never could. He took good care of her, I'm tellin' you." That was, as far as Carl knew. "Every need that she ever had. But they didn't have any children, 'cause it was too late in life. And then she developed uterine cancer. She was 44 when she died. I'd still see her occasionally when I'd go north in the summer, up until the early '50s. She spent a few summers out in Amagansett after she married Larry, when the kids were growing up. She took 'em out there and they rented a place."

In the winter of 1999, Carl, Gail, and I sat in their comfortable living room just down the street from the Edison Museum in Fort Myers Florida, and while we talked I tape recorded the conversation for my Oral History. Gail brought out a copy of the old illustration of my father's that they had saved, the old black and white drawing on newsprint that Ray had done as charity for the Hundred Neediest Cases Charity of the New York Times, a charcoal sketch of my sister and me looking like two ragamuffins staring out a window, me holding a teddy bear. We were looking as pitiful as we could, to entice the Times' readers to send money. Then she brought out a print of a photograph of Mary Anne sitting on the floor in Ray's studio in a polka dot dress, in front of the white backdrop, holding her infant daughter, Carol Lynn, and the torn-out page of the magazine in which the illustration had appeared.

We talked about life after high school. Carl had gone to New Paltz State Teacher's College, and his girlfriend and future wife Gail went to Ithaca College, both in upstate New York. He came home from college in the fall of his freshman year and said goodbye to old Will Cartwright, "Pop," for the last time. Pop died that winter, 1947.

Because he'd worked summers fishing he had enough money to buy a car, an old Oldsmobile with a bad clutch. Several weekends a semester, with the clutch slipping all the way, he drove through the Catskill Mountains, from New Paltz to Ithaca, to see Gail. "By the time you got to the top of the mountain you were going about five miles an hour. I mean you could walk faster than that damn car would go. I mean that clutch would slip something terrible. Outside of the mountains it was fine. Let it slip, you know. No big deal. It would go along forty, fifty mile an hour, no problem."

Though he had always wanted to be a fisherman he also wanted a college degree, and once he got it he felt he had to use it for something, so as soon as they both graduated (Gail was a year ahead of him), they got married and, for about a year, they lived in Southampton, where Gail taught in the grade school and Carl in the high school.

"The two of us together livin' in Southampton was kind of expensive, but we could make it. I really liked it. But there wasn't any money. So, eventually, I had to quit. It was Gail's second year. She had started the year before me. But then she got pregnant. So I called my dad. They had moved down to Florida and were gettin' into the shrimp, and so I called him up and I said, 'Do you think I can make more than twenty-eight hundred? Next year I'm supposed to get a hundred and fifty dollar raise, I'd get twenty-nine fifty.' And, he said, 'Well, I think you can do better than that if you come down here and work for me.' So we quit teaching and came down here and the first year I made over eight thousand. So I was real happy, you know? In those days, back in 1952, that was real money."

Little Carl had lost touch with much of the change that had gone on in the fishing community up in the East End, but he still had strong connections among the older fishermen. For instance, he had, over the years, kept track of what folks like his uncle Johnny Erickson and Harry Stannard were doing. Harry and Mary Stannard were well known characters in Montauk. Mary had been the Erickson's housekeeper for years, both in Amagansett and at the Fishing Village. When little Carl was young, Harry had a boat and always went into Perry Duryea's to unload his fish. "He had a small boat out there next to Duryea's dock. They lived, he and Mary, right alongside Duryea's house, which was across the street from the dock. One time I remember, Bill Milligan and I were fishing off the dock, and Bill got a fish hook right through his hand, all the way through. And in those days, there was no doctor in Montauk. None in Amagansett either. You had to go to all the way to East Hampton to a doctor. So I took Bill, with this fish hook right through his hand, to Babe. And she says, 'Go to Harry Stannard, he'll get it out.' And we went looking for Harry, and found him down by the Montauk Yacht Club, and Harry took one look at Bill's hook in there, and he goes, 'Aha!' and grabs Bill's hand and twists the hook like that, and bam, it's out. Just like that. Happened so fast Bill didn't even know it happened! It was great! Tough? Oh, he was as tough as they come.

"Harry was a regular at Mary Gosman's little coffee shack. He was caretaker down there for one of the docks, traveled everywhere by bicycle. And in his later years, he did very well pinhooking for porgies. My uncle Johnny (Erickson) used to go with him. Used to go out to the buoy there at Great Eastern Rock. When he got older, Johnny went pinhooking all the time. He and Harry, they knew all the places, and they had the technique. They always used a little rowboat or a skiff. And hand lines all around the boat. And a case of beer, or something to drink anyway."

I asked Little Carl, "What if I was someone fifty years from now and I never heard of pinhooking, how would you explain it?" He said, "It's just a line with a baited hook on it, no rod. Hook, line and bait. And you just pull 'em in. Let the line coil up on the deck, or wind it around a stick or something. One hook per line, or maybe two or three. There's, different ways, you know. Johnny did it for quite a few years. Sometimes they'd get two hundred pound of porgies a day. He'd make himself two, three hundred dollars a day, easy. And you've got hardly any overhead. Just a little gasoline to run wherever they were running to, with a little tiny outboard engine. They'd go out half a mile or a mile. Not more than that. They probably used skimmer clams or somethin' like that. Frozen junk fish. Pinhooking, it's ninety-nine percent profit. And porgies were, even way back then, close to a dollar a pound."

Little Carl's favorite celebrity was Liebert Lombardo of the Guy Lombardo Orchestra (The Royal Canadians). "He played in the band. Guy had about four or five brothers. Liebert played the trumpet in the band. And when I lived in Montauk, Ruth King and Budd lived next door and Liebert would often stay with them. He'd practice his trumpet and go fishing. In fact, one time, when my father had a party boat, Liebert paid me five dollars so he could take over my spot as mate on the boat. So I'd stay home. Liebert retired in Sanibel very near Little Carl's home, and eventually became a town councilman for Sanibel. He was very well liked. He died there a few years ago at 88."

When he was growing up, all the men Little Carl looked up to were fishermen; his father, both his grandparents, the men of the Edwards family; "So it was really no surprise that I went into fishing. I was drawn to it. You know, one of the men I admired most was Sam Edwards. I could tell you a number of stories about him, ya know? He had the *Magdalene* at Promised Land. The *Magdalene* was a hundred and ten foot sub chaser. And every day, he would come down to go fishing, believe it or not, with a suit jacket and a necktie, and wearing Boss gloves. He always wore gloves. You wouldn't believe it! That's the way Captain Sam went fishing!

"I remember when the Long Island Railroad used to terminate at the old Fishing Village, it'd come in to what we called the Excursion Dock. The Railroad brought all these trainloads of people in from New York and they would come pouring out of the train towards these boats. The biggest boat out there then was the *Montauk*, owned by Capt. Sam. And all the city folks, they would run down the docks and jump in these boats and they'd get charged three dollars a head or five dollars a head or whatever. And Capt. Sam always had the most customers. I can still see him today, with his jacket and his tie on. And his gloves. He was just somethin' else. I remember he had a guy by the name of Andy Semb that used to work for him a lot. And Johnny Erickson worked for him at different times. He always had the best people.

"But Norman Edwards, I don't remember if he ever worked for Capt. Sam or not. I remember when Norman got blown up though, with his hundred and ten footer. He went down and started the engine one cold morning, and he ignited the heater and the engine blew up. Blew him right up through the deck. And he lived to tell about it! I can't think of the name of his boat now. If I thought about it some, I could remember."

After Mary Anne got married, Little Carl went shrimping in Florida, and Bill moved to the other end of the Island, Hooker Hand (the guy who drove the laundry truck) kept in touch with them all. In fact, he was the conduit to Mary Anne, and Babe and Carl and Little Carl and Gail and Budd King and Ruth, and Leonard and Theo. He was their pipeline for all of East Hampton, Amagansett and Montauk. He'd deliver laundry and the news, especially the Babe and Carl news and the Mary Anne news, to people like the Prohaskas and all the Erickson friends, the Tillinghasts, and the Osbornes and the Edwardses, and others that I don't remember that were on the Hooker pipeline. Hooker would collect his information by mail and by phone and by periodic visits to Ft. Myers, and disseminate his information as part of his laundry delivery. I always felt growing up, that if you had access to Hooker's pipeline, you were somebody.

Babe and Carl had enjoyed more than a decade of retirement, playing golf and traveling around the country in a big motor home. Babe had continued to played golf often with one of her best friends, famous golfer Patty Berg, and she would still occasionally fly off somewhere to judge a field trial.

Then Big Carl died in 1989, and Babe remained healthy for several years until she was in a serious car accident that left her in a coma for six weeks. "When she came to," Little Carl said, "Her mind didn't work. She had been in intensive care and now she had to be put into a rehab, where after some weeks, everything clicked and she was back to normal. She remembered the accident, she remembered everything, and she was fine for a year, and then all of a sudden her mind started deteriorating again. For what reason, I don't know. Whether it was old age or due to the accident or what. At eighty nine she was healthy as could be, worked out in the yard, planted flowers and did all that stuff. And then she began to deteriorate, fast. Gettin' worse and worse. In just a few weeks, she was dead."

Though he continued to go to the office every day, Little Carl, now, finally, just Carl, had recently turned over his part of the shrimp business, Erickson and Jensen Shrimp Company, to his son Grant, who was already managing their extensive real estate holdings. The office and dock were in Fort Myers Beach not far from his home. At the time, with their equal partner Mr. Jensen, they had over a dozen shrimp boats and a complete packing and freezing plant. Carl died on December 23, 2010 from Parkinson's disease.

JOHNNY MAXWELL

The studio across the hall from Ray's at 51 West 10th Street belonged to another illustrator, John Allan Maxwell. He was a southerner from Johnson City, Tennessee. He had studied at the Corcoran School of Art in Washington D.C. and with George Luks at the Art Students League and had been at 10th Street since he took over the studio of painter-poet Khalil Gibran in 1925. He was an illustrator in much the same vein as Ray, with an affinity for watercolor and gauche. Both have been referred to as romantic, as well as painterly, painters. Maxwell, though, in addition to magazine fiction, was also known for his book jacket covers, particularly those of writers popular at the time, such as Joseph Conrad, F. Van Wyck Mason, Pearl Buck and Booth Tarkington. When Ray and Johnny met, both had careers that were going well.

Years after the fact, in a conversation with Carolyn, Johnny's wife Stella let it be known that in her opinion, Ray had "led Johnny astray." Ray, she believed, had been a bad influence on poor Johnny. It may have been true, too, but nonetheless, Johnny was an alcoholic. Though relatively little was known about alcoholism in those days, it was pretty much considered okay to be one if you stayed out of trouble and got your work done. For the average middle class Joe, in those days at least, staying out of trouble meant keeping it in your pants. But on 10th Street that rule didn't apply. At The Studios, there were more models who posed nude then there were paintings of nudes. (Not that there wasn't legitimate drawing and painting of nudes going on; in those days drawing from the live nude model was considered an important exercise for an artist, sort of like doing scales was for a musician.) As Carolyn stated it, there was even (speaking of nudes) a mother and daughter act, a mother with twins, who were models and screwed pretty much everybody.

But Johnny Maxwell was unlucky. Ray came home one night from a typical evening of drinks after work and told Carolyn, "Boy, that John. He's got this beautiful dame that's crazy about him, a doctor's wife." A doctor's wife she wasn't, though she was beautiful, or at least had been at one time, this dame. Her name was Joy Fender. She was the wife of Willie Fender who was, according to Carolyn, "a con-artist of sorts."

John had a nice house on the north shore of Long Island in Sea Cliff and "Doctor" and Mrs. Fender and Mrs. Fender's small daughter had moved in and established squatter's rights. Johnny Maxwell was, according to the Fenders, the father of the little girl. And Willy Fender, well, he didn't care about the paternity thing or the ongoing affair; he just wanted the house, and, eventually, he ended up getting it. Johnny never admitted that the child was his and when questioned about it by Carolyn, "Now John, what is it, why are you so ham-strung by the Fenders? Any reason? Any guilt?" And he'd replied, "Why Carolyn, how dare you! How could you even suggest such a thing?" spoken in his perfect Southern gentleman way.

"Poor Stella, of course, she couldn't live with that," said Carolyn, "so she ended up taking her cats and moving home to her family's house in Red Bank, New Jersey. Fender was a dreadful little man." Whether the child was Johnny's or not, the Fenders got a nice house out of it.

SPORT WARD

Carolyn's studio was a small building, about 14' by 20.' In winter, she would heat it with a kerosene heater. In summer, the breeze off the ocean was all the cooling necessary. Hanging just below the roof peaks on either end of the building were two carved wooden figures which as time went on caught the attention of the neighborhood children. Each figure was about 5 inches wide and 18 inches long, darkened gray-brown by age and showing bare breasts. To the minds of these country kids of the 1950s bare breasts were cause for snickering, which Carolyn considered stupid and insulting.

The figures were a gift from "Sport" Ward, Leroy P. Ward, an architect, who ran in the Artists and Writers circle. Though not an illustrator, he was also a member of the Society of Illustrators. It was Sport who found the building at 128 East 63rd Street where the Society of Illustrators had been housed ever since that organization had moved from the old 23rd Street clubhouse, which they had sold to the Alcoholics Anonymous Foundation. The wooden figures, meant to portray angels, were part of the elaborate ornamentation carved by Italian artisans, to be part of the interior trim of a Manhattan building designed years ago by Sport and later torn down and replaced.

Sport Ward was a figure who loomed large in the parental narrative of New York past which haunted the household as the Prohaska children were growing up. It seemed he had been there when every bon mot was uttered at The Club, or The Society, as they referred to the Society of Illustrators. One could almost say Sport was an Angel for the club. He functioned as a P.R. man, getting the club mentioned in the papers and bringing influential people to its luncheons and gallery shows. He was also a major character in the Dutch Treat Club, whose membership co-mingled with that of the Society.

The D.T.C. put out a book called The Dutch Treat Club Annual, a hot item for a curious child to get his hands on, being full of ideally-figured pen drawings of beautiful naked girls. The books were conveniently placed in the big bookcase in front of the darkroom, for my surreptitious perusal from an early age until, well, I still have them.

Ward was a man-about-Manhattan often mentioned in the columns. He had been involved with Gloria Swanson before she took up with Joe Kennedy and continued to act as a "beard" for that none-too-secret couple. Ward was also a big contributor to the Society of Illustrators annual Artist's Ball. The show was comprised of a series of humorous skits, risqué and full of bare-breasted girls, and always played to a packed house.

After Sport worked on Preston's barn (May and Jimmy), in the estate section of East Hampton Village, he built two houses for a fellow named Everett Bacon, who had been involved with the Prestons' crowd as a congenial investment counselor. Bacon seemed to have strong opinions on painting and would barter paintings for investment help. He was then married to his second wife, Ramona, who had been the governess for his two children by his first wife. Ramona (Ray called her Morona, not nice) enjoyed buying paintings and furniture, and decorating, which was probably why they needed a second house as soon as the first one was finished.

The first house was at Beach Hampton and the second one was on Highway Behind the Pond in East Hampton Village. For years, after going to the Amagansett Post Office, Bacon would drop in on Ray in his studio unannounced. He would be free with his criticisms, both pro and con, and often got himself thrown out, but was never daunted and continued to be friendly over the years.

COCKTAILS

When I was small and Ray and Carolyn had cocktail parties, I hovered and milled about, horning in on conversations, until at last I'd be sent upstairs. I was fascinated by the whole idea of cocktail party drinking and associated it, or had it conflated with, not well thought out fantasy ideas about grown-up sex. While sitting on the top step of the second floor landing, ears straining to hear individual conversations, I tried to understand complicated subjects; art criticism, psychoanalysis, Trotskyites, rumors about affairs. I felt excluded and resentful about it.

If my father received wisdom from his mother's knee, as he seemed to imply, I received lots of information from a long list of cocktail parties, from the mid-1930s up till whichever was the last one Carolyn had attended. When she made notes, as she had a habit of doing, they were often about things that had happened or had been discussed or overheard during cocktails; she was a great eavesdropper. She kept her notes, written in her elegant, nicely legible half script with her own fine-nibbed Parker pen, along with small drawings, dried flowers and scrap she would save for her infrequent delving into collage, in books that she was reading or that she saved because they were particularly treasured; books such as *Delacroix's Journal*, or Ben Shahn's *The Shape of Content*. (Ben Shahn was a friend.) After she died I collected as many of her notes and assemblages as I could find and put them in a shoe box. Among them was this one about a famous party in Bridgehampton:

"There was a party that was the big party mentioned in last year's bio of Pollock. I believe it says that Jackson was not invited. I expect that was correct. They wanted a nice party; but Jackson got wind of it and showed up! It was a year in which de Kooning's mother was visiting from Holland, and Ludwig Sander and Franz Kline rented the Red House (a Victorian house located across from the grade school in Bridgehampton.) Big talk for weeks and weeks before was about the great festivities. The Ward twins were decorating, with paper flowers on trees, shrubbery, all over the place. Luds (Ludwig) invited us. Other friends of ours were going; Fran Weiss, Fred and Audrey (Hurdman), Julie and Hoffman Hays; Julian came with us. Jean avoided most functions of this sort.

I remember Ray having a long conversation with a very pregnant woman. They were lamenting the demise of the magazine "Today's Woman." She had been an editor, or the editor, or an Art Director at that rag. Ray had been a regular with them. Was she Paul Brach's wife, Miriam Shapiro? I've wondered. Were the Ward twins just visiting, or in residence?"

Joan Ward and her twin sister and their mother were fixtures at 51 W. 10th, where all three modeled and had allegedly had affairs with the artists. Joan was the mother of de Kooning's only child, Lisa.

BREAKDOWNS

One topic that came up occasionally in Carolyn's conversation was that of the nervous breakdown. People in the literary and painting crowds seemed to be prone to "breakdowns." None of these events were ever considered to have any relationship to alcohol or drugs, but were simply part of the creative process. After a period of intense creative activity, a person would quietly become unhinged and go into a hospital for a few days, or even a few weeks. To me it didn't seem unattractive. I can't remember a time when the idea of having a nervous breakdown wasn't part of my regular thought process, and I must have got it from my mother. She's the one who went to a shrink and who believed in, and talked about, analysis. Not Ray, who always maintained that fishing was sufficient therapy for him. (Family members of course, Carolyn, my sister and I, felt that all the fishing in the world wasn't sufficient. His anger was something we thought he could "work on" though people didn't speak that way in those days.)

Carolyn thought Ray was a hypochondriac. "Remember when he had bursitis?" she said to me in one of our later conversations. "He could lie in bed for weeks!" (She was exaggerating.) Then, after a long pause, she talked about a doctor friend of Ray's. "I remember, it was a year or so before we met but he told me about it. He was separated from Dolly and he landed at Neurological and they examined him to see if he had a spinal cord tumor. He told me this. He was having bad neck pain. So this young guy came in, Dr. George Katinak, and said, 'You know, this operation on the upper spine canal is very risky. I think we should examine further, and if we can rule out the tumor, I'd say it is just occupational, and you should change your posture.' And that's how he became friends with George. God, it was only my third date with Ray when I got to meet George. I thought, 'Ha, I'm really in now, I'm getting to meet his shrink.' We used to pick George up and we'd go to The Onyx Club. But George would get a little tired of the loud music. He was awfully sweet. When they met they were both separated from their wives, so they became buddies. But he always said George saved his life."

George actually took up surfcasting and would come out and rent a bungalow in Montauk and fish with Ray. Carolyn said she figured

George probably shrunk him a little bit on the sly. "What do you mean by that?" I asked her. "Well, I think he just helped Ray get rid of some of his fears, like becoming incapacitated or sick, that kind of thing. He couldn't deal with anybody's being sick. It was almost a phobia. Like when I had my back surgery, or when you kids had the flu, or colds, he'd have to go fishing, or out with the boys."

When she got angry Carolyn never failed to include the information that she was being "driven crazy." She was an avid reader on the subject of analysis. There was a bookcase against one wall in the second floor hallway which I perused almost every time I went by on my way to my attic bedroom. There was Freud and Fenichel and Otto Rank; and Reich; and a several volume collection by some madman named Harry Stack Sullivan. Not that she read all these books cover to cover, but she had interest and the intent to read them all; and I picked this craving up from her. There were also a few art books, though most of those were in the studio, and art magazines like *Art News*, and some anthropology; Margaret Mead and Ruth Benedict; and political books and magazines; like the *Partisan Review* and *The Nation*. There was the complete set of Carl Sandburg's *Lincoln*, which I never saw leave the shelf. She used the word neurotic to define most people she thought had any intelligence, including herself and me. I thought she was right. Everyone that is, except Ray, about whom she said, "He just doesn't care to deal with anything." After which, I suppose, we both quickly came to the conclusion; "Why should he? He's an artist!" In our value system, we had that completely ingrained.

I clowned and dreamed and read a lot; the standard fare available at school and snatches of books and magazines from Carolyn's bookcase. But my reading and perusing and thinking remained secret, perhaps for no other reason than that all kids have their secret worlds. I didn't realize that I'd begun a lifelong secret study of Psychoanalysis.

I also read snatches of the short stories in the *Saturday Evening Post*, even the ones not illustrated by Ray, and the writing under the photographs of naked natives in my *National Geographics*, the stack of which was the heaviest thing in my attic bedroom; the sex parts of Margaret Mead; and when I slept in my father's bed when he was in the city, I'd peek through the books on the bookshelf behind his headboard. I figured these books were part of what made the Old Man tick, so I thumbed through them; Andre Malraux's *The Voices of*

Silence, which had lots of pictures, Ernest Hemingway (I read all of *The Snows of Kilimanjaro,* probably the first adult story I ever read), snatches of Emile Zola, and the gory parts of Mickey Spillane.

I was a voyeur and a constructor of secret fantasies that had no adult supervision, guidance or interference. When I think back on the books I actually read cover to cover, though, what I remember mostly are the Walter Farley Stallion Books. My absorption in his books was intense, in particular, I read *The Island Stallion* several times, and much preferred life on that island to reality; and other books about horses.

It may have been my intention to cure the family neurosis by my sneak-reading on analysis. I was aware of anxiety and Oedipus complexes; sexual obsessions and obstructions; transference and acting out, long before I knew my multiplication tables. In this regard I probably had something in common with some of those kids I would meet casually and infrequently in the summer who were the children of shrinks or the children of writers who had shrinks. (The abstract artists mostly didn't have kids.) But I didn't have anyone to talk to about it, so I never got to work on the vocabulary. Among my pals there was no interest in anything Marxist or Modernist. They were practical people. Looking back I feel safe in saying that I began self-analysis in pre-adolescence. I did discuss it with my mother. My sister thought I was nuts.

SCUTTLE

As a kid, I had what today they call "social anxiety," which means I had fears. My father, a demonstratively loving man but an artist focused on his work, a narcissist with an excuse, was not above coming out of his studio if my sister and I were too noisy, and smacking me in the head. Nor was he above chasing me into a corner and using his doubled-up belt if I did something particularly bad, like hitting my sister, or saying "fuck you" to my mother, which wasn't something you ordinarily did in the Fifties; in fact, I may have invented it as a kid strategy. It was a long belt too, he being 6' 2" inches tall and weighing anywhere from 225-250 (and me being a small, skinny kid.) So in the back of my mind I always had the expectation that if I weren't careful, I could be hit.

Before I was ten I had mastered crawling out of the scuttle door onto the roof, grabbing on to the roof peak and edging across to the eastern peak where I'd hang down and drop onto the roof above my sister's room, from where I could walk like a mountain goat onto the studio roof. The skylight and its support structure was higher than the studio roof peak and formed a barricade from being seen from the street. Behind this barricade was a valley where the furnace room connected to the studio, and behind the valley, a little shed roof that covered the furnace room, where the oil heater and later the clothes washer were. From there, I could leap onto a long springy branch of the big Black Maple in the back yard, from which I would hand-walk until I was close enough to the ground to drop. (I had named the tree Blackie. All of us, Ray, Carolyn and Elena always referred to it as Blackie.) Then I was off to play, while the Old Man cooled off.

I remember the first time I escaped from the Old Man that way. I came up with the idea that climbing out onto the roof would be romantically heroic. I don't know why, but at the time it seemed like destiny. I was little and skinny. I remember the black asphalt shingles seemed warm and welcoming. It didn't seem too dangerous. But it was. If I had fallen, I would most likely have been killed. It was forty feet from the peak, from which you would slide down the roof to wooden rain gutters which would not hold you long enough to slow the fall, and you would land not on grass but on a cement grouted flagstone patio. Neither parent knew about this gambit for some time. When they figured it out they were angry, but impressed. In old age I am not fond of heights; my feet and hands sweat when I go over the Verrazano Bridge. But at eight or ten or however old I was then, it was an adventure.

Being chased by my father up to the attic wasn't all terror and trauma, it was also a game. Although there was a part of me always half expecting to be killed, there was also that part of me which filled with joy at the excitement and the attention; the competency I displayed in beating him to the staircase and foiling him there was part of that. And of course he too must have enjoyed the game, as witnessed by the way he huffed and puffed at the door but insisted, most times, he couldn't get in. What game was it? Brinksmanship? Bullfighting? Rodeo Clown?

When I got to be too tall for the attic so that my head bumped the ceiling unless I stood under the peak in the middle of the room, a new bedroom was made for me out of the part of the studio that had been used for storage. The storage wing was cut in half. A small hallway was created between the dining room, the new bedroom and the studio. I was happy about having a new bedroom, but apprehensive about being in the line of fire. When Ray's work was in full swing the new bedroom was too close to the studio to be a good place to daydream or read. In spite of a new storage room separating my room from the studio, I could still hear the music, the phone calls to New York, the parental arguments about money, the loud sneezes, the blowing of his nose, the bell-ringing sound of his brush being rinsed in a glass beaker. Some days I felt like a fine-tuned old barometer, gauging the approach of a hurricane and waiting for it to get to where it read, "Run for cover."

ERICKSON BREAK-IN

Experts use the term Middle Childhood to define the period Tommy and I were going through during the years the Ericksons made the transition from Amagansett to Florida's Gulf Coast, to my mind a sea change in the history of Main Street. In those days, the late '40s to early '50s, children were not supervised nearly as much as they are today. There was no such thing as a play date and child psychology was considered trivial. It's supposed to be a time for exploring, for taking on or experimenting with moral judgments, for learning to cooperate with one's peers. So, that's what we did.

In 1950, when we were eight years old, Main Street was our turf. We were curious about the empty Erickson house. Babe and Carl were huge in their absence, according to our keen kid's sense of the immediate world around us. They were as much a part of the local zeitgeist as if they were still living next door, rather than making a once a year appearance in their pink Cadillac. Word on the street was that they had "struck it rich!"

We took the back way onto their property, first to the back of our garage, which was actually two garages, a lean-to addition was for Ray's beach buggy, then through a small path between the garage and a large compost heap, and then under the branches of a fence made of tall arborvitae which went from about twenty feet in from the sidewalk to back where the abandoned dog kennels began. Both sides of the Erickson's property were fenced in this way, though the trees on our side were older and taller. We went to the back screen door expecting it to be open. We'd gone in that way many times when Babe was home, to visit her and to be given cookies and milk.

The screen door was locked, but I managed to pry loose the screen and get my tiny fingers at the door hook, which let us into the back porch. On the porch was an abandoned old-fashioned ice box, some empty soda bottles and a dried-up mop and bucket. The kitchen door was open and the kitchen had a musty, kitchen smell; old linoleum with a tinge of propane gas, mixed with sun baked dusty lace curtains. We had left our embryonic consciences on the other side of the fence and were excited to be in unoccupied territory.

I wish I could go back and visit the scene of that crime with my adult's eye. I would more carefully notice those things, like the appliances, obvious ones like the stove and the big console radio. But what my middle childhood mind chose to file was mostly the emptiness and the smell. Part of that smell, I now know, was from the slow shedding of lead paint dust from the paint all houses were painted with in those days. But the emptiness and the quiet were what registered most. A child's first break-in.

We were in the previously untrodden territory of grown-up space without grown-ups; walls without ears. An adult might look around for something to steal, but we, as kids, were in over our heads. We started a fire in the fireplace just for something to do, and then went upstairs and jumped on the beds. Then we went into the bathroom and tried Big Carl's cologne. That was when we heard the fire crackling and went downstairs and put out the smoldering patches in the carpet where the fire had begun to spread because we hadn't put up the fire screen.

And then Ray appeared. Someone had seen smoke coming out of the chimney and called him. He gave me a good cuff on the ear and dragged the two of us outside and sent Tommy running home, saying his father was waiting for him. Ray dragged me back to our property just as far as the back of the Jeep garage and then gave me quite a few whacks with his doubled up belt.

The Ericksons were notified, someone was called in to clean up the mess we made, and Ray offered to pay for the rug, but Babe and Carl were just glad we didn't burn the house and ourselves to the ground. Tommy's father scolded him a little but didn't beat him. Tommy was always lucky that way.

Babe and Carl never came back though, except for an occasional short visit, a wedding or a funeral. The house was eventually sold to a retired Hungarian couple, named Sajo. The name was pronounced

"Shayo", but in deference to colloquial style, they were always called the Sajos (Sah Joe.) Mr. Sajo was a retired Brooks Brother's tailor and he set up a little tailor shop in the house.

RAY AND ABSTRACTION

Ray had always preferred painting to illustrating, but when he began to merge his enthusiasm for the experience of fishing in the surf with a brand of abstraction that he got from observing some of his artist friends, particularly Philip Guston and Julian Levi, his enthusiasm grew. Although among the new art crowd that Ray got to know, he was tainted with the label of commercial artist, and he must have felt the ranks close in on him, he did have his friends and admirers and his fishing, and so he sloughed it off. I didn't. I was the family's gatherer of resentments.

The mystique behind abstract painting seemed to me to have the power of religious fanaticism; there were concerns about purity and loyalty, as well as talent. I was aware of all this throughout those growing up years of the 1950s, particularly as I went from eight years old to twelve. I heard the dogma and the catechism from Ray and Carolyn and heard it discussed at cocktail parties where I was the wall that had ears, and gleaned it from my occasional perusals of *Art Magazine*. And I was interested.

The abstractionists were followed by critics and groupies who incorporated their interest in art into the leftist politics of the day. Purity was a guiding principle for them, too. The New York Left, who dominated the intellectual world, had backed away from Stalin and become obsessed with ideas about Marxist purity. Many had Trotsky as their patron saint and martyr. They were a mixture of varying types of Marxists. It seemed to me at the time, at least to the extent that my childhood mind could grapple with it, that the Stalinists called themselves Communists, the anti-Stalinists called themselves Trotskyites or something else, and still others called themselves Socialists or Liberals. I think my parents had a fair amount of respect for these intellectuals, but considered themselves merely Stevenson Liberals. Of course I think that many people felt in those days, perhaps wishfully, that Stevenson was a secret Socialist. I don't think I ever thought that I had a place in this spectrum.

Probably the most unique thing about my adolescent years, from a historically significant perspective, was the influence of the atomic bomb on me and my contemporaries; on our little cranial cavities. All the cliché things having to do with bomb drills in school and public service announcements and government propaganda, applied. But the last thing in anyone's mind, including mine, was that the cultural explosion going on within the Pollock and de Kooning fan base and the growth of Modernism as an important slice of the American pie, was being substantially paid for by money that came out of the taxpayer's pockets (which included of course our local families) and disappearing down the National Security rabbit hole.

Aside from occasional mention of the time that the FBI came to visit Dad in his studio to ask him if he knew any Communist sympathizers, and the occasional references to certain people possibly being (not in a bad way) "Commies" or "Red," I didn't give much thought to the possibility of leftists in our local art and intellectual scene being involved in any international intrigue. My only real concern was that I, personally, and my parents, not be labeled anything too threatening or dangerous by the local populace.

I didn't know, for instance (and neither did any American who wasn't an insider), that the CIA had originally intended to set Clement Greenberg up with a Paris literary journal, but decided to back Peter Matthiessen and *The Paris Review* instead. I didn't know that while Prince Sadruddin Aga Khan, son of Aga Khan III, was thought to be publisher of *The Paris Review*, that the money really was funneled through Saddrudin from the CIA.

In 1967 *The Saturday Evening Post*, as well as the magazine *Ramparts*, reported on the CIA's funding of "a number" of anti-Stalinist cultural organizations aimed at winning the support of Soviet sympathizing liberals world-wide. These were articles written by people within the intelligence system itself.

"A number" doesn't quite cover it. The Congress for Cultural Freedom subsequently re-named The International Association for Cultural Freedom had its genesis in the minds of the heads of the CIA, going back as far as the Frankfurt School, originally spawned to promote an American conceived de-Nazification agenda. The Congress was founded in 1950 at a conference in Berlin. Though it was an anti-Communist advocacy group, virtually all of its members were politically left wing. Its reach went well beyond anything the "man in the street" could ever have been led to believe, with branch offices and sister organizations all over the world. Many members, including its top guys, were Marxists or somewhat reformed Marxists. Malcolm Muggeridge was a member, as were George Orwell, Max Eastman, Dwight Macdonald and Mary McCarthy. So were at least several of the Abstract Expressionist scene, including Pollock. So were many of the stars of the poetry scene. The CCF's stable of magazines included *Kenyon Review, Sewanee Review, Poetry, The Journal of the History of Ideas, Partisan Review, The Paris Review* and *Daedalus*. The Ford Foundation and the Rockefeller Foundation were two of many instruments through which CIA money was laundered and funneled to the CCF.

Eventually, The Congress had offices in 35 countries where it functioned both as a cultural arm for the U.S. and as a back-channel to the CIA. The Congress's British sister, the British Society for Cultural Freedom, whose founding members included Isaiah Berlin and T.S. Eliot, also received help in its forming and funding from the CIA.

POLLOCK

The Abstract Expressionist painter Jackson Pollock had made a fast reputation among the locals as a character. He acquired a Model A and a pet crow. Both items were popular in those days. The crow followed the heavy-drinking artist around the area, flying above the Model A or sometimes riding in it to the nearby saloon, Jungle Pete's, sometimes following all the way into the village of Amagansett to The Elm Tree Inn and to the post office. My early interest in Pollock had mostly to do with his pet crow. In grammar school, one of the older boys had a crow that followed him to school and waited for him, perched in one of the big Horse Chestnuts out front, crying out with a loud caw once in a while, just often enough to cause plenty of snickering and ruin any period of studious quiet. Back on Oak Lane where the boy Stuart Vorpahl lived, it was felt that the crow served as a sentry for the Vorpahl territory, which besides the parents, included two boys and a girl, the house they lived in and a complex system of tree houses and foxholes, referred to as "huts."

Pollock's crow covered the area between Jungle Pete's, the closest saloon to Pollock's house, and the Elm Tree Inn on the north end of Main Street. As a kid, I thought of the Elm Tree as the northern boundary of the Vorpahl crow's territory. I visualized a countryside linked up with crow reconnaissance.

Pollock would often appear on foot at Julian Levi's house a few doors down from his, preceded by his crow, who would light in a tree in the backyard then hop from the fence to his Pollock's shoulder, when the artist had gotten himself righted after reeling in, drunk, from the bluestone driveway. He would help himself to a drink and a boiled potato or a piece of chicken from the refrigerator, and then stagger back toward his own house, the crow circling above.

Or, if he was not on foot, but in his Model A, he might head for Jungle Pete's or The Elm Tree, or, at least on one occasion that I remember, to the Amagansett post office, the closest post office to his house. One particular day as I sat on the front fence watching people come and go from the post office, I noticed Pollock's Model A parked out front, with his crow perched on the windshield. I saw him come out and, instead of getting into his Model A, he climbed our fence at the other end from the gate, and went up to the Old Man's studio door, knocked, and went in. Expecting to see some kind of commotion, I went in through the kitchen in time to see Ray making a stiff bourbon on the rocks filled to the brim, which he carried with care back to the studio. I stood in the background and watched with amazement as the Old Man listened respectfully to this drunk, wild looking guy. Pollock critiqued the illustration on the drawing board and then went to a large abstract that was on a big easel behind the drawing board, and discussed it with the Old Man. They talked and gestured the way I'd seen Julian and Pop do with each other.

The loud talking stopped. I went to the back window and climbed a small beech tree that grew near the back wall of the studio and looked in the window. The man had a cigarette dangling from his lip. While the two men talked I suspended myself in the tree and enjoyed spying and trying to interpret a picture with no sound. Then he left, climbing over the fence the same way he came in.

Who was this drunk and why was he so important? He wore cowboy boots and was from somewhere out west. He was a drunk and he had a pet crow. At one of the exhibitions at Guild Hall, when a couple of art lovers were standing in front of one of his paintings rhapsodizing, he had, according to rumors, walked up behind the patrons and hollered "bullshit" and left. But if he was a cowboy, how bad could he be? I guessed he was alright. The Old Man shut the studio door.

Jackson's visit seemed to cause a slight change in the Old Man, changing the chemistry in the air. I understood at some level that my father understood this other man's importance. To me, my father owned the world. To my father, this man belonged to a bigger, newer world.

Pollock was a magnet, but not the only magnet; the urban mythology notwithstanding. East Hampton was attractive in its own right, and attracted artists and non-artists, geniuses and the rest of us poor shlubs. But, to an increasing extent the town and specifically Springs, not long after Pollock moved in, took on a sacred air for many of those people who considered themselves the New York Intelligentsia, in part because his move coincided with the beginning of his sudden, explosive fame. The Intelligentsia descended, slowly at first, like the first early geese in a cornfield. Analysts and critics and wealthy bohemians followed the first wave of abstractionists, along with writers like Dwight McDonald and Harold Rosenberg and soon after, a group who had jumped from radio to early television. Among the group were several who had been blacklisted in Hollywood and returned east, some with professional aliases.

ARTSY KIDS

It was at a summer cocktail party in Springs, where members of the Abstract Expressionist movement were mingling with other New Yorkers, writers, poets, psychiatrists, when a kid, the child of a writer, asked me who my father was and what he did. When I said my father was an artist, the kid said, "Aw, he's not an artist, he's a commercial artist," with "commercial" spat out with the utmost contempt. I had already by then absorbed some of that hatred of commercialism from my parents, who accepted the artists' prejudices of the times, which were anti-commercial, anti- anything bourgeois. But I knew the truth was not that simple, that I was justified in being angry, and I talked to my parents about it later. They seemed much more accepting of the prejudice than I was. They were painters. They admired the Abstractionists. They were going to vote for Stevenson. And they weren't going to be reactionaries! God forbid.

My father was an illustrator, so he was branded; it didn't matter that he painted on the side. (My mother's painting was realistic or, as they said then, representational; that is, recognizable stuff.) But they weren't crushed by the criticism. They were adults and they could handle reality testing. Anyway, they were friends with most all of the artists who lived in the area. If art was the religion of my parents, the Abstract Expressionists were the deacons of the church, the in-group, and that was something they never quite belonged to, though they were certainly believers.

ADJUSTING AND COMPLAINING

I was miles from any serious thought of having therapy for myself. I would have died of embarrassment if I'd been subjected to that. In my Amagansett, that would have been tantamount to being locked away in an institution. But my imaginary grown-up-self had a shrink which he, I, attended with regularity, and in that daydream mode I became whatever heroic being I could imagine.

These privileged thoughts would spill over into my conversations with Ma and I'd hammer away at my tragic past. I would drone on about how other fathers played catch with their sons, and Carolyn would point out that not every father plays baseball and that anyway, "you don't like baseball."

I had some inkling that they weren't showing me how to live. I give myself credit for knowing at least that much, though I wouldn't really put my finger on it until I was in my thirties and I read Alice Miller's book, *The Drama of the Gifted Child,* about narcissistic parents. "You don't associate with the other parents," I would say, stating the obvious. I knew that would get me nowhere. Neither of them had any intention of becoming friends with any of my schoolmate's parents. For Carolyn it was enough that she employed Tommy's mother and that she occasionally participated in a Cub Scout meeting and even more infrequently, went to a P.T.A. meeting. For Ray, his fishing friends were enough.

To the Old Man most of the local people, in fact most people in general, were Magimper and not worth his time. The term Magimper came from a cartoon that had been in the San Francisco papers back around 1918, when he and his two buddies Dan Butler who would become an engineer, and Ray Sullivan who became an in-house illustrator for Standard Oil, were the men about town. The cartoon featured Joe Magimp who was just an average Joe who did stupid things.

Carolyn, if she was pushed into a corner, could get mean. Moronic, imbecilic, snot nosed, these were words she could fling at anyone she wanted to avoid. Though it wasn't completely true, it seemed to me that aside from the few transplants and part-time resident artists, the only friends my parents had were these poor disoriented New Yorkers that they knew from the Thirties. So much older than anyone's parents ever were, most of them were childless people who all drank too much expensive undiluted whiskey or martinis. They all seemed to have one affectation or another, whether it was a pompous way of talking or wearing a jacket and bow tie in the country, or talking about the locals as if they were these terribly humorous oafs.

DEATH OF ANASTASIA ILICH, 1955

I remember the day my grandmother died. My father was crying. I knew, because there had been a phone call from California that morning and then a stillness descended on the house. I didn't see him cry, I could not imagine him crying I wanted to peek into the studio but I was afraid. I knew that she must have been old. It felt strange that I'd never met her. There was a small portrait of her, 18 by 16 inches with a nice ornate frame, in the hallway between the living part of the house and the studio, done by Ray in 1924 when he was twenty three years old. A dark skinned woman with a great hooked nose and her hair curling in around the base of her neck, some sort of black peasant dress on, the painting was done with the realism, the gloss, of a Flemish master. That portrait is now hanging in our bedroom in Florida.

I tried to imagine what his life with her had been like but it was too remote. He had two sisters who still lived in California. I only met each of them once, briefly. Ray rarely talked about growing up. He had mentioned several times that he had once won a medal for broad jump; that his father beat him because he said he wanted to be an artist; that his mother and his Uncle Sam had bought a fig orchard in Walnut Creek, where they'd raised figs as they'd done in Yugoslavia; that his mother was a wonderful woman; that she had faith in him.

Blue Jetty, 5' x 3'4"
See more at rayprohaska.com

A while later, when the studio door was opened, he came out for a cup of coffee, went back into his studio, and I wandered in behind him and sat silently while he worked on a large blue canvas of rocks and forms in an abstract, ocean-like background of blue. He worked on that painting, which he named "Blue Jetty," for a year.

ELSIE JOE AND THE BANTIES

Somewhere in the mid-50s, Tommy's mother Eileen Scott went to work for Mrs. Austin up on Bluff Road, where she would get better pay and be able to work more hours. Carolyn had cut her hours back as living got more expensive. Elsie Bennett from the East Side, came to take her place. Elsie's husband Joe ran the poultry farm for the Bell Estate.

Joe gave me a half-dozen Banty chickens and I decided to design my own coop for them. It was clever, I thought; a one piece thing with a little box at one end with a hinged top to get at the eggs, and with the pen attached to the box as one piece so that the whole thing could be moved around. When they'd scratched the grass enough, it could be dragged to a new spot.

I asked Ray for help. He had built a nice dog house for Suzy and surrounded it with a big pen, meant to keep her from wandering. The pen was built against the Erickson's old chicken wire fence that was the back wall of all their dog runs so their champion Chesapeakes couldn't jump out. Suzy didn't like being locked in the pen though, she preferred wandering the neighborhood or sleeping in the green velvet chair in the living room in front of the TV (when we got TV), and also preferred following me around or running across Main Street to chase the cats behind Joe's restaurant.

We bought the necessary boards and nails and chicken wire at Shorty's Lumber Yard, and began assembling. I began hammering and sawing away, and Ray, seeing me fumbling, grabbed the hammer out of my hand and said, "You don't know what you're doing, let me do that." He put the whole thing together in less than an hour and it was beautiful, just as I'd envisioned it, but not having helped build it took some of the joy out of it for me. Still, it was the best looking miniature chicken coop in town. I raised several crops of chicks over a couple of years and on occasion I ate scrambled Banty eggs for breakfast and had the pleasure of feeding them scratch feed and letting them loose to fly into the big Greening apple tree in our yard.

Elsie Bennett, aka Elsie Joe,* was what we called a real Bonacker, someone who still lived in the East Side and had a real, old fashioned, thick, Bonac accent. She was a heavy cigarette smoker, stipulated a six-pack of beer be in the fridge when she arrived, and didn't do any heavy lifting, which was left to Carolyn, about the same size and age as Elsie but without the beer belly. Ma always seemed to be in the middle of some difficult chore, whether it was wrestling with turning over Ray's big mattress that dwarfed her little frame, or waxing antiques with steel wool and Butcher's Wax, making curtains, making some obscure, difficult meal requested by Ray, or working in the garden. She bravely managed to save some time, never enough, for painting.

Bonacker women and women in that neighborhood tended to have their husband's names attached to them. The other one that readily comes to mind was Mary Jimmy, who lived on Neck Path in the East Side. Mary Jimmy cleaned for the people who bought our Hand Lane house; she mowed their lawn too. She reminded Carolyn of the old character actress, Marjorie Main.

SHAGWONG PICNIC

Except for his few closest fishing buddies, Ray's socializing with fishermen was mostly limited to having a few drinks at a favorite watering hole for sport fisherman and charter captains, the Shagwong Tavern on Montauk Main Street.

Besides being the name of a tavern, Shagwong is the name of a place. There are several smaller points to the north of Montauk Point that jut out from the land as the beach rounds the corner to head east. Behind the dunes there are several ponds, the largest one, Oyster Pond, which opens up periodically to the sea, and two smaller ones, Big Reed and Little Reed. The ponds are surrounded by hilly grassland. One hill, the highest, gave the place its name. The Indians called it Shagwong, or Village Beside a Hill. (There must have been a permanent encampment there at one time.) Shagwong was our family's favorite picnic place. It was kind of a tradition to go there once a year with a picnic of fried chicken and potato salad and a couple of bottles of Pouilly-Fuissé. Occasionally we would bring a family friend or two.

To get to Shagwong we drove the Jeep north off the Main Highway onto East Lake Drive, the road that borders the east side of Lake Montauk, to the bay beach, and then for several miles along the beach. Gin Beach, where some gin washed up more than once, was not then the popular bathing beach it is today and before you drove very far you felt the impact of wilderness. It was quiet. A distance down the beach, there was a barbed wire fence that came down to the water. The fence was there to keep the cattle from the nearby Dude Ranch on the east side, all property leased from a development company to the ranch.

I would get out and open the fence and my father would drive through. Sometimes there would be cattle milling around near the fence and occasionally you'd see riders on the beach, or just a cowboy hat visible bobbing along behind a bank of beach plum covered dunes.

About a half mile before Shagwong Point the beach becomes rocky, before making a ninety degree turn at the point to curve south in a cove that reaches around as a white sanded crescent beach as far as Rocky Point, after which the beach is rocky all the way towards the end of Long Island, Montauk Point. The Cove is the most beautiful place for swimming, sort of half ocean half bay, deep, often calm, but with a bit of a rolling swell.

Along this curved stretch, called Shagwong Beach, 60 years ago, there was often not a soul in sight. The peaceful atmosphere, interrupted only by the song of Redwing blackbirds and seagulls, was where I first learned to drive, following the tracks in the old beach buggy along the unpopulated sandy beach while the Old Man fished.

Sometimes when we went out there, instead of driving along the beach we would turn off the road a quarter mile before the beach, where the dunes meets the grassland, into a large reserve of land called The Benson Estate. This way, we would save time getting to the fish, bouncing along in two wheel drive some of the time, where the ground was more solid, less sandy. Parallel to the beach but behind the dunes, we would have to stop to close another gate, part of the same barbed wire fence that went down to the water. Then, over a couple of big hills, including one with an adobe hacienda on top, and we came into a little valley taken up mostly by Big Reed Pond. It was a savanna, like something out of Africa. The Old Man would start scat singing a medley of Benny Goodman jungle rhythms, the *Hawaiian War Chant* or some Boogie Woogie beat, drumming his hands on the steering wheel. We pretended we were on safari going past a watering hole on the Serengeti Plain. I expected to see a herd of zebra gallop past at any given moment. In fact we did see hawks and osprey, rabbits and white tailed deer, foxes and grazing White Faced cattle.

FISHING WITH RAY

Not all the time, but once in a while, I went fishing with my father. It was a way we made peace with each other in between battles. It was how I said I was sorry when I wished he was dead and how he apologized when he'd been too rough on me. He should have had a bumper sticker on his beach buggy saying, I'm spending my kids inheritance. In some circles he was more well-known as a fisherman than as an illustrator. Fishing accrued enough down-time to explain why he never got rich. But for Ray it was enough to say that it was where he drew spiritual sustenance for his painting. I bought into it, and I still do.

    Alone or with his fishing buddies, Sam Cox, Vic Mohns, Jimmy Amaden, Duke Doucette and *Daily News* columnist Bob Sylvester, he fished up and down the sandy beaches and on the rocks in Montauk and even in the creeks and harbors on the bay side. Sometimes they would chase the bass as far north as Provincetown and as far south as Hatteras; staying overnight in motels. A couple of winters they broke the pattern and took the Orange Blossom Special south to fish for tarpon and bonefish in The Keys.

I had been immersed in his work since I could remember. His illustration jobs were the life blood of the family; but I understood, intuitively, why he had to do his abstracts. Standing next to him in the studio you could feel that it renewed his spirit. He would ask me how I felt about a painting and he seemed to appreciate my criticism.

Being tuned into him and standing just outside his center of gravity, I could sort of tell what his next move would be before he consciously knew, and I would say "over there," and he'd do something to that area and say, "Yeah!" I suppose it was the equivalent of playing catch with him in the backyard, which was something he'd never do. "Too Magimper."

There were days when he'd been working on something, either an illustration or a painting, and I could sense that he was feeling as if he'd done enough for one day; that he'd come to a place where he could let it sit for a while; come back to it with a fresh eye. I knew he was about to call it a day and go fishing and I'd ask if I could come along. Sometimes we'd head straight to the ocean beach near our home and drive along the sand in the beach buggy. (Over the two decades of the Forties and Fifties he went through a half dozen beach buggies, first the Model A, then a surplus Army Jeep, and then a series of Willys Jeeps.)

Before I was big enough to see over the windshield, I was driving the old Model A along the beach, starting in second gear and standing on the seat, using the throttle on the dashboard and popping it out of gear without the clutch. Chugging along in the tracks made by the haulseiners in their big army surplus power-wagons, I'd follow him as he'd walk along following a school of fish down the beach. Those were the times I felt closest to him; when doubts about being able to measure up receded into the background.

I remember once, I was thirteen and we were in the Jeep. We went down on the sand at Amagansett by the bath houses and headed east towards the Coast Guard Station. It was a gray, early fall day and there were gulls working along the beach concentrated over a crew of haulseiners just east of the Coast Guard beach. There were often a few kids hanging out with the seiners and today was no exception; Mickey was there with his father, and everyone over fourteen had a cigarette in his mouth. The Old Man talked to Ted Lester, who was captain of the crew and who was Pop's friend and subject of several paintings, while I milled around with the kids, feeling the least grown-up. I would feel better when we got back in the jeep and headed east toward Montauk.

We moved east following in reverse the tracks of the big power-wagons, then broke out to make tracks of our own across a broad stretch of beach going way, way east, in the direction of Montauk. All along the coast the dunes were higher then, the beaches wider, before joy riders and tourists and the forces of nature wore them down. We had covered the length of Beach Hampton and could now see about two miles down the beach to where it bent around a slight curve near the Napeague Coast Guard Station. We rounded that bend and continued along, down the beach, now in sight of Montauk still six or eight miles away.

When we got to a place where the dunes gave way to bluff, a place the seiners called the Transformers because of the electricity transformers on the power company poles that line up on the bluff, bluefish were breaking very close to the beach. Instead of having me follow him along in the jeep, he told me to take the extra, smaller pole. On the first cast I hooked into an enormous bluefish and "horsed" him in slowly with a tight drag, just like I'd seen the Old Man do. Pop yelled encouragement, but he didn't stop fishing. We were in competition. With almost each cast I hooked into another one. Each time I would tighten the drag and then loosen it, letting the fish tell me what to do, using the force of the white water, the waves after they've broken, to help me pull in each fish as it tired, getting each one up out of the water where I could grab the line in one hand and drag him up onto the dry sand where I would then fit my hand into his gills for better leverage and drag him up a few more yards next to the Jeep, to lay flopping on the sand. Six in all, not one under ten pounds. The captain of a charter boat not much more than a hundred feet off shore was giving my father a wry smile and applauding me. And then I made several casts and nothing. They had moved off shore. In a matter of a few minutes, the fish, the bait, the gulls, and the charter boats were all working way out past the sand bar, drifting farther and farther out past where our casts could reach. The Old Man was proud of me. I was exhausted. "Well, you skunked me, Chum," he said.

Another time when I was still quite young, nine or ten, I went with him to Montauk. It was late fall and rather cool. While he fished, I huddled in among the rocks. He was casting into the surf just under the lighthouse, where there was and still is an apron of gigantic granite boulders at the foot of the cliff to limit erosion. At sunset it began to get colder and I amused myself finding little caves to hide in. Earlier I had been leaping from rock to rock around the point in my sturdy high-top sneakers, going out of sight of my dad to where the granite bulkhead turned into a mixture of rocks and sandy beach, then I'd run back using his parka hood as a reference. The way his hood came to a peak made him distinguishable from the half dozen other fishermen. When it got dark I made a home in the cave closest to him and peered out, watching him haul in one big striped bass after another.

He fished on. In the dark I could just make out the chain he wore around his waist that held the gaff hook, and the swirling of several big bass tethered to it, the brass chain threaded through the gills, while he stood there in the moonlight, up to his waist, on a rock, flipping the heavy home-made plug three hundred feet into the surf. Finally I was so cold and damp I started calling out to him. "Hey Pop!" A few minutes later, "Hey Pop, let's go." After a few seconds the Old Man would holler back, "Just a few more casts."

For the next hour my misery continued to increase. I was cold. My teeth were chattering. He was having fun and didn't know I was miserable, or didn't care. Times like that he loomed larger and larger. I was the incredible shrinking boy, huddled like a spider in the rocky crevices. The magnitude of distance between my smallness and his uncaring became cosmic. I would spend my life in this cave. I stuck my hands in my pants and warmed them between my legs. I imagined building a fire. I imagined killing him.

By the time he came in and gutted his fish in a shallow below me, using a light like a coal miner's lamp which was clasped to his head by an elastic strap, he began talking to me casually about how we should come back tomorrow and fish the early morning tide, as if I were one of his buddies and had been fishing beside him. I was stiff with cold, my feet numb, but too weak to complain. Heading west in the dark in the old jeep, me with my socks flush against the heater, cooking my feet, he at last realized I needed attention. As we drove through Montauk village, he swerved into Bohler's Restaurant. He bought me a banana split and got himself a hot fudge sundae.

I have never forgotten how I felt later that evening, still reeling from the bout of self-righteous self-pity that I'd gotten myself into earlier, in my cave. Now, sitting in a hot steaming tub, going into an altered state listening to the blood pounding in my ears, mostly sugar-rush I'm sure, or maybe it was part incipient hypothermia, my mind was buzzing, ringing. It sounded like the warbling hum of an old refrigerator and had me convinced I was in touch with some cosmic vibration.

WRITERS AND FISHERMEN

There is a book by John Cole, with almost a cult following, *Striper*, about the striped bass and the adventure of fishing for it. Cole, a childhood member of East Hampton's Maidstone Club and the son of a founding member, went on to be the publisher of the *Maine Times*, one of the most prestigious small town newspapers in the country, and a respected writer on conservation and ecology.

    The Maidstone Club had a slightly more high-toned beginning than the average American country club. Its main purpose seems, to decidedly unclubby people like me, to provide a place for middle and upper management to play golf and dress up in funny-colored pants. The Club was started almost as a summer camp, a home away from home for people from New York who enjoyed golf, tennis, swimming and various forms of rustication. It expanded out of a Tennis Club which was already in existence, and became clubby enough to attract those who were simply social snobs, but also appealed to outdoor types who enjoyed picnics, sailing and fishing, and were attracted to the area for both its charm and its people. Each generation of club members has had its few members who went local, to one degree or another, by fishing, hunting, fraternizing with the locals, and by staying in residence, at least part time, during the winter season.

    The Coles, John and his wife Cynthia, moved into a rented house in Springs in 1951. John Cole was one who went native. With his friend Pete Scott, another Summer Colony kid, Cole came back to East Hampton after The War because it was the place he felt most at home. In another book about fishing, *Fishing Came First*, Cole describes a day of fishing before The War, with a fellow Maidstone member and a lover of fishing, an older man in his sixties. Cole was sixteen and had ridden his bike the several miles to the Town Dock at Three Mile Harbor. He was standing at the dock next to Emerson Taber's Lobster store, watching the baby bluefish, called snappers, chase bait. The man came by and recognized him and asked him if he wanted to go fishing. He said yes, and the man pulled up to the dock and let him come aboard his custom-made sixteen foot runabout. As Cole put it in the aforementioned book:

"There is a confluence of elements on Long Island's East End in late August and early September that creates crystal air. As summer glides toward the autumnal equinox and high pressure builds in the heavens, certain mornings become complete units of hours suspended, as if nature has succeeded in generating a timeless moment, a shimmering souvenir of a passing season, saved and pinned in the book of elements, motionless, perfect, intoxicating, and touched with the tragedy of its own fragility."

His fishing companion's name was Wyman Aldrich. They went out of the harbor and east toward the bay-front of the Bell Estate and fished the bottom for blowfish using clams Aldrich had dug that morning for bait. When they had half a dozen fish, they pulled anchor and headed for Cartwright Shoals. They talked about Gardiner's Island and Captain Kidd. They beached on the shoals and made a fire out of driftwood and cooked the blowfish on an iron skillet with some salt pork Aldrich had brought along for bait. That day was a highpoint in young John's life, and led him to become a life-long fisherman.

After The War, John's sister Jane opened a small antique shop in the village of East Hampton. She had gone to Chatham Hall, an all-girl school, and then to Smith College. At both Chatham and Smith she had been friends with a pretty blond Boston girl named Patsy Southgate who later married a young writer, Peter Matthiessen, while both were studying at the Sorbonne. Matthiessen was from an upper-class east coast Wasp family; his father was a wealthy architect. His father's cousin, F.O. Matthiessen was a famous critic and authority on Henry James.

Fresh out of college, Yale and Smith respectively, and after a short trip down to Washington to receive some Cold War training from the CIA, Peter and Patsy had gone to Paris to become part of the post-war literary scene. Peter had been asked to start a literary review which could become a base for anti-Stalinist writers and intellectuals. Instead, he had taken over one that had already begun, *The Paris Review*. They had become popular members of the artist and writer's post-War American expatriate scene in Paris, and Patsy became known as the most beautiful American woman in Paris.

Cole, Matthiessen and Scott, who were all from well-to-do families but seemingly without enough income to live on, began haulseining with a local crew and quickly decided they could make a living at it, which would allow them to live their lives out on the East End. They went native. When Ted Lester saw how gung-ho the three were, he asked them to join his crew.

They were strong, healthy young men and, just as important; quick studies. They soon became capable fishermen, accepted and well liked. It was Milton Miller, my friend Mickey's father, who was the most history-minded of the crew, who educated them concerning the history of fishing off the beach, and filled them in on Bonac lore and legends and Milton's passionately held opinions on everything under the sun.

Milton had entrepreneurial dreams and had tried a few things, like owning a dragger, starting a small cement block plant, and doing some carpentry. Becoming friends with these sophisticated and preppy writers didn't negatively affect his expansive way of thinking. He already saw himself as larger than life; a characteristic not limited to people in the creative arts; something I discovered in a eureka moment in my youth.

Peter and Chloe Scott (Chloe was a dancer and years later became a member of Ken Kesey's Merry Pranksters) found the wing of a mansion with a room large enough for a dance class and had the house mover Robert Kennelly move it to the far reaches of the Accabonac wetlands. The mover did this by floating the structure on a barge from a beach in Southampton to the shallowest part of the harbor and then dragging it the rest of the way with a bulldozer. Milton, a capable carpenter, helped with the remodeling. When their Border Collie had puppies, Jackson Pollock got one and Milton got another, which he gave to Mickey. Mickey, a connoisseur of comic books, gave the puppy the name Spike, after the *Looney Tunes'* bulldog character.

The Coles had moved into a house in Springs that had last been rented by Berton Rouéché, a *New Yorker* writer who was renowned locally for having written an article about the Amagansett fisherman and off-shore whaler, Capt. E.J. Edwards. (*The New Yorker*, Sept 1949)* Rouéché, a handsome, well dressed, tweed-clad mid-westerner, came to the *New Yorker* from the *St. Louis Post Dispatch*. He and his wife Kay, an attractive niece of Dwight D. Eisenhower (who became President in January of 1953) bought property on Stony Hill Road in Amagansett and built a modern, green-oriented house, half a century ahead of its time, modeled after a potato storage house, with its rear end built into the side of a hill and walls partially underground. The Rouechés had one child, a son Brad, who was my age, and briefly (for one year) went to Amagansett School before being sent off to a private boarding school in Connecticut. The Rouechés lived in Amagansett for 45 years until his death by suicide.

*Roueche's article on E.J. Edwards, a surf whaler who was one of the three founding brothers of the Edwards Fish Company, gives another peek at the subtle, wry, interactions between cultural New York and the wilderness of the East End, with a description of the taking of a photograph of the old whaling captain by the famous and sophisticated photographer Arnold Genthe, in which Genthe calls the Captain "the handsomest man in the world."

After spending a year in the former Roueché home John Cole and his wife Cynthia moved up the street to another smaller rental a few doors from the Pollocks, and Lee Krasner Pollock and Cynthia, introduced by John's sister Jane, who met Lee when she came into her antique store, became friends. The Matthiessens took over the now former Cole house and Patsy also became a friend to Lee. John did some house painting for Lee and while he was working Lee confided in him about Jackson's drinking (which was no big secret) and her fears about his driving while drinking.

LUCIA AND ROGER

Another artist who appeared in the area after The War was Lucia Wilcox, always known only as Lucia. Ray and Carolyn met Lucia through Julian Levi, who had been friends with Fernand Leger in Paris in the Thirties. Lucia and Leger may have been friends with benefits, or just friends, but they arrived together in New York Harbor precipitously (in a rough sea) on the *Normandy*, on the same day the '38 Hurricane made landfall on the East End. The trip was arranged and paid for by Gerald and Sara Murphy whom had known them both in Paris.

There is a beach in East Hampton that the locals refer to as Wiborg Beach. The owner of the estate originally, was Frank Bestow Wiborg, of Ault and Wiborg Ink Company in Cincinnati, which later became the International Printing Ink Corporation. The property included a large, stone mansion on a long stretch of ocean-front that went almost to the public beach, called Main Beach, and back to the shore of Hook Pond, so that it was bordered on two sides by water and took up almost 600 acres.

Roger Wilcox, who would become Lucia's husband, whom I interviewed in May of 1994, told me that all those Toulouse-Lautrec posters one used to see everywhere, which were said to have been printed in Paris, were actually printed in Cincinnati by Ault and Wiborg. The lithograph stones would be sent to Cincinnati, where the printing took place, and then the prints and stones would be sent back to Paris. Any number of artists in France did the same thing, but they didn't want to be thought of as traitorous so they kept it quiet. "But the printing," Roger told me, "you can see the difference. I've seen posters that were printed in Paris before they made this deal with Ault and Wiborg, and boy there's a difference. The French didn't know how to print at all."

Sara Murphy, Frank Wiborg's daughter, and her husband Gerald Murphy, an artist, had been part of the Hemingway and Fitzgerald crowd in the Paris of the Twenties, and had come home to the U.S. when Gerald was called in to help save his family business, the company that made Cross pens. A great book has been written about them, *Living Well is the Best Revenge*, by Calvin Tomkins.

The Murphys had inherited the Wiborg property from Sara's father. The mansion itself was in bad disrepair, so they had torn it down with the idea of rebuilding it someday, which they never got around to. They renovated the six-space carriage house, which was about four hundred feet behind the main house, and made it their living quarters, leaving space for a one car garage. In preparation for an influx of artists from Europe as The War neared, they had leased a studio building at 80 West 40th which had artist's studios and living quarters in it. It was on the south side of Bryant Park and all the big windows faced north with a view of the park. They had reserved a studio for Leger and one for Lucia. Because the studios weren't ready when Leger and Lucia first arrived, they were put up for six weeks in a nice hotel on Park Avenue. When they moved in, Lucia was on the third floor, Leger directly above. The building was almost all artists. Among others, Kurt Seligmann was there.

Though they owned a big apartment in New York, in summers the Murphys came to East Hampton, and for the summer of '39 they brought Lucia with them. They had a guest house, similar in size to the carriage house, which they had painted pink and called the Pink House. In its back yard the Pink House had a miniature playhouse, also pink, which had been built for their daughter, Honoria. The ceilings were six feet two inches, the doors were about five two; altogether, it was about half-scale when matched to the guest house. Lucia, who was barely five feet tall, decided it was just right for her, and moved in. She stayed there all that summer.

ROGER

Roger Wilcox, b. 1910, d. 1998, grew up on the shore of Snapper Creek, an estuary fed from the Everglades, near Cutler Ridge, Florida, south of Miami. The water was full of manatees, alligators, and water snakes. It was a place full of wildcats, rattlesnakes, and eagles, where you had to take careful notice of your surroundings.

In Akron, Ohio, at the turn of the century, his father, a house painter, had developed lead poisoning, possibly because he made his own paint. His doctor had suggested moving to a warmer climate. Sight unseen, he bought land in the boondocks of south Florida, thirty acres for which he paid practically nothing, about ten cents an acre, and on which he intended to farm. He took some "wags" advice, as Roger told it to me, that the best crop he could grow was celery. The fellow didn't mention that you should first find a buyer for the crop.

Roger and his older brother started school the same year, walking the three miles from home to a one room school house with a total of 12 students. They had two older sisters going to the school too, so together they made up one third of the student body.

During the summer before high school he hitch-hiked to New York City for fun. The following summer he returned to the city and got a summer job at the Claude Neon Laboratory in Long Island City, across the East River from Manhattan. He did that for a couple of more summers, and then without a high school diploma, began to work there full time. His boss, George Claude, b. 1870, d. 1960, was a French engineer who had patented the first neon lighting tube in the U.S. in 1915. His first sale was in 1923, when he sold two signs reading "Packard" to a Los Angeles car dealership, for $24,000. Claude had convinced Roger that he could do without the diploma from high school. "America is full of public libraries," Claude told him. "You can get any book you want. All you need is a book list, which I'll give you." So Roger went to the New York Public Library and borrowed every book on the list, one by one, and Claude gave him tests, guided him, and taught him how to learn.

Before long, Roger had a good education and, to boot, knew everything there was to know about making neon signs. Claude made him a partner and moved him to Los Angeles to run a plant there. The company became a corporation with three partners; Claude, Roger, and a financial backer. Roger put half his salary back into the company to buy shares and within four years his stock was worth three million dollars.

When the crash came in '29 Claude Neon lost a lot of money, but rather than close down, he sent Roger, who by this time had gotten married and had a daughter, to Denver to rescue the franchise there by consolidating the crew. "I went in there and taught three guys how to do everything. The sheet metal man became, in addition to his regular job, the electrician and the painter. We had all these guys who just did the glass part, see, and I taught three guys to do the whole schmeer!" He had made a deal with Claude to streamline all the branches, cutting down the labor costs. He would talk to the men and find out which ones were willing to learn, willing and able to do at least two, maybe three jobs. For each franchise that he streamlined, he got a bonus.

During the Thirties, Roger, having tired of the neon business and having given most of his wealth to his first wife in a divorce (he had no appetite for saving money), was living in Key West, working at the naval base as a designer and draftsman, when he ran into a friend from New York whom he hadn't seen since before the crash, Marion Logan, a former Vice President of B. Altman & Company, a New York City department store. While still at Altman's, Marion had gone to Paris every year and had gotten to know quite well a designer of fabrics named Lucia. On every trip she and Lucia would spend time together.

Marion was married and retired when Roger ran into her. She and her husband, who'd been a producer and director in Hollywood, were living in Mexico and had just bought a second home in Key West. They asked Roger for help in remodeling it, which he did, putting together a crew of carpenters and decorators, and in four months he had the house just as she wanted it, modern on the interior and old Key West on the outside.

Roger was in his late twenties at the time, living in a rooming house with a small suite to himself, one bedroom and one sitting room; "Anyway, she and her husband were both very nice," Roger said. "She decided I should move in with them. She said, 'You know, George and I have talked it over and decided that it's silly for you to be living alone and going out to every meal and all that. You come over here every day anyway, and I cook every day, so,' she said, 'you can eat with us. If we go out to dinner, you can go with us.' They sort of adopted me," he said.

It was now 1940. He was thirty years old, living in a beautiful house designed by himself, with bright and charming company that doted on him like a son and kept him well fed. There was another spare room so that guests came and went. Marion talked about Paris and frequently brought up her friend Lucia, a beautiful girl, a talented designer who also had ambitions to be a fine artist. "Roger," she said, "Too bad she'll never be coming to America, because you two would get along wonderfully together. She has all this personality, but she's a little too flighty. People think she's a flibbertigibbet, but she's serious and you being the kind of guy you are, who's practical and down to earth and real, you see, you could benefit her."

Then one October day (in October it's usually still hot in Key West), he was taking his siesta and he heard loud talking outside his window. Marion had run into Lucia on the street. "They hadn't seen each other for nearly ten years, you know. But of course they recognized each other and so, of course, she had to come to the house. And that's how I met Lucia."

Roger thought "Maybe I've been set up!" but he would never know, or care. Perhaps Lucia had written Marion that she was coming to the States. Lucia, though married, was living with Fernand Leger in New York. Though they had come over together, there didn't seem to be any real romance, or at least there was no possessiveness, because there was never any friction between Roger and Fernand.

Lucia, of mixed Middle Eastern heritage, was born in Lebanon and had been married to her husband when she was fifteen, in an arranged marriage. They had immigrated to America and stayed two years, and during that time had a child. Although she didn't know it at the time, the law in those days made both Lucia and the child citizens. Though born in Lebanon, Kabbaz (first name I don't know), Lucia's husband was of Italian parentage and had Italian citizenship.

Although he was an artist, he was, according to Roger, "Not a very good one, as it turned out."

Lucia and Roger began living with each other almost immediately. Kabbaz came to New York and took over the studio that she had been gifted with through her relationship with Leger and the Murphys. He was easily talked into a compromising-photo adultery divorce, and then, along with his allegedly meager talent, he went on his merry way.

Roger had become good friends with the Commander of the Naval Base at Key West and had introduced him to the Logans, and Marion had invited the Commander for dinner on several occasions. With the Commander's help, Roger gained a year's deferment from the draft. He and Lucia met in October of 1940 and The War started just over a year later. For the following year, while she was working in New York in her studio and Roger, as part of his deferment deal, continued his job at the Naval Base, Roger would periodically take time off and go up to New York City to be with her. During one of those trips, they married.

Eventually, though, The War caught up with him and he was drafted. His first post, in the summer of 1941, was at Lowry Field in Colorado, where he would be stationed for four months. He was in the photo lab, learning about reconnaissance, when he got a call from headquarters. Lucia was in the office of the Base Commander. She had told Roger she was coming to visit, but he hadn't believed her. But there she was. She told the Base Commander she wanted Roger to spend the night with her at the Cow Palace Hotel and that he'd have to have the next day off so that they could look for an apartment. The Commander agreed. Roger said, "Lucia was like that. Nobody could get to that guy, but she did." Roger was then a corporal.

Lucia looked at several places in the neighborhood of Lowry Field and found a beautiful little cottage owned by a Yugoslav man who spoke no English. But Lucia had this facility for languages. How she knew Serbo-Croatian God knows, but she did. (She spoke it with Ray.) She and this Slav hit it off and he gave her the best of the several cottages he owned and fixed it up just the way she wanted. "So as soon as she finalized the deal I moved over there," Roger said, "And every day I'd travel the two miles from the base. Here I'm a corporal and I'm living off the base! And I'm still in training! That was Lucia, that's what she could do."

From '42 to '45 Roger was in the Pacific in a reconnaissance squadron, first in Bougainville, then Tinian, the Solomons, and in New Guinea. Since the Squadron had to be close to the intelligence headquarters because they made target charts for raids, they were always close to the airport. And, because MacArthur's headquarters were always near the airports, Roger saw plenty of The General.

Roger always had a huge capacity for booze, which never seemed to affect him negatively. And he didn't like that whenever they were under MacArthur's command, there was nothing to drink. Plenty for the officers, but nothing for the men. According to Roger, every enlisted man in the Pacific hated his guts.

"He was Gay! Absolutely! And if you saw him, you know, a few times, you'd recognize that. He had this retinue of young guys, lieutenants, captains and majors hangin' around, everywhere he went. All they did was help him put his makeup on! I witnessed some of this shit because, you know, I was there. He'd come to the air base and I'd see him waiting for the press, and he'd get these guys to smear some mud on his Irish mug. He wore beautiful custom made clothes, including his shirts and ties. He would do all this makeup and stuff, and then the press would show up, you know, with the cameras and all that shit, and they would smear mud on his face. And his guys would get everything ready and then someone would say, "Yeah, alright, alright, no, your pipe is too straight. Let it go this way, that's good. That crazy corncob pipe bit, you know."

Roger got to Red Beach on Leyte on the day after the U.S. invasion. "O.K., here's what happened. I'm going to tell you the truth. Two days later the Marines took Leyte Island in the first attack. Not the Army. The Navy and the Marines, okay? And our outfit went in and worked off the beach the second day after the Marines got the Japs back into the woods. We started our operations there. The Marines took the island on the third day. On the fourth day MacArthur arrives, and he puts on this show on that same big Red Beach where the first attack was, see? You know, you saw that, all the newsreels. 'I have returned.' And there again, all the makeup and all the other shit that went down, you know? Incredible! The people at home, from the newsreels and the newspapers in America, they thought that that was the day of the attack, you know, MacArthur taking Leyte. They thought that he was there that day. They falsified the dates!"

Although he was in the Army Air Corps, Roger hadn't been eligible for flight training because he was too old, which was why they'd made him a photo analyst. But there came a time when they weren't getting in enough reconnaissance flights. A pair of Japanese paratroopers had gotten in and blown up thirty-one of their airplanes and killed twenty-six pilots. They had only three planes and three pilots left. So he went to the commander of his squadron and pleaded with him. "I said, 'Listen, I can fly one of those damn planes, why don't you let me go up?' I had gotten a pilot's license before the War, and had flown PBYs while I was a civilian working for the Navy, so I knew how to handle a twin engine plane."

The Commander said no. There were too many negatives. And besides, these P-38s the only ones that were left, were not rigged as fighters, but as photo planes. And there were no fighters for cover. And besides, he said, Roger was not checked out on any plane. "Have you ever been in the cockpit of a P-38?" the Commander asked. Roger said, "Sure. Just sitting there looking at it, you know, making sure the camera's installed right and all that kind of stuff." As they continued to talk, the Commander became obstinate. "No," he said, "absolutely not. You know what MacArthur would do to us if he found out that we had a guy flying a mission that's not checked out? We'd be busted, the whole squadron would be busted." Roger said, "How the hell would he know, unless you told him?" To which the Commander replied, "No, and that's final."

Roger spent a sleepless night trying to figure out what to do, and went back in the next morning and said, "Look, I'm going to let you off the hook. I'm going to steal the damn plane, alright? You've got one that's in good shape. I talked to the mechanics and they say it's in tip-top shape. All we've got to do is load fresh film on it. And you don't have to know. There's nothing you can do to me if you don't know, if you don't have any guys watching it, which you don't have." I said, "You know, I'll just go down there in the morning and steal it. And I'll fly the mission and come back and there doesn't have to be anything on any record about who took the photographs. We never do have any marks on the photos about who was the pilot, anyway. It's all automatic, you press a button and that turns on the camera, and it starts takin' the pictures, that's all. You know!" So, he said, 'All I can tell you is I never heard what you said.' So the next morning I stole the fuckin' plane. But once I did it, see, before they got enough pilots and planes back on line, I flew twelve missions."

According to Roger, he was attacked only once by Japanese Zeros. He climbed to fifteen thousand feet, put on his oxygen mask, and the Japs lost sight of him. He stayed up there until he was close to home and landed safely. "No big deal. That was a beautiful airplane to fly, I'll tell you. When you push that pedal down, those big Allison engines, *Vroooooooom!* Terrific airplane. No maneuverability though. You couldn't do any sharp turns or anything. But the controls were simple, unlike a B-26 bomber, which I flew once, just sittin' in as a co-pilot. The B-26 you had to throttle the right and the left engine separately. P-38 they were locked together and you don't, you rarely had to do anything about it, you know. Never had any trouble with those engines. They were the most dependable aircraft engines that we had, actually. In-line, straight-eights. I don't know, three hundred horsepower something like that."

Near the end of The War, Roger's outfit had been attacked and he had been wounded; shot through both ankles by one bullet, and had part of his scalp torn off by a piece of falling shrapnel, probably by falling ack-ack. On V.E. day he was in the hospital in the Philippines.

With Roger still overseas, Lucia spent the last two summers of The War in Amagansett with her friends Max Ernst and the American writer Jane Bowles. Bowles had rented a cottage on the Main Highway, just west of Abraham's Path, next to the realtor, Tom Scott. (Tommy Scott's uncle.) The house belonged to a plumber, Fillmore Miller (the Prohaska's plumber, until he retired), who lived across the street on the corner of a little dirt road called Handy Lane.

Roger returned to New York and was discharged in September of '45, expecting to go back to Key West, where, before he left, he had paid cash for a house. But by then, Lucia had fallen in love with Amagansett.

THE HOUSE ON ABRAHAM'S PATH

Tom Scott found just the right property for them. It was down the road on Abraham's Path, half a mile from the little cottage she'd spent the last two summers in, with twelve acres of land and what Roger termed "a little old Bonacker house." An old fisherman who had died a year or two earlier had been living there in what amounted to little more than a shack. "A real mess," said Roger. Because the original part did have two stories, he built a second story wing with a foundation around the circumference. He jacked up the middle of the old house to meet the new. "I was known as a crazy man around here, because I was trying to build this house all by myself, you know?" Roger said. They moved in on Lucia's birthday, April 8, 1946.

Lucia, still working as a textile designer, began to ask Roger for help with some of her carpet designs. She thought he would be good at it. It seemed that neither the designers, like herself, nor the carpet companies, had enough knowledge of geometry to make some of her designs work well with the weaving machines. Roger had a good mathematical mind which he had sharpened at the New York Public Library at Bryant Park, and he put it to work.

"Jesus, but she was right. I was a hit immediately. Every fuckin' design I made, it sold. You know, I forget now, it wasn't very much money, fifty bucks a shot, something like that, you know? I could do maybe six a day." But Lucia had an agent whom Roger thought was ripping them off. "He was taking, like, forty percent of the thing, and I wasn't gettin' much money out of it, so after I'd been doing this for a couple of months, makin' all these designs and going through her agent, getting some money back, but having to wait and all that, I just felt it didn't seem right." He decided to become his own salesman. "So that's how I met with the guys at Bigelow."

In no time at all he had a consulting contract with a twenty-five thousand dollar a year retainer fee with the Bigelow Sanford Carpet Company. "Anything I'd do, they'd have to cover expenses! Three hundred dollars a day every time I lifted a finger." He would go around to carpet companies with a portfolio, showing them his stuff, and gradually found which ones they liked best, and he'd work to suit their needs. One day while at Bigelow Carpets showing them some things, the buyer challenged Roger with the statement that no way any loom could actually make the relief effects that he had in his drawings.

When Roger protested that he'd seen such rugs and carpets, the guy explained that those were hand-made. Roger said he'd like to learn more about looms, so they gave him a pass to their company library. He spent a week there. A week later he told them he could design a loom that would work. His design idea was a modification of a velvet loom. They sent him to the Vice President for Engineering, after telling him, "He's going to think you're crazy. But he's the one who's knowledgeable, so he's the one to talk to." Roger convinced the V.P. that he could build a small loom, big enough to reproduce a carpet square the size of the sample drawings he carried around, and that if it proved to be functional, the company could have an industrial designer build a full size one.

He went back to Amagansett and thought, "I'll probably never hear from them again." But three days later the Railway Express truck drove up. The driver, whom he was friendly with by that time, had two big boxes for him from the Bigelow Sanford Carpet Company. Inside were spools of yarn in every color imaginable. Roger began making the loom immediately. He built it to make the sample squares he'd been designing, which were thirteen and a half inches wide. When it was ready, he practiced for a while and then made twelve different pieces, all of different patterns, and brought them in to Bigelow. Lucia went with him.

"She loved the idea of flabbergasting these businessmen. To carry these samples we used an old shirt box. And when we got there, Lucia starts unwrapping them, and all this tissue paper is spread all over the office floor, and the Vice President takes the first piece and he puts it on his knee. And he says, 'You made this on your loom?' I said, 'Yup.' He said, 'You mind? I've got to do a little unraveling here to see how you wove it.' I said, 'Well, okay, go ahead.' And about then somebody, tap, tap, tap, walks into in his office, and he hollered, 'Get the hell out of here. Hey, wait a minute! I want you to get Security up here. I don't want anybody in this hallway. I don't want anybody walking near this office. I don't want to see anybody, okay?' He had gone nuts!"

At the time, in spite of all the money he had made over the years, Roger was broke. He didn't even have money for the train fare back to Amagansett. So he made a deal. One thousand dollars in cash, and fifty thousand a year for ten years, as a retainer fee. He also would get five hundred dollars a day, plus expenses, any time they needed him as a trouble shooter. "Now I was rolling in dough! That was in '49. So by 1950, a year later, I had enough money I thought hell, I'm going to remodel the house. I'll have a brand new house." He tore the roof off and spent three years having fun, re-designing the house by himself. Bigelow spent seven million dollars developing the first loom and they made fifty million dollars the first year they had it running.

Roger and Lucia became year round residents of Amagansett about the same time as the Prohaskas, and the two couples hit it off from the beginning. Lucia loved to cook, as did Ray. (Although Carolyn was a good cook, she'd just as soon let someone else take over.) Some of my earliest memories are of the gypsy-like Lucia telling me convoluted stories about tigers and snakes that sounded like her paintings looked. Her paintings were neo-primitive, magical and sometimes spooky.

Though the Wilcoxes continued to socialize with the Murphys, Ray was a little too earthy for Gerald Murphy's taste. Gerald was very aloof. Juan Trippe, founder of Pan Am, who lived near the Murphys, had tried to befriend him on several occasions, but was rebuffed. Gerald never gave a reason for not liking someone. There was a man who was a Librarian of Congress and a poet. He was a "very nice gentleman," according to Roger and Lucia, but he was persona non grata at Gerald's home and Gerald wouldn't appear anywhere that he was going to be.

Roger told me, "I don't know why Gerald didn't like this librarian guy. But how I know that he didn't is, Lucia had invited the poet and Gerald to dinner, and Gerald was always careful to ask who the other guests were before he ever went out. He was that kind of person. He would do it in a way that you wouldn't be offended by it. So, when Lucia told him this man's name, Gerald said, 'Lucia, I really appreciate the invitation, but, honestly, I do not like that man. It has nothing to do with you. You can like him all you want to,' he said, 'but I don't want to see him. I don't want to be in his presence and have to deal with being polite to him, which, if I'm in your house, I would have to do, because I could not do otherwise in your presence.' And that's about all there was to that. Amazing, you know? Gerald was kind of spoiled in that way.

"It wasn't a class thing, though. Gerald was very friendly with a young man whose mother worked for the Murphys for years and years. Her husband worked on the Village Highway Department and their son often came to work with his mother. Gerald treated him like a member of the family." The son, Kenneth Wessberg, grew up to be the Mayor of East Hampton.

According to Roger, "If Gerald liked somebody, it didn't make any difference to him who they were or what they were. He treated them all the same way and Lucia was the same way, I think she may have picked up some of that from Sara and Gerald." They were very democratic snobs.

Roger had always come by money easily but never held on to it; never invested. He was incredibly generous to his friends, mostly artists. He went for long periods without making any money, and he never thought about getting old. On the advice of several friends, and for Lucia's security, if anything happened to him, he had signed the Amagansett property over to her. When I visited him in May, 1994, he was eighty four, and again, nearly dead broke. Before she died though, in 1974, Lucia had given Roger life estate to the property. After that, the property went to her only son and her grandson.

BRODOVITCH

In February of 1958 a giant snow squall hit the East End. Fifty mile per hour winds and temperatures near zero brought life to a standstill. Church services were canceled and schools were closed for the next two days. On the cover of the February 21, 1958 issue of the now defunct *Bridgehampton Press*, there is a photograph of the gaunt ruin of a chimney, with a caption that reads in part, "...amid the debris of what once was the Simmons house..."

Up near the ocean in Sagaponack on the day of the storm, maybe two hundred yards back from the dunes, there had been a big house fire. All six trucks from the Bridgehampton Fire Department were stuck by drifting snow, half a mile from the fire. The trucks were stopped near the house of Cliff Foster, a potato farmer. Foster took the Chief to the fire in a tractor equipped with chains. Three trucks took an alternate route, along Bridge Lane, a road parallel to the ocean that goes over a little bump of a bridge crossing Sagg Pond Dreen, a stream joining Sagg Swamp to Sagg Pond. Two of the three got through to the fire, but by then the house was too far gone. The brick-faced front collapsed into the ashes. Soon, the remains of the house and the orchard and gardens surrounding it would grow wild.

Local people still called it the Simmons house. A former president of the New York Stock Exchange, old man Edward Simmons had been greatly admired locally. He was one of those who had the foresight to withdraw his money and go on his honeymoon just before the crash of '29.

Frank Brennan, retired Bridgehampton potato farmer, remembered as a child bringing potatoes to the Simmons family and later, watching the daughters and grandchildren grow up. His memory was vague though, about the particulars of the strange family that bought the house from the Simmons Estate sometime in the mid-Fifties. They were people the neighbors would never learn much about, but would remain suspicious of, until the strangers moved away. They were Russians.

The new proprietor of the Simmons property was someone I had first heard about in the summer before that fire. Frank Zachary, then Art Director of *Holiday* magazine, had, with his family, wife Kay and two daughters Amy and Jennifer, rented the Milligan house next door to us, for the summer. Frank came over for coffee almost every morning and he and my father would talk about art and about the magazine business. Around this time Ray did an illustration for Frank, that is, for *Holiday*, which he thought was one of the best he'd ever done. As an Art Director, Frank was one of the good guys.

On one of these mornings I was headed out the door to feed my horse, who was stabled in our back yard, when I overheard Frank and Ray talking about a mad Russian, a Cossack, who lived in Bridgehampton and rode around drunk on horseback. The words horses and drunk both caught my attention, and that the man was Russian. It was the Fifties and Russians were feared, suspect, and much talked about, especially there in Eisenhower country. So that morning I lingered at the breakfast table and listened to the two men talk. Frank talked frequently about the man who I continued to think of as "The Cossack." His name was Alexey Brodovitch, and to both Frank and Ray he was considered a genius.

Brodovitch had been a Czarist cavalry officer in his youth and had fought against the Bolsheviks. A White Russian, he was exiled in Paris, where he had become a graphic artist and photographer, first designing sets for his fellow émigré, Diaghilev, and going on to design textiles and pottery, interior design and layouts for magazines. He came to America in 1930, to the School of Industrial Art at the Pennsylvania Museum, to start a department of advertising design, and a few years later became Art Director of *Harper's Bazaar*, where he stayed for almost 25 years.

From 1949 to 1951, he was Art Director and Art Editor of *Portfolio*, a graphic arts experiment that called itself a journal. Frank Zachary was editor. *Portfolio* was in fact more than a journal, it was a bold visual manifesto which declared Graphic Art to be Fine Art.

Our whole family loved Frank Zachary. I loved him because, sitting there in his khaki shorts and sandals, sipping coffee with my Old

Man, he always allowed me to be part of the conversation. He didn't seem to think it strange that on a hot summer day, a thirteen year old from a beach community was dressed in blue jeans and western boots, a polyester cowboy shirt, straw hat and spurs. "Hey," he said, in a stage whisper, as if someone was there who might take offense, "One time, back when he had the farm in Bucks County, I saw Alexey ride his horse right into the dining room!" This Russian, I thought, was a man right after my own heart!

One morning I asked Frank what happened to Brodovitch's farm in Bucks County. "The house burned to the ground," he said; "Suspicious circumstances. Maybe the wife was smoking in bed, or maybe it was the kid. They had a strange kid."

The day of the Bridgehampton fire, Brodovitch had been in New York, having left his wife and his son alone in the big house. Did she start the fire smoking in bed, or did the son start the fire, on purpose? Of the local kids who saw him occasionally, some thought Nikita, or Niki, was retarded. Others said he was slow or disturbed. Nancy Ford, who saw the fire from her bedroom window, a big orange ball behind a screen of blowing snow, remembered seeing him occasionally, a big and fat older boy with a big head, at the General Store sipping a coke, or driving his family around in a big Packard with his parents sitting in back.

Nine years before the conversation in our living room, Brodovitch had been run over near his office in Manhattan by a Hearst truck. The accident left him with a broken hip which never quite healed. He couldn't sue, because he worked for Hearst.

The year of the Sagaponack fire he lost his job anyway. Though officially he retired, most likely it was his drinking that had finally caught up with him. In 1959 his wife died. He was still in great pain from his hip injury. He became despondent and drank more. His mind began to go. At one point he was institutionalized. His friends gave up on him. In 1970 he died alone, at his home in Le Thor, France.

Alexey had been coming to the East End since the Forties. One summer during The War, he'd rented in Amagansett, at Quail Hill, and a couple of summers he'd rented in Bridgehampton. His career had run parallel with Ray's. They both started out in commercial advertising art and made it to the content part of the magazine business at about the same time, in the mid-Thirties, one as an Art

Director and the other as illustrator.

For many years Alexey had conducted design workshops that were attended by the best people in the graphic arts; photographers, art directors; people in commercial art and the fine arts. Those who were influenced by him included many people who came to visit or to live on the East End, including Otto Fenn, Richard Avedon, Bob Cato and Irving Penn. He was an artist who didn't paint. He was someone whose entrance into the Twentieth century was abrupt, shocking, and traumatic. His theory, if there was one, was connected to film. He believed in action and in the value of shock. "Astonish me," he would say, borrowing an oft repeated statement from Diaghilev.

He had been a horseman, a warrior, and a fighter of what I saw as my father's battle, the skirmish between commercial and fine art. When I first heard about him, I was having trouble fitting my father's world of art and illustration into my local world of horses and heroes, and as time went on he began to have a symbolic meaning for me.

A decade later, in the late Sixties, I was living in the renovated barn in Sagaponack that my parents had bought when they sold the Main Street house, sponging free rent. I was drinking and getting high, too much for my own good, a caricature of that decade. Occasionally, in the gloomiest part of the winter, trying to ward off depression, I would walk south towards Sagg Cemetery, where I'd commune with my maternal ancestors who had once owned all the surrounding property. Then I'd head over toward Sagg Swamp, where I'd hope to flush out a wood duck or some-such magical creature. On these walks I'd always think of Brodovitch, and in my mind's eye I'd see a ghostly presence; a uniformed man, monocled (he did wear a monocle), riding a white horse; the horse steaming and puffing in the cold, nervously sidestepping his way across the black-top, horse and rider finally disappearing into the frozen potato fields.

ALEXEY MEETS ROGER

The Murphys had known Brodovitch in Paris. In fact, Gerald had worked with Alexey on Diaghilev's scenery. Also, of course, Lucia had known everybody in Paris, including many members of the White

Russian community, including Alexey.

In Amagansett, Roger and Alexey became friends. As Roger tells it, "We used to have dinner at each other's homes occasionally, both out here and in the City. We talked about mostly art. I was interested in art and music in those days, you know, and vision. The visual arts were part of my thing possibly because of my brother having lost an eye when he was six years old, and me, I got focused in on the study of vision, see, and I'm still, well, up with that. And so that led to an interest in art, you see? And I met a lot of artists, even before I met Lucia. And when I met her, of course, all the artists that she knew were Europeans. There was a whole European colony in New York, you know. She knew them all. So, when I came home from The War, I met all these people, some of whom she had told me about when she'd written to me, you know, and so I knew something about most of them."

Roger specifically remembered that Brodovich's house, which reminded him of Gerald Murphy's original old mansion, had been built partially of stone, the kind of stone that had to be imported. "It came from New England, you know, this kind of gray stone; it had dark and light striations to it." He made the observation that there was another stone house of that type in town, the house in Montauk that locals called the Stone House; originally built by, "that guy, the lawyer who became a senator." That guy was Harrison Tweed. The house was later owned by Peter Beard, who entertained the rich, the famous and the decadent, including Mick Jagger and Andy Warhol.

Nina was Alexey's wife. With seemingly no more presence or sense of propriety than a cleaning woman, she took care of the interior of the house. She rarely went outside except to go back and forth to the city. The interior of the house was simple, with no fancy furniture or expensive art collection. There were a few Russian icons which she kept dusted, but they didn't seem to have any big importance for Alexey as they did for some of the other Russians, so Roger figured that Alexey had saved them for Nina. "She was very nice as I remember," Roger said, but neither he nor anyone else knew Nina well.

Most of the time, Alexey was in the city all week. Niki would pick him up at the train station in the Packard on Friday afternoons. Roger, who had a thing for Packards, believed Alexey's Packard was a 1940 model. "Pre-war, I think, yeah. That was a good car. Beautiful car, too. Even the last Packard they built was a terrific automobile.

Absolutely innovative all the way through. And they failed, you know, they couldn't sell enough of them. They were too expensive, for one thing. Did you know that that last Packard had automatic levelers, which became standard on other cars, maybe twenty years later? And automatic jacks if you had a flat tire. All four wheels. The jack was built in, somewhere back in there near the wheel, you know. And, a lot of innovation like that. It was terrific."

The son took care of the grounds. He mowed the grass, using a hand pushed small mower for the lawn part, and a big hay scythe for the back lots. He seemed to enjoy working in the fields. He also took care of the horses, feeding them, grooming them, and checking to see that their feet were okay. Niki was about sixteen or seventeen when Roger knew him. "He was a big fellow, like his mother, not fat, but kind of husky. He was a little retarded, but not seriously. He could take care of horses, and he could ride. He wasn't going to become an intellectual, though, that was for sure."

Roger had seen Alexey ride, and had even been offered riding lessons. "The boy can teach you," he had said. Roger remembered that he always referred to Niki as "the boy." I asked Roger about Alexey's horses. "There were six horses, I believe, when I first went there, and a horse barn, and an exercise ring, and a fenced in pasture. Each horse had his own stall. There was a large thing like a veranda that the horses could congregate in. It was fenced, but it had a roof on it. It must have been twenty feet, probably twenty-four feet wide, and the length of all those six stalls. Each stall was maybe ten feet, twelve feet. So, it was big. That barn was a quite imposing thing, you know, but not tall. A low roof. Horses don't need height. And it had a fan at one end of the stable, for ventilation. It was a nice job. A very beautifully built thing. It was maybe a hundred feet from the house. When you approached the house as a guest you couldn't see the stable because of the shrubbery and all that. But from the kitchen, you could see the horses.

"One thing I do remember is Brodovitch did not have what you'd call landscaped grounds. It was sort of wild. He liked landscaping that was natural looking. None of that special bush here and special bush there, none of that. So the upkeep was small."

One day Roger and Alexey were having a conversation and Alexey said, "I'm going to go down to Mexico next week because I've got to see this fellow Jake Spencer. He doesn't want to come to New York and there are some important things I have to talk to him about."

Harper's Bazaar had a caricature page every month and often used Spencer, one of the top New York caricaturists at the time.

Spencer had lived in Greenwich Village in the 1930s and was a friend of famous Greenwich Village Poet-Alcoholic and member of the Raven Poetry Circle, Max Bodenheim. Ben Hecht wrote a play about Bodenheim's life, titled *Winkelberg*.

"I'll only be there a couple of days," Alexey said. It happened that Roger knew Spencer and had been to his house in Oaxaca, so Alexey invited Roger along, all expenses paid. He offered to pay but Alexey insisted. (*Harper's Bazaar* gave Alexey a substantial expense account.) They flew to Mexico City and then took a bus to Oaxaca, a couple hundred miles from Mexico City. Spencer's house was on the same street as the Oaxaca Cathedral. According to Roger, "It was a marvelous house that he'd designed himself and had local craftsmen build. It was on ten acres of land overlooking a ridge. Today, it's some sort of museum."

Alexey had asked Spencer to do a caricature of somebody, "Some famous person that Jake had met and didn't like," according to Roger. The trip was a success because Alexey convinced him to do it. That was the only purpose to the trip. "So he did it," Roger said, "But, Jesus Christ, it was so insulting, this caricature, that when Brodovitch published it, the guy threatened to sue Brodovitch and Spencer and *Harper's Bazaar* for defamation. He sure as shit was a good caricaturist. That's all he did! And he had fun with it!' And Alexey loved it too, the caricature and the whole uproar."

During the winter that the Brodovitch house burned, Roger was in Florida. He and Lucia had a winter house in Sanibel then. It was Roger who got Rauschenberg to come visit that area first, some years before he bought in Captiva. They returned in mid-May and drove over to see the wreckage. They saw what was left of the stone wall and the chimney. "But the house was gone, there was nothing left. Absolutely nothing. It was just a charred mass. Very depressing. And I don't remember when I saw him after that. But, it was so sad. I do remember that the last time I talked to him, he'd rented a house on Hedges Lane, near where it connects with Sagg Road. I think it was second from the corner. He was planning this Long Island paper. It was next to Ludwig Sander's house. The two houses were similar. Not big. Only Lud had added a studio onto his."

What Roger and Alexey shared was a broad concept of art, different from that of a painter. They were both interested in physics and in what we today call hi-tech and its relationship to art. Early in their relationship, Alexey asked Roger why he had so many artist friends. "Why didn't I have more friends in industry, you know? And I said, 'Because they're boring people.' Art was so interesting, that's why I liked artists, you know? They're the most interesting people, as a class, if you wanna call it a class. They know more about life and about the world. They have a broad unity. Most artists have a broad knowledge of everything. They know something about music, literature, in addition to art, history and geography and God knows what all, you know? I think that's characteristic of artists in general. I have never found one that was narrow minded, you know, ignorant. But I don't remember very many businessmen I ever met who knew anything other than their fucking business. That's it. They didn't know anything about music, they knew nothing about art, nothing about literature, poetry, whatever, anything. Just their business, that's it."

According to Roger, Alexey admired many artists, but his favorite was Gorky; "And, of course, Alexey could meet any artist he wanted. But he knew Gorky and I knew Gorky, you know? Lucia spoke Gorky's language, too. Armenian. And Gorky was a great guy. I liked him. He was a lot of fun, but he was apparently one of those, what do you call it? He'd be depressed, then he'd be on a high, then he'd be depressed (manic-depressive.) He never went out when he was depressed, you see. He didn't go out to parties, or he rarely did. But he'd come to dinner at our house when he was out here, or we would see him in the city."

KLOON AND DE KLINING

When I asked Roger, "When Alexey thought up this idea about a Long Island magazine, was this going to be a real magazine? Not a newspaper?" He said, "Well, he wanted a block format, similar to PM.* PM had better printing and better editing than any of the other dailies. And he wanted to use magazine stock, you know, coated stock. So it was a great idea. Instead of a magazine that's got a limited size and all that, and stapled together, all that shit, he just wanted it to be loose, with good color printing, good quality paper, and, you know, the art would be the main thing. Maybe put a big de Kooning or a Gorky or whatever, on the cover, you know? Each week a different artist, with one picture. The whole page, you know, that would be that. He wanted to tie together Long Island and painting. He was aware of all the artists around here. And, I remember talkin' to him about having big quality color photographs of paintings in it. I said, 'Well, one week you won't need any color, for Franz Kline!' We laughed about that. But before he could get the magazine off the ground, he came down with dementia.

*In mid-century there were several radical newspapers in New York, including "The Daily Worker," PM and "The National Guardian," which became "The Guardian." PM was, like "The Daily Worker," backed by The American Communist Party. "The Guardian," started in 1948 by backers of Henry Wallace, though also radical, was more independent from the Communist Party than PM.)

"I remember another incident when we talked about Kline and de Kooning," Roger added. "That's when Kline started putting color in his black and white paintings, not, you know, all over the place, but he began to put some patches of color here and there, and at the same time, de Kooning began to paint some black and white paintings. So Alexey said, 'Well, I'm going to have to call them Kloon and de Klining!' We had a lot of laughs over that. But when I told Harold Rosenberg about that remark he sniffed. 'That's demeaning. Insulting to the artist.'" I said, "No, no. You don't know Alexey. He'd never insult an artist."

I told Roger that I thought some of that Art Crowd were terrible snobs, and that I was going to say so in this book. I said, "I mention in the book that when I was a kid, the local kids that I grew up with in Amagansett Grade School, they would make fun of my father's abstracts. And then in the summer, when I would run into some of these city kids whose parents were part of the Manhattan art world (Le Monde, as Tom Wolfe would call it), they would insult my father by saying, "He's just a commercial artist." And so I was always sort of pissed off at them, because of course I knew that the kids were getting this from their parents, and they, most of them, it seemed to me, were junior elitists. Some of these painters and critics, like Harold Rosenberg, thought that what they represented was such high culture (and I guess my parents, and therefore, I, agreed with them about that), that everyone who didn't accept it was selling out.

And of course that was related to a political revolution. And yet, when offered, the artists lined up for the big bucks. Wasn't that selling out?"

To which Roger said, "Oh yeah. Some of them were like that, but not all of them. Bill (de Kooning) was the least interested in money of all those artists. I know that for a fact, because I knew Bill for fifty, sixty years. Even before the War. And, it's amazing! He was never interested in money. He didn't give a damn. He used it when he had it, but it wasn't something that was on his mind. He never calculated how to make paintings that would sell. He never thought about the money. And I think he's the only artist that I ever knew who didn't have any interest in the money, in the worth of his work. He was always a little surprised when he got a bunch of money."

And Roger went on to site examples of Bill's profligacy, tales which are legendary and legion on the East End, but which someone like Roger would be in a position to know about first hand. And I believed him, still believe him, sort of. I knew de Kooning well enough to believe that his personality was pretty set in its ways, and that he believed in his painting and loved to paint. When he wasn't working he didn't have another life in which he planned and choreographed his career, worked the room, played the political games; he went straight to playing. Women, booze and good conversation; about painting. That, I think, was why he was loved so. But of course booze eventually put the period at the end of his life, as it has for more people than I care to think about.

"Kline didn't care much about money, either," Roger added. "But a lot of them did, you're right about that. A lot of them were real money conscious. And they'd do all kinds of manipulations to get a good review, a good gallery and all that. But Bill de Kooning never did." And he didn't have to, because his wife, Elaine, even when they were separated, was a dedicated manager of his career.

"He never did, and he didn't care about clothes, either," Roger said. He went on to tell me about the time he gave him a brand new overcoat one winter, at a time when Bill had plenty of money but just hadn't thought to buy a coat. "But you're right about the others, Tony. Painters and sculptors, they were always thinking, scheming, how they were going to get more money, what the prices were going to be, how they could get the prices up, get a good criticism and so on and so forth. Buttering up critics and shit like that, you know.

"I'll never forget an art critic by the name of Sam Hunter was working on a book on contemporary art. He had written articles in art magazines and was now a professor of art history at Princeton. A real pain in the ass. But he was an influential critic, and I remember a party we had at my house. And Sam Hunter was telling everybody, oh, a whole gang of artists, you know, he's standing there talking to two or three others, and they're all like waiting for every fucking word out of his mouth, because he's an influential critic. And I'm sitting on the couch next to his wife, Hunter's wife, and she was a nice lady. Anyway. So he says, 'Well, the reason Ad Reinhardt is probably the greatest artist in this particular period is because more students imitate his work than any other artist.' And I thought that was such an idiotic statement that I jumped up and I said, 'Sam, you're absolutely full of shit and you know it! That's ridiculous! That's an insane remark!' And, he was furious, you know. But his wife was sitting there and she started applauding. She was clapping! Said, 'Bravo, Roger.' But, anyway, he huffed and puffed and he walked away, and the whole group that was hanging on his every word, they didn't know what to think!

"I never did like the man. I didn't like what he wrote, he used his imagination when he wrote criticism. He attributed titles, and, you know, motives, for an artist's work or whatever. 'Oh, this painting is obviously influenced by the green of the trees in the spring and and la la la, all that kind of stuff. Had nothing to do with it, just because it had some green. You know, had nothing to do with it. He didn't ask the artist. You know, he just imagined. And a few times he got called out by other critics, you know. Not very often, though. He was a famous critic and art historian. All shit, you know? Now that was a guy who was really snobby.

"Rothko was another good guy (like de Kooning.) He was just a kind of a straight-faced guy. He reminded me of Buster Keaton. He had a deadpan face like Keaton. Very seldom saw him smile. He was alright. All the good guys commit suicide you know."

JEFFREY POTTER

By 1950 Babe and Carl Erickson were gone and there was a glamour vacuum in the little village of Amagansett that was quickly being filled by the emergence of two handsome young couples, Jeffrey and Penelope Potter and Peter and Patsy Matthiessen. From a kid's perspective, they seemed to just suddenly be there, since I wasn't then concerned with the logistics of adult's lives.

Jeffrey Potter and Peter Matthiessen were upper-class men who could have belonged to the Maidstone Club but did not. They were of a more liberal mind-set and traveled in too cultured and bohemian a social circle to be comfortable among bankers and corporate executives.

Potter had come to the East End in the late fall of 1948, and fell in love with and bought a house with a lot of land to the north of Amagansett Main Street; a dairy called Stony Hill Farm. He met Matthiessen soon after and before long had rented Peter and Patsy a renovated barn on the property.

Pollock had been living in his house in Springs for several years, and the Matthiessens had already met him and Jeffrey met Jackson when he was just in the process of buying the Hamlin Farm. Mrs. Hamlin, recently widowed, was still living in the main house on the property and Jeffrey was turning one of the barns into a livable rental home. Potter and Pollock met when the artist was driving through the woods in his Model A Ford on one of the many dirt roads in the woods of the farm property, doing what today is called off-roading. Pollock stopped and the two had a friendly conversation about cars. It was the winter of 1948, during the period, 1948 to sometime in 1950 when Pollock had two years of shaky, intermittent sobriety and during which he completed some of his best work. Jeffrey would become one of several male friends in the area who tried to help Pollock with his drinking problem. Among Pollock's other helpers in those years were Dr. Heller, a local G.P. and Roger Wilcox, who befriended and, in his own words, practiced amateur psychotherapy on Jackson.

In their fanciful book, *Jackson Pollock, an American Saga*, the writers Steven Naifeh and Gregory White Smith make the following grossly untrue statement about Jeffrey. "To Potter, Jackson embodied the elusive blend of artistic sensibility and hands-on, masculine efficacy (he could fix a car and wield a hammer), that Potter himself, the would-be writer-engineer, aspired to." To say the least, that's just plain not true. Jeffrey was a certified master mechanic who had been enamored of cars all his life and first learned to love them through his friendship with his father's chauffeur.

Born in Manhattan in 1918 to Mary Barton Atterbury, the daughter of John Turner Atterbury, and J.W. Fuller Potter Jr., a stockbroker and a governor of the New York Stock Exchange, Jeffrey was the youngest of five, with two brothers and two sisters. He was seven years younger than his next youngest sibling and grew up as an only child in a large L-shaped townhouse house at 133 East 55th St. on the corner of Lexington Avenue in Manhattan. Because his parents divorced when he was very young and because his father was working, he was raised by servants, a half dozen Irish people from County Cork, in a sort of upstairs/downstairs kind of a household.

The most important figure in the household for Jeffrey was Mike, a big man with an enormous belly, who had been their coachman before they switched over to cars and had never learned to drive very well. All the cars had to have the steering wheel raised so that he could get his big belly behind it.

Jeffrey said, "Mike taught me the proper way to wash a car. In those days car bodies were varnished and very delicate. They scratched easily. Which meant you had to have a special sponge for the running gear, the so-called wheels and chassis, and a different sponge for the body; and then, also for the body, a chamois. And lots of brass polish! Even as a small boy I did a great deal of brass polishing." And, Jeffrey added, he took great pride in it.

Jeffrey told me that Mike humanized cars meaning, it was clear that he anthropomorphized them, adding, "Even while driving them, he would talk to his cars; about their behavior and so forth, which in fact I've found myself doing throughout my life. And if I really hate something, some Thing, and I can see it as a natural being, well, I find that very useful."

Jeffrey was a friend of my parents and I knew him from the time I was a small child. Over the years I talked with him on many occasions and always found him to be an engrossing conversationalist, for his knowledge, his sense of humor, and his wonderful manner of speech, which was a snappy, humorous mixture of Groton and old fashioned upper-class East Coast English.

He had attended St. Bernard's, a day school with an English faculty. He intensely disliked school and took some hard knocks as a result of a bad stammer, which he was grateful to have outgrown. "In our classrooms we had free standing desks. The teacher, called the Master, kept a soccer ball on the floor beside his desk pumped up till it was rock hard. If you failed to pay attention he would throw it at you and when it hit you it knocked you backwards in your chair, and the desk would tip backward and the inkwell would empty into your lap. Then when you got home you had to explain why you were covered in ink."

He did so poorly at his studies that he wasn't allowed to graduate, and thought that he'd get out of going to Groton; he was therefore very disappointed when the headmaster informed him, "Potter! Don't you know? All Potters go to Groton." And so he went.

His father had inherited money and had added to his wealth when he married Mary Atterbury. As Mary Barton Atterbury continued through life, she had four husbands, and with all those stepchildren it became complicated as to who was step and who was half and who was zero. His maternal grandfather, John Turner Atterbury, who had died in 1912, before Jeffrey was born, had been an investment banker, "In the true sense of what that then meant," Jeffrey added. "What they would do, is invest your money for you, but on the basis of a bank as opposed to a brokerage firm. It was much more conservative. They particularly liked bonds and so forth. And no big return.

One of the Atterbury cousins had been president of the Pennsylvania Railroad and had left each of Grandfather Atterbury's four daughters a considerable fortune. The line of inheritance became confusing though, when Mary Barton and her sister married Jeffrey's father and his brother, resulting in their children being double-first cousins.

Jeffrey's father's maternal grandfather, Dr. Eliphalet Nott, had been a partner in the Fuller-Welling Stove Company in Troy N.Y. and a builder and designer of coal stoves. One of twelve children and self-educated, he grew up on a farm, got his doctorate of divinity at 24. He spent 60 years as president of Union College, and during that time educated 66 college presidents. He was a punster in Latin and Greek and an inveterate designer of stoves, and developed a special stove for using anthracite coal. When he died in 1866 he left what was considered a huge fortune of over a million dollars. Most important to Jeffrey as a child, though, was that he gave Troy its first fire engine.

Included on his father's side were a long line of Episcopal bishops, including Bishop Horatio Potter who was the founder of the Cathedral at St. John the Divine in New York, and Horatio's son, Henry Codman Potter, under whose leadership the cornerstone of the Cathedral was laid.

Jeffrey's sisters Polly and Helen both went to Fermata School for Girls, in Aiken, SC, a very genteel little school that, at the time, was even more horsey than the Foxcroft School, also nearby, in Middleburg Va. Helen Fuller Potter was the oldest. She served in World War II as a Red Cross Club driver in England, and then, after D-Day, on the continent. After The War, in order to keep active, she bought a motel outside Aiken. It was a disaster. Within a month of her buying the motel, the highway there was closed. Helen, a very funny, witty woman, according to Jeffrey, "liked alcohol rather too much." She also loved animals, and devoted her life to them.

"Next came Polly, the younger sister and also a horsewoman of note," Jeffrey added. As a child Jeffrey was very attached to Polly, partly because she had boyfriends who had wonderful cars; Bubastis, Isotta-Fraschinis, Minervas, "I mean, Mercedes were kind of boring, really. Her boyfriends' cars were really great."

Tommy Hitchcock, famous polo player and WWI flying ace, was just one of many famous horsemen who pursued Polly, who eventually married an Englishman by the name of Ivor Balding. Balding's grandfather, a Brit, supplied horses for European circuses and for the London Public Transportation. Ivor David Balding, b. 1942 is a circus consultant for theater and film. Balding, along with his brothers Barney and Gerald, were the top polo players in the world in the Thirties. Ivor later became the manager of Sonny Whitney's racing stables.

Fuller, Jeffrey's oldest brother, was an artist. "He studied in Paris," Jeffrey told me, "and then in New York with Paul Kuhn. When he was 31 he married a fourteen year-old Appalachian girl he met while on a painting trip in the hills of Tennessee." According to Jeffrey, this charming young girl was, the last he knew, "still alive down in North Carolina. A petite blond with brown eyes, she had not learned to read or write when Fuller met her, and had never seen a movie or worn store-bought clothes. She had two children with Fuller, and then, while the children were still small, went back to the mountains, leaving the two kids in New York, where they were raised by Fuller and his mother. The older child, a boy, was an alcoholic and went back to the mountains after growing up in New York. The girl, Mary Barton, also went back to the mountains and worked with the poor in social services. They were close with their father and stayed in touch with him."

When Fuller died, in 1990, it was a great loss for Jeffrey. "We had this lovely psychic thing between us. I almost always knew if when the phone rang, it was he. One of those strange things. We were very close. He was a funny man and charming."

Fuller had another son, by his second marriage, named Daniel Potter, who at last count lived in Stonington, Connecticut. Dan Potter is a sculptor who's married to a woman, "Who's very high on Zen. In fact they've built a Zen temple there. Like his father, he's a charming guy. His younger brother was the Maharishi's (Transcendental Meditation) right hand man, aide de camp and so forth."

"Incidentally," Jeffrey added, for my benefit, "Fuller met Jackson Pollock down here at our house at Stony Hill Farm. Jackson had come by for a drink and Fuller went back to his studio that afternoon with him to look at some of the work he'd never seen except in reproduction, and he didn't get back to the farm until about two in the morning. The next day Fuller went to New York and joined Alcoholics Anonymous.

"So out of all these rather neurotic tendencies in the family some interesting people come. And then the last one is very prickly, which is fine by me because I never liked him; my hideous brother Charlie, who was the hero of Groton School. Captain of the football team. He's the reason I've always hated athletics. Captain of everything you can be. All his life he worked for a trust company which belonged to the family of a Groton friend. He was a foundation executive taking the Concorde back and forth to Paris. That's how they spent the foundation's money, money that was supposed to go to the poor. He had a daughter by a fine woman, an actress, a charming woman, but when he married a very rich woman in Chicago, he abandoned the girl. We had a great falling out, he and I.

"Charlie's daughter, a charming woman herself, is a psychotherapist. There are other hideous tales about Charlie which I won't bore you with. I just can't believe that with the kind of education and background and all the rest of it, that he turned out the way he did. Particularly Groton School, which is supposed to be teaching you the ethics and morality of Christianity. To end up that way is very sad."

Charlie died two years ago in the airport in Chicago on the way to come to see Jeffrey, to see if he could somehow heal the breach. "It was a nice little flicker of fate, because it, Charlie's death, obviously made me feel guilty. He hadn't been well, had a heart condition, and had had an amputation for circulatory reasons." Finally, he was coming to see his little brother. "He was a drinker too, though he wasn't incapacitated by it, as Fuller was."

Jeffrey's involvement with the East End began in 1919, at the age of one, with summers at the family's summer home at Shinnecock. Grosvenor Atterbury, Jeffrey's mother's first cousin, was a famous architect of that period, and, as Jeffrey said, "A very, very good one, indeed."

Atterbury had built a great many private houses in New York City and also summer houses in Southampton; long, rambling versions of the "Shingle Cottage" type. In Shinnecock, Atterbury owned Sugar Loaf Hill, which overlooks the bay, and on the east side of the hill he had built and designed a house for himself which had lovely views of the bay. On the west side of Sugar Loaf, Grosvenor had built a house for Jeffrey's father, which also looked out across the bay and over the barrier dunes that Jeffrey's father owned.

His father had plans for those dunes. "They were land that he was going to someday build his dream house on, those high dunes. But he never accomplished that and there were two reasons for it. Number one being that the '29 crash took care of the dreams. And secondly, there was the '38 hurricane when the dunes went out to sea.

"There were all of six houses in Shinnecock in those days. It was really wild country. In fact for my brothers and me it was magical. It was very much like the moors of Scotland and was loaded with Indian artifacts, arrowheads and flints and so forth. And the guide to the artifacts was our gardener (though we didn't have much of a garden), a Shinnecock Indian named Anthony Beaman who was a nice old man. He claimed to be the medicine man for the tribe. And it wasn't until about ten years ago I found out he was not the medicine man at all. But I always believed him. And he had a lovely, lovely black bottle and whenever we asked about it he said it was oil for the lawn mower. But what he really kept in the bottle was some of my father's Jamaica rum.

"Summer at Shinnecock was a great and simple life. We had a windmill, which is where we got our water from, which didn't pump when there was no wind, so of course, we used to run out of water, which was fine, because then we didn't have to wash. All the servants, Mary O'Brien and the whole gang, came to Shinnecock with us, and every Sunday morning they would go in the Model T to Mass in Southampton, taken by old Mike. Mike would cover the cars with blankets at night to keep the dew off. They would go to the Stone Church (because his father insisted upon it), the rich people's church, not to the wooden church, the one known as the Polish Church, where most of the servants of the summer colony went."

Though Jeffrey was seven years younger than his brothers, they would on occasion, take him along with them on camping trips to Montauk. "In the early days, when we first went down there, it was a sand road still, not paved. And the car we had then, which was great for that terrain, was a new Model T Ford station wagon. They were great for that, you know, because you could slip the speed bands, almost like an automatic transmission, and get through sand pretty well.

"It was like a foreign country, you know, there was such great adventure, lots of game, ducks and so forth, and we had tents too. It was all to do with the great outdoors, you know. Though we sometimes slept in tents, we were always near the hunting lodge of a friend of father's, Jack Prentice. And of course even there, one could get a cocktail. One time my father almost got drowned down there in the surf, and, as always, I think his bravado with the surf was encouraged by martinis. It was just pure luck he got washed in, because he was out cold. And that was traumatic for all the kids, both me and my siblings."

It happened that I interviewed Jeffrey at a time when I had recently read a book about the Southampton Summer Colony, a bastion for the Catholic rich at the turn of the century and up into the mid-Twentieth, so I asked Jeffrey if he'd known any of them. "Did you know any of the McDonalds or Harrises or Murrays?* "Oh yes," he said, "Old Charlie McDonald, a fellow founder of the National Golf Club in Southampton, was a friend of my father. I knew him as a child."

*Though they were Irish (The McDonalds, Harrises, and Murrays) they were not considered nouveau riche because they were second and third generation, and they'd done very well in the stock market. So they were somewhat accepted by the Wasps. And, according to Jeffrey, his father was so gregarious and open that he was more accepting of people out of his class than might have been the norm.

"My father was a broker and a club man. He founded the Links Club in New York. And he wasn't really a member of the Racquet there, but I think that what he was doing quite a bit of with some of his big customers was helping them along socially, helping them to get into these clubs and so forth. Which I'm glad he did, you know. He was a much-loved man, was my father. But he was a child. He never left Groton School. He loved it so. He brought a Groton mentality with him to the Stock Exchange, lots of practical jokes and things. Of course, that's why he was so ill-equipped to handle the '29 crash. He remained convinced it was going to come back. And within a week, everything was gone, and indeed it didn't come back.

"He lost a great deal. And what happened there was, a lot of his customers, big customers, Whitneys and Vanderbilts and so on, had huge domestic staffs. And he loved servants, was very nice to them, and vice versa. Therefore, what he did was, because they wanted to invest money, he would, you know, invest it for them, on margin.

"This was before The Crash and, therefore, he would buy stocks and trade for them on his own account, but for them. And when the crash came he told them not to worry, you know, he'd guarantee all their accounts and he'd take care of it. And it didn't take him long to be wiped out.

"But his brother, my uncle, was a fellow partner in the firm. He, luckily (financially, that is, for his family), died. He died in July and the crash was in September of '29. So when he died, they had unloaded a lot of stocks quickly because of things coming up like taxes and so forth, so his kids were not hit like our family was.

"Ultimately, though, what happened was that my father got into such bad shape that everything gradually went, one by one. We were left with three very nice people in the staff of our house. Mike never left and the cook never left, because it got that bad that they had no place to go. At least there in the house they had a bed and they got fed. And there was always the chance of a job coming up. And dear Mike, in my father's last years, this sounds incredible, but he was giving my father an allowance of five dollars a week to help him with small stuff. And then for a while my mother, his ex-wife, helped him financially. And when she no longer did, the children, all five of us, helped him. I was only then about fourteen.

"How it was done legally, I don't know. But all of us assigned our interest in the family trusts, there were two of them, to our father, to guarantee his seat. And of course when he couldn't pay the dues on his seat, then the trusts went, and I ended up, as a kid, with nothing left but a small savings account at Corn Exchange Bank, which also went, eventually, to my father for, as he said, petty cash. And when I demurred a bit, he said, 'You know, after all, Jeff, you wouldn't have even that money if it hadn't been for my friends.' So, it went.

"By that time, of course, because of alcohol, he was really half mad. His main concern at this time, I think, was to not declare bankruptcy, which he maintained a gentleman would never do. It had nothing to do with what a gentleman might do to his children in order to avoid bankruptcy, of course. The same moral code didn't apply there."

When Jeffrey went to Groton, his mother paid some of his tuition costs, and, unbeknownst to Jeffrey, The Reverend Endicott Peabody, a friend of his father who knew about his financial condition, gave him a scholarship.

"Mind you," Jeffrey said, "I was doing so badly, that out of the mandatory eight courses, I was only at that time taking four. And the only ones of those that I passed were English and Sacred Studies. But I was allowed to stay on because of being a Potter. There had been a Potter every year at Groton since the founding bishop on the board, who was a friend of the rector. And just the other day I discovered, to my amusement, there had been fourteen Potters at Groton before I got there. And the same was true of the Century Club in New York, fourteen Potters before I got there. At the Century Club, though, alas, there is no scholarship."

Jeffrey never finished Groton. Instead, he joined the work force. At seventeen he went to work as a cub reporter, just above a copy boy, on a daily newspaper in Columbia, South Carolina. He was a Yankee come down there in the Depression in 1936, not a bit popular either, as a Yankee and for getting a job that could have gone to a Southerner. On top of that, the job had been gotten through social influence, through friends of his mother who owned a paper company and had bought the newspaper to control the news and lessen the heavy criticism they were getting for poisoning the local rivers with their paper mills. His first story was about a Brownie troop, and then, as a promotion, he was assigned to do one on the Girl Scouts. In spite of a hostile work environment though, he soon became friendly with the Fire Chief, and did several features on the firemen, fires they had fought and on the fire trucks themselves, some of which, to Jeffrey's mind, had fascinating histories.

Eventually they sent him out to the local prison's death house, to visit a very young black man, a minor, who had been found guilty of murder. During his discussions with the boy, Jeffrey saw he was illiterate, immature, and, "Unquestionably gay, not that we used that word then. He was a harmonica virtuoso!"

The young man was sentenced to the electric chair and Jeffrey was given the assignment of covering the electrocution, which was very gruesome. "When the signal was given to turn on the juice, which the warden did by tapping the floor with his cane, everything seemed to be working, the switchboard and rheostats came on, but nothing happened at all, except the poor kid lurched from the chair. They had forgotten to connect the ground cable. So there was no juice. I thought, oh well, hurray. Justice has been carried out and the guy can go free. Nothing of the kind. They connected the ground and this time they really gave it to him, to the extent that smoke came pouring out of his helmet. A vicious tale.

"They took him out in a sitting position and as we passed the room where they had placed his body, there on the table he was still in a sitting position, but on his back. Then, for our benefit, the twelve witnesses and the press, being myself, a large jailer with a wooden mallet broke each of the joints in his limbs to straighten them out. And then the sheriff said to us, "Now, folks, let that be a lesson to you. That's what happens to bad Darkies." And that was not that long ago, you know? That was in 1938. Astounding.

"I wrote my article, and of course, put that in, and my long column was whittled down to one paragraph, captioned, "Justice was Carried Out."

After that, Jeffrey left South Carolina in a rage, and began his next career; engine building apprentice. Again, it was through social contacts that he got the job at a factory in Ohio that made Diesel engines. The plant owner's wife happened to be a former girlfriend of "My evil brother Charlie," as Jeffrey routinely referred to his oldest brother. Charlie knew the young woman, whose father happened to be Charles E. Mitchell, chairman of the National City Bank (later Citibank), from the Southampton Summer Colony at Shinnecock Hills. "By the way," Jeffrey added, "That fellow, Mitchell, should have gone to jail for tax evasion. But with a good lawyer, he didn't. But anyway, that's how I got the job."

Most of the skilled laborers at the plant were Germans and very skilled mechanics. They were building engines for ships and for locomotives. It was, Jeffrey assured me, good training for a Groton boy. The men were hard taskmasters. They worked ten hour days, six days a week. All the fitting was done by hand. It was an intense, in depth course in working-class values and pride. He stayed there for six years and earned the equivalent of a PhD in Diesel Mechanics.

After being an apprentice for the first three months, he was promoted to helper, which meant more money. Instead of getting 33 and a third cents an hour, he was getting 95 cents. He began sending four dollars a month to his father. Although the factory wasn't union, the men did have an informal committee and they appointed Jeffrey to be their liaison with management, and that led him to a job as Assistant Works Manager. From his boss the Works Manager, Jeffrey learned Machine Shop German.

From there he was promoted to a very nice job which he liked a lot, as engineer of a revolutionary locomotive. He was the guaranty engineer and demonstrator on railroads in the mid-west for a Diesel Hydraulic Locomotive which was far superior to its predecessors. The War, unfortunately, killed further development of that machine, and the shop became more and more geared toward the war industry, growing to about 2,000 men.

4-F from the military for being blind in one eye and color-blind, Jeffrey landed a job as assistant to the engineer on a merchant ship, where his Groton accent and youthful demeanor caused him serious grief from the ship's mean and tough crew. After a couple of trips he used family connections to get himself out of that unhappy situation by joining the American Field Service. He was assigned to an Ambulance Unit attached to the Royal Indian Army, part of the British Army, in the India-Burma Theater. Though he was supposed to be an ambulance driver, there were no ambulances available, so he had to be content with being a stretcher bearer.

With no Commander, he was able to continually reassign himself, going from regiment to regiment whenever one pulled out; staying at the front. He went out on night patrols with squads or platoons and brought in the wounded, and quickly developed a good rapport with the Indian troops.

"The Japanese had overrun Burma at the start of The War, the whole way out. They came up to Rangoon and Siam from both sides. They controlled that country for almost four years. We were part of the first wave going back into Burma after the British had been routed, the units going into Burma, about 20 battalions in all, were mostly Indian. Five, perhaps six, were still British. In most cases, one company would be Hindu, one company would be Muslim, and so forth, mixed that way into battalions."

Of the three or four different battalions he was with, the last was the Gurkhas, the Sikhs, and it was they who he liked the best. He found them "interesting people to work with," partly because he was fascinated with their religion. He stayed with the Gurkha battalion until they took Rangoon just after the Armistice. The war went on out there five more weeks after the signing because the opposing Japanese thought it was a trick. During that time, none of the troops wanted to stick their neck out, and so they took very heavy casualties.

Before he went home, Jeffrey decided to spend some time in Hyderabad, the center of the Sikh faith. He accomplished this by using the excuse that he wanted to find some Field Service people who seemed to have disappeared. Military discipline had become very casual and disorganized. He found no Field Service personnel, but did manage to stay on for a month.

Even in non-Sikh battalions, many of the doctors were Sikhs. Two of the medical officers that he served with, and with whom he became friendly, were Sikh. They encouraged Jeffrey to go with them to Amritsar, in the northwest, which was the Sikh capital and the home of the Holy Golden Temple of the Sikhs. Jeffrey decided that after first returning home he would return to take instruction in the

Sikh faith, but he never went back.

PENNY

When Jeffrey returned from Southeast Asia, his brother Charlie's connections came in handy again. Charlie happened to know Richard Aldrich, the husband of Gertrude Lawrence, a great star of the theater at that time. Jeffrey liked the theater and had just been trying his hand at writing a play. With Charlie's help he applied for and got a job as stage manager at a theater in Dennis, Cape Cod, doing a production of *Pygmalion*. The play went on to Broadway and Jeffrey went with it, still as Stage Manager. He was there for three years and it was there that he met his first wife, Penny.

One winter weekend in 1948, just to get away from the city, he and Penny drove out to East Hampton and checked into The 1770 House. It was near dusk and starting to snow when they arrived, but they decided that before checking in, they would sightsee a bit. They headed east to Amagansett Main Street and then up Old Stone Highway, toward the highland of the village. The snow had become heavy and the visibility poor. They turned west onto Town Lane through some old timbered woods and then past a white fence, and, "Just barely, through the snow, I could see a sign saying 'Farm for Sale, 100 Acres, Three Houses,' and I thought, Jesus, how about that!"

That night at The 1770 House, Jeffrey kept thinking about that sign. The next morning he dragged Penny out to look for it again. In the peaceful and countrified landscape of new fallen snow they lost their bearings and ended up going round and round, ending up way out in the Northwest Woods where they spent all morning retracing their own car tracks. It was early afternoon before they finally found the farm. They drove up the driveway to the side door of the main house, where they came upon an old man shoveling snow off the porch.

As Jeffrey got out of the car to say hello, thinking this might be the owner, the old man leaned on his shovel, "And he said this remarkable line, which was, 'Ah! It's come you are at last!' And, really, my hair practically stood on end. And he told us it was for sale, had been for a long time, and he knew the place was just right for us. Then he said, 'I'll tell ya, come and take a walk.' And we walked up to the hill by Stony Hill Road where there was a wooden water tank." (Years later Jeffrey tore it down to use the wood for paneling in a new house.)

"Anyway, on this clear day, looking toward the ocean clearly visible a mile away, I saw what seemed to be, up in the sky above us, a freighter going along the shore. Of course, it's a very strange optical illusion, you know, that somehow you know you are looking straight out but yet you're looking up. I thought, 'God, this is the place, it must be, if it has this magic.' And I turned to the old man who said, 'Ah, you saw it!' I said Yeah."

'Well,' he said, 'it's like the place. Wherever you look, it'll be yours. Come on.' We went back, and he introduced us to Mrs. Hamlin, who was where she spent most of her time, on the sofa in the living room in front of a big fireplace kept going by Jimmy."

His name was Jimmy Mundell and he was what they used to call a black Irishman, a Protestant. He had been Mr. Hamlin's right-hand man on the dairy that Hamlin had run until his death. Jeffrey made a deal with Mrs. Hamlin according to which they would rent the house for the summer, with an eye toward buying it, and the rent for the summer would be the cost of fixing the plumbing. The plumber they employed was George Schellinger, a plumber and a hunter and a trainer of dogs, at that time Brittany Spaniels. He was also a reputed ladies' man.

"All the plumbing in the house was rusted out and so was everything else, and the floors were giving way. It was kind of a creepy summer, no screens and a new baby, and a not very happy bride, and over the summer we had a great many meetings with Mrs. Hamlin because, as I remember, the place was on the Previews market for a hundred and forty thousand and we ended getting it for thirty one thousand, with a hundred acres, three houses and about five barns, including that exceptional one, the old dairy barn, which at the time was being leased by a local farmer, Roy Lester."

Lester continued to rent the dairy barn, another barn he used for raising pigs and some pasture. Roy and Jeffrey became instant friends, since they both shared a love of vehicles, both internal combustion and horse-drawn. Lester eventually became Jeffrey's tenant; "because we needed a tenant. Roy was married, and, I think he had his daughter by then, too. And since we had the plumbing fixed, I figured we were okay. But then the next problem, since he was going to be there year around, was the heat. The furnace in the main house was shot and so were the radiators and everything else, so we had to do that. Every time I turned around in that place, for years, we had more expenses.

"The next thing I heard was that Mrs. Hamlin, at some tea at Guild Hall when Mrs. Woodhouse, great benefactor of East Hampton Village, was still alive, with her white gloves and all the rest of it there, at Guild Hall, had said to several people that she'd sold her dear Stony Hill Farm to this young couple from New York and she was very worried because she was afraid we'd have artists living up in her trees. End of Stony Hill."

The main house, which Jeffrey and Penny lived in, had originally been on Amagansett Main Street next to its twin, the Baker House, which had been home to the owners of Baker Brother's Dairy. The Hamlins had moved the big house in the winter of 1915, pulling it, the way it was done in those days, with oxen, block and tackle, and a capstan, across the frozen fields between Main Street and the Farm.

In 1953 Jeffrey moved a Main Street barn belonging to the Conklin family up to the farm. He intended it to be a garage, replacing the previous garage which had been made into a home and was being rented by the Matthiessens. But as soon as the new building was in place Jeffrey decided it too should be a rental house, and began fixing it up. Eventually, they had four barns converted into houses. One summer, Arthur Miller and Marilyn Monroe rented one. The rental business had become quite profitable.

Jeffrey hired several local fellows to do the carpentry. One day, Penny and Jeffrey were in the car heading out to do shopping and one of the men, a retired mason, was coming up the road, walking to work. It was October and it was blowing like a hurricane. He signaled for Jeffrey to roll down the window, and uttered this phrase which began Jeffrey's fascination with the local vernacular. He said this lovely line, which was, "Stormin, ain't it?'"

JEFFREY'S BUSINESS

While he was building the rental business, Jeffrey also took over the dairy barn from Roy Lester and converted it into a riding school, named it Stony Hill Stable and hired an attractive young woman, Liz Bogert, as riding teacher. She was later joined by another beautiful woman, Mimi Matzner, and when Mimi left, possibly to go back to school, she was replaced by yet another beautiful young woman named Maggie Kotuk.

The stable had five horses strictly for the young riding students, plus a big hunter, which was Jeffrey's personal horse, a matched pair of carriage horses named Jack and Jill, that could also be used as riding horses (though they were very tall, seventeen hands), and a pony.

He bought a Gravely garden tractor with a rotary mower for clearing brush. A few people saw the cleared brush and decided they needed the same treatment on their property. It became an instant business. As he got busier, he added a Ford tractor with a big rotary blade, not the apparatus that Ford made but a larger one made by an independent manufacturer and called The Bush Hog. Jeffrey said, "The only trouble with that little gimmick was that when you'd grind up these heavy stalks, the brush, and you'd come back another time, these spears were sticking up from the soil and that was not so great for your big tires on the driving wheels, which are darned expensive tires, and hell to change. So, what I did was, which worked out pretty well, I bought a set of tracks, with an idler up by the engine and then this track would go over the driving wheel in back. That made for good protection, plus you could then get into very marshy ground, too. Of course once your front end went down, you'd have to back out. So I would keep the tire pressure low in the front end, and I did very well with that rig. Very well indeed."

The jobs kept getting bigger and eventually he was knocking down trees, for which he needed a bulldozer. For that he got an International TD9, and eventually a front end loader, a Michigan 75A, and an International TD14. He put up a small building for an office and hired a full time bookkeeper, Betty Schellinger. He also, by this time, had a couple of young guys working for him, Willard Mahar and Harry Cullum, who were both "very talented mechanics," according to Jeffrey, as well as very good looking guys. Perhaps, he suggested to me, being a stage manager had made him more conscious of looks.

Always, watching out of the corner of his eye was Jeffrey's only real competitor, Pete Bistrian. Pete had worked his father's potato farm and after The War had started in the trucking and contracting business. As a teenager and into his twenties, Pete had been known locally as a good amateur boxer, with quick hands and fast on his feet. He was way ahead of Jeffrey and growing fast. About Pete, Jeffrey had this to say; "One day in the fall I heard a hell of a racket down in the woods on the farm and I went down, and there was Pete, with a really nice big Cat, a TD 24, brand new. And what he was doing was he was going right down the ditch line which marked the property division (Pete owned the adjoining property), knocking down big beautiful oak trees. So I went down to ask him to lay off. He said, 'Yeah, just a minute,' and just at that time he turned the machine and a branch clipped him and he said, 'By God, I'll get that tree,' and down went the biggest and most beautiful damn oak you ever did see. So I said, 'Pete, you know, we don't have a fence here but we do have this trust, and I trust you not to go any further with this rig, because if you do you're going to have to trust me for stuff much more serious than a dozer.

"He was a tough guy, Pete, you know? And I wondered, is he going to come down off the dozer or is he going to stay up there, and maybe just keep coming. I told him to back off, and he laughed and then stopped the big machine, just before the blade got to me." Pete, Jeffrey figured, was testing him, to see what he was made of.

Jeffrey continued buying up the land around Stony Hill; any land that Pete hadn't gotten to first. Most of this land had, into the early 20th century, belonged to the Edwards family. They had sold off some but still retained quite a bit. Land didn't seem quite as valuable in those days, particularly after the end of the wood stove era, in the 1930s. (The land on the Glacial Moraine had poor soil and had been useful mostly for firewood.) Jeffrey was then paying about $50 an acre.

At one point he had wanted another piece of Edwards property, 40 acres to the north of what he already had, and had contacted Clifford Edwards, his lawyer, who was also the trustee for the estate. He had received a verbal agreement from Clifford to buy the piece, but had not yet seen a contract. (He eventually added 300 acres to his original purchase.)

"But I didn't worry about it because I thought, he's my lawyer, you know, and he was the trustee for the estate. So one day I called him and I said, 'You know, I think we ought to close this deal, and get it done, so I know where I am financially. 'Oh,' he said, 'Hell, I can't do that because Pete was after me for it, you know, and I get a lot of work from him.' Mind you, Clifford was my lawyer, old family, Edwards, and all that. I really couldn't believe it. And that's how Pete got it."

A few years later, at a meeting at the firehouse, Pete came up to Jeffrey and said, "You know, you'll never make it as a contractor." "Why is that?" Jeffrey responded. "Well, because you don't move fast enough!" Recalling this to me, Jeffrey laughed and said, "And you know, he was right. Pete ended up with all the biggest rigs you can buy, and a helicopter to boot!"

Once Potter began to spruce up the farm, people began to realize what a lovely spot it was, the Stony Hill woods. One day on the way to the dump, which in those days was north of that acreage, where the top of the glacial moraine begins its decline toward the bay side of the island, my father, Ray, saw a for-sale sign along the east side of Stony Hill Road, near its highest point.

When he got home he called Herb Mulford, a real estate broker and also the Town Supervisor at the time. Ray said he'd like to buy the piece and would Herb please find out what the owners wanted for it. What happened next no one will ever know for sure, but a week later Ray called Herb again, and Herb said, "Oh, Ray, Joe Hren bought it." Ray was sure that Herb had "sold it out from under me," but couldn't know for sure. Since it was too late to dicker with Herb because the property was already sold, Ray called Joe. Joe said, "That property wouldn't have been good for you, Ray, it's a pig-in-a-poke. It has an old deed and a very old survey, with very poorly defined boundaries. But I need land to plant my Black Pines." (By that time his pines were selling like hotcakes.) Ray asked Joe to come over, "For a cup of coffee, to discuss it."

I waited upstairs where I knew I'd be able to hear everything, and when Joe parked his car in front of the house and walked in over the flagstone walk and through the inside gate and was standing under the trellis that he had built, I went to a side window in Ray's bedroom, where I was almost directly overhead, and could see, a little, through the winding trumpeter vine that covered the trellis; and listen. Ray, a head taller than Joe, threw him against the side fence and boxed his ears and then swore at him for what seemed like five minutes but could have been a mere thirty seconds. I'm sure he said "I thought you were my friend and you screwed me, you son of a bitch!" and something to the effect that he should never darken our door again. Joe left. They never spoke again. My sister and I stayed friends with the Hren kids, I guess feeling it wasn't really our business.

Many local people remember with fondness those days when Jeffrey was running his business. He had class and charm, and he was a very knowledgeable mechanic. Pete Bistrian quickly realized that he'd always be one jump ahead of Jeffrey, and that there was room enough for both of them. "He realized that in the long run I wasn't going to be any serious competition; wouldn't ever put him out of business," as Jeffrey put it.

Though he could be tough, Pete was a very likable guy. He employed many people, had a wonderful family and could be very generous. And, eventually, Pete grew to respect Jeffrey, as many locals did, because he was, unusual for a man from the upper-crust, a good mechanic, an expert on diesels, a man who had had his share of hard knocks, treated people fairly and was not afraid of a hard day's work.

At its peak the business had eight or ten men, with an ordinary amount of turnover. Men would occasionally quit Pete and go over to Jeffrey, or vice versa, looking to work their way up and to bargain for a little more money. And that worked to everyone's advantage because it created competition and higher skills.

Keeping men busy year round was tough, and so Jeffrey bought some plows, five at final count, and began plowing snow in the winter, both private roads and public. For the highway plowing jobs he depended on Roy Lester, who also did some trucking, because Roy had the State contract. Jeffrey could never have gotten involved directly with the state because he was a Democrat and in those days Republicans were in firm control. But he could subcontract through Roy. (Roy's father had done road work for the Town with teams of horses.)

When there was nothing else to do, he kept the men busy by moving or demolishing buildings. "Which was tricky because of no insurance, you know, that's a special kind of liability; wrecking. So with all these things we would try to get by, and we'd get some money in, but boy, those monies were scarce indeed, and with a payroll to meet, it was never easy."

Getting up before dawn, he would write for a couple of hours, before the men arrived at seven. Then he would be out with them; gone all day. Penny liked to have cocktails after dinner and talk, but Jeffrey, exhausted, would collapse early. Every morning, he would wake the children before he left the house, to say goodbye. Sometimes, Penny would wake up and be annoyed. "Yes," he told me, "there was some strain on the marriage."

JEFFREY THE WRITER

Jeffrey had a life which I could in some ways identify with. He had interpersonal relationships with people who were arty and literary, but he also had an ongoing rapport with the local working men. "I felt at home with the men, you know, because we had a common interest in engines. And also because of lack of education. Harry Cullum (one of the men who worked for him) was another dropout, too, you know." The lack of a college education, which one might think his private school education and reading had compensated for, was something he also seemed to share with at least some of his artist, writer and actor friends. In fact when he began selling pieces to *The New Yorker*, he was told he was the only writer they had who hadn't at least gone to one year of college. He said, "And that was probably true because, except for the newspaper job during the year down south, I was mostly self-taught.

"But I always did some writing on the side and it was terribly important to me and it came with a lot of psychological stress, always. There was the fear of rejection and at the same time the tension that came with acceptance, you know. And having to rewrite while meeting deadlines; I would freeze on that, thinking maybe it wouldn't work. I don't think I ever wrote easily, probably, until the Pollock book. I'd done three books before then, but they were all hard work, not fun."

Today Jeffrey is known primarily as the writer of the book about Jackson Pollock, *To a Violent Grave*. Written in oral history style, it was not unanimously well-received when it first came out, but became the basis for a movie of the same name and, as time went on, it has become popular with art students and young artists, for its accurate and descriptive picture of Pollock in his last days.

During The War he had submitted an article to *The New Yorker* and it had not been rejected outright; rather, they had asked him to come in and talk. That was his introduction, and so, after The War he sold them several articles. "William Maxwell, then fiction editor, was himself a very good writer and I loved the way he edited. There was really no discussion about anything, either the thing worked or it didn't. And if it didn't work, he would simply turn the pages up by the piece and then he'd pause and look at something, and I didn't necessarily see what he was looking at but I knew intuitively what it was. And I'd nod and I'd go fix whatever it was and that needed fixing. A great way to work."

When the Potters first moved into Stony Hill, the first friends they made were Berton Roueché and his wife Kay. "As far as I know, Berton Roueché was the only other *New Yorker* writer down here at that time. The rest came later. Harold Rosenberg, with his art criticism, for instance." The following is Roueche's obituary, from the The New Yorker, May 16th 1994.

When Berton Roueché died, at the end of April, he had been writing for "The New Yorker" for almost fifty years. He was born in Kansas City in 1911, and worked as a newspaper man there and in St. Louis before joining the magazine, in 1944. A year later, he began a series of sparkling pieces about people who were left over from the nineteenth century - rural people who made maple syrup or grew potatoes. Then, possibly because his grandfather had been a doctor and he himself had had polio, he wrote his first medical piece. It dealt with the discovery of a hitherto unknown disease, Rickettsialpox fever, and he wrote it as a tale of suspense. Reports on gout and sodium-nitrite poisoning followed, and the flow continued until 1991. (To refresh himself, he occasionally went back to the nineteenth century and wrote, for example, about trains and small towns and harvesting wild rice.) Roueché's medical pieces became doubly famous: lay readers found them scary and exciting, while doctors, impressed by their learning and clarity, used them as medical texts. William Shawn once wrote about his style, or non-style, "Certainly his is the art that conceals art. His words are so plain, his sentences so chaste, his rhythms so natural that one can overlook the presence of the writer and see straight through to the matter at hand."

Roueche was handsome, courtly, out-going, and a lover of anecdotes. He wore Brooks Brothers' clothes when he came to New York from Amagansett, where he lived for forty-five years, but he considered shined shoes an affectation. A kind of urbane country boy, he liked nothing better than gleaning new potatoes, then closing things down with a couple of Martinis and a glass of wine. (He was scrupulously cared for by his wife of nearly sixty years, Katherine Eisenhower, a niece of Ike's, and they had a son, Bradford.) He had grown up with the Kansas City jazz of Count Basie and Joe Turner, and he once said that he tried to imitate jazz rhythms in his writing. He relished the original he had of a 1963 Steinberg cover, showing a giant, blocky "E" sitting on a clump of grass and dreaming of a delicate capital "E" with an accent aigu.

JEFFREY'S ACCIDENT

From the East Hampton Star, Thursday, June 2, 1955:

A tragic accident occurred on the Montauk Highway between East Hampton and Amagansett about 8:45 a.m. last Friday. Dane Hansen, seven year old son of Mr. and Mrs. Claude Hansen who live on the north side of the highway across from Joseph Hren's nursery, was hit and killed by a 1945 Chevrolet dump truck filled with topsoil, owned and operated by Jeffrey Potter of Stony Hill Farm. Witnesses said it was something that could happen any time on any highway.

It seems that the school bus operated by Peter Rana takes high school students from Amagansett to East Hampton every school morning, and on the return trip picks up small children at the west end of Amagansett village and takes them to the Amagansett Grade School. Three young children; Dane Hansen, his sister Claudia, 8, and James O'Brien, 7, saw the school bus approaching and started to run across the highway. They came out from behind cars parked on the north side of the road. Claudia and James made it, but Dane hesitated, as Mr. Potter, going west in his truck, approached. The bus was coming from west, the truck from east, and the small boy was confused. There is a sharp curve to the road just there; this, complicated by the parked cars, made it hard to see him. He was hit in the north lane of the highway and dragged about 15 feet before the truck could stop. He was probably killed instantly.

The parents of the little boy came originally from Greenport and bought their home which stands 75 feet or 100 feet back from the road only a few years ago. Mr. Hansen's sister married Francis Lester of Amagansett. The Hansen's are prostrated by their loss. Mr. Potter, *himself the father of small children, is also crushed by the terrible accident. He knew the boy. Dane was a classmate of and playmate of Mr. Potter's own young son.*

Mr. Potter had slowed down, noticing the bus headed east round the curve. Coroner John Nugent has not set the date for the inquest, as this is written.

The funeral service for Dane Hansen was held in the Amagansett Presbyterian Church at 2:30 Monday afternoon. Rev. George Nicholson conducting. Burial was in the cemetery at East Marion, L.I. The little boy was dressed in a cowboy suit, something he had always wanted and which he would have received next Christmas.

PATSY

After the accident, he arrived home with Penny still asleep in bed. When he walked into the bedroom with the child's blood still covering him, she looked up from her pillow and said, "Oh, Jeffrey, what have you done now?" Jeffrey stayed in the shower for a long time, scrubbing the blood out of his skin. He said, "And in the meantime, out of sympathy, people came to visit me, and of course they should have been going to see the family of the child, but they didn't. And down comes Penny, cheerfully, into this room full of people and said, 'Ah, let's all have a nice Bloody Mary.' That was no help. And the next day I just sort of stopped functioning."

Pending the investigation, Jeffrey's driver's license was suspended. Patsy Matthiessen, aka Southgate, who was an early riser, volunteered to drive him to his jobs in the mornings and then in the afternoon Penny would pick him up. "And then, as someone once said, Patsy drove me to more than my jobs. And it was very bad," Jeffrey added, "because, you know, her husband, Peter Matthiessen, was a good friend and they were tenants on the farm."

Jeffrey wasn't telling me anything that I didn't know. The affair between Patsy Matthiessen and Jeff Potter was, with the help of the party-line, burning up the telephone wires in Amagansett, and spreading out from there to the growing community of abstractionists and their writer friends.

I don't think there was any intention on the part of Jeffrey and

Patsy to break up their marriages. It was intended I think as a discrete affair, but it was hard to keep a secret in Amagansett, as it still is. To my mind it seems they found themselves in a precarious situation and succumbed. Jeffrey was a naturally sensitive man, who was not closed off about his feelings. Probably he got a more nurturing childhood by being raised by the Irish domestic help than he would have otherwise, and the natural inclination which led him to become a medic in the Field Service, and his subsequent experiences there, as well as his attachment to the Sikh doctors, no doubt served him well too. Jeffrey was not a devotee of the Hemingway school of masculinity to the extent that Peter and John Cole, and in fact my dear old Dad, were. He had a more nuanced view of manhood.

In a culture that had many full time muses Patsy is considered by many to have been the chief muse of the abstract expressionist movement and its surrounding culturati. She set the gold standard for muse, not only with her blond hair, golden skin and blue eyes, but with her conviction that being treated badly and greeting it with amused stoicism was justified if the object of love was a capital G Genius.

It was a year before Pollock died. Patsy and Jeff shared a fascination with and a concern for both Pollocks, Jackson and Lee. Jeffrey was the son of an alcoholic. His father had been destroyed by both alcohol and the force of nature that was the stock market crash, and Patsy had by then become a source of strength and support for Lee, as well as companion in the experience of being the wife of a dominant, and suffocating, male ego.

Though they were not divorced until 1964, Jeffrey and Penny separated that year, and Jeffrey moved into a small, old saltbox house, on a hill opposite Three Mile Harbor Boat Yard, in the area known locally as the-head-of-the-harbor, because it is the most inland point of that body of water. He paneled one room in the house with weathered cypress boards from the dismantled water tower at the farm, made a few other minor improvements, and lived there for the next six years while he slowly down-sized his company, and eventually sold all his equipment. A few years before he shut down, he had changed the company's focus to building docks and bulkheads and changed the name to East Hampton Dredge and Dock, using the motto suggested by Patsy, "Your bottom is our business."

When he divorced in 1964 he moved a larger house onto his new property and moved in with his second wife Diana, with whom he had a son, Robert Hitt Horatio Potter.

One positive thing, Jeffrey felt, did come out of the brief affair with Patsy. It got him into formal analysis. It was his good fortune, he felt, to be the patient of Dr. Rollo May. I told Jeffrey that I had read several of his books and that *Love and Will* in particular had a positive effect on me. "Oh, yes?" He said. "Well, he really saved my ass. His office was up at 103rd Street and Riverside Drive, on the uptown corner. Twenty four stories. Very strange building. The Roerich Museum was downstairs and then small suites upstairs. In fact, his definition of psychoanalysis, as opposed to psychotherapy, is that it is a form of learning on a deep level. And that's what it was for me, very educational; absolutely.

"And, after seven long years, we finished, and I was looking around trying to find a place to live in the City and, however odd it might have looked from an analytic standpoint, I found myself an apartment in that very building, a really nice, small, two room apartment, with two terraces, five floors below the very office from which I had graduated. Very strange, indeed. God, the views of the Hudson and New Jersey were amazing."

BEACH HAMPTON

Before WWII the Coast Guard Beach on the East End of Amagansett village had only a few fishermen's homes nestled in the dunes around the Coast Guard Station. After The War, these homes, little more than shacks, were bought for summer homes by adventurous city folks who expanded them. Further to the east, along this wider than normal swath of dunes sometimes called the second dune, was a small beach-house development called Beach Hampton. These were nice little Cape Cod houses, mostly summer residences. Begun in the mid-Thirties, McClelland Barclay had been one of its charter residents. He had built a cozy place on the ocean front next door to the community's private club house, a beautiful, large, modern place with dozens of cabanas and a fancy art moderne style restaurant. The Beach Club, from topmost shingle to last floor joist, was turned into match sticks during the 1938 Hurricane, leaving Barclay's house with hardly a scratch.

When Mac died in The War, his house was inherited by his mistress, Marty Hoff, daughter of the illustrator Guy Hoff, who eventually, in the Fifties, sold it to a famous TV personality of the time, Robert Q. Lewis. (Lewis later sold it to the powerful NYC Transit Union boss, Mike Quill.)

During the Fifties my parents became friendly with several Beach Hampton families. There was a middle aged lesbian couple, very much a Stein-Toklas type of pairing, though the Stein figure was somewhat less portly than Gertrude. One, I think, was a teacher and the other an artist. There was an architect, Albert Scheffer, who built many of the buildings in the community as well as throughout East Hampton, Amagansett, and Montauk, often pairing with Kay Perkins for interiors and Joe Hren for the landscaping. There were a couple of families from the New York City suburbs, with a small flock of children. All were part-time residents, summer, spring and fall weekends.

Then came the Ruby family, Jack Ruby, his wife Leticia (Letty), who was a Castilian Spaniard from Puerto Rico, and their three daughters, Meg, Susan and Jaqueline. At first the Scheffers and the Rubys were the only year round residences in that small development which had been built for vacation homes. It was an all sand and beach grass landscape; a holding place for winter fog with lots of Joe Hren's Japanese Black Pines and no sidewalks. In the winter it was cold and raw.

Jack Ruby had left an executive job in New Jersey to become manager of Gobel Aircraft, a small aircraft parts plant that had opened in Montauk, in the Government buildings built during The War on the site of the Old Fishing Village. My sister became friendly with the two Ruby girls as soon as they moved in. The two girls marked the beginning of a more diverse, less local-dominated student population, and made the school seem, to my sister, more normal. Within the next year or two, the Ruby girls were joined by children of two other families, that of a Jewish novelist and a psychiatrist writer with a rich wife.

In the summer, most local people who went to the beach went to the one that was nearest their home. Many of the older locals didn't even go to the beach, because to them beaches were for fishing. Kids went to the beach the way today's suburban kids go to the Mall, to be with their own kind. They would agree on a common meeting place, girls being followed by boys.

Since we lived on Main Street, by custom we should have gone to either The Coast Guard Beach or Amagansett Main Beach, at the east and west ends of the village, respectively, which we did in the early years, into the first few years of the 1950s. Main Beach* had a food concession that sold ice cream and hot dogs, and lockers and bath houses were available for rent. Eventually, though, Ray and Carolyn decided it was too Magimper. Meaning, in this case, people who are just ordinary; who don't "talk painting," but instead talk about things like baseball. Now that there were people around who read, or at least pretended to read, the "Partisan Review," and "Art News" (and who could at least pretend to be interested in Ray's painting), there was no need to be desperate about socializing.

One of the lifeguards at Main Beach was a popular kid named Jim Eckes, who distinguished himself at the evacuation of Saigon, when, as an employee of Continental Airlines, he ferried refugees to freedom until the last minute.

The beach, when we weren't going on a special off-road picnic in the Beach Buggy, could mean the bay or the ocean, depending on air temperature, insects, wind and time of year. The bay was usually for early spring and late fall, when the water was warmer and there were less flies and mosquitoes, or for days when the ocean was too rough to swim in. As time went by though, my family became connoisseurs of subtle beach differences. When an inlet on the south shore was cut open to drain a pond, the whole family loved swimming in "the cut," as it was called; today, this is considered criminally dangerous.

"The cut" could have been as far west as Mecox inlet, or as far east as Oyster Pond on the north side of Montauk, near the area of Rocky Point, Shagwong Point and Gin Beach where the water was half ocean, half bay, protected by the ocean swells only by being in the lee of the very end of the Island. The water was deep and there were small swells and Ray could fish while the kids and Carolyn swam. (It was also a place where the whole family swam naked, though that was probably perverse and dysfunctional and not something I would have told friends.)

Napeague Lane was the eastern border of the Beach Hampton area and the beach parking area for that development. Eventually, probably around 1954, we settled on this place as our official family beach. Only we called it Pig Beach. Locals pronounced Napeague, Nahpig. New residents now call it Nahpeeg, with the accent on the second syllable. They also often call Amagansett, Amaganzett, which irks locals.

In summer there were a handful of umbrellas with small families attached to them, mostly Beach Hampton residents, and then west a few hundred yards, after a small open space, another sub-group beach community, a one-road development separate from Beach Hampton, called Beach Lane, had a few families. After Napeague Lane the beach was empty but for sky, water and sand. As a child, to my mind's eye it was like the end of civilization, leading eastward only to water and, over the horizon, to Montauk, a frontier town.

In between family fights and amidst the parental narcissism, the general chaos, there were times when my father, my mother, my sister and I were a cozy little nuclear family. That was usually the case when we went to the beach. We thought of Pig Beach as a unique place. It was not terribly popular, and had lots of open space and therefore privacy. It was unofficially, a place reserved for the people of Beach Hampton. Before Beach Hampton existed, this section of beach had been unused except for fishing and, during prohibition, for the landing of illegal rum.

East of Napeague Lane was so private that in 1957 Marilyn Monroe and Arthur Miller were able to frolic there almost unnoticed, in mid-summer. Of course someone obviously took a picture of them, once, because there is a famous photograph, but for the most part, all that summer they were left in peace.

TELEVISION

Bob Costello was a Dartmouth man who had been in the O.S.S. in WWII and after The War had gone on to Yale Drama School. At Yale he studied under Connie Welsh, Carolyn's old mentor and friend. He described her as "an old maid, not too attractive, who lived with her sister." (Assuming for a moment that it wasn't actually her sister, and at least according to Carolyn's surmise, Connie may have been what we describe today as gay.) He then went on to Stevens Institute in

Hoboken and studied theater engineering and worked in summer stock. After that he and another fellow wrote a book on the technical side of theater, which ended up being his ticket into a new industry.

"Then, they invented television for me," he told me, when I interviewed him for my Oral History. "And just in time! I needed a job." He started out, in 1950, on a show called *Your Pet Parade*, which featured pets that did funny stuff. His job on that show was not specified but eventually became Unit Manager, which was, "sort of the production manager; they watched the money; they were the gofer for the producer; and I don't mean for coffee, but just, well, we were at the beginning you see, so there was no prototype. We were the prototype. It was hit and miss."

At first, when I was interviewing him, Bob reminisced; "No one knew what to think of television. It was live, therefore was it theater? It wasn't the movies, yet it was really a combination of theater and film, and all most of us knew about in the 50s was what we had learned going to the movies. Well, some of us had some theater experience. So anyway, for about eight years it was purely an art form of its own. It lasted just about that long. Like the Pony Express! And then it was gone. And I don't say it unkindly."

From there Bob went to NBC as an official unit manager for a group of shows, in fact for an endless series of shows over a period of years. At NBC he met Fred Coe, one of the founding fathers of television. Coe was producer of *Philco Playhouse* from 1948, when practically no one had a television set, so that they were broadcasting into thin air, to 1955, by which time TV was becoming a going concern. "Fred Coe* was there at the beginning. So was David Sarnoff. It was a pretty intimate art form, I mean you kind of knew everybody, or if you didn't, they knew you, that sort of thing. And you still signed off at night about midnight, the show went off the air and it wasn't until they started rolling movies, that the programming stayed on. Then as a unit manager I was assigned to Fred's show, *Mr. Peepers*, and because Fred had bought a house in East Hampton, he'd say to the guys, 'Hey, fellas, come on out and we'll have a conference.'"

See; "The Man in the Shadows," by Jon Krampner. Biography of Fred Coe. Krampner also did a biography of Kim Stanley, the great actress, and member of Costello's early TV social crowd.

It was through Fred Coe, that Bob Costello met David Shaw and Bob

Arthur, who were writing for television, and together the whole group began renting on the East End, in either East Hampton or Amagansett. "And then, out here (meaning East Hampton-Amagansett), I met Hoffman Hays and Joe Liss, two other writers and some non-TV writers, and some artists.

"The first year I was here, which was either '52 or '53, I can't remember, I rented a house on Further Lane, and the next year I rented this house, and the next year I rented out at Montauk, and then this house came up for sale, and well, it had never occurred to me to buy a house, so I don't know why, but I did."

Bob's house was built by Rose Hadel, daughter of Bart, the potato farmer who farmed the lot behind the Prohaska house. She built the house around 1951, intending it to be a rental property, in part to help finance her father's dotage. Bart was going senile and Rose had gotten power of attorney over him. She built the house using a carpenter-builder named Kendell Leek, a gravelly throated man with a crew cut like my father's and great big, purple lower lip, a permanent disfigurement that he'd gotten in some sort of accident. Leek's son Kendell Jr. was a year or two older than me and was the lone altar boy at St. Peter's, our little Catholic Chapel, during my tenure there.

But when the local bank, The Osborne Trust, found out she was building a house and hadn't filled them in on her plans, they were disconcerted and demanded she sell it right away, which put Bob Costello in the right place at the right time. The house, right on the dunes, has, since then, withstood more than a few hurricanes, including two bad ones for the East End; Carol, and Donna. Leek, fearing his reputation had been ruined because he partook of a project behind the bank's back, moved, according to Bob, "to Shelter Island or someplace."

From *Mr. Peepers*, Bob went to the Patti Page musical show, which he would share with other unit managers, working shifts; and then, when *Kukla, Fran and Ollie* came from Chicago, Bob became their man in New York. "They were really a wonderful, wonderful group, all really very nice. One night Sarnoff gave a party for them up in the Rainbow Grill. Their producer, Beulah Zachary, asked Sarnoff, 'Well, can I bring the company in?' referring to me and the unit and the Chicago stage manager, and Sarnoff said, 'Well if they don't come, we're not coming!' So there we were at the Rainbow Grill in our sneakers and everything. Beulah died in a plane crash. Burr Tillstrom died a few years back."

By this time Bob had married his second wife and had two more kids. Now there were Martha and Julia and Kate and Ned. And because television was live in those days, everyone took a vacation at the same time, in July, and the whole TV bunch would be on the beach in Beach Hampton in front of Bob's house. Fred Coe and Hoffman Hays were the only ones living in East Hampton Village. Fred lived in the Georgica section, next door to the artist Arline Wingate, and Hays on the edge of Georgica.

"David Shaw was near me, on Surf Drive in Beach Hampton and Bob Arthur bought a place in Springs. Neil Simon rented in Beach Hampton and so did a Canadian writer, Brian Moore, who wrote *The Lonely Passion of Judith Hearn* and any number of marvelous books. He was a first-class writer; an Irishman who became a Canadian; his wife's name was Jackie. Bruce Ruddick, the analyst, was up the street here on the dunes, with his three daughters, and Joe Liss and his family were on Accabonac Creek. And then there were visiting friends like Mordecai Richler, big Canadian writer, who would come down; and Bob Fosse and Gwen Verdon became part of the group, and they would rent at various places. And of course, these people had different levels of importance, Bob and Gwen were really big deals, but we were all kind of young and we were all kind of doing whatever we were going to do, and we got a kick out of each other so there was absolutely no stratification at all. The Shaws had two girls, as did the Coes. Bob Arthur had three kids, the Ruddicks had three kids, Joe Liss had two daughters, Doc Simon had a daughter, and all these kids, some played more than others, but they all knew each other.

"The kids as you might expect were kind of theatrical, so I built a little stage out on the sand dunes and they put on performances. And you'd either have a party here and we'd swim on the beach, or we'd go to David's for something to eat, and also Barbara Bel Geddes and her husband were out here and they lived just up the street. And nobody imposed their citified pretensions on the locals, if you know what I mean. Wink and David Shaw and Brian Moore and I would split the tab on Frank Mundus'* charter boat and go shark fishing. It was all very casual. I mean, we didn't expect to be accepted as locals, but we liked what we had here and we didn't want to change it."

Mundus, a world-famous shark fisherman, was the inspiration for Capt. Quint in "Jaws."

Walt Hackett, who ran a body shop in East Hampton, was the only local that Bob Costello hung out with. Walt ran a car body shop and was one of Ray's favorite models. He was married to a Lebanese woman who gave piano lessons. The couple were Prohaska family friends. He was a tall handsome man with a great head of salt and pepper hair combed to a substantial pompadour. He had been in the Ambulance Corps of The American Field Service during The War and had served with a Yalie named Charlie Pratt, the heir, as Bob put it, to the "Pratt Gazillions." Bob had known Pratt at Yale.

Robert Q. Lewis lived up the street from Bob in Mac Barclay's old house. Robert Q. was gay, no secret in Amagansett since he went everywhere with a coterie of flamboyant young men who could be seen from the dunes by nosy children splashing in R.Q.'s pool. He was, according to Bob, a very nice guy. He often invited Bob and the others over for a drink or a dip when the ocean was too rough for swimming.

When David Susskind and some people at MCA (a talent agency) went out on their own with Talent Associates, TA felt they would need to have Fred Coe. Bob said, "They were planning to do dramatic stuff, not game shows, and they knew Coe had the credibility and the clout they would need. Being good with money, Fred knew he'd need someone at TA to keep an eye on them, and talked me into being his man at Talent Associates."

Bob stayed with TA for ten years and began producing his own shows, some with Fred and some not. Eventually Fred got more and more into Broadway, while Bob stayed with television. As he told it to me, "Susskind's career was really taking off by then and we were selling shows to *Code Justice* and *Appointment With Adventure* and all these things. At that time you had little shows that were half hour dramas or half hour adventure shows and that was the market; how things were done in those days. So, we would do those shows and David would produce them, and then he'd get bored with them and I would step in and I would produce some of them. We did specials of the classics. We did the *Family Classic* series of shows, like *Vanity Fair, Les Miz*, and stuff like that, which we'd compress into an hour and a half.

"We did an awful lot of stuff that, fifteen years later, somebody thinks this is the first time it's ever been done. And some of it didn't work, but some of it did, and it was never without effort and never without a certain amount of class. Our big show at that point was the *Armstrong Circle Theater,* a half-hour show which David had gotten from the advertising agency BBD&O. He talked them into turning it into an hour show, so we did a half hour for one year and then it became an hour show, alternating with the *United States Steel Hour* dramatic show.

"David was tired of it after about the second show and I produced it then for the next eight years; about a hundred and twenty-some dramatic shows. That kept me pretty busy. And every now and then I'd pitch in and help with other shows within the company. When Susskind was doing his *Open End,* the first program we did was in Chinatown because *Suzy Wong* had opened on Broadway, so we got the *Suzy Wong* cast to come down. And that went on forever. Jesus, was it open-ended! And he got good people! I mean, he got Khrushchev! You got to see Khrushchev and David sparring! Anyway, his show lasted for a long time. But then the business changed, and Talent Associates went defunct, and Al Levy died and David was a one-man show. He really preferred to operate alone anyway, so when *Armstrong* went off, that was the end of the company.

"The one place the television crowd liked to go to was The Elm Tree Inn, the main place where the locals and the artists and writers met. They would bring their kids and eat on the outside patio, or come in the evening to listen to a Jazz group that included a local fisherman and WWII flying ace, Jimmy Reutershan on trumpet, an artist named Eliot Atkinson on piano, and Larry Rivers on sax.

"During that time, the Elm Tree changed hands, and was taken over by Sam Liss, brother of the writer Joe Liss. Liss took the liberty of promoting the place to the late night gay crowd, which at that time had reached a bar in the back woods of Bridgehampton, but had not yet moved east. Of course, the word gay, for homosexual, wouldn't be coined for years. These folks were called either homosexuals or queers, and that was it. I don't know how "very" it was, but it was gay. We'd take the kids and everybody and, uh, Jimmy Reutershan was up there playin' away and Eliot Atkinson was on the piano, and you could dance and you could have a good time.

"But Sam Liss got nailed. They set him up. The Liquor Commission, or some other political body, they sent some guy in with a lot of muscles and a tight tee shirt who allowed himself to be solicited. So Bob Arthur and I, of all these people, we went down to the trial to testify for Liss, downtown, it was either the Federal Building or the State Building. And, uh, I think he got his license back eventually, but, uh, it was pretty stupid.

"And, then after that I was unemployed until, with a little help from Bob Arthur I got the job of producing *The Patty Duke Show* when it came to New York. The reason it was in New York was because California's child labor laws were a hell of a lot stricter than New York's. I don't know if you knew the show but she played a double character, and in California they could only work her three hours a day, which meant losing money so, in New York they could work her till she dropped. Not that they abused her or anything, she had a school teacher and she had everything else that was needed.

"I had used her a lot on the *Armstrong* show when she was a little girl. She was cute as a bug's ear. And now here she was all grown up and a star and kind of a pain in the ass; that type of thing. I should say, by the way, she's grown into being a very nice gal. She became president of the Screen Actors Guild! Anyway, they took the show to California when she turned 18 and they had all the help they needed in California, so I didn't go. A lot of TV people went out to California at that time but, I liked my house, my children were here, I figured I'd take my chances. So from that point on it was whatever came down the pike. Soap operas or series for PBS or movies for television or no work at all or whatever, but I stayed."

At the time of my interview with Bob he was married to his third wife, Sibyl. They met on a show called *Dark Shadows*, "which I put together for ABC. The guy who owned it, named Dan Curtis, was a sports enthusiast and he had come up with a golf show and that was his claim to fame. It was a good idea, but he also sold the idea through another guy I knew named Art Wallace. It had originally been Art's idea but he sold it to Dan who then sold it to ABC. At that time ABC as a network was sort of nothing, and their pitch to build themselves into a big network was to appeal to a certain class and that was the young people. So *Dark Shadows* appealed to them. It was the first daytime show that ever dealt with vampires. I brought a lot of people with me on *Dark Shadows*; my designer from *Armstrong*, who was out of work, and the costume lady, the musicians, a whole bunch of us. And I put together the show for Curtis, and we had a lot of fun, great fun."

Toward the end of Bob's career he did a series for PBS, called *The

Adams Chronicles, which was about the Adams family (the founders, not the ghouls), and after that he worked on several soap operas, *Ryan's Hope*, *Another World* and *The Doctors*. "By then I was getting a little weary, so when I was offered a job to teach at NYU in the film school I took it and I retired from there after six years as a full professor with tenure, and the rest is history. Or just loafing around. Sibyl though is still working. She's a post-production producer at CBS on *As the World Turns*. After the show is edited, she then puts in the music and the effects.

"Well then, bit by bit, this place built up. Doc (Neil Simon) moved out, David (Susskind) went to California, Bob Arthur died, Fred (Coe) died, but not before he had divorced Joyce and that was a big mess and the house went someplace and now living in the house is a writer. I can't think of her name. The area has changed. You haven't asked me, but it has changed considerably. It's now a resort, where it used to be a village that just sort of allowed summer people to visit. It's not what it was."

PART II: HORSE PEOPLE

On Strawberry at Woolnough's ca. 1951

WOOLNOUGH'S

The summer of 1951 I was eight and at my mother's suggestion, I took riding lessons at Woolnough's riding academy. She came with me the first time and a few times after that, but she'd gotten to the point where she coveted her free time for painting. Woolnough's was an elegant old place, situated on a side street on the edge of the East Hampton Village summer colony, owned by a hunched-over old man in steel rimmed glasses and his daughter, who was the riding instructor. I looked forward to the lessons. I quickly developed a crush on Sue, my teacher.

If I got there early I would wander around, checking out the horses and the tack room. Old man Woolnough was friendly. I never felt like I was getting in the way or intruding on somebody's private turf. The horse world seemed like a neutral country; like an animal version of Switzerland. Then the daughter would appear, either walking across the paddock from the house, or I'd hear her horse's hooves ringing on the tar road out front, coming in from the lesson before me. Strawberry, the big sorrel mare, was the horse I always rode. In fact, I would find out a few years later, she was well known in the community, having taught numerous older boys and girls to ride.

I had to use a mounting box to get up on the mare, but that didn't embarrass me. My usual self-consciousness and my phobic fears about athletics seemed to fall away when it came to horses. I wanted up; got my feet in the metal stirrups with a great feeling of satisfaction. Once I got over the momentary self-consciousness of being eight and about to embark on a trip through the woods with a pretty lady in her mid-twenties wearing jodhpurs, her blonde hair done up in a net, I settled my skinny little frame the best I could into the rather large English saddle and we headed off down the street to where we crossed Pantigo Road and headed up a hill and into the woods.

For two summers, barring rain, I rode Wednesdays and Fridays. Sue hardly had to teach me at all. We trotted along through the oak woods and before long, during that first season, we were cantering. Coming out of the woods on the north side of the railroad tracks we would lope through a meadow where the trail twisted around some stunted pine trees and where once we caught the red blur of a fox that had its den in the high grass.

After two years Woolnough's Stable closed and I discovered, through an ad in the newspaper, a new place to ride; Rocking Horse Ranch in Springs, on the Three Mile Harbor Road. The owner was a woman named Fanny. Lean, weather beaten, with a toothy smile, and a way of talking that was old fashioned, a bit of Connecticut Yankee and a bit of John Wayne, she dressed like a cowboy and was, according to local mothers and proper ladies, "Somewhat coarse, like a man."

The little farm was dominated by her brand of androgynous femaleness. Her husband Phil was a quiet man, not in good health, who stayed in the background doing small chores, functioning, it seemed, as a kind of stable hand. The two daughters had the run of the place and tore around on horseback like a couple of Plains Indians. The young one had a pony, and the older one, about my age, had several horses, but that summer was favoring a big Tennessee Walking Horse named Tony, after an old horse of Fanny's.

At first I rode at Fanny's as an anonymous, quiet customer, but in a few weeks I got to know the girls and the kids and older people who hung out, who were, to some extent, Fanny's followers. Then I too developed a case of hero worship on Fanny, half love and half wanting to be like her. She impressed me as a natural aristocrat. In fact she was descended from an original settler, the man who had bought most of the town from the Indians and left his own private Island to be fought over by generations of descendants.

Fanny and her daughter Fran
in front of the Gardiner Brown House
Main Street, East Hampton, NY

FANNY

By her story telling when I went riding with her, Fanny Gardiner was the one who first got me interested in local history. When I got older I continued to run into her at a local coffee shop (she seemed to live on coffee and Camel cigarettes, which may be why she died at a premature 92.) It was natural that I would interview her for my Oral History. I had to get my facts straight, if only for her sake. I both loved her and was terrified of her scolding, which was just a kind of snappish correcting, "No, no, no, the barn was on the *other* side of the property!" that kind of thing. There was definitely a world according to Fanny.

She was a direct descendant of Lion Gardiner, who was one of the first settlers of East Hampton and first Lord of Gardiner's Island, a beautiful island just off the coast of East Hampton in Gardiner's Bay, which was granted to Lion by the English Crown. Lion was an engineer and member of the British Military, who came to America in 1635 to set up and run a fort at Old Saybrook, Connecticut, for a company of noblemen who had invested in that area with plans to build a plantation.

After setting up the Fort and assisting some of the local Indians in the Pequot Wars, the Indians gave Lion the island which they called Manchonake, which was situated between the two eastern forks of Long Island. Lion's daughter was the first European born in what is now Connecticut, and his first son was the first born in what is now New York State. Though Gardiner called the Island the Isle of Wight, it eventually became known as Gardiner's Island. Lion ran the island as a plantation, raising corn, wheat, fruit, tobacco and livestock.

For generations of local East Hampton people, Gardiner's Island had the character of sacred ground. The only land in what eventually became the United States that carried an unbroken line of descent from an original royal grant from the English Crown, that of Charles the 1st, the Island gave East Hampton a long historical continuity, as well as a pretension to nobility and to royalty. And because the Island was private property, it had mysterious qualities, so that the deer were said to be bigger, as well as the clams, the fish and the birds. On occasion, adventurous people managed to get themselves stranded there overnight; it was kind of a romantic thing to do.

In 1919, the year Fanny was born, the Gardiner family still owned most of the real estate in East Hampton. Though born in her parent's New York City apartment, she spent the first decade of her life at the Mill Cottage, a small house with a windmill in its yard near East Hampton's Town Pond. In 1924, Fanny's father, Winthrop, inherited the Gardiner Brown House, so named because it was brown and to distinguish it from the Gardiner White House, a white stone house a few doors down which had been the summer White House for President Tyler, who was married to a Gardiner.

Winthrop was a distinguished looking man with a Van Dyke beard. On his birth certificate it says, Winthrop Gardiner, born Gardiner's Island. He was the last of the line to have been born and raised on the Island. As a boy he rode the Island on horseback in snowstorms to find snow-buried sheep, sometimes spending a week searching before finding steam puffing from a hole in the snow and a covered sheep which had been eating its own wool to stay alive.

Winthrop's father, John Lion Gardiner, had inherited the Island from Uncle David, father of First Lady Julia Tyler, who had inherited it from his father Samuel Buell. Thinking he could do a better job with the Island, he had told Buell, "Why don't you give it to me? If you don't, I'll take it away from you in court," said David. Generations of sometimes spiteful but usually civil litigation make up a big part of the Gardiner family's history.

John Lion needed an isolated place to raise his trotting horses. Fanny's daughter still has a medal dated 1894, which says, "Best four year old colt, Suffolk County Fair, Chieftain, raised Gardiner's Island."

In his log book is a notation made by John Lion, "Best colt I've ever raised."

When Fanny was a child her father was around most every day, mostly supervising work on the garden at the Brown House. During the depression, he was the sole source of support for several local families. He was a country squire, but with a garden rather than a farm.

Winthrop went to college in England but came home to the Island when his father became ill. Fanny gave me this anecdote from her father, to explain what taking care of her grandfather had entailed. "One day he (her father) left the Island with a northwest wind blowing like hell and when he came into Three Mile Harbor, the wind and water were so high the boat went right over the breakwater! He went into town for medicine and went straight back. The worst part of the trip was getting out of the channel!"

Winthrop's wife, Isabel Lemmon Gardiner, was a good horsewoman from Virginia's horse country, who rode side-saddle. When Fanny was "about four years old" her mother sent her to Woolnough's riding stable, where she learned to ride English style. (When she began to ride on her own with friends though, she rode Western.)

Her brother and sister were both older and more interested in the social world. But, although she would occasionally appear at the Maidstone Club for a swim in the pool, Fanny preferred to be riding. When her sister Isabel, called Babe, had a coming-out party at the Brown House, Fanny, in a dress to suit the occasion, jumped on a horse bareback and rode into the front yard.

During the summer of 1935, when she was fifteen, Fanny went out west to Wyoming, with her cousin, Margaret Tyler, to the Bones Brother's Ranch, a dude ranch sixty-five miles outside of the nearest town, Sheridan. (Margaret was the daughter of Julia Gardiner Tyler and President John Tyler. Her grandfather, David, was killed when a canon blew up during a cruise on the Potomac and the aftermath of that accident led to Julia meeting and eventually marrying President Tyler.) They liked it so much they went the following summer. Each summer they stayed six weeks and Fanny spent most of her time working with the cowboys and copying the things they did. She watched the way they rode and the way they threw a lariat and the way they tied their spurs down. When she came back, she taught her new skills to her friends (all boys) at Dan Huntting's stable next door to her home.

Brother Winthrop, called Win, was very interested in cars and later, airplanes. He was a well-known playboy, often mistaken for a movie star, and a frequenter of the society pages. He was a friend of Howard Hughes. Over his lifespan he was married five times, including once to the ice skater and movie star, Sonja Henie. On an old film that was digitized and was lent to me, there is a shot of Hughes' boat, the *Southern Cross*, anchored off Crow Head in Gardiner's Bay. "Was he actually here, or just his boat?" I asked Fanny. Annoyed (Fanny did not suffer fools), she said, "No, no, no, he was here, staying at our house! My brother used to fly with him all the time! They were both into air racing! He probably came up on the boat with half a dozen airplanes flappin' along behind it. He (Hughes) was in the hospital for a while. He disappeared out of the hospital and the news guys were all looking for him. He was at the house hangin' out with Winnie."

Win had a friend named Smitty, a local fellow who was a motorcycle cop, who was assigned the job of looking after Fanny when big brother was off traveling. She wasn't allowed to play with, or later, date anyone, unless Smitty approved. Smitty, whose father had been an engineer on the Long Island Railroad, was a race car driver and had been an ambulance driver before joining the local police force. Up until the time he was killed in the line of duty in 1937, in a motorcycle accident, he taught Fanny, as she said, "Everything there is to know!" about cars.

In high school she had five best friends and they were all boys; Phin Dickinson, Roy Lester, Charlie Osborne, Buddy Mullane, and Ern Schellinger. The hang-out, where they met after school, was Dan Huntting's Stable. One of several horse rental businesses still operating in those days, it was one door down from the Brown House. Dan was a man who had inherited money and ran the stable for something to do. When Teddy Roosevelt was at Montauk with his Rough Riders in 1898, Dan's father had taken him to meet Teddy. (During those days Teddy's family had stayed at the Dickinson boarding house at Ditch Plains.) Dan was much taken with Roosevelt and the Rough Riders and passed his affection on to many of the local young men. Horses and Teddy Roosevelt were Dan Huntting's lifelong fascinations.

L to R: Phineas, Frank, Phineas II

DICKINSON FAMILY

In the 1890s a man named Phineas Dickinson Jr. had a small farm on the east side of East Hampton Village near Lily Hill, which he had inherited from his father, Phineas Sr. At the same time, he also owned a rooming house at Ditch Plains in Montauk that had been used by Teddy Roosevelt during the time the Rough Riders were at Montauk's Indian Field. Phineas Jr. had a son named Frank who married a Sag Harbor woman, Loretta Kelly. In 1914 Frank and his wife moved into the vacant and falling down Third House in Montauk, which had been the residence of keepers of the cattle for the Town of East Hampton during much of the Nineteenth century. They lived there until 1926, and had four children; Eleanor, Phineas, Frank, and Jack, in that order, all of whom were delivered by a Dr. Lewis, who came all the way from Sag Harbor for each delivery.

To supplement their income, Phineas and son Frank worked for Jack Prentice, who owned a house near the Third House, and rented some 600 acres on the east side of Lake Montauk from the Montauk Development Corporation. Prentice loved to hunt and ran his place as a sort of hunting lodge for his friends and the Dickinson men worked as guides. The Prentice house was full of stuffed animals; deer heads, stuffed mallard and black duck, and a flying goose hanging from the ceiling.

Third House at Montauk

Life at Third House was primitive. There was no indoor plumbing, only a pump in the front yard and an outhouse in the back. The Dickinson kids loved going to visit their grandparents in East Hampton. It was a long trip. Before 1925 the road was paved with cinders from the railroad trains. The kids loved going to the movies at Roy Edwards Movie Theater, where the boy's favorites were Tom Mix and Hoot Gibson, and afterward getting ice cream at the Candy Kitchen.

Frank Dickinson had been an important participant in rum-running during Prohibition, storing large quantities of off-the-boat booze in the Third House cellar. For his legitimate job, he raised and broke horses for riding and light driving, which he sold locally. He raised horses, cattle and hogs, and quite often had as many as 50 foals on the ground in one season. His cattle and horses ranged free from the Point to the Great Plain; all that land around Fort Pond where Montauk village is now. In 1925, when the State bought what became Hither Hills State Park, Frank became its first superintendent. Shortly after that, in 1927, he moved into the first of two houses built for him by the State. He continued though, to rent the Third House property and to buy and sell cattle and horses.

Goodhue Livingston, born and raised in Manhattan and a member of the old Hudson Valley Livingston family (a Livingston had signed the Declaration of Independence), was a life-long member of the East End summer colony. Goodhue, who had a Groton accent, lived at his small but exclusive estate in the Georgica section of East Hampton, with his fourth wife, Dorothy, called Dody. (She was the daughter of Albert Michelson, renowned for his measurements of the speed of light and the first American to win the Nobel Prize for science.)

Goody (everyone who knew him seemed to call him that) was born in 1898 and had been a friend of Jack Prentice. When I interviewed him for my Oral History he told me, "Well I don't remember exactly how I met Prentice. He had two daughters and I knew them, and one of them married Freddy Cromwell, who later married my sister, so maybe that was it." (In upper-class society, in Goodhue's younger days, there was always a social connection.) "And also," he went on, "Jack Prentice's wife came from Philadelphia, and one of my best friends at Groton came from Philadelphia and he knew her! So I got to know Jack Prentice quite well! In fact, I later worked for him a bit at his bond brokerage in New York City." Prentice was also a friend of Jeffrey Potter's father.

Goodhue often went hunting on Montauk with Jack Prentice, back in the days when a horse and buggy would meet you at Montauk Station. "You drove out and there was this cabin to sleep in. That must have been 1919, '20, '21, I don't remember the dates. Shot more ducks and geese than you can imagine. Montauk was a wild place then. Practically nothing down there. Of course, Teddy Roosevelt had been there, right after the Spanish-American War. With his Rough Riders. Teddy was a great friend of my Grandfather Robb. Grandfather Robb was the Park Commissioner in New York and he was in the State Senate for a number of years. Teddy was a friend of my family and his sons all went to school with me!" (Goodhue had a very gravelly voice and said almost everything as an exclamation. He was delighted with his own life, and with its longevity.) "I got to know Kermit (Roosevelt), particularly. He was one of my best friends!"

When he went abroad to drive an ambulance for the French in the early days of WWI, Goodhue's father called Teddy Roosevelt and asked for a letter of introduction for his son to use in his travels. "He gave me a one page letter. When we (the U.S.) got into the War, I wanted out of the ambulance corps. Wanted a commission in the field artillery. I had to appear before a colonel with the marvelous name of Marlborough Churchill! Told him I'd been in two military camps and been driving an ambulance as a foreigner for the French. Then he said "How about letters?" And that's when I produced that letter from Theodore Roosevelt. He looked at me and said, 'That does the trick!'"

Goodie had visited Jack Prentice at a field hospital in France during the First World War, when he was in such bad shape they didn't know if he'd live. Prentice lived though, until 1925, when, on a day that he and some friends had been out hunting in Montauk, he went out on the veranda and dropped dead of a heart attack.

Prentice had once told his caretaker, Frank Dickinson, that he hoped the last sound he ever heard would be the honking of a goose. He may well have gotten his wish.

For more than two centuries, until sometime in the early 1900s, eastern Long Island farmers had held spring and fall cattle drives, taking their stock to Montauk for summer grazing. It was a communal grazing ground, with keepers of the cattle paid for by the town government. It had worked well until Montauk began to have full time residents.

In the spring of 1935, fourteen year old Phin Dickinson (son of Frank), having decided to revive that tradition, persuaded several local families to participate by including their cows in a drive from East Hampton to the Indian Field near Third House. He organized his friends and some other local people into a band of drovers. Buddy Mullane, whose father was a caretaker of a large estate on Main Street, rode one of Fanny's horses that was always on loan to him.

On the evening before, to be sure he'd wake up in time, Charlie Osborne, who lived next door to Fanny, set two alarm clocks. When the clocks went off the next morning he could hear the horses' shoes clanking on the pavement in front of his house. The drive, which probably included more cowboys than cattle, had started at the Mulford Farm, next to Home Sweet Home, on the southwest side of Main Street. Charlie was on his horse and had joined the procession before it passed his house. The drive was enough of a success that they had it for several more years and achieved a small increase in the number of farmers turned cowboys.

RODEOS

In the summer of 1938 nineteen year old Fanny, along with her male pals, put on an exhibition of western riding at the East Hampton Riding Club's annual horse show. A member of the audience, a partner in a real estate group responsible for the new Tiana Beach Development near Westhampton, proposed to the group of friends that they stage a rodeo as a publicity stunt at Tiana Beach. Because he was older, in his thirties, Fanny and the boys put Harold Govier a local horseman and electrician, in charge. Govier had been raised in East Hampton and as a child and young man had ridden at Dan Huntting's. He had worked in refrigeration on merchant ships and had become a refrigerator repairman when he returned home. The event, which included a parade through Southampton Village, was such a success the group decided they'd put on their own rodeo at Montauk over the coming Labor Day weekend.

Bill and Mary Bell, the children of Dr. D.M. Bell, of the Bell Estate, had ridden at Woolnough's and at Dan Huntting's, often with their mother, who rode side-saddle. The two Bell children, having spent summers in Amagansett all their lives, knew the others, though not well. Mrs. Bell had gone to great lengths to encourage her children to interact with the local kids. (For years she was instrumental in helping stage entertainment for the local young people, including plays, parties and dances at the local gathering places for social events, the Presbyterian Session House, Miankoma Hall, and Guild Hall.) The Bell kids had gotten involved with the group during the planning of the Tiana Rodeo and were enthusiastic about the next one.

Bill Bell, with his girlfriend Sally, drove around in his big blue Cadillac putting up posters for the Rodeo. Because it was, in those days, against the law to do business on Sunday, they made Dr. Nugent's Southampton Hospital the beneficiary, making the show a charity. Through Phin's father they got snow fence from the State Park, and made a big ring inside Indian Field. Kids appeared from all over to pitch in.

Fanny Gardiner on Tony

The first Montauk Rodeo was written up in all the papers, including *The New York Times, The Herald Tribune, The Brooklyn Eagle*, as well as *The East Hampton Star*. *The Eagle* had several large pictures, including one of Phin roping a calf, and one of Harold riding a bull over a jump, and one of Fanny with her horse Tony rearing up on his hind legs.

That fall, while out riding with Bill Bell near Third House, and possibly inspired by Fanny's talk about the trips she had made to Wyoming, Phin said to Bill, "This would be a great place for a Dude Ranch."

THE DEEP HOLLOW RANCH

In the 1920s, Carl Fisher was one of the best known real estate speculators in Florida. In 1925 when the Florida real estate market crashed, he shifted his attention to Montauk with the intention of turning it into the "Miami Beach of the north." In 1925, he bought the entire peninsula of Montauk, 10,000 acres in all for $2.5M. When the stock market crashed in 1929, he lost everything. His Montauk Beach Development Company went bankrupt in 1932 and by the mid-1930s, Fisher was penniless. He died in 1939 of complications from alcoholism.

In the fall of 1938, Phin Dickinson and Bill Bell bought the Third House, the barn and about four acres, from the Montauk Beach Development Company, then a group of real estate speculators based in New York, and leased hundreds of the surrounding acres. More than likely, Phin got the money to go in with Bill as partner in The Deep Hollow Ranch from his father Frank Dickinson, part of Budd King's crowd during Prohibition. The Third House had been an important way-station and storage facility for Prohibition's life's blood.

A building contractor from Bridgehampton came out and built a bunk house and several cottages. To save on materials when they added several rooms to the Third House, they used lumber that they stripped from a nearby sheep barn. Carl Fisher had used the barn to house the sheep he'd acquired to go with the Scottish shepherd he'd hired and brought over from Scotland to accentuate a Scottish Highland's mood. In the middle of Indian Field (a large flat plain that Fisher had used as a polo field and which was surrounded by a race track with a privet hedge closing off its infield), they built a large rodeo arena.

Most of the livestock, the horses and cattle, came from a ranch in Waterford, Connecticut, the C Lazy Y, owned by a man named Morgan Chaney. At one time Chaney had been a supervisor for Fred Stone, the owner of Stones Ranch in Flanders, Connecticut, and had traveled with Fred Stone's Wild West Show, which performed around the country, including at the Globe Theater in New York. Fred Stone, born in 1873 in a log cabin in Colorado, started out as a circus performer, then became a Vaudeville star, played the Tin Man in the first Broadway rendition of "The Wizard of Oz," in 1908, and had a long career in motion pictures. His father had been in Buffalo Bill's Wild West Show.

Through Stone, Morgan Chaney had gotten to know Tim McCoy*, Will Rogers, Tom Mix and other movie stars. Chaney operated the riding school at Connecticut College for a number of years and sponsored rodeos and horse shows at his ranch. At one time he had a government contract to supply horses to Camp Trumbull in Niantic, Connecticut. In 1909 he visited the Big Bend area of Texas and bought a ranch there. For the rest of his life, he spent part of each year there, in Marathon, Texas, at the place he called the San Francisco Ranch.

Timothy John Fitzgerald McCoy, born in 1891, lived until 1978. He had been an officer in the Army in both the First and Second World Wars, had retired as a Brigadier General and had served as Adjutant General of Wyoming. He appeared in almost 100 films, including one made from the very popular Zane Grey story, "The Thundering Herd." He was linked with several female stars, including Joan Crawford, with whom he starred in "The Law of The Range," in 1928. He was a friend of Chaney's and along with Chaney visited the ranch in Montauk several times.

In one of his last appearances, McCoy played himself in the 1956 version of "Around the World in 80 Days." During the 1950s he hosted a local TV show in Los Angeles, in which he showed old Western movies and taught lore of the Old West to his audience of children. More recently, he gained notoriety from the disclosure in a book by Seymour Hersh, titled "The Dark Side of Camelot," that his wife of 28 years had been linked to both Adolph Hitler and JFK. In spite of her past, he was married to Inga from 1945 until her death in 1973.

The horses that Fanny and the boys bought from Chaney included horses with names like Butterfly, Piecrust and Yellow Hammer, and a mule named Dynamite who was a bronc. Ern Schellinger bought, for himself, a stallion named El Capitan. Called Cappy, he was small, spotted, Mexican-bred, very pretty, built somewhat like a Paso Fino. Ern, Roy, Fanny and a man named Pars, leading the little stud from horseback, brought Cappy over from Chaney's on the Orient Point Ferry. They went across Shelter Island and rode all the way home to Montauk with Cappy in tow.

Altogether they bought eleven wild horses out of the wild horse event at the Madison Square Garden Rodeo. Bill ended up selling several to kids who began hanging around the ranch. Roy Lester bought one they named Jimmy. Frank Eck, the saloon owner from Amagansett who owned the Elm Tree Inn (later to become a hangout for artists), bought one. Ern bought a Dun mare. And Bud finally got a horse of his own, a brown horse they called Buster. One gray mare that was never really broke was used as a bronc for a while until she became Shank's horse. Shank eventually bred her to Cappy and she had a sorrel colt, a mare with a blaze face that Shank kept and rode for many years.

The rodeos were held weekly, at night under floodlights. They had calf roping, steer riding, saddle bronc and bareback bronc riding. Bill Bell and Pars Fournier were the pickup men, riding up to the riders who stayed on till the buzzer and taking them off. Pars sometimes made it a little too dramatic by barreling into the bronc and rider at full speed, often as not squashing somebody's leg.

Phin and Ern were the best bronc riders. Norm Quarty, who later became the building inspector in East Hampton Village, did some good rope tricks as part of the entertainment, and there was a fellow named Billy Keen, who toured the country, who would jump a convertible touring car while Roman-riding a pair of horses. There was a black man named Tony Travis from over at Chaney's who was the best calf roper and did a trick roping exhibition, including the one where you jump through the big loop, and another where he'd rope three horses at once.

Roy Lester talked Bill Bell into buying a stagecoach from Chaney. Chaney had gotten it from Tim McCoy, who bought it from Fred Stone. It may well have been an original, though restored, relic of the Old West. On its side was painted the words Deadwood-Cheyenne Stage Coach. (A rumor circulated that it had once belonged to Buffalo Bill himself when he toured the country at the turn of the century with his Wild West Show; though that part of its provenance was never confirmed.)

As part of the opening for the Rodeos, Roy would take the stagecoach, hooked to a four-in-hand team, and make two turns around the arena at a dead run. After that he would come down the middle from the far end and dash through the gate. It was Roy Lester's idea of heaven. At one show, someone had neglected to open the gate and in trying to make a sharp turn, the stage flipped over. Roy jumped clear of the wreck and managed to land on his feet with horses well in hand. The stage was a bit banged up, but no one was seriously hurt. Buddy Mullane jumped in the ranch pickup and went to the barn to get a thick rope to right the stage and, in his haste, managed to flip over the pickup, supplying some comic relief for the attendees.

Josephine Rutkowski remembered the Rodeos well. She would take the train from East Hampton to Montauk and either take the stagecoach, when Roy came to pick up the Ranch guests, or if there was no room, someone would pick her up in the ranch's old wood paneled station wagon. At the rodeo shows on Saturday and Sunday night, she would meet up with all of her friends from Joe Loris' bar. "It seemed like everyone in East Hampton was there," she said. "Jimmy Grimshaw and Georgie Stolberg were there, riding broncs; Bepo Bennett rode George, the jumping steer, and there were barbecues and square dances. Hoot Gibson would come out from the city to shoot dice on the bunk house floor and a man named Woodbury, who owned the Woodbury Soap Company, would come with his two sons who loved to ride." There was no question but in those days, the Deep Hollow Ranch was the place to be.

Aside from riding, gunning was another thing that the guests and the help and the hangers-on liked. In those days any pond bigger than a puddle had at least one duck blind and there were several nice ponds between the Third House and the Point. All three ponds, Little Reed, Big Reed, and Oyster Pond, had blinds that the guests could use. Socially prominent people like Jack Chrysler and Jock Whitney would come out to shoot. The best gunner, though, was Len Edwards, the man who owned the East Hampton Movie Theater.

One day, in August, 1939, Harold Govier and a fellow from Southampton were skeet shooting in Indian Field and when they were through they left the gates open. Fanny's horse Tony was turned out in the big field with a few others. All the horses got loose. Nobody went after them. Following Tony, they all started making their way back towards East Hampton. As they came onto the highway at the Eastern end of Napeague beach, in the fog, a Coast Guard man heading west hit Tony with his car. His leg and his back were broken. Someone called Bill Brockman, the local State Trooper in Montauk and he killed the horse with his pistol. Fanny was so devastated that her mother packed her up with her other horses and shipped her to her grandmother in Middleburg, Virginia where she stayed for three months. When she came home, she had a headstone put down on the beach where Tony was buried.

That first summer of 1939 The Ranch made a nice profit and by the following year it was booming. With the War heating up, people couldn't go to Europe and the Ranch, with capacity for 45 people was, during the big weekends, 4th of July and Memorial Day, jamming in as many as 60.

One summer afternoon in 1940, on a day when everyone except Charlie Osborne was out trail riding, a man drove up in a big Cadillac. He stopped and asked Charlie what they did around here. Charlie told the man it was a dude ranch and that they had a skeet field and all that, and as the man was leaving, he recognized him. He was Gary Cooper.

When I repeated this anecdote to Fanny she had to one-up Charlie. She told me the story of the day she was shooting skeet in Bridgehampton with Harold Govier and a man named Elding Warner. She felt something tracking by her ear. She turned to see Warner, who was following the bird with his gun. Angry, she stalked off and when she got safely back away from the point of his gun, she gave Warner hell. From behind her she heard a man chuckling. It was Gary Cooper, there shooting with his wife Veronica Balfe, a Southampton socialite.

THE HURRICANE OF 1938

I once owned a copy of an old *Life* magazine dated Dec. 28th 1942, my birth date, with the caption, "Rommel driving hard into Egypt," with a picture of his advancing troops on the cover. My best drinking and pot smoking buddy during the Sixties was born that same December, which made us both Capricorn, which was part of the data input I used to make some sense out of the nonsense we were up to in that decade, but even so, 1942 never seemed to work as the beginning of my life.

As I believe I've said, my parent's lives bled into mine. And since I have internalized the history of my town to such an extent, as well as my parent's histories, I don't in all honesty feel that my personal history began in 1942. It doesn't scan well for me. (Is this how lies begin?) 1938 was the year the ranch was started. It was the year of the hurricane. And it has always seemed to me like the beginning.

The history of the East End is punctuated by big northeasters and hurricanes. I grew up in the shadow of what people then referred to as The Big One. It has been written about, at least one documentary film has been made (in which much of the voice-over is that of my pal Mickey's father, Milton Miller Sr.) and people have recorded their memories of it in at least several oral histories. I remember the idea of it as exciting and I remember hoping that there would be a big one in my lifetime, so that I could have bragging rights to it. There is something about storms being responsible for a sea change in people's lives, evil winds blowing through, slates being wiped clean. And then too, the '38 storm was closely followed by the Second World War. The Hurricane killed 682 people in its path from Long Island through New England to its final dissipation in lower Canada, and, in today's money, did the equivalent of five billion dollars in damages.

Phin Dickinson was in East Hampton with Roy Lester, Fanny Gardiner, Charlie Osborne, and Buddy Mullane, when the wind began to blow. Phin insisted on being taken home to Montauk. Charlie drove him as far as he could, to the place on Napeague where, by that time, the ocean had broken through, making Montauk into an island. There, a Coast Guardsman brought Phin across in a dory and he walked the short way to the State Park House, his family's home at the time. Bill Bell spent the night of the hurricane with Roy Lester at his family's Pantigo Farm, between Amagansett and East Hampton Village. Several of Roy's horses were pastured about a mile away (in what Roy called the Maude Taylor lot on Town Lane) and broke out and came running home during the big blow.

PARS AND JOSEPHINE

The Hurricane hit at three o'clock in the afternoon. That night Josephine Rutkowski, a waitress at Joe Loris' Restaurant at the East Hampton Hotel, met Pars Fournier, who would become the love of her life. Pars came in with his friends the Stolbergs. He was a man in his fifties, craggy faced, rugged looking, wearing a cowboy hat and Western boots. He was drinking and dancing and giving Josephine the eye.

Pars, whose last name was Fournier, was never referred to locally as anything other than Pars "Funyon." That was as close as any East Hampton local was willing to go in pronouncing any sissy French name. Pars was no sissy. Born in the horse and buggy era, in 1886 in Sag Harbor, he had traveled to Texas in his teens and worked as a cowboy there. During WWI, he worked in New London making torpedoes at Bliss and Company. In New London Pars had gotten married and had a daughter. He abandoned his wife and daughter, but never bothered to get a divorce. He was a scoundrel.

He now lived on the Sag Harbor Road where he raised Foxhounds and, with the Lester boys from Round Swamp in East Hampton, scoured the Northwest Woods hunting foxes for the skins. When he was really hard up for cash, Pars might also do some carpentry.

At the hotel that night Mrs. Stolberg dared Josephine to sit on Pars' lap but she was too busy waiting on her customers. Until, that is, wind knocked down the power lines and the lights went out. The crowd continued on, eating and drinking under kerosene lanterns and candles. Pars made the following comment to Josephine, the poetry of which never left her; "Well how are you tonight, sweetheart, in all this darkness?" "Well, I'm doing pretty well, I guess," she said as she plopped herself down on his lap. That was the beginning and she went on to live with him for thirty-one years.

At the time that I talked to her she was having trouble remembering certain things about those days, but about that night she remembers who ate what (soft shell crab was the favorite dish) and who drank what and what time it was when Pars came in and where he was sitting; over in the corner by the telephone booth. Josephine worked hard all her life and still does and she took good care of Pars. She worked cleaning houses and at Bannisters Laundry and waitressing at Loris's and later in Montauk at Bohler's, a luncheonette, bakery and soda fountain, in business all through the Fifties.

When I visited her in the 1990s she had a nice little business doing washing and ironing of shirts for some of the richest men in the summer colony, including Steve Ross of Warner Communications. She was also boarding horses in her back lot, where Pars, long dead by now, had kept his horses, including a very pretty little Quarterhorse stallion, named Honky Tonk.

WORLD WAR II

The War was coming and Ern Schellinger was the first to enlist. He had joined the Navy and had his tour extended till the duration. Bud Mullane and three other local fellows went in together in 1940. In 1941, Charlie Osborne went off to the University of Texas. Bill Bell went into the Navy in March of '42. Before he left, the Army requisitioned the Indian Field, leaving the ranch with no arena and no flat grazing land. Roy Lester had a heart condition and was 4-F. He bought the Deadwood Coach, another coach called a Waggonette Brake, and two motor vehicles, a platform truck and the pickup. At the end of the War he became Superintendent of Highways of East Hampton Town and spent the rest of his life either in politics or road construction and collecting wagons and coaches as a hobby.

All three Dickinson boys were in the War. Phin went to Italy, Shank to China and the South Pacific, and the youngest, Jack, was in the infantry in Northern Italy. Shank spent ten months in the China of Chiang Kai Shek as part of a support group that serviced B-29s. Phin, in a scene reminiscent of the movie *To Hell and Back*, was hit by shrapnel. There were seven soldiers holed up at night in a farm house. They took a direct hit. Three men were killed and the rest were wounded. Phin lost an eye and part of a finger.

Charlie, the kid in the gang, was 20 years old and in the Air Corps. After what seemed an endless series of schools, from South Dakota to California to Texas to Arizona and back to California, he ended up in Torretta, Italy, on the Foggia Plain, in a B-24 group. He flew 35 missions, mostly as co-pilot. On his 31st mission, they were shot down over Austria, somewhere between Munich and Vienna. They were in their usual plane, called Knockout, and Charlie was co-pilot. As they came in for a crash landing, they put their wheels down as a signal of surrender, but the Germans kept shooting. They came down between the line separating the German and Russian troops. Some Russians appeared, who picked them up and took them to Bucharest, Romania. Charlie noticed that the truck they rode in was a Ford, a Model A made in Russia, with the Ford medallion in Russian lettering.

The guys who weren't captured, including Charlie, spent five days in a boxcar, traveling 75 miles. They lived on what food they could scrounge, including bread, sausage and wine. In Romania, they caught the Orient Express and took the overnight ride to Bucharest. (The five that were captured and became POWs were liberated in about a month, by Patton.) "We had a bit of a hard time," Charlie said. In Bucharest they were picked up by a South African DC-8 and returned to Italy, where they flew several more missions before the War ended.

PINCKNEY ISLAND

During the War, Harold Govier and Pars Fournier, both too old to serve, were approached by a man named James Bruce, who had a house in Southampton and was head of an outfit called International Dairies in New York City. Bruce wanted them to go down and manage a cattle farm he owned on Pinckney Island, off the coast of North Carolina near Hilton Head. Harold and Pars went down first to check it out and when they came back, Pars asked Josephine if she'd like to come down with him and she said she would. "If you don't think I'll be in the way," she added, in her usual self-effacement.

So she quit her job house-cleaning for I.Y. Halsey, a local car dealer, and with Pars and Harold already back down there she, all by herself, loaded Pars' belongings and all of hers into the one horse trailer he owned and hitched it to the back of her old Plymouth and headed down U.S.1. Along the way, she made herself useful to the war effort, giving lifts to hitchhiking soldiers.

In spite of the heat and the snakes and the mosquitoes, to Josephine the place was a tropical paradise. From the cabin that she and Pars shared they could watch through binoculars as the Marine recruits trained on Paris Island. She had always enjoyed keeping busy and there were lots of things for her to do. While the men were de-horning cows, she would count heads and put sulfur on the wounds. Because there were lots of snakes on the island, everyone wore high boots and had to learn how to inject themselves with antidote. It was Pars job to kill the snakes and keep a record of what kind they were. And there was a tame wild turkey that came to the door to beg. He was Josephine's pet. He ate from her hand. She named him Tom.

Other than an on-going struggle between Harold and Pars over who was the boss, all went well on Pinckney Island until one night when they all had dinner together at Harold and Alice's* cabin on the other end of the island. After dinner they stayed up late playing cards and Pars and Josephine ambled home late, in the cool of the evening, walking off the big meal. Pars woke up early the next morning in a fit of anger. "Son of a bitch killed our turkey," he said. "That was Tom we ate."

Back in Montauk, Alice had very briefly been married to Bill Bell, but had quickly been stolen away by Harold, in what would have been a scandal if there had been anything like a real town in Montauk in those days, and if Bill had ever let himself be ruffled by any idea that his life was ever anything but sunshine and roses.

The turkey incident was a sad one for Josephine and an ego deflating one for Pars so, not long after, the couple headed home. Harold called Fanny in Virginia and asked her to come down to replace Pars. That was in the spring of 1944. Not one for sentimental goodbyes, Fanny left mother and friends without fanfare and headed south. She drove down Route 15 through Warrenton, Virginia and Upperville, her mother's family's ancestral turf, and stopped overnight to visit with her relatives. She had two passengers, a dog and a baby. The baby was two years old.

No one had any idea where the baby came from. Fanny had a gruff persona, that discouraged people from asking her personal questions. No one ever said "Who's the father Fanny?" People just made up stories. Most of her close friends assumed it was Phin. Other people had other ideas. There were several versions going around. The baby, Frances, who is my age, told me she always assumed it was Phin, until finally, in middle-age, she got up the nerve to ask Mom, who told her without hesitation.

During the War, with only the Inn part of the ranch still open, Fanny had taken a turn as manager. In April of 1942, she had a brief encounter (possibly as brief as one weekend) with a radio writer-announcer whose name was Gardner, not spelled the same, but still a coincidence.

Ed Gardner was the voice of Archie the bartender on *Duffy's Tavern*, one of the most popular radio shows of all time; a serial which ran from 1941 to 1951 back in the days before television. Gardner wrote and starred in the show which he produced with Abe Burrows, a well-known Broadway comedian. The show was an Irish joke made into a running gag. (It was said that Gardner was an Irishman who had changed his name because you had to have an English name to work in radio.) Its theme song was *When Irish Eyes Are Smiling*, and it always began with Archie answering the phone in a New York Irish accent, saying "Hello, Duffy's Tavern, where the elite meet to eat. Archie the manager speakin', Duffy ain't here. Oh, hello, Duffy." Then Archie would tell Duffy, who never appeared, the latest adventures of the staff and patrons.

The regulars included Gardner's first wife, Shirley Booth, the first to play Duffy's daughter, and Eddie Green, who played Eddie the waiter. Guest stars included Fred Allen, Mel Allen, Nigel Bruce, Billie Burke, Bing Crosby, Bob Hope, Boris Karloff, Alan Ladd, Veronica Lake, Peter Lorre, Tony Martin, Marie McDonald, Gene Tierney, Arthur Treacher and Shelley Winters. Larry Gelbart, who much later wrote "M*A*S*H," and Dick Martin, co-host of Rowan and Martin's "Laugh-In," also did some writing for the show.

Duffy's was a direct inspiration for *Archie Bunker's Place*, Jackie Gleason's "Joe the Bartender" sketches, as well as *Cheers*, co-created by Abe Burrows son, James.

The baby, who grew up to be my lifelong friend Fran, has only a vague memory of a night when she got out and wandered around in the snake-filled subtropical night, unnoticed until Fanny heard the screen door close and her daughter came toddling back in. During the day, she would follow her mother around while she worked, mostly staying out of trouble, except for the time she threw a shotgun shell into some burning trash. Until she saw the blood trickling down her own arm, Fanny didn't realize they'd both been hit. Fran said it was no worse than a mosquito bite.

Fanny's job included trapping hawks, killing snakes and clearing brush. Once, with the rifle she'd been equipped with, she took a shot at a big gator that lived near where she was using a tractor to mow a field full of something she was told was called coffee bean weed. She shot at him once and never saw him again. Though there were no horses on the island, Fanny noted to me that occasionally they were visited by a black man named Chiz who went from island to island in an old tin boat that he used to transport both his mowing machine and his small, scruffy, old stallion that pulled the rig.

POST WAR

Bud Mullane stayed in the Army until retiring and lived his whole life in California. Bill Bell met his wife, Betty, in Sherman, Texas before The War. After The War he still owned the Ranch, but didn't re-open it. He and Betty lived in a large apartment in Manhattan and engaged in a mild mannered life of charities and social functions, but he always loved to talk about his "Ranch Days."

Phin married and built a house on the Montauk Golf Course and worked for a while for the town as a foreman of the Montauk division of the Highway Department. In 1947 the Ranch was sold to a restaurateur from Bay Shore, Long Island who ran it successfully for some years as a restaurant, inn and guest ranch. The youngest Dickinson brother, Jack, managed the inn for Bill Cooper, the new owner. Phin worked a deal where he could raise cattle and horses on the Ranch property, which added to the Ranch atmosphere. He bought the cattle in Texas, had them shipped by rail, and sold them in the fall.

Shank married and became the State Park Policeman for Montauk and moved into the State Park House at Montauk Point.

By 1947 they were all home, including Eleanor Dickinson's husband Dave Baker, a local East Hampton man who had become a dentist. Dave had been over in France with a dental outfit. (According to one source, he worked on General Patton's teeth.) Eleanor and Dave Baker moved to a house in Amagansett.

Charlie Osborne built a thriving real estate and insurance business in East Hampton and raised a family, and though he hadn't ridden in years, he continued to wear his boots and cowboy hat to the office until the day he died.

After phasing out of potato farming Roy Lester started a road construction company and served for a time as Town Highway Superintendent. He continued raising horses and cattle. He died in 1977 after a long bout with heart disease.

Around 1948 or '49, Phin helped start the Montauk Quadrille Team, a square dance on horseback that had 16 local riders including Roy, Phin, Ern, Jack, and some of the wives, some other local people who had been part of the old ranch crowd, and several newcomers. The Team performed at Eastern Long Island horse shows throughout the Fifties.

FRAN

Other than the vague memories of being stung by bird shot on Pinckney Island, Fanny's daughter Fran's earliest memories were all of living with Mom at the Brown House on Main Street in East Hampton. She remembers being in the barn behind the house and being kicked by a horse and having the wind knocked out of her and being given a tetanus shot with a needle that was first boiled on the stove. She remembers getting a hot bath in a big, dark colored tub by grandmother, a handsome woman and a Virginia aristocrat.

Grandmother and her friend Mrs. Shy were spiritualists. They had been involved in astrology and seances and had been made to burn all their books when they joined the I AM religion. Fran was ten years old, the only child among dozens of adults, when with grandmother, she visited Mt. Shasta, California, the center for the I AM. The leaders of this group of mostly wealthy people, gentiles only, who met among the tall pine trees and deep ravines of the Sierra Mountains, were Mama and Papa (Guy and Edna) Ballard. Mama Ballard, in a white fox fur coat, stood on a stage decked out with an abundance of flowers, a huge white gardenia pinned to her bosom. No one protested the white fox fur, though live animals were banned from indoors when the I AM got together. The adherents believed that animals could get mean when disoriented by the power given off by the higher beings that showed up at these meetings.

The I AM believed you could be reincarnated and become so holy that you needed no sustenance. They placed special value on certain colors: red was dangerous and white was good; and purple was powerful. Superior beings, effeminate, with gigantic pastel lavender eyes peered out from pictures in the books and charts that Fran and her friend Robin, Mrs. Shy's granddaughter, inherited. Fran showed me a picture of one of the beings carrying a sword enfolded in flames.

In 1949 Grandfather Winthrop, nearly bankrupt, having spent many years rebuilding the estate, was forced to sell the Brown House to pay his debts, after which he "ran off," with a Southampton woman to spend the rest of his life in Connecticut. Then in her seventies, grandmother went to live a short distance down the street in a tiny house behind her son Winthrop Jr.'s Windmill Cottage. The little house had several small rooms and a living room dwarfed by a large crystal chandelier. She used a sideboard for an altar, for her I AM worship.

Fran stayed with "Grandmama" often. As a little girl she loved sitting at her grandmother's dressing table and playing grown up, trying on her jewelry, or sitting quietly while her grandmother brushed her hair. She would often join in saying the I AM decrees. "Mighty I Am Presence," they would begin, "Charge me with the violet consuming flame of divine love...," and on in that vein, beseeching the higher power for envelopment in a cloak of white light. There were countless sayings and altogether, according to Fran, it was a protective and loving environment for a young girl to grow up in.

After a few years at the Brown House, Fanny and Frances moved to Three Mile Harbor, to a very small and very old house on a large piece of scrub oak acreage. Fanny married a local dog trainer, Phil Collins, and they had a daughter Mary. Fanny kept two horses, Tony and Indian, but didn't ride that much. Phil liked to fish, and Fanny and Phil spent a good deal of time fishing in the bay. They had fishing for bluefish down to a science and would fish two poles at a time each, and in that way caught more fish than they could give away.

Though Phil's reputation as a trainer came mostly from Chesapeakes, he had Coonhounds too. According to Fran they had, "Coonhounds all over the place, in kennels out back and tied up in the yard." But not in the house; these were not pets. Along with a veterinarian from Riverhead named Dr. Goode, they spent many nights Coon hunting. After putting the two girls to bed, they would wake up Fran in the middle of the night (she wanted to go), and they would go "running all over hell and gone," as she put it. She would sit in the car while they drove after the baying of the hounds, till finally they'd tree a raccoon and he'd be shot out of the tree. "Then, we could go home!" she told me.

One of Fran's favorite memories is of a day when she was still a little girl, when Tony and Indian got loose. Fanny drove Fran and a young neighbor boy over to where the two horses were, in the woods off Springs Road. The boy put Fran on Tony, a Tennessee Walker named after the horse who was killed by a car in Montauk, and the boy rode Indian. They started back, the kid in the lead, Fran following, without bridle, halter or lead rope. The boy wasn't looking behind him when Tony veered off and headed for Amagansett, where, the year before, the two horses had been turned out at Stony Hill Farm. Tony took off at a good clip in his smooth running walk. He was remembering the sweet grass.

Fran rode through scrub oak woods and meadows, over the high land between ocean and bay, and down Stony Hill Road past the old fire tower and into the deep woods and big trees behind Stony Hill Farm and came to a halt in front of the barn and out stepped a man so handsome he looked, to Fran, like the Cisco Kid. She thought she was in a dream. It was Jeffrey Potter. He asked what her name was and where did she come from and where was her saddle and bridle, and then he lent her a bridle and sent her off back home. She says that she remembers that day as one of having no fear and of experiencing only the magic of something new around every corner.

Fanny's house wasn't without its charm. There were some fine antiques around that came from the Island. In corners were pieces of fine china and some pieces of cut glass that were very valuable and had dried flowers stuck in them. On the rafters hanging by nails were shotguns, rifles, pistols, and even an elephant gun. There were trophies and ribbons from horse shows, saddles, bridles, Navaho blankets, open jars of peanut butter, and wandering in and out, chickens, ducks, geese and goats. There were boxes and boxes of what Fran today refers to as "crap and corruption. Wherever there was a spot, there was junk. And a kitchen full of dirty dishes. Mom never once thought about keeping house."

But Fanny's sister Babe, the elegant socialite Mrs. Isabel Mairs, would come to visit occasionally. She had one child, a boy, and she adored Fran and she decided one day that Fran was just too backward in social graces, too much of a bumpkin. In fact, she felt that Fanny was neglecting Fran, and so she convinced Fanny to ship her down to the southern family for some polishing up.

So when she was twelve, Frances went to spend a year with Great Aunt Neville and Great Uncle Tom who lived on a farm in Virginia. (They were from Grandmama's side of the family.) They were both sixty-six years old. They had two daughters who had left home, who were about the age of Fanny. The place, which was vast, was set in a vista of rolling hills with the Blue Ridge Mountains off in the distance. Everyone rode; it was hunt country. Aunt Neville rode side-saddle, and Uncle Tom was training a three year old colt as a hunter.

It was the opposite of being with mother where they lived in a tiny house with little money and Fanny never gave a damn about what people thought. Propriety here was everything and everywhere. At dinner Uncle Tom wore black patent leather shoes with little bows on top and a smoking Jacket. Aunt Neville wore what looked like a long, wrapped, velvet dress. And she wore pearls. It was more than Fran could have been exposed to in Springs in a hundred years. There were servants. You rang a bell and one came in. And you had to eat breakfast, which she'd never ever done. And you had to go to church on Sunday.

She was sent to a private progressive school called the Calverton School, where she read *Lorna Doone* and a bit of Greek mythology, quite advanced compared to Springs School at the time. Students had to speak in front of the whole school at assembly, which almost frightened her to death. A year later she was back at the little house on Three Mile Harbor Road, a baptized Episcopalian with a trace of hunt country Virginia in her speech. The little house took some getting used to now that she had become accustomed to the grandeur and the order of Aunt Neville's.

Fanny lost interest in fishing when Phil developed cancer in the early Fifties. She started buying horses when he got sick. In 1953 she named her property Rocking Horse Ranch and started a "hack line," a horse rental business. Partly because it coincided with the Western fad in films and TV, kids from all over the area began to ride there.

The kids loved Fanny, who dressed like some Wild West heroine, in boots and hat and silver belt, dark hair waving in the wind. Trim figured and elegant with her tanned, long fingered hands holding the reins lightly, her emerald and diamond ring sparkling in the sun, she would lope along slowly, instructing the kids with patience and care. Phil died in 1955.

Fran gained confidence in her riding while in Virginia where she was coached in English horsemanship, and because she gained self-confidence from the more disciplined environment, her mother began to give Fran horses. The first one was Indian. Then, when she turned twelve, Fanny decided to give her the Tennessee Walker, Tony. Fran became horse crazy.

Every horse had a story. There was Butterfly, who had been Winston Guest's polo pony. Guest had rented Gardiner's Island and had brought over his horses and Butterfly was one of them. And soon after that she was given Peaches, a small, pretty Palomino. Then there were the Pixies, three look-a-like sorrel horses that Fanny and her daughters rode in local shows as a family group. One was Fanny's, one was Fran's and one was Mary's. As I remember, they were Pixie, Little Pixie and Pixie Three.

But her favorite horse, the one she loved most, was the one I remember seeing her on the day we rode over to play broom polo. Skinny Fran in a pixie haircut, rolled up jeans, a dirty tee shirt and dirty bare feet almost made me swallow my heart. And Star was a perfect match for her. She had a very long mane, a forelock that went down to her nose, long eyelashes and eyes that were rimmed with black, as if she were wearing kohl.

Star was Fran's pet more than anything else. They had gone up-island to a horse dealer named Paulie James in Lake Grove, looking for a horse for her friend Tink. James' place was ramshackle, with sheds and barns spread all over. The two girls went running from stall to stall to see what was what and in one barn in the last stall was a sickly horse with an unusual coloration, a bay with dapples. Under her jaw she had a nasty sore from a condition called strangles, a type of strep infection. That was Star.

Star put her head down and Fran began talking to her and petting her. Fanny told her not to touch the horse, she'd give the disease to all the others. The horse was friendly and sweet but untrained and according to Paulie it was not worth a goddamn. But that's the horse Fran wanted. Star, though, was problematic. She mixed her leads, what Fran called cross-fired. She had a bad back. And her bad gait hurt Fran's back too. And the mare had tantrums. She'd work herself into a sweat standing in her stall and only Fran could calm her. She was a one person horse. Eventually, though, she just became too much trouble and had to be sold.

Horses came and went. One did a little dressage and could jump. Another "cantered in a teacup and stopped on a dime. When you reined him he came right up off the ground. But he was sour, whenever he saw a show ring, he'd go on strike!" In 1958 on Skip, the best handling horse she ever had, she won the Long Island Reining Championship.

CHAMP

Abe Katz was an East Hampton dairy farmer who now and then sold a few horses. Carolyn took me over to his place and I picked out a little Arabian gelding. The horse's name was Champ. I boarded him at Emil Gardell's barn in Amagansett. Mr. Gardell was a man who, even then in the 1950's, made his living with a team of horses, plowing people's gardens, mowing hay, giving hay rides, and in the winter, plowing the sidewalks on both sides of the street all the way up to East Hampton Village, a distance of several miles. He had an extra box stall and an old half rotten English saddle and bridle that he agreed to let me borrow until I could buy my own.

The first morning after he was delivered by Abe, I was there at Gardell's brushing him down at six o'clock. I had never ridden a horse alone, but I didn't let on to anyone that I was scared. I remember feeling a kinship with Champ who was also noticeably scared. I was confused about which way to go and was ready to head down toward the beach and changed my mind. I rode out the driveway past the boarding house that was Mr. Gardell's home and headed out across the Main Street macadam and into a huge vacant lot that now houses the Amagansett Farmers Market, a fancy vegetable and "balsamic vinegar" emporium. Champ went prancing across the street in true Arab fashion, tail up, nostrils flaring; he was in a hot sweat before we got a hundred feet into the big, ragweed-filled lot. Then the background noise which I hadn't paid any attention to before changed its rhythm. It was the Cannonball, the local name for the 7 AM train to New York City.

The train, one of the big diesels that had replaced steam locomotives only a few years earlier, was just leaving the station, revving up the way diesels do. The combined noise of the revving engines, the clanking of the cars following up, and the thunder of the heavy train rolling across the tracks, made a noise that both horse and boy could feel through the ground. Champ got one look at that gigantic noisemaker coming his way and spun around and took off like a shot back towards Gardell's, bucking and snorting all the way.

I'd lost my grip on the reins and lost both stirrups and was trying to readjust when he slid on the macadam, going down on his left hip, and I fell on my back on the pavement with my sneakered left foot stuck in the stirrup. I still had hold of the reins but was dragged across the street and over the curb before he stopped to eat grass and I was able to get my foot out. I knew it was a nasty near-miss. I could have been killed. But my first thought was, "Did anybody see me?" As far as I could tell, there had not even been a soul peering out a window. Not to be embarrassed was all that mattered. No one must ever know.

Champ was a problem which I faced willingly and willfully. He never bolted again but he stayed nervous and so did I. After a couple of weeks I met up with a group of riders, local people from the village, all riding Western, and rode along with them, enjoying their company until Champ kicked a few times at their horses. They insisted I put a red ribbon in his tail and, after I'd ridden with them a few more times and he'd proved himself to be very nasty, kicking and biting and having his ears back nearly all the time, one of the men, named Roy, said I should return Champ to Abe and swap him for a more serviceable horse.

ROY LESTER

Having been declared 4-F because of a heart murmur, Roy Lester had spent the coldest part of the first winter of The War at Deep Hollow, acting as caretaker. He was fending for himself for the first time, without his mother and two sisters to cook and take care of him. During that winter and again the following year, he twice bred his mare Topsy, a Mustang given to him by Dan Huntting, to El Capitan, the little stallion they had gotten from Chaney, getting Pawnee and Blackie, a horse and a mare. The pair were almost identically marked. (Roy called them "spotted horses," but technically they would today probably be classified as Dominant-White Tobiano.) He kept both horses for the rest of their lives. Pawnee was his main riding horse, but he also paired him with full sister Blackie as a handsome team with which he drove many of his smaller vehicles, including a two-horse hay mowing machine.

When I first met him, Roy was just forty years old, short, balding and slightly overweight; a condition he always referred to as "stout." (Stout could mean either heavy or strong, as in "hitch up that block and tackle to a stout post," or fat as in "That boy is awful stout.") He was no taller than me; we were both still a half-foot shy of my Old Man.) He had good self-esteem, though, and thought of himself as looking something like Tom Mix. He was still a boy when his father died and left him Pantigo Farm, 22 acres of farmland, thick, dark, chocolate colored Bridgehampton Loam, with a homestead, a big barn, several out-buildings, several teams of horses, and farm equipment.

His mother and two unmarried sisters lived in the homestead their entire lives. One sister was a school teacher and the other a secretary in an insurance office in town, and mom and both sisters were devoted to Roy and treated him as the head of the family. While still a young man he had expanded his business to include raising pigs, dairy farming and then mining gravel and running a small trucking company. He was one of the town leaders, active in the Republican Party. For entertainment he collected and drove horse drawn vehicles.

Roy was a person you would think held a patent on being down to earth. He regularly made proclamations to me which he meant to be on the Q.T, and which he would preface with, "Now, between you me and the lamppost," which might have been about a certain person not being too bright, or some attitude of someone's being "a little too communistic." I always agreed with him, even if I also quietly carried alternate opinions in my youthful and malleable brain.

He craved political position, and after being Superintendent of Highways, would run a couple of more times in his life, spending a small fortune in a futile attempt to make everything right in his world. (He was very right wing; a member of the John Birch Society.) He kept a half-dozen men busy in his trucking business, kept his barns and machinery insured, his horses well cared for and all his equipment well maintained. Like the old men he grew up admiring, he believed Teddy Roosevelt had been the last great president.

Roy had responsibility thrust upon him at an early age but had settled into the burden easily and taken his pleasure in being hard-working and successful. Some of the men who worked for him (often relatives) were from fishing families and would quit periodically when fishing was good, to go back "on the water." He didn't exactly look down on them but took more of a paternal approach. He always tried to have employment ready for them when they needed it.

He broke his horses both to ride and drive, kept them "hog fat," as he called it, and when riding, he liked a fast walk and a slow lope. He did all his own training and shoeing. Pawnee, who was well aware that he was boss horse at the farm, was Roy's personal riding horse. He and Roy had an affectionate though manly and gruff relationship. Once or twice, when Pawnee was antsy to get out of his stall or, when in harness, to get working, I saw Roy yell at him, and Pawnee would snap to attention and act terrified, but I felt it was an act, because overall the horse handled so well; around the barn, roping calves or herding cattle, driving single, double or four in hand, getting in and out of trucks and trailers, and especially, Roy was very proud of this, the way Pawnee and his sister worked pulling the clackety old hay mowing machine. Roy's two favorite topics of conversation were working with horses and politics.

On Roy's advice I decided to trade Champ. With my mother, I went back to Abe Katz's Dairy in East Hampton and Abe showed me a very gentle, snow-white albino gelding, two years old, fifteen hands, with one blue eye and one brown, green broke, that someone had named Jerry. He should have been called "Unflappable," because a bomb going off wouldn't have startled him. (That's a small exaggeration, he didn't care much for groups of backfiring motorcycles, or the ocean when it was very rough.) I remember Abe had me ride him out from his farm into a field to the west which was wild grass then, but which grew into a full forest of forty foot tall pitch pine and oak, and finally became a housing development. Abe took Champ back and gave me Jerry as an even trade and trucked him to Roy's Pantigo Farm, where I would board him.

Roy had just recently gone into the boarding business and I boarded with him for the same price as Gardell's, $25 a month. There were a couple of other boarders, and Roy lent me a saddle till I got one for Christmas. My father wasn't too pleased that I needed a new saddle, a rough-out Western saddle with a Latigo leather foam-rubber lined seat, but he did buy it for me for Christmas. It cost as much as the horse. Along with the new saddle he also bought me a nice Navajo blanket. To be honest, Jerry was a somewhat clunky horse. His head was too big, his knees a little knobby, and he had trouble keeping weight on. But in those days most kid's horses were not perfect specimens. He was scrawny like me, difficult to keep fat on and difficult to keep clean.

Roy had some good horses. Not fancy and expensive, these were farm horses and pleasure horses of differing types and assigned to no registry. (He did have one thoroughbred filly that he'd bought at a sale in New Jersey, who had a benign tumor on one leg; and he planned to breed her when she was older.)

He kept his father's farm going in a way that suggested that there was still a need for horses that drove farm vehicles. When he had time, he would use a team to harrow or mow a field, or to pull a manure spreader, or pull a tree stump. He hired out his vehicles for parties and parades; and he took friends for rides. Keeping alive the days of a working horse-and-buggy day's farm was his mission in life. He needed driving horses for his wagon collection and his wagon collection needed horses. It was circular reasoning that worked perfectly. I'm also sure that, in part, keeping the farm alive was an homage to his father and his father's times; an effort to carry that set of knowledge and skills forward.

I owned Jerry from the winter of 1955-1956, when I was in the eighth grade and about to graduate from Amagansett Grade School, till shortly after I graduated from East Hampton High School in the spring of 1960. During those years I experienced most of the physical phase of adolescence, the growth part. I grew from about five foot zero and under one hundred pounds to 5'8' and 125 pounds. Being busy and responsible for my own horse, I didn't have enough time for an identity crisis, or any of the adolescent problems that a nervous, complicated kid from an artsy family had a right to, and in fact would get around to later. In my first year of horse ownership I made several friends who would help smooth the way for me in my transition from the little Grade School in Amagansett to the slightly bigger high school in East Hampton.

With the post-War economic boom and the proliferation of Westerns on our black and white television sets having contributed to a Western oriented horse riding and ownership boom on Long Island, it seemed every kid who'd gone riding at Fanny's suddenly had a horse stashed in a backyard pen with a corner stall in the car garage. It was inevitable that someone would organize a club.

At first I was Roy's only boarder at Pantigo Farm and rode mostly by myself or with him. Through January and February of 1956 we rode every weekend and sometimes after school I'd get off the school bus at the Pantigo corner and go for a short ride by myself, often with snowflakes flying.

Roy and I became friends. He talked to me man to man, ignoring the fact that I was probably the youngest looking twelve year old within miles. But within a few months there were three more boarders and, with Roy's horses, the barn was full. Roy took us on sleigh rides up into the Amagansett Woods, where his wife would join us with hot cocoa and cookies.

By spring there were several more kids and the Pantigo barn had become an informal riding club. There were two new boys; Dave, whose family owned a liquor store, and Jamie who wasn't a boarder, but was Roy's cousin's son and lived next door with his own barn and pasture. His father had bought him a small spotted horse that was quick and agile. Jamie, Dave and I had all ridden at Fanny's the year before we got horses. Dave had a big Palomino. And there were two girls, Peggy, who had an Appaloosa, and Peggy Lou, who had a sleek, chocolate colored mare. We were all about the same age.

During that first spring at Pantigo, David, Jamie and I often went riding with the two girls. Peggy, who had the Appaloosa mare, was a shy, pigtailed redhead, whose Italian father ran the vegetable section at the A&P. Her mother was Scottish, which explained the red hair. Peggy Lou, whose father was from one of East Hampton's founding families and who had been part of the Deep Hollow Ranch crew, was a little older than the rest of us, we were all twelve or thirteen, but she acted even older.

Peggy Lou was a serious tease, precocious and provocative, with a well-developed body. All three of us boys fixated on her, letting the other Peggy tag along as the third wheel. Jamie, Dave and I were at the constantly horny stage and Jamie, the brave one, wasn't afraid to yowl about his boner. David and I felt brave along with him. With Tommy I'd already established my habit of letting a brave man/boy lead the way; a habit I would keep through my twenties.

Peggy Lou's well rounded hips looked good in her blue jeans and molded well to the cantle of her expensive Western saddle. Her horse, the best looking horse of the bunch, a Quarter Horse mare, was the color of milk chocolate. Whenever we went out riding as a group and the groups got larger with time, Peggy Lou trailed a wake of boys and men, whoever happened to be along that day, jockeying to see her from behind; or just her behind.

Peggy Lou's father, J. Harrison Mulford, treated both his daughter and her mare in a heavy handed, mean-spirited way. He rode herd on his daughter, whipping her whenever there was half an excuse. He did the same with the mare, though she had come so well trained there was never any real need for it. (Roy put a quick stop to the mistreatment of the mare, reminding Harrison that it was his barn.) The only affect the whip had on Peggy Lou was to put a rebellious gleam in her eye, meant to let her father know he was making a fool of himself. Soon enough it worked and J. Harrison, frail anyway from having one lung removed due to lung cancer, gave up his reign of terror.

According to the standards of horse ownership in the Hamptons today, our horses were mostly just plugs. (In those days there were more plugs around than expensive pleasure horses; now that's very much the reverse.) I use the pejorative plug loosely, because no single handle would pin it down. Outside of the few small horse dealers in the area, like Phin Dickinson and his father, for inexpensive horses most people went to either Milton Potter in Northport, Long Island, or to a horse auction in Metuchen, New Jersey. There, you could find Mustangs, caught wild in the west and shipped directly east, as well as "Remount" horses, those that had been bred for the government during the days leading up to the Second World War, before the Cavalry was disbanded, as well as Thoroughbreds, Standardbred and farm and pleasure horses that were being sold cheaply for one reason or another.

In a few years, when some people in Montauk would start raising Registered Quarter Horses, prices would go into the thousands. But for now we mostly paid two or three hundred dollars for a horse. These horses were what were called Grade horses, or Mustangs, or were tagged with a name that was more often a physical description, like Spotted Horse, Paint, Palomino, Hunter, Quarter Horse, part Thoroughbred, or what not.

The South Fork Trailblazers Riding Club was started by the mother of three boys and the wife of the owner of the largest remaining dairy in East Hampton, Mrs. Frank Tillinghast. The first meeting was held in the remodeled basement of Bart Hadel, son and heir of the Amagansett potato farm of Bart Hadel Sr., who had also been Postmaster after Pop Cartwright. Bart Jr. had bought two horses, one for each of his kids, Midge and John.

That first year, The Trailblazers organized at least one trail ride a month. These rides were a good opportunity for a kid like me to listen in on adult conversations, something I had a natural talent for. Probably I'd inherited that talent from Carolyn, who loved to eavesdrop. Kids weren't so much a part of the adult world in those days and it was easier to go unnoticed. These were the other kind of people, non-art, non-citified, not poor or rich, just normal. I learned local gossip that most kids weren't even interested in.

Most rides called for members to join the group-in-progress as it came near their stable, and to continue traveling along a trail that the Long Island Railroad maintained alongside the railroad tracks. The trail, originally cleared to put out fires that the old steam engines caused, was now used to facilitate track repair.

Often we met at the greasy spoon shack that adjoined a golf

driving range on the East Hampton-Southampton boarder, an area called Sagaponack. It was all woods along that trail from Amagansett to Southampton and back, and we would meet up there with the Hand family from Wainscott and a group from Southampton who also traveled along the train trail. The Greasy Spoon, a borderline den of iniquity, catered to locals and a handful of eccentrics, including a sign painter, one of the owners, named Willie Whitehead, a self-proclaimed Beatnik who had his own zany posters on the walls advertising the cuisine. They served burgers, hot dogs, and ice cream. Country folks, in those days including the adults, always seemed to be big on ice cream.

On one of these night rides, as our East Hampton contingent wound its way home through the dark, one of the lead riders heard a noise in the woods and, riding in to investigate, found a downed airplane, its radio crackling, with its pilot and a passenger inside, both injured. There were no cell phones in those days, so one of the men rode ahead to the nearest house and called the police.

Abe Katz, the man I'd bought my horse from, went on the rides often, along with his girlfriend and her two kids, Charlene and Billy. Abe was a Holstein breeder and a pioneer in selling frozen bull sperm. He had customers as far away as South America. Over the years that I knew him, he had several girlfriends, always blond, and always among the most attractive women in the community. They were either divorcees or widows. The story was that being Jewish, and with his father presumably still alive somewhere, he couldn't marry a Gentile, so he was condemned to live his life unmarried, something for which he should, everyone seemed to agree, be forgiven due to the circumstances. Why he didn't just find a nice Jewish girl was a question I suppose no one thought to just ask.

Abe was a nice guy; liked by everybody. He had the same toothy movie star smile that all my heroes among the horsey crowd had, probably due to the ministrations of Dave Baker, the favored dentist for the local gentry, who as you might remember had married Eleanor, the sister of the Dickinson boys. Abe had acquired his farm with its acreage and house and barn during the Depression from the owner of Manhattan's McAlpin Hotel, Gen. Edwin A. McAlpin. Abe changed the name from McAlpin Farm to Dune Alpine Farm, a clever name change since there were (and still are) ancient dunes under the earth in that area. See the excellent book about the area, *The South Fork,* by Everett Rattray.

ED WELLES

In 1940, Roy bought and began to renovate a large barn with several acres of land in Amagansett. The building, which still stands and is now an Art School, is on Indian Wells Highway, the road to the Main Beach and Bathing Club, right off Main Street in Amagansett. In the 19th and early 20th centuries the building had been a Livery Stable owned by a man named Nichols. The back of the building opened into a tiny valley, with the barn doors opening out of the cellar, while the front entrance opened from the first floor, back from the street, with a paved parking area out to the road. During the War, Roy had used the Livery Stable cellar as a potato storehouse. He had broken out the stables and the concrete floor so that the potatoes would have a dirt floor to lie on, and had lowered the door space at the rear of the barn so that big trucks full of potatoes could back into the cellar.

The main floor was used as a machine shop for his trucks and to store his collection of horse-drawn vehicles, some of which he'd inherited from his father, and others he'd picked up in his travels. (I went with him on occasion to rummage through old barns.) The collection had grown to fill the second floor and the attic as well. In the attic, mostly in advanced disrepair, were sleighs, sleigh runners and numerous two wheel carts, gigs and sulkies, which he rarely if ever used.

Roy married Bernice Adams of Amagansett, in November of 1946. When they were first married, they lived in an apartment that was attached to the side of the livery stable. The apartment had been where "Old Nichols" lived. Roy made a few improvements, adding a bedroom and a small sitting room and enlarging the bathroom. The apartment, which was a shed roof addition to the large barn, ran the length of the building, a good sixty feet; something like a railroad flat or a large mobile home. It had a front door and a small yard with a picket fence to the side of the main building, and another door that opened onto the machine shop and storage space on the main floor. When I first met him though, Roy was living in a house on Stony Hill that he had been renting from Jeffrey Potter since the late '40s and was getting ready to move into a new home next door to the Livery Stable, which came with several acres of land.

Ed Welles, Roy's cousin and foreman of his four man crew, was living in the stable apartment. Ed was a Jack of all Trades, but his main job was to keep the trucks and dozers running. Though he was chronically overweight (he slid up and down from 250 to 300 for much of his adult life and was usually too heavy to ride any of Roy's horses), he was a very capable horse handler. He was also a good bulldozer and crane operator, truck driver and excellent mechanic. During the time when I first started hanging around, Ed was digging a cellar out from under Roy's new house, which entailed very careful digging and placing of jacks and support structures for the house. After the hole was dug, the cellar walls were built out of Belgian Block from New York City streets.

I interviewed Ed as part of my Oral History in June of 1998 at his home in an East Hampton mobile home park. He was then 76 years old. We started out talking about when he lived in the little apartment in the Livery Stable. I reminded him that I had been in the apartment a few times having coffee with him, and that it was a cozy place. "Yeah, yeah," he said, "It wasn't bad. It was pretty nice. Except, once he started stabling horses downstairs, why, come a rainy day, 'cause he didn't clean the stables every day, but come a rainy day, he'd put Albert down there to clean out the stables, and I'll tell you, it wasn't none too pleasant upstairs. It got kind of ammoniated. Ammoniated somethin' fierce, it was."

Ed was born in West Mystic, Connecticut in 1922. But, as he says, his mother "was a Bonacker, one of Josiah Lester's daughters, born down Pantigo. See, Irving and Josiah Lester were brothers and they were born at Pantigo. Irving was Roy's father, Josiah was my mother's father. And these two Lester brothers, Irving and Josiah, married sisters, who were Kings, from Springs. Let's see, Hiram, Clifford, Uncle Al and the two girls, Ada and Hattie, that's all there was, And Uncle Al (Alfred) King was the brother that had moved over to Connecticut. My grandmother's name was Hattie (Hattie Irene King.) I never knew her, she died before I was born. And, uh, 'course, Roy's mother was Ada (Ada Gray Lester, nee King). Now, Irving (Roy's father), he lived there in Pantigo, at the old original farm. And Josiah, he lived right next door on the southeast side, the side closer to Amagansett. And Hattie King, my mother (daughter of Hattie Irene, Josiah's wife), was over in Noank one time (just below West Mystic) visiting my Uncle Al, who was workin' for the State of Connecticut as a bridge tender, and my father (Edward R. Welles), an old Mystic boy, he was cruising around in his Model T and they met up and ol' Ed Welles he started coming over here to see Hattie, and eventually they got married.

"Right after I was born we moved to Old Mystic, 'cause my father's aunt gave him an acre of property up there off the farm. He built a twenty-by-twenty house and started from that. And, of course, we used to come back here very often on the old steam driven side-wheeler *Shinnecock*; from New London to Montauk."

Concerning those side-wheelers, Ed had this to say; "They had a number of 'em. The first one was named *Shinnecock*, just like the bunker steamer. When they took her off, they had another side-wheeler, the *Yankee*, I think it was. And that one was kind of a leaky old tub. It sank at the dock couple times over in New London. Then later on, why, the old *Catskill*, they put her on runnin' back and forth. It had been a Hudson River boat, used to go up the Hudson River at night. 'Course, now, it was kind of a rolly tub."

Ed's father, grandfather and uncle all worked at one time as machinists at Lathrop Engine Company in Mystic. "My father worked his way up in the shop, building engines and eventually got promoted to sales and service and went on the road. And every time he went away, why Mom she'd pack a bag and we'd head for Bonac! So I been going back and forth all these seventy-six years."

When he first came to work for Roy, in the summer of 1941, when he was 19, Ed lived with Roy and his family. "I called her (Roy's mother) my aunt but she was really my great-aunt, my mother's aunt. Aunt

Ada and Uncle Irv, I stayed there with them and with Roy and his two sisters, Ruth and Mary Emma." He was in college at the time, Becker Business College, in Worcester, Mass. "My father always hollered at me, 'Get above the grease line,' he says, you know, 'Do something different.' He didn't want me to be a mechanic, which I really loved and, of course, I had it served up to me, the talk of it, with prit'near every meal, when grandfather was around."

That same summer, when he came home from Worcester, he found a job on a dude ranch in Connecticut, the C Lazy Y, owned by Morgan Chaney. About Chaney Ed said, "He'd got into supplyin' horses to the Army during the First World War. He would go out west and buy a bunch of half-broke horses and send 'em east here and then sell 'em to the Army. That's the way he got his start, and then later he took a job at Connecticut College running the stable up there. The college was where he met his wife. She was a girl half his age, maybe twenty-six to his fifty-two." But then, Roy had called Ed and asked him if he could give him a hand for the summer. With the War coming on, Chaney realized that farming was more important than clearing trails at his dude ranch and let him go with good wishes.

It was the beginning of World War II and Ed was just coming to draft age, but the President had said that any young men who were working on farms could be deferred until the crops were in. Roy asked Ed if he would do that. "I told him sure, so I stayed with him until the potato harvest was in, and then come October (1941), when I turned the right age and the Draft Board sent me a notice, Roy suggested that I apply for a Farm Deferment, and by God, it wasn't long, before it come through! So I stayed, and except for a few periods when we argued over money, I stayed on for twenty four years." He married Martha Edwards and they moved into the apartment in the Livery Stable.

At that time Roy had a contract with the Town, inherited from his father, to mow the sides of the highways in some parts of East Hampton and Amagansett, which he did with a horse drawn mowing machine. One day, after having been out all day mowing the roadsides, he came home, and since there was still plenty of daylight left, he sent Ed out to disc a four acre plot just a few hundred yards down the road from the farm. The disc arrangement was built for a four horse hitch, four abreast, so they hitched two fresh horses in the middle, and put the two tired horses that Roy had been using all day on the outer sides.

And, as Ed related it to me; "I went to discin' and, let's see, I had Pete and Badlands on the outside, and Brownie and Jack Filer in the middle. And Roy, he went home; he was doin' something else up on the farm up there, and I was discin', and at the end of every row, why, I give 'em a blow. (Let them rest for a few minutes.) I'd go down and come back and then I'd give 'em a blow, 'cause that disc pulled hard. So anyway, I was, oh, three quarters of the length of the lot comin' back towards Skimhampton Road there, and all of a sudden Old Pete went down! *Slammo!* I thought I'd killed him surer then hell! I unhooked him, got him out of the harness and started home with the other three. But before I got halfway home, I hear this cloppity-clop behind me, and here comes Pete on a dead run! He was home before I was! He'd had enough discin' for one day! He was tired and he laid down and got a rest, then he got up and come home. But I'll tell ya, it kinda spooked me for a while. I thought I'd killed him!"

When Roy took over Pantigo Farm in September of 1939 after the death of his father Irving Otis Lester, he was planting potatoes and raising a few pigs, at that time only on the farm itself. Then he noticed that a dairy farm up on Stony Hill in Amagansett was going to waste. Its owner, Mr. Hamlin, had recently died. From Hamlin's widow, Roy rented the farm's dairy barn and some of the pasture, and bought and installed twenty-five cows.

That was at the time Ed had begun working for Roy, and I asked him about it. "Milkin' all those cows by hand, God that was some job. And then there was the pigs. Roy moved what pigs he had at Pantigo over to Stony Hill, and got more. We collected garbage from the Army base in Montauk. We'd go there every afternoon, and also to the Navy base down to the dock there, and the Air Force Academy at Signal Hill. We had a flatbed truck with fifty gallon cans on it. They'd bring the stuff out in the garbage can and dump it in. They called it garbage, but it was fit to eat when it come to the truck, I'll tell ya. They didn't save much for leftovers, you know, everything went in the garbage can. There'd be whole loins of pork and tray on tray of mashed potatoes and stuff like that." No, the pigs didn't pick out the pork, they ate it with gusto. All the produce, the milk, and the pigs, were sold locally. Joe Dreesen's Market in East Hampton was at the top of the list, but other butchers also bought the pork, and the milk was sold to other dairies around town for distribution.

The biggest acreage they planted with potatoes was behind Roy's farm, 22 acres. But as demand increased from the Government during The War, Roy expanded, renting several smaller lots in the neighborhood, including one small plot inside East Hampton Village, which had the best soil and the highest yield. The lots were usually referred to by the name of their owners, or by that of an earlier owner; the lot in the village was the Cort Mulford lot; a lot on Town Lane north of Pantigo was the Maudie Taylor lot, for its owner Maud Edwards Taylor, and the larger lot across the road where soil was poorer, mostly sand, it was on the edge of the Moraine, was the Jeff King lot.

Like all the Long Island potato growers, they bought seed potatoes from Maine and Prince Edward Island, Canada. A local man and a couple of women were hired to prepare the seed for planting. They would cut the potatoes into several pieces and store them in half bushel peach baskets so they could breathe, sometimes coating them in lime, particularly if they had to stay un-planted more than a couple of days. "We used to put on about a ton of fertilizer to the acre then," Ed said. "And that was a miserable job, especially when the wind blew. Cuz the potato planters (pulled by horses), they had these bins on the front, you know, for the fertilizer, and you'd have to toss these hundred and twenty-five pound bags off the truck onto the planter and dump 'em in these bins and so forth. And the seed, we used to cut our own seed by hand. Then Virgil (one of Roy's men, and another cousin) and I would do the planting."

LIVERY STABLE

In the spring of 1956 after having his men renovate the stables back to the way they had been in Nichol's day, Roy opened a horse rental business operating out of the Livery Stable. He had a sign-painter refurbish the Livery sign that hung above the barn doors, and moved all his horses over from Pantigo Farm and bought several more. He suggested that with a small patch of land behind the Prohaska house going to waste, I should move my horse over there, just two hundred yards from the Livery Stable, to make room for the expansion. In order to bribe me into moving, he promised I could work at the stable. My father went along with the deal. Even with the twelve dwarf fruit trees at the back end of the property, there would still be room for a one-horse stable and a tiny paddock.

With the help of a local kid who was a couple of years younger than me, about eleven, I set about building a stable. Most of the lumber we used was scrap lumber left over from a demolished Navy building that had stood on the site of the Old Fishing Village in Montauk. The lumber was given to me and delivered, by Jack Ruby, the manager of Gobel's Aircraft, an airplane parts manufacturing plant that was built over the old site.

The little building was a rickety proposition, which I was amazed to find lasted years after it was abandoned when I went off to college. It was four beams stuck directly into the dirt without cement, one more in the middle of each side for sturdiness, and the whole thing covered with the grey planks from the old Navy building. We used the size of the short boards as the guide to the placing of the beams.

I didn't want a repeat of the Banty coop episode, so I kept the Old Man out of it until we had a somewhat square four-sided structure with no doors or roof. Then I decided I'd let Ray help. He quickly banged together a square platform out of two by fours and plywood; something similar to a small dance floor, and we lifted it up and settled it onto its support posts, which we'd measured carefully and cut on an angle, with a slope, so that the rain would run off. We covered it with roofing tarpaper lapped over the sides and sealed with roofing tar and tacked down with roofing nails and put a nice piece of metal trim around the edge. Ray built the two Dutch doors so that Jerry could stick his head out during the day, and we painted the whole thing barn red with white trim. It was a beauty.

Then, we built a small paddock, using barbed wire and locust posts that we got, with his permission, from Roy's woods. We chopped down enough small locust trees to make about thirty fence posts, and stretched the barbed wire with Roy's block and tackle. We were full of cuts and scratches at the end of that job, but it was a serviceable fence. In the shed-roof Jeep garage that was an extension of the car garage, Ray kept a workbench for his fishing stuff, with his rods and plugs hanging along one wall. I would share the space with the Old Man, with never any bad repercussions; a saddle rack, a fifty gallon drum used to store feed and bales of hay piled to the ceiling against back wall.

The Livery Stable opened on Memorial Day Weekend 1956, and I was busy all summer working as a trail guide. Roy paid me $2.50 an hour and I often got tips. With the money, I was able to pay for my horse's hay and grain and to always have a small wad of cash in my pocket like all the other boys my age, all of whom worked at something, mostly fishing.

I established myself as an apprentice horseman attached to Roy, so that he knew he could call on me whenever he needed a hand; a hand that is that didn't have to be strong as an ox, highly skilled, or with a driver's license. When not on horseback I did other farm chores like cleaning stalls, pulling the manure spreader around behind the little Ford tractor, and cleaning harness. Though at home I was often a petulant adolescent, at Roy's farm I was a working fool. As time went on I added driving a team to my resume, taking out hayrides and driving coaches and surreys at special events and parades. The trail ride business boomed. Six times a day either Roy, his friend Francis Smith, or I would take out riders, either down to the beach or up into the woods. Much of the time we were on Roy's property. He owned hundreds acres of woodland not yet labeled as "The Hamptons."

Often we would move horses from one place to another using his International flatbed which was rigged to carry horses and cattle. It had a cow horn that made a loud moo which could be elongated by pushing it down harder. We might take a couple of horses to a pasture, or from pasture back to the stable or, sometimes we'd truck someone else's horses or cows somewhere. Occasionally we went to the few horse shows that were in the area. Whenever we stopped at The Cream Queen, the soft ice cream place on Pantigo Road, Roy would give a loud moo as we pulled up.

I subscribed to *Western Horseman* and *Horse Lovers* magazines and read them from cover to cover and knew the names of the top ranked rodeo cowboys and the top ranked Quarter Horse stallions. I practiced reining, following the pattern used in Western horse shows, which included fast turns called roll-backs, a figure eight and a sliding stop called "marking eleven," for the marks the horse left in the dirt when he slid on his back feet. Roy put up barrels in the Town Lane lot so we could practice cloverleaf and slalom races. We tried to practice calf roping, but he banned us from chasing his small herd of a dozen cattle that he was trying to fatten.

On days when I was using my own horse to take riders out, I'd saddle him up in the morning and head over to Roy's, through the small acre-sized hay lot that had once belonged to Carl and Babe Ericson, across Hedges Lane, jumping the bramble covered embankment on the other side of Hedges, into another lot, twenty acres of timothy hay that I'd cross at a dead run, to the back of Roy's property, and through a small junk yard, one of several he had spread around town, this one with a couple of old cars and some farm machinery and an old bulldozer rusting in the weeds.

One cold winter morning running across that lot, in mid-field, Jerry went into a sudden fit of bucking and threw me ass-over-tea kettle. I landed on my sitz-bone on bumpy frozen ground. I limped for weeks, made light of it, said I was just stiff, and identified myself with Casey Tibbs, who was World Champion Cowboy at the time, who had had every bone in his body broken. My right hip went permanently cockeyed and after twenty years became a reliable forecaster of bad weather.

When I left Jerry at home, I often tied him out in the neighbor's lot next door, the lot where the Erickson's Pony had formerly grazed. That lot was now owned by a wealthy widow, the imposing, blue-haired, stiffly coifed, wool-suited Mrs. M. Gordon Frazier, a wealthy widow from somewhere, who had built a small but elegant little bungalow with a big bay window facing south, out of which she enjoyed the vista of a grazing horse from her living room window. For Jerry it was an easy job keeping the square acre trimmed and manured.

The stable kept getting busier and Roy soon realized he'd need more help. He hired an older boy, a senior in high school, to work full time as a stable hand and rider. His name was Harry, and we hit it off. Harry was not insecure around girls the way I was, so whenever a teenaged girl came to ride it became more fun. He could be charming and engaging, where I would have just slipped into that ridiculous trail guide persona that kids who work at hack stables employ, a bossy pretend grownup yelling orders to hold up or slow down or to watch out for branches.

Roy had contracted with a boarding school and a summer camp for underprivileged kids to each bring a bus load of kids three days a week. They were the two biggest groups we had. The school, a Sag Harbor Catholic boarding school for girls was run by nuns, and the girls were delivered in a bus driven by a nun, which was probably a first in Amagansett. The camp was Boys Harbor, a camp for underprivileged boys that was run by Anthony Drexel Duke, and which was probably one of the first of its kind and possibly the best run, ever. Duke often went on the rides with the boys and so I got to know him, a wonderful man, easy to talk to, always a person among persons, never the upper-class snob that he could have been. Raised in a wealthy family (he was a cousin of Doris Duke), his father had lost his money and so Tony had gone off and made his own fortune developing property in Florida. He had started Boys Harbor on a shoestring before WWII, and continued it upon return from the Pacific.

John Belushi wasn't the first one to call nuns Penguins. It was Harry. I'd never heard that before and thought it was very clever. The Catholic group was the most difficult bunch, because the younger girls rode without the nuns along to offer support (the nuns didn't ride.) The girls were often frightened and occasionally started crying out on the trail, so we usually took them along the ocean beach where, if they fell off, they'd land in the soft sand.

One morning, with ten or more young girls in tow, aged ten to fourteen, we reached the beach and let the girls bobble on ahead, while our two well-exercised cow ponies shuffled along behind on the hard sand where the foam washes up toward the dry beach. My horse Jerry was amusing himself snorting at the foam, when behind us the wind must have been blowing the wrong way and blocked out the noise until they were very close, two big Navy helicopters came roaring down the beach heading west, directly overhead maybe a hundred feet up. The horses stampeded. It was a slow-motion melee, since none of these horses at this point in the summer was bursting with energy, but they loped along, startled enough to have all the girls screaming. Several fell off and landed safely sprawled on the sand and most of the rest fell out of their stirrups, glued to the horn like so many rag dolls. Harry and I galloped up ahead on the hard-packed sand till we reached the front, grabbed the reins of the two lead horses which halted the procession, then dismounted to brush the sand off our scared little Catholics, and became heroes to a small portion of the future generation of suburban Long Island womanhood.

The youngest riders were Sara Jane and Bobby Newton. (They were about four or five years old.) We had no ponies, so we put child saddles on two of the gentlest big horses, Pal and Paul. When out in the pasture, Paul loved to buck and Harry and I had once put a bucking strap on him and played rodeo. He had a nice, authentic but not crazy buck. But with kids he was gentle as a lamb. How Roy was so sure of this I don't know, but in the two years that the stable was operating Paul never bucked and not one rental customer ever got hurt. (I think Roy felt that his horses knew they were representing him and so had an image to uphold.)

Sara Jane and Bobby were my special charge. Whenever they came, if they went with a larger group I would always ride close to them. I felt that Pal and Paul and I were babysitting them. The Newton kids lived in a new development between Amagansett and Springs called Barnes Landing. Their father was a psychologist and part of the artist, writer, and psychoanalyst community that was by then in its prime. Dr. Newton was a Sullivanian. The critic Clement Greenberg had gone to a Sullivanian, and had recommended that therapy to Jackson Pollock, who went briefly. (They both went to

Sullivanian Ralph Klein.) Though Harry Stack Sullivan himself had died in 1949, his heirs advocated many of his more radical ideas, such as avoiding monogamous sexual relationships. In the Sixties, on the Upper West Side of Manhattan, a cult made up of self-styled Radical-Marxist Sullivanians was involved in a scandal which involved sex and drugs and the psychological manipulation of couples and children, which was disastrous to Sullivan's reputation. In the Sixties, Bobby was part of the West Side Sullivanian cult led by Dr. Newton, and acted as his father's enforcer, allegedly strong-arming people who broke the rules.

Sara Jane and Bobby were precociously bright little kids as shrinks kids often are. But we, rightly I'm now sure, assumed that their parents were crazy, being shrinks, and that we needed to be good examples of normalcy. Children brought out the cowboy best in us.

I remember the first time Roy and I had a political discussion. We were on a ride with a small group of rental customers, and apropos of some political point he was making, he said to me, "Well, of course I know you're a Communist, but..." I protested, "No, I'm not!" and I had to pause to think what I was. "I'm a Democrat, I guess, that's what my parents are." Roy allowed as how Stevenson was a Democrat, but he was also a Communist. That was when I began to see that politics was a complicated business.

I assumed my parents weren't Communists, but had been told by them that some of their friends were, and that Communism was only feared by Republicans. I knew that my parents felt that Republicans were unsophisticated and backward. Democrats thought that fear of Communism was at worst dangerous; at its best quaint.

I felt there must be something to Roy's side. (There were, in those days, continuous news items about Soviet spies being arrested and prosecuted.) I knew Roy wasn't stupid, though his prejudices were as one-sided as were those of some of my parent's Communist-friendly friends. Roy's view centered on private property. He'd inherited land, he farmed land, he profited from land. He was also an employer. He profited from the labor of his employees and to do that, he had to be tough and fair, had to take responsibility and risks. And he had to face stiff competition when bidding on jobs; things like that.

On rainy days, or whenever I wasn't working for Roy, or going to school, or cleaning my own horse's barn, or being hounded into doing chores for my father, like raking leaves, or filling the firewood bin (we had someone who mowed the lawn, and Carolyn weeded and fussed with the garden), I'd be hanging out with Roy. He didn't seem to mind. He had regular visitors anyway. It seemed to be a natural part of country life to go visiting, especially for the older men. I would sit in Roy's office and listen as he shot the bull with these older fellows, former town leaders, men who remembered when road construction and farming (and other jobs, like conveying whiskey off the beach), were done mostly with horses.

DRIVING HORSES

Roy closed the horse rental part of the stable after two years because the insurance got to be too high, but decided to expand the coach and wagon business. He broke all his new horses to drive. His system entailed the use of a three horse hitch, with the green horse between two heavy poles, and an experienced horse on either side. For smaller horses Blackie and Pawnee were used, and at least during my time, bigger horses were sided with Pal and Paul. To break a horse to drive, we would put him between the poles (which were similar but heavier than the shafts of a single rig) and drive the three horses from the livery stable to the beach, about half a mile, then take the rig, usually a farm wagon, down onto the sand, where it would be heavy and hard to pull, and we'd drive a short way down the beach, turn this way and that; stop and start; turn around and come home. The next time the green horse would be hitched to a two horse rig and would invariably walk off like an expert. We broke my horse Jerry to drive that way and I drove him around town in various gigs and carriages belonging to Roy. I liked driving.

 He had a horse that we called a Norwegian Dun; he was yellowish with a brown stripe down his back, small and stocky with a short neck and thick brown mane and tail. One day when we were still at Pantigo Farm, I was helping Roy put a sick cow in a stall that was part of an outbuilding behind the main barn; we were pushing and pulling at the wobbly cow who turned out to have something called "Hardware Disease." She had swallowed a piece of metal. Randy, the Dun, who was loose in the surrounding field, came up and nipped at the cow and shoved her along till she was in the stall.

 During the summer of 1957, after Roy taught me to drive a team, I became the official hayride and parade teamster. That July 4th, I drove Randy, single hitched, in a surrey-with-a-fringe-on-top in a parade in Sag Harbor, with the two guests of honor, Hurd Hatfield and Magda Gabor. They were two aging movie stars who were already has-beens by then, but they were still glamorous enough that I considered it an important mission on my part. Hatfield starred in the movie *Picture of Dorian Grey*.

Driving the Omnibus with Paul & Pal

During the summer of '59, Roy contracted to have a group of his horse-drawn vehicles used to cart guests around at a convention at the big old hotel in Montauk, The Manor. Anybody who could be trusted to drive a single horse or team was drafted for the drive to Montauk which took most of a day. I drove Pal and Paul, the "yellow pair", on an English coach called an Omnibus. Perched high up on the driver's box in an old stove-pipe hat, I looked like an old-time teamster. After that weekend event, The Manor management decided they'd like the Omnibus and a surrey for the whole summer, and Frank Tillinghast and I were given the job. Sometimes Frank would pick me up in the morning and we'd ride down to Montauk together, other times, since by now I had a license, I'd use Roy's Willys Jeepster, a cute little car that looked like a Jeep but was a two wheel drive convertible with overdrive. There was one steep hill as you entered Montauk after the several miles of flat isthmus known as the Napeague Stretch; on the incline when you let up on the gas the car "free wheeled," coasted with no friction whatsoever; sort of a slingshot effect; which was fun.

We kept our horses, Pal and Paul, and Frank's brother's horse Omaha, with whom he drove the surrey, at the Manor stable, a building later bought by Edward Albee and made into an artist's colony.

PART III: COCA COLA, CIGARETTES & BEER

BEATING

When I was 12, while riding my horse, my secret life as a romantic hero played itself out on a background full of open spaces and with live characters willingly though unwittingly playing supporting roles. It was a separate world in which I was protected from the harsh reality of school and its simpleminded plans to prepare me for post-war industrial society. In what was for me the early part of an extended adolescence, drinking beer and smoking cigarettes was an occasional way to blow off steam and rebel. But the most fun, besides riding horses, the thing that made the prospect of growing up really seem worthwhile, was the cheap thrill of driving. I had started learning to drive on the beach, in the Model A, its official name was "The Gut Bucket," and then in the Jeep when Ray graduated to it. I even managed eventually to extend the privilege to include driving up and down the driveway, a distance of less than a hundred yards from the garage to the sidewalk in front of the house.

The Model A had an accelerator that was hand-operated and was where the directional signal is on most cars today; and it was easy to double clutch, meaning you could go from one gear to another without using the clutch by going at the right speed and leaning on the gear shift till it popped in. So, before I was tall enough to reach the pedals, I would drive along the beach standing on the seat, popping it into second gear from a standing start, then to stop, just popping it out and then quickly turning down the accelerator. Steering was easy since the front tires stayed in the tracks already made by other beach vehicles, of which there were always at least one pair. Fishermen, commercial and sport, tended to use the same track, as it made the going smoother.

Driving was no big deal for a country kid. Kids who lived on farms, including several of my friends, were enlisted to drive their father's tractors as soon as their feet could reach the clutch. In some cases, they put blocks on the foot pedals to make it easier for a smaller kid to drive, thereby increasing manpower. Several kids around town had old, cut-down jalopies, called Woods Cars, which they drove around on the extensive "Scallop Roads," in the woods. These roads were old walking trails, sometimes Indian trails, which often evolved into places where people dumped household garbage, dead horses or, most often, scallop shells. Scalloping was a fairly big industry in those days, in the fall and winter, and the shells needed plenty of isolation because after a few days in the warm sun they stank.

One day I was driving up and down the driveway in our several year old Ford station wagon and I decided I needed a cigarette. I was afraid that someone would see me driving the Old Man's car with a cigarette in my mouth, I was 12. So I backed up and drove into the back lot along the edge of the potato field.
    After letting the potato farmer who farmed the acreage behind our house plow into our property as he'd done for years, it being a corner of his field, a few days earlier Ray had a surveyor put markers up, and Joe Hren (before their falling out) had come in and smoothed out the dirt and planted nine fruit trees in a square, three each of pear, apple and peach. The farmer, Bart Hadel Jr., had been pissed because it spoiled his run, taking a half-acre corner chunk out of his crop. But the property was ours, part of the original Cartwright property, so Ray felt within his rights.
    I drove out along the western edge of the property to the end and turned left, inspecting my new orchard. At the next corner, maybe one hundred feet, I turned back toward the house but I turned too tight and the side of the car, the car door area, crunched into the new concrete property marker that the surveyors had planted so recently the concrete had barely had time to dry. I was probably high on the two or three cokes I would have consumed by that time of the day, early afternoon, and on the cigarette I'd been puffing, and on the "here's the big man driving his car" fantasy I'd been having till five seconds ago. I leapt out of the car to see what had happened and in sheer terror saw a dent about a yard wide and four inches deep on the right hand door.

It was almost dark and I was in my bedroom when the Old Man came home from fishing. I'd been hiding there all afternoon. I heard him come tromping up the yard in his waders covered with fish scales and sand, heard him hose himself clean and then come into the kitchen and place a couple of fillets in the kitchen sink. I could hear a quiet conversation going on. I undressed and got in bed and pulled the covers over my head and wrapped myself up like a mummy. And just as I was tightly wrapped he burst into my room, dwarfing the space, the door latch rattling as the door crashed open and hit the side wall and I flew out of bed as if to fly out of the window and ducked into the corner, in my underwear, screaming and pleading, while he laid into me with his long leather belt; leaving a dozen or more thick, throbbing welts that lasted for days.

I remember being surprised after the first few strokes that I could withstand it. I'd been sobbing and pleading and then I wasn't. For an instant I felt some pride that I was bearing up under it. Then I had what later I remembered as an out-of-body experience, feeling myself safe hovering at ceiling level, witnessing the scene. I suppose it could have been a mental trick, something innate that I hadn't needed before. Or, if I imagined it, it might have been my first really abstract, creative thought, before my thinking degenerated into getting even.

I felt that my mother had betrayed me, too, when she told him. Granted, I'd wrecked his car and he had a right to be angry, but that didn't enter into my thinking. He'd tried to kill me, is what it'd seemed like. At least I felt he'd given himself that option.

After the beating there was a period of truce; a time when he felt remorse, after my mother had gotten to him, persuaded him to realize that he'd gone too far. He'd apologized and I'd apologized, in a more reasoned way than when I was being beaten, which had been just, "Stop! Please! I'm sorry!" and we then went through a chummy period where I actually felt safe in his presence. There had been something Oedipal about it; I had fucked his car. The cost of damage would be more than the car was worth.

I had paid with a good beating. But the part of me that was capable of resentments, self-pity and revenge was left un-addressed. Underneath, it festered, and I stayed wounded. I nursed my wounds and incubated a radical scenario. It was the 1950s and the timing was just too perfect for development of an angry young man.

CHRYSLER

The Old Man was very particular about his coffee, switching brands every year or so. I used to love going with him to the A&P when they still ground their coffee fresh. I loved the smell. There had been a time, I call it the Maxwell House period, when he'd done a series of four illustrations, one for each season, pictures seen from above of yards in suburbia, children playing, raking leaves in the fall, in winter making snowmen, that kind of thing; with a tilted coffee cup at the top, good to the very last drop. During that time, we drank lots of Maxwell House. Now, unrelated to any illustration job, but just due to his quirky taste buds, he had changed to the A&P fresh ground.

It was several weeks after the beating and it seemed like I'd been hanging around with the Old Man quite a bit. The two of us were in some sort of amnesia about that rage, me sort of disembodied, a shadow brain, a yes-man, aware of the good feelings he was giving off. One day, after shopping at the A&P in East Hampton, we came out of the store with coffee and some of Ray's favorite snacks, Fig Newtons, Mallomars, apple juice, pickled herring, Rye Crisp crackers, and because it was almost lunchtime, a half dozen slabs of minute steak, A-l sauce and some new potatoes.

"Hey, who's that dame selling chances?" he wanted to know. That year the Ladies Village Improvement Society was raffling off a brand new, bright red, Chrysler Windsor at their annual summer fair. He thought I knew everyone, but I didn't know her. She was summer people. "She'd be just right for the job I'm doing," he said. I figured he'd ask me to go up to her and solicit; but I was out of my element being the front man in this case, and I held back. By the time he got up to the card table he was all charm and he had this handsome, tall, white haired sixty-ish woman all full of blush and giggle and she'd agreed to pose for him if he'd buy one ticket. And she did pose for him later that week, but that event is overshadowed in my memory, by the car.

Several weeks later. Labor Day weekend, 1955. Everyone had gone to bed. Late. Maybe midnight or after. The phone rings. In bed in my room off the studio, I awake with apprehension and run into the kitchen in the dark and listen on the extension; I pick up just in time to hear the Old Man yelling at someone; something to the effect of, "Oh go to hell you drunk." Then he hangs up. As I'm walking back to the bedroom, the phone rings again and I lift the receiver quietly again; "Ray, it's no joke, it's Jack Chrysler, you won the car! Here at the LVIS Fair. C'mon down and pick it up!"

It was the only time I ever saw him knock off a shot of whiskey neat. Ordinarily he was a mixed drink drinker. Scotch and water; bourbon and soda; wine, beer; but never a shot. That one shot; it made an impression on me. He seemed to need it.

He didn't talk much about his superstitions, but I had heard him say, more than once, that his mother believed he had a guardian angel protecting him; ever since the miracle of the bell back in Yugoslavia. There is nothing, after all, like a new car. As we drove out of the fairgrounds he said, "This is our lucky charm, buddy boy."

1956

I went from boy to teenager in the time it took Jackson Pollock to rise from obscurity to fame and then die in a car crash on Springs Fireplace Road, coming home from a party in East Hampton with two pretty young women in his car. Along with Pollock, one of the girls died too. I wouldn't begin shaving for another half dozen years (I was a late bloomer), but 1956 would be the beginning of a protracted adolescence and an eventful year for me. Two important things happened that year; Jackson Pollock died and I began to idolize Elvis.

Pollock's spirit had suffused itself through the countryside of Springs and Amagansett and become the inspiration for a new generation of talent in the art world. His death affected me because my parents were shocked and sad; because to me he was somewhat of a hero, and because it was national news in our small town. But there was really no one among my peers to discuss this event with, since none of them seemed to care one way or the other about Pollock. They didn't recognize him as a hero. This hampered my attempts at building a personal mythology having to do with the world of art and culture. Or, seen from another perspective, it might have made my fantasizing more creative. I imagined myself as a future cowboy-artist-writer, lover of women, who would someday (when I grew up) attach himself to a worthy female who was a cross between Penny Potter and Patsy Southgate, or Ava Gardner and Corinne Calvet, and a nice small-town girl with a smart mouth and tight jeans and bobby socks.

By now I had developed some ideas about artists. Some of my ideas were sophisticated, reflections of my parents thinking and things I heard their friends say and things I picked up in books and in the resident art magazines that I leafed through. Some ideas were simplistic and developed in my own countrified noggin, such as: Artists are different from you and me. They don't go to work with a lunch box. If they can help it they try not to have a job. If they have to, they teach. Teaching allows them to be in the studio, see what the less talented are doing, and study a nude model. An art student needs to learn how to draw. An artist is born knowing how to draw, but likes having a nude around. Artists are drawn to any flat surface. An artist's studio wall is always fascinating.

I had a split screen view of the local social world; I saw two types of cultural behavior. To illustrate; imagine an aerial view showing two cocktail parties, one populated by locals, possibly at the Amagansett Fire Department (not today but before it was culturally integrated), and another a view of a cocktail party in the sprawling yard of an art speculator's rental house in the Summer Colony; place these parties both in the time frame of the mid-1950s.

At the Fire House, women and children are noticeably separated, for the most part having the sense to sit in lawn chairs or frolic under the shade trees. The men are standing around the bar or in evenly distributed groups, hands in their pockets or wiping sweat from brow, getting stoically drunk, discussing the joys of trolling for bluefish.

Meanwhile, on someone's posh but low-key estate, pockets of frenzied people are being led by casually dressed men and women who are gesturing like band leaders. If you had one of those mikes they use to pick up the cracks and grunts on pro football, you'd hear the creative one talking about "my work," a key phrase in the understanding of the Art World. It means something more than my job, or my car or even my philosophy, or the product they create which other people pay good money for. Carolyn called it breast beating. One such artist we knew actually caressed himself, wiping his hands across his sagging chest, as he groaned on about "His Work." He spoke as if he was just finishing up the final explanation of life. But why were people listening to him?

Because he was *selling!* Selling didn't mean selling. Not like when you have to sell your Harley to make the next month's rent. That's just the business of life. "Selling" implied that you were being lionized, being made a member of the ruling elite, something you can't simply buy, though you did have to sell it, that is have someone pitch it.

Am I being a little bitchy? Mean spirited? Of course. Is this just the whining of another failed artist? Who would care anyway? Neither the artist nor the buyer. I refer you to Otto Rank's seminal book *Art and Artist*. If you want to get to an artist, you've got to attack the work. And I ain't going to do that. Because, odd as it may seem, I'm prone to respect the words of critics.

But watch out for the camp followers, the significant others and the other members of the art world's inner circle. When I was a young voyeur, being dragged around to parties from Water Mill to Montauk dressed like a midget cowboy, invisible, feeling tense and paranoid, isolated even from the glib New York educated red-diaper babies, the more important cultural guard dogs were usually women; wives, mistresses, camp followers. Each artist had his own. Some had several, but not usually more than one at a party. Other members of the entourage might be covering different parties. In those days, at least, there was a special type of woman who married or otherwise ministered to an artist. For one thing, she had to be able to say "He's a genius," in such a way as to let you know that: A: She's pretty smart herself, and B: You're not.

Why did I go to these parties? I was curious, obsessively curious. And a big part of that of course was the overt sexuality of the art crowd that registered with me even before adolescence. The other part was that, from the festering unconscious of my two parents, I was told in no uncertain terms that these were the people who made the world go round.

SICK DAYS

From dawn till dusk, on weekdays, when I caught the bus to high school across the street in front of the post office, till I fell asleep at night, and on days off, riding my horse alone, especially in the woods in the winter when the air was still and only an occasional snowflake drifted by, I drifted in and out of grandiose, heroic and romantic daydreams. I had my own, brazenly imagined adult world. A by-product to all this dreaming was guilt. I had a privacy deficit in my existence that hadn't allowed me to grow a capacity for secrets. Having grown up in what was for me a sort of fish bowl existence, in a house in the middle of the Main Street of a small country village that was producing pictorial narratives that would be seen throughout the nation, and whose production required a big sky-lighted studio that blared Jazz and Classical music, I felt I must be somewhat suspect to the outside world, that I was being closely watched, maybe even under surveillance. So I was always engaged in a rear guard attempt to cover up my world of fantasy with some cool cover-story, a narrative made up on the fly without anything like the attention to detail of my daydreams. This amounted to building a house of cards.

When I wasn't a cowboy I was still a boy, and that played itself out most transparently in the way I dealt with being sick. I remember a time while still in grammar school, it was during the winter when I came down with something that seemed like a bad cold or the flu. Perhaps it was Rheumatic fever, or even Lyme disease, though that hadn't been discovered yet. It has been the source of some conjecture that Lyme may be the same illness that used to be called Montauk Knee, because it was, and is if it's the same thing, often accompanied by a swollen knee.

I was sick for a week with swollen glands and aching joints and I spent whole days lounging in my pajamas feeling nurtured and important. From the living room window I would watch the people coming and going across the street at the post office and feel the pleasure of being in an ivory tower. I took many naps and read the paper and news magazines. I got well reluctantly, in the meantime working on and elaborating my fantasy life, particularly my when-I-grow-up fantasies, which revolved around being a rancher or a farmer who also wrote or painted and was either a spy or an inventor and was married to a sexy and sophisticated wife. I would be someone similar to Peter Matthiessen or Jeffrey Potter with a little Roy Lester thrown in. When I was well enough I continued this creative work while sitting on the white fence drinking Coca Cola, which still came in the green glass bottle and was kept cool by the case in the dirt floored cellar beneath the kitchen.

HIGH SCHOOL

I looked so young in high school. It was a big source of shame for me. In my daydreams I was older, bigger, and without an inferiority complex. It seemed like all the kids except me were bathing in growth hormones; I felt like what Mickey Miller's sister Lila called me; "Howdy Doody," the perennial pre-adolescent. I wasn't prepared for the larger classes, compared to those in grade school. More kids meant more complicated social interactions.

East Hampton High was a district school and I was part of the bussed-in crowd. In the petty simplistic way of kids everywhere, the kids who came from close by, inside the boundaries of the Village of East Hampton, considered it their school. Those of us who rode the bus from Wainscott, Amagansett, Springs and Montauk, were outlanders.

Among the East Hampton Village kids there was a bigger ratio of clean-cut, short haired, "Ozzie and Harriet" types. There were no Nelson Family kids from Amagansett or Montauk. Further, I was drawn to those who didn't study, considered smoking cigarettes a sport, and spent lunchtime in front of Marvin Conklin's Candy Store next to the school, eating hot dogs and candy and smoking.

I continued to grow slowly, without the addition of facial hair and voice change, and I got skinnier and skinnier. The Old Man began calling me Mahatma Gandhi. Carolyn initiated a program of trying to fatten me up by feeding me milk shakes with bananas and a raw egg, and sometimes a big hamburger without the bun, for breakfast. I burned it off quickly with nervous energy, amped up with Coca Cola and cigarettes. Since the Old Man smoked occasionally, as in when he needed a kick start before starting a new job, or to keep the bugs away while fishing, he couldn't exactly condemn tobacco, but he didn't like the habit. (He said it was Magimper.) He didn't want smoke smelling up the house, bothering his sensitive nose, making him sneeze, ruining the taste of food. And smoking still made me dizzy and self-conscious, so I felt no compulsion to smoke when alone, when it wasn't going to make me look cool. And I couldn't smoke around Roy Lester because he had quit smoking years ago and complained that his wife still smoked. And anyway, smoking around the barn was dangerous.

But I needed cigarettes as a badge of adulthood. So I smoked on the school bus and in front of Marv's and as time went on I would light up while out riding on the trail, out of sight of my two father figures. More and more liking the biting sting on the lip, the rush, the smell and the way I thought it made me look. (Whenever I took a piece of tobacco from my tongue with my fingers I was rather sentimentally reminded of Jean Levi doing that while holding her glass of whiskey in her other hand, her silver bracelets jangling as she talked baby talk to her big Foxhound, Vicky, and let the dog take a lap out of her glass.) Smoking was a distraction from adolescent rumination, not unlike hitting yourself on the head with a hammer. And getting jacked with nicotine and the sugar and caffeine from Coke, probably helped me to process my transformation of childish tantrums into repressed rage.

I was a failure at sports, a real klutz. After a year of goofing off in high school Gym, smoking cigarettes behind the playground fence, I dropped myself out of Gym and hid in the library-study hall for the three remaining years. It took some negotiating between my parents and the school Guidance Counselor when it was time to graduate and I came up short on grades and class credits.

Tommy Scott participated in both sports and drinking. Sometimes he mixed the two, managing to crunch a few heads while numb on beer and aspirin, making himself more powerful than his modest size should have allowed. He was still my link to what seemed like the real world, that which began and ended at school. It was no small thing that the boy who best understood power, at least in a local sense, was my bodyguard and my diplomatic aid whenever I needed his help.

Mr. Thayer, 6'4", with a large belly that he used as a battering ram, taught math, all the advanced stuff like algebra, geometry and trigonometry. If you weren't careful, he'd "queer off" with you. My first year in the new school he was my homeroom teacher and he always seemed to be torturing someone, usually a girl, asking them impossible, difficult questions, making them cry, then ridiculing them in front of the class.

For the most part, he left me alone, in part, I suspected, because of my prominent, not to say aggressive, father. He had his pet for each period. In some classes more than one. These were always boys, and they always sat to the rear, next to the window. While the class was quiet, doing homework or occupied with a problem, he'd be in the back of the room, bent over one of his boys, helping him with a problem, breathing his hot breath down their neck. His boys always got good grades. Some also went on camping trips with Harry.

On the few occasions that he focused on me, either physically or by calling me to the blackboard to work out an equation, I would go pale and break out in a cold sweat. If Harry didn't give me homophobia, at least he gave me a good start. My suffering in the face of mathematics was so great that it became apparent to him that I had no redeeming characteristics. A couple of months into the first year, after several days of being focused on as the class dunce and after several occasions of squirming at his fondling attempts, abruptly, in the middle of one of my blank responses to an algebraic riddle, he told me that I should go down to the nurse's office and tell her I was sick. When the nurse, Miss DeCelle, took me back to the classroom door, he locked the door and pulled the shade. I was not allowed back into the class and had to take algebra over again with another teacher during the summer.

By now I was pretty much satisfied with my hair. It was combed back on the sides and there was enough in back so that without looking too Magimper I could comb it into a subtle, perhaps minimal is a better word, D.A. (duck's ass), when the situation called for it. The guy I sat next to in homeroom had a full D.A. which hung over his turned up collar, and sideburns (I couldn't grow sideburns) that came down to his earlobes; a fine head of hair. His name was Gary Schellinger. He lived on Abraham's Path in Amagansett, just north of the area called Poseyville. He affected a toothpick and a perfect hood look but didn't have an ounce of surliness or hostility. You couldn't imagine him in a fight. Like many kids from fishing families he was absorbed in getting to be sixteen so that he could quit school and go fishing. Any rise in fish or scallop prices increased his enthusiasm towards his one goal.

One reason we both worked intently on combing our hair and being sure our collars were up was because every morning Mrs.

Haas, our homeroom teacher, would leave her desk to come stand behind each of us in turn and carefully, and in my remembrance of it now rather sweetly, turn our collars back down and brush any unsightly dandruff off our shoulders. It was a subtle, sexually nuanced thing, which calmed us down from the morning's coffee and prepared us both for a day of not concentrating on schoolwork.

Gary Schellinger was not a "Rebel Without a Cause." He hoped to fish along with his father, on Ted Lester's crew. By the end of the year several people would have left this homeroom and quit school, feeling that what they could learn working on the water; in the surf, on the bay, or off-shore, was special, a traditional education, well worth the sacrifice of any book learning beyond the fundamentals of reading and arithmetic. Gary's idea of success was to be part of the crew when it hit a bonanza, something that happened occasionally, sometimes once a season, sometimes more, and pulled in enough striped bass in a morning's work to fill a hundred fish boxes.

HAIR

Up until around my twelfth birthday, the Old Man forced on me the same haircut G.I.s got (I suppose they still do) when they went into basic training, what my friend Mickey called the tennis ball haircut. All his life, until he hit forty, my father had a great head of wavy black hair. Then, around the time I was born, he'd developed an aversion to what he now called "the grease ball" look. His new look was a brush-cut, or a crew-cut, rounded, but similar to a flat top. So, what was right for the goose, I suppose, was right for the gosling. Whenever he was away, in the city on business or on a fishing trip up in Cape Cod or down in the Keys, I would try to sneak-grow my hair by getting just a trim. But when he returned he would make me get scalped. For Mickey and Tommy, hair length was optional. In the summer they'd get crew cuts just for fun, then let it grow out whenever they wanted. I was stuck with haircut fascism.

At least once a month the whole male portion of Amagansett could be found at Pete Rana's barber shop. For a small group of men who always seemed to be there it was almost a club house. Among the heavy frequenters were a fellow Italian who was a stone mason and deacon at the little Catholic Church up the street and the man whose full time job it was to sweep the street with a broom and the

Chief of Police, Harry Steele, who got a shave from Pete every morning.

The few times I went to Pete's for a haircut someone would ask me a question about sports and I'd say I didn't know and that would start me sweating. By the time I was in the barber chair I would be blushing and my hands would be slippery on the arm rests. Pete would pull out the oak board he used for little kids to sit on and then put it back saying, I guess we don't need this; getting to be a big boy. Then he would run the machine over my head at what I thought was too fast a speed. Was I oversensitive; because my father was an artist? I was afraid he'd drive it through my skull. Tears would start leaking out the corners of my eyes when he used the scissors.

But I felt that if I could get my haircut from him it would make me more of a citizen of Amagansett. He treated the other boys, like Tommy and Mickey, like men, putting soap around their ears and shaving it off. But even though Pete's was just across the street from our house, Ray drove to East Hampton to Nat's barber shop, and he brought me with him. Though his explanation was that he thought Nat gave a better haircut, I thought it was something more sinister, something never discussed, something perhaps that had started with just an unintentional slight, and that might someday blow up into a vendetta. (Carolyn thought it had to do with the day the FBI came.) I felt that they eyed each other, from opposite sides of the street, with suspicion.

Don't get me wrong. Pete had a lovely family; his wife kept a beautiful house; she collected antiques, they had two beautiful daughters (both of whom baby sat for my sister and me) and a handsome, bright son who became a successful local builder. Occasionally, Pete and the white haired old lady who taught fourth grade would give concerts at the school, Pete on the mandolin and she, Miss Ward, on guitar. Perhaps, the tribal animosity was just some Mediterranean thing. Or maybe it was all in my head.

When I started high school I pleaded to be allowed to grow out my hair. Carolyn sided with me, trying to be the voice of reason. I wanted hair like Jamie's, whose pompadour seemed to be part of his personality; confident. I began stalling about going to Nat's but eventually Ray would insist. "Get a haircut after school, and I'll pick you up," he'd say.

If Pete had just a tiny bit of artistic pretension, with his mandolin resting in the corner (he would play it occasionally when not busy), Nat's place was a museum; a particular kind of Italian-American monument. A small one-story building of concrete block and brick, with a granite store front and an apartment in back, the shop itself was floored with fantastic inlaid linoleum depicting scenes of local interest. The Hook Mill Windmill. Home Sweet Home (the home of John Howard Payne.) A swordfish. A sunrise. The whole thing having been done by Nat himself. So Nat was an artist. And he gave the Old Man the treatment. He called him Maestro.

When it came my turn in the chair, when Nat was through giving the Old Man the maestro treatment, he would begin giving me a kinder version of the same obsequiousness; something I never liked and found hard to distinguish from condescension, the "So, is he going to be an artist like his Papa?" treatment. It was something I occasionally got from adult locals on first meeting, which made me feel like a trapped mouse.

Nat was gentler, though, than Pete, and slower, much slower. And careful, snipping the scissors four times in the air for every follicle of hair he'd snip off. And then after what seemed like an hour and I had paid the dollar or whatever it was and was on my way out the door, he'd hand me a piece of Double Bubble gum. Though I tried to speed up my retreat so as to miss the gum, he kept at it, until one day when I was about fourteen, with great embarrassment, I was able to refuse.

MAIDSTONE CLUB DANCE

By my freshman year in high school my romantic fantasies had become sexually charged soap operas that went straight from the Hollywood clinch in the moonlight to being married and having kids. I wanted to be Ozzie Nelson. (I thought Harriet was hot. I liked Moms.) I had seen myself so often in the *Saturday Evening Post* that I believed there must be a Norman Rockwell world out there somewhere that I could become part of. I was sure that all I needed was to become an adult, something I hoped would happen soon.

To the encouragement of that kind of thinking, one day in school, Fran Gardiner (she was still calling herself Frances in those days), came up to me at my book locker and putting her long tanned fingers on my arm, asked cheerfully, "You wanna go to a dance?" The way I looked at her with such a shock of disbelief, she must have thought it needed more explanation. "I'd ask Jamie but he's too crude. It's at the Maidstone Club."

I knew Frances would have preferred to take Jamie, or I figured as much, but I was willing to think she was thinking positively, giving me a chance. I thought that maybe since my parents were not locals and had some sort of status, however ill-defined, she was betting maybe I could hold my own against her family's posh friends up at The Club.

I didn't have my driver's license and so we'd have to be driven. I knew it looked dumb and would make me look like a kid. I'd rather have foregone that kind of dating till I could drive. But the next day I had more than that to worry about. When I came home and announced I had been invited to the Maidstone Club, a fancy club for rich summer people, the Old Man took notice. He was impressed. He knew Frances was a young dish, in fact she would soon become one of his models. It never occurred to him though, that I might need some sort of coaching through this. It didn't occur to me either.

My hair was growing out. A pompadour was just at the crest of its wave, with porcupine sides. Another week and I'd be normal. I thought about my hair all the time. In the back of my mind I was hoping he'd just let it be; let it keep growing. I must have been giving off those vibes because mid-morning on the Saturday before the dance, Ray hollered from the studio, surprising both myself and Ma in the kitchen, who thought everything was calm, and who like me had no idea even that the studio door was open, let alone that he had been thinking about me, or my hair, "Hey, Tone, we're going to Nat's. You're not going to the Maidstone Club with a Magimper haircut." He must have been giving it some serious thought, though you could never tell where his reasoning came from because he'd never sit down and reason with anyone, just always seemed to be concentrating on his painting and approaching everything else peripherally, according to some internal logic.

I let out a guttural groan, like a man dying at the bottom of a ravine. My heart plunged. Ma, my defender against injustice, came to me and put her arms around me. There wasn't going to be any family discussion. He came out of the studio, said, "Let's go, sonny boy," and five minutes later we were at Nat's Barber Shop. I had to pretend I was just getting my summer haircut, rather than being symbolically castrated by an emotionally blind patriarch. All hope was gone. I might as well go to the dance as not. Protesting, canceling, any action at all would take too much effort. Nothing mattered. Today I suppose some might call that depressed.

The dance was a triumph of courage. Nothing good happened except that nothing bad happened. The dancing lessons at Guild Hall had paid off. It was the one and only time I would ever see or hear from Lester Lanin in person. Someone said I seemed like a pretty nice guy for a "townie." Frances' Aunt Babe, Isabel Mairs, assured several people that my father was famous and not Jewish. I danced surprisingly well. So did The Dish. We had pulled something off. So, though we didn't talk about it for forty years, we'd established some sort of a bond.

Unaccountably, shortly after the dance, I was able to convince the Old Man that I shouldn't look like a weirdo in my new high school environment. (If I'd been wiser, I'd have just said that it wasn't good for his image for me to look like a prisoner of war.) I then had to muster up the courage to tell Nat to not touch the top at all.

Several haircuts went by where I'd come out looking like a whitewall tire. I used Butch Wax to train it. Once I even bought a jar of Dixie Peach Pomade, but it smelled so strong I had to wash it out. Carolyn was supportive, helping me with my unruly cowlick by licking her hand and pressing on it whenever I walked by.

After what seemed like months, I had long hair, almost Elvis style, but without the sideburns since, unlike many of the boys in school who were shaving at thirteen, I had no facial hair. The pompadour, of course, could be pumped up after getting on the school bus. It was my first year in high school and I looked like a real human being. A young man. Someone with a personality. A mind of my own. A little bit cool. It was the spring of 1957.

Until the day I started basic training, I never got another crew cut. Having hair long enough to have a wave in front (like Jamie and like Elvis) and to be able to comb it back on the sides was, I felt, my greatest life achievement to date. The older guys I admired were the ones with pompadours and D.A.s who wore their collars up and their pants down low. The ones who had taps on their shoes.

SPRING FEVER

The first warm spring day I would wake up in the morning with a feeling that I could take in the whole world with one deep breath. When no recent family fights were leaving reverberating aftershocks, the house's well-appointed charms stood out; Audubon prints in the dining room, the silverpoint drawing of the Old Man by Julian Levi that hung next to the big 1938 portrait of Carolyn sitting in the wing-backed chair with her feet curled up; the raking light coming through the muslin curtains and the wide old pumpkin pine floorboards creaking to the Old Man's steps as he came out of the studio for a cup of coffee. I'd run up to the attic and look out the scuttle to the ocean and sniff the earthy aroma blowing in off the potato fields. I'd put on my boots and my Western hat and prepare to enter my separate-from-the-family world; my *Riders of the Purple Sage* persona. Carolyn, in her ongoing effort to fatten me up, would hand me one of her "Tony Specials," a cup of coffee in a large glass of warm milk with an egg beaten into it. Spring fever, probably assisted by caffeine, was my first major addiction.

I suppose I rode regularly partly out of responsibility. A horse trapped in a small space all the time without exercise will go crazy, so if you own a horse and you don't have much pasture, you have an added motivation to go riding a lot. But it was also a time when I breathed the air of what I thought was my own, self-created world. Any day when there wasn't school, my first order of business was to go for a ride. Even if I had other things to do, I could always take an hour to get Jerry and me some fresh air. I rode with Roy, or any friend with a horse who wanted to ride, and I often rode alone. I rode in the winter when it was snowing. I'd go up into Potter's property where the wind and snow were muted by the heavy woods, or to the west into Roy's woods, or east toward Montauk, into the lowland at the edge of Amagansett. When it was warm, or less cold, I'd go down toward the beach.

Between the garage and the horse barn, there was a small vegetable garden where I would set my Banty chickens loose from their little coop to scratch. Behind the garden was the smokehouse, which from twenty feet away, even when cold and not being used, gave off the succulent aroma of smoked striped bass.

After first letting Jerry out of the barn to get a drink of water at his trough, I'd scoop out a few quarts of horse feed for his feed bucket and put a flake of hay under my arm. While he was having breakfast I'd brush him. Then I'd throw on the Navajo blanket and saddle I'd gotten that first Christmas and I'd be ready to roll.

Out the driveway we went and across Main Street at a speedy trot, a pace determined by the need for us to be invisible, out of synch with the human traffic at the post office and the barber shop who would barely catch a blur of white horse and rider. We'd head up Cozzens Lane, past the village water tower and up a field that inclined imperceptibly toward the farm on the hill at the highest point in the village, Stony Hill Farm.

Behind a thirty acre pasture on what was called a hill but was really just the top of the long slow rise from the ocean across a mile of thick loam to the beginning of the glacial moraine, was a colonial style farm house (still there, now owned by the actor Alec Baldwin), and in back of that big house was more pasture and several smaller cottages and the dairy barn that Potter had transformed into a riding academy, a posh alternative to the Livery Stable. Here, a new, more social-conscious group of summer people could send their children to learn the English style of riding.

It wasn't simple aimlessness that often had me heading up towards Potter's, as the place was then called. There was a hint of curiosity and expectation. The hilly woods behind the horse barn were full of old-growth trees and trails that were kept neat, like an English park. The first winter I had my horse, I had stopped there a few times. There'd been no one around but the old groom, Jimmy Mundell, who had eyeglasses so thick that when he looked at you it made you feel as if he were looking at you through a microscope.

Most of the horses seemed oddly tall; huge hunters and jumpers the likes of which I had never seen close up. There were a couple of ponies that seemed lost in over-sized stalls; stalls that were kept absolutely clean. You'd no sooner hear a thump of manure hit the ground then Jimmy would have it scooped up into his wheelbarrow with his manure fork.

The first time I made the approach on a spring day there were cars down by the barn which caught me by surprise and made me fear I might be told I was trespassing, so I went on past the main part of the farm, along the outside of the big pasture that fronted the main house and over the high crest of the hill that looked out toward the ocean, into a little valley, a huge glacial pothole that bordered on one side a potato field and on into the woods behind the farm. At the edge of Potter's woods were miles of moraine, with scrub oak, sassafras, sumac and blueberries growing over millions of tons of gravel scraped off the top of Connecticut during the last Ice Age.

I opened a gate and went into the dark woods on the jump trail, the Park Avenue of local woods' trails. Jerry loved to jump and we took off at a gallop up the slightly washed-out incline that was the beginning of the trail to the first jump, Jerry checking himself and sailing over one jump after another. At the end of the series of jumps I did a quick turn, spinning around like Casey Tibbs when I saw him at the Madison Square Garden Rodeo, to go back over the same jumps, this time from a slightly down-hill grade. I noticed some riders coming along a trail that converged at the bottom of the slope, out of the thick woods on my left. Two handsome, tanned young women in jodhpurs and hair pulled back were shepherding several rich looking children all done up in English garb and looking a bit intrusive for what I had a moment ago thought were my private woods. I waved to them and they smiled pleasantly; then I backed my horse up ten feet, cowboy style, turned and loped away dramatically.

Twenty years later on a borrowed horse I crashed into Dick Cavett on that same trail, thank God not injuring him, just bumping knees as we passed too close; he wasn't pleased and we didn't become best friends.

In the summer of 1957, Marilyn Monroe and Arthur Miller were staying in one of Jeffrey's rental cottages. One day I rode my horse to a hill in back of the stable to where I could see into their fenced-in yard. I saw her sunbathing and watched Miller walk out of the house with a drink.

Tony and Jerry

THE FOX

One morning I woke up remembering that I'd been dreaming of a little brown dog. There was a southerly breeze and I could smell the ocean, so I took a ride to the beach. I rode up Hedges Lane to a dirt path that led into a ten acre field of fresh plowed ground-coffee-colored loam which I traversed, galloping along the neatly packed tractor tread that bordered flush with a hedgerow on the side of the field. At the south end, where the loam ends abruptly and turns into dune, there was a high thicket with a tunnel-like pathway through blooming shadbush and honeysuckle vines that led to a broad expanse of marshy beach grass through which ran the asphalt road leading up to Main Beach.

    A fox appeared out of the brush and stared at me as if it was an oddity to see a boy on a white horse. Without thinking, I let the reins go loose and Jerry dropped his head like he wanted to sniff the fox. Jerry stepped a few steps forward nervously. The fox sniffed the air, made for the brush on the east side of the road, changed his mind, went back to the middle of the road, and trotted slowly, staying just a few yards ahead of me as I followed him down towards the beach. Jerry trotted along behind, curious, his ears pricked up and his head down. The fox never did bolt, all the way up to the Beach Club building, where he disappeared under the boardwalk.

    When I saw my friend Jamie later and told him about the fox and the dream, I was never one to think anybody wouldn't be interested in my dreams, he said I was crazy and that I was a liar. He called me a lying turd and began to go into what almost amounted to a fit, grabbing my hat and throwing it on the ground and stomping on it. He seemed to think I was insane as well as retarded and found my story offensive if not down-right dangerous. I was taken by surprise, grabbed my hat and turned and walked away and went home deflated and hurt and full of resentment. We were about the same size, but on his little spotted horse not much bigger than a pony Jamie looked bigger. To me, he looked like a real cowboy, like he knew what he was doing, wheeling around, doing lots of sliding stops. He was cocky and brash, and I envied him.

MOVIE BREAK

Mickey, Tommy and I had a favorite way to inaugurate the weekends on Friday nights. We would hitchhike into East Hampton to watch the movie break. Once, after standing under the street light at the corner of Oak Lane, Tommy's street, for a good half-hour, we got a ride from one of the "hoods" from Montauk, really just a sleepy eyed overweight kid who was the mate on his father's party boat and made more cash than he knew what to do with, other than to sink it into his what would now be a priceless 1951 Mercury, which he had nosed and decked and lowered in the back, and painted an elegant gunmetal gray.

We smoked a cigarette in front of the theater till the ten or fifteen people from the first show ambled out. We took note of any attractive females or any strangers that happened to be in town. Then we went over to the Candy Kitchen and sat in the back, avoiding the stuck-up village kids, wisecracking with a small group of fellow outlanders who, as it happened, had a pint bottle of whiskey they were sneaking into their cokes. When we'd had enough we'd hitch a ride back home.

DANCING, CARS, AND BEER

Rheingold Ben, as he was called, was a successful local businessman who commanded the respect of the general population because he was a functional drunk, maintaining his respectability while holding up space at several of the local saloons on an almost round the clock basis. A real estate broker and man-about-town, he was known for always ordering Rheingold beer in a can at the one saloon in town where they had a large selection of beer on tap. Several times a year he sponsored and ran a dance party at a community center on the outskirts of East Hampton Village.

Known as the Neighborhood House, it looked very similar to a private home except for a larger than usual addition which, in fact housed a gymnasium. It was set back from the highway, with a flagpole out front, on Three Mile Harbor Road, a macadam road that heads north from the village into what were then the boondocks, years before the whole town became posh. The nondescript shingled building was still there the last time I looked. These dances were more important than the school proms because they weren't run by the teachers and the buttoned-down kids.

Mickey, Tommy and I would hitchhike to East Hampton Village from under a street lamp on Main Street and then again from the Three Mile Harbor side of the windmill at the north side of Main Street. By the time we arrived at the dance and paid our dollar admission, the three of us would have convinced each other that our purpose in being there was to look for girls that would "put out." What we would do with them then was anybody's guess. We would meet in the back of the hall near the men's room and share a swig of Seagram's from the pint bottle that Tommy would have gotten from his friend on Oak Lane; a Korean War veteran who was teaching him how to play Pinochle. Then Tommy would mingle with the other boys who were active in sports. Mickey would spend a half hour in the bathroom trying to get his pompadour right, when it was right it was close to perfect, and then he would stand around on the porch with several other guys recounting practical jokes they played on the senile teacher in shop class. I was so self-conscious that I couldn't just stand on the porch or on the sidelines in the gym, but would walk back and forth, pretending that I had some agenda. If the word dork had been in use in those days I suppose I'd have known what I felt like, but as it was, I just had a vague feeling of being clueless.

Tommy was always the first of the three of us to dance. I remember his smiling face, a vision of glee looking over at me with his arm out straight, one-stepping a girl with pimples, his white bucks straddling her dainty little high-heeled feet. I danced mostly with girls I was friendly with, one dance per girl. There was no glamour, no high fallutin' posturing. The girls were dressed in the Rock n' Roll style of the day which still included bobby socks and crinoline slips under the skirt. The boys wore jeans and sometimes Wellingtons or Engineer boots, with their blue jeans a little low, resting on the pelvic bone, a Garrison belt if you thought you were tough, and maybe a cigarette behind your ear.

The dance to do circa 1957 was the Lindy. The best dancers were Bill Pitts and Joan Cantwell, two kids who were dance partners, but not, I think, a couple. Sort of pros, I guess. A Chuck Berry record would lead to everyone doing a heavy stomp on the second beat that would get louder and louder until the dance hall basketball court floor would start shaking under the weight and it would feel like it was going to shake the building down, like things were getting out of control, "Blackboard Jungle" style. At that point Rheingold Ben would take the needle off the record and stand at the front of the stage looking as fierce as he could considering that he must have been stewed to the gills by that time of night. The hall would go quiet, the lights go on and everyone would take a few breaths and then a slow record would come on and the lights would go out again and the dance would resume again, post peak-experience.

The cars parked in the cinder paved parking lot out front were Fords, Mercurys, or Chevys, some customized in the style of the Fifties, lowered in back and with some of the chrome removed, particularly the hood ornament. Some kids came in the family car or in their father's pick-up. When the dance ended at ten o'clock, the guys with suitable cars would spend ten minutes or so in the parking lot revving their V8 engines which, with glass-packed mufflers, straight pipes and whatever other Rube Goldberg exhaust pipe rigs they could put together, made a beautiful thunder of backfires and rumbling. Then, one by one they would leave, burning rubber on the road out front while heading either north or south, to one of the make-out beaches, or into the Village of East Hampton to the Candy Kitchen.

After one of the dances the three of us hitched a ride from Ike, an Amagansett boy who drove a late 1940s DeSoto with old scratchy Moquette fabric car seats. The car belonged to his mother. Ike didn't have a girlfriend, in spite of his tall Elvis good looks and the four and a half years of high school he had under his belt, but he was 18, old enough to buy beer, and between the three of us we scraped together four dollars and fifty cents and bought a case.

In those days beer came in a hard steel can and required a sharp, steel can opener, which someone, of our generation probably, had named the "church key." Tapping the top of the can with the church key was a ritual that helped lessen the spray. Cars driven by kids and often adults not uncommonly stank of beer spray and cigarettes.

After buying the beer at what would today be called a Mom and Pop store, we hit the beaches to see who was necking with whom. All communities have their lover's lanes. Some towns, that don't have a lake or ocean, use the Town Dump, or did until dumps became more institutionalized and began to be locked up at night. In our town, the older and more serious parkers who didn't want their cars to be spotted at the beach at night used the scallop roads in the woods north of Town. There were enough of those roads so that everyone could stake out his own special place.

At Main Beach we picked up an older woman, a well-known barfly, who was walking back to the town from the beach parking lot where someone had abandoned her. Elvira had once been pretty and popular, but was now known as a town drunk; and we were as ignorant and prejudiced concerning alcoholism as the rest of the world. I should have had more sympathy, because I knew, for instance, that for artists, heavy drinking was a side effect of a tormented, tortured soul bursting with unconscious messages that needed to be laid out on canvas. But that, I reasoned, didn't apply to ordinary people. Elvira had no teeth and black hair with long gray roots. She sat in the back seat between Tommy and me. She gave each of us an extraordinarily wet kiss and a drag off her equally wet cigarette, and drained a can of beer quickly, probably wondering why she hadn't had to give a blow job yet.

Tommy and I finished our beers and got to work on another one. We'd split the pint of Seagram's earlier so I suppose we both had a good buzz on. She gave each of us a muscular leg rub. She was used to sharing beer with rougher customers than we were. By now either one of us could have gotten what she felt expected to give, but we were both in new territory and too lacking in back-seat skills to make the next move, so we drank and smoked faster and when Tommy got out to puke Ike told Elvira to come sit in front seat between him and Mickey.

We switched our attention to the music coming from WKBW in Buffalo, loud and clear though three hundred miles away, and when she was settled in front she began giving Ike a blow job, which I noted out of the corner of my eye when it was my turn to get out and puke.

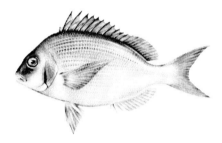

CARTWRIGHT JUMBOS

The porgie, also called scup, is a money fish. For fisherman on the East End, it's always been a dependable source of income, though not popular as food. The Indians used it as fertilizer. The fish's only drawback is its ultra-thin, hard to pick out bones, which my mother got around, as a big cold food lover, by poaching them and letting them cool in the fridge overnight in their own juice. The bones were then easy to peel away, the meat being cool and firm. Jellied porgies. I loved it, but wouldn't have told any of my friends that; too weird. She was also big on Jellied Madrilene and any kind of cold soup, Gazpacho, Vichyssoise, Schav, or any pot luck mixture she could come up with, whipped up in the Waring Blender, the invention of a 1940s Big Band leader, Fred Waring.

One fall Mickey and I, and a couple of other friends, decided we could make some money fishing for porgies, "Jumbos" on Cartwright Shoals. Mickey assured us it was a potential gold mine. His father went along with it, probably figuring we'd learn something. All we lacked was a net and a boat. Mickey's father Milt gave us the half-rotted wings off an old trawler net and Mickey showed us how to patch up the worse parts. We found another kid, Jake, who had an old sharpie with an outboard engine, and we were ready. We did a couple of practice runs in the Accabonac Creek channel and had some luck, catching over the course of several hauls a bushel full of trash fish; dogfish, skates, small flounders and a few porgies. The next day we headed out to Cartwright. Over the course of our career, maybe three or four trips, we probably netted a box or two of dogfish, small sharks and maybe a couple of bushel of porgies. It was beer money. That was important because we were typical American boys hooked on beer and cigarettes.

The last trip to Cartwright was the most eventful. We had Jake and another friend Barry, and Mickey and I and a younger kid from Sag Harbor named Bobby. On our first set we hit a snag and tore the net all to hell and had to call it quits. So before going home we sat on the beach and drank some beer. A thick fog began to roll in and the water developed a slight chop. Fog and stormy weather don't usually go together, so this seemed ominous. We decided to get home fast, back to Bonac Creek.

When we were a hundred yards off the Cartwright shore we were bobbing up and down into what seemed like a good two foot chop and couldn't see any shore in any direction. We figured if we kept cutting into the waves at the same angle we'd end up somewhere near Louse Point where the channel was, so we kept on. And on. After twenty minutes we decided we should have seen the beach but there was nothing but deep water and the same old pea soup fog. Then, after an agonizing time which seemed like hours but was probably half an hour, in calmer water but still heavy fog, we came to a big tidal rip which meant we had to be between the Fort, a tiny island with a wrecked brick building on it that had been used for years as a bombing target by the military, and the top of Gardiner's Island. Looking ahead, the water to the west was rough, with a southeast cross wind. We decided the safest thing was to head back around the east coast of Gardiner's, try to make it back to Cartwright and stay till morning. We knew we could land on Gardiner's Island if we had to, but we didn't want to be caught trespassing. Jake was with us and his father was now the Chief of Police. Harry Steele had retired.

Soon after we landed back on Cartwright the fog cleared and the water calmed down and we could see Bonac Creek and the flashing headlights of a car. We headed straight for the lights and were home, that is back where we started, in twenty minutes. The flashing lights had come from a police car. It was Jake's father, also named Jake, who'd been out looking for us, half mad with worry, figuring he'd find his son and the rest of us washed up on the shore. Jake Sr. was as rough and tough as a Police Chief could be and known for his salty language, but he was nothing but sweet to us when we got in, saying, "I was a little worried about you," and leaving it at that.

VIRGIN

My first real date had been in the eighth grade, with a twelve year old girl named Beth, who swooped down on me by telephone, having met me at an adult supervised dance at Guild Hall in East Hampton, a cultural center that in those days was shared by the local people and the summer people, but has since, and for many years now, become "Culture Central" for the entertainment moguls who are the new top rank of the summer people food chain in my particular Hampton.

Beth's mother drove us to a roller rink in Hampton Bays, a ride of about 45 minutes even in those days before heavy traffic became commonplace. I remember the date as feeling mostly like an educational outing. Beth was nice though and we eventually became friends. Then, at another of those supervised dances the following year when I was a freshman in high school, I met a little blonde named Margie, with whom I "necked" at the movies twice (but who's counting), if putting your arms around a girl and kissing her a few times with lips sealed qualifies, and had a number of hot telephone calls, in which she led me through some of the steps of the now obsolete teenage courtship ritual of talking about "caring for me" and "caring for her" and "do you think I'm cute and how cute do you think I am? And etc."

I remember having a couple of these conversations while lying on my father's bed, using his overhead wall phone, a remembrance which immediately brings up, "Did I tell my shrink about this?" I was allowed to sleep in his bed when he was in the city, when I became the man of the house, at least in terms of getting away with stuff. The wall phone hung on the side of a pine combination headboard and bookcase and I remember being excited, having a kind of glow, and being intoxicated by a vision that this talented little blonde girl painted with her powerful little voice.

That relationship ran its course in about three weeks, partly, I suspect, because I was afraid, and therefore I didn't push hard enough to the next step, where ever it might have led; first base, second or third, but she shook me loose easily by taking offense at some little inanity of mine which I have mercifully forgotten, and the next thing I knew she was seeing a junior who had a car.

I remained a virgin throughout high school. But there were other kids, the faster developers, almost everybody but me or so it seemed, anybody that counted anyway, they were doing second, third and home plate, in cars, at the beach, in the woods and, favorite place for those sneaky clean-cut kids, at the Nature Trail, the little park in the village, a fact it took me twenty years to discover. I knew that everyone wants to get laid, but it took me a long time, many years, to figure out that all you have to do is ask.

BARKER

By the spring of 1960 when graduation and college and having to sell my horse seemed imminent, my anxieties took on a new edge. Along with an acceptable level of adolescent jitters, which could always include regressive silliness among friends, there came a new, absolute horror of impending manhood's large shadow. With great difficulty, I was able to attempt an explanation of all this to my mother, who recommended I go see Wayne.

Wayne Barker was a psychiatrist, a slow moving, slow talking sort of a guy, a renaissance man, always dabbling in some new thing. He was married to a wealthy woman so he wasn't under the gun financially. Around the time I went to see him he was doing imitation Pollock paintings, learning to surfcast with my father, and hunting pheasants and ducks with some of the local guys with a much envied, brand new, expensive Browning Automatic 12 gauge shotgun. He was also writing a book about ideas and how they resembled epileptic fits, and how Jesus might have been epileptic.

He was from Southern Illinois, had gone to the University of Chicago and had treated shell-shocked veterans during The War. He was part of the cultural crowd and was a good interpreter and ego booster for the area's growing pack of neurotic, boozed-out painters and intellectuals. Wayne, it seemed to me at the time, gave the East End the comforting feeling that it was under careful and uncritical observation.

He lived in a Danish Modern style house, on a corner of a street that was also a neighborhood, Poseyville, the home of the Posey Lester clan. Behind his house was a six acre potato field that had been lying fallow for several years and was covered with long-dead rye straw, once a cover crop and now sparsely overgrown with short cedar saplings, the tallest of which, out in the middle of the field, was draped by a large bittersweet vine. The lot, which, unlike most open fields in those days had no name as far as I knew, and which I therefore called the Barker lot, was at that time connected through hedgerows and backyards and other lots, to my backyard where I kept my horse, so it was convenient for me, after Carolyn made an appointment, to ride over on Jerry.

Wayne's studio was built on stilts above a half-open carport/shop and separated from the main house by a neglected and overgrown Japanese garden. I tied Jerry to one of the building stilts and mounted the stairs to his studio. A little apprehensively, I hollered up to him. "Wayne?" He was standing at a tall table looking at some papers. "Waall," he said in his southern Illinois drawl, "so, I understand you're having some anxiety." I nodded yes, and said, "Mm hmm." "Well now, what do you think is causing it?" he said, as if he had opened up the hood of an old car and was about stare into space for an hour.

If only I could go back to that time and divine what was going on in his mind during my visit, concerning my appearance; at five feet eight inches, about as tall as I would ever get, lean and gimpy like any good cowboy, smelling of horse. I wonder if he thought I was nuts. I was at the end of what for me had been a very real five year career as a teenaged cowboy.

I was intuitive enough then to trust, and I wasn't very trusting, that this wasn't going to be the same kind of buck passing that occurred when my parents tried helping me, which always ended up feeling like a group paralysis. I had a secret sophistication about psychology which only Carolyn knew about, since it was only with her that I discussed what I gleaned from her library, which included snatches of Freud and Fromm and Anna Freud, Otto Fenichel, and the voluminous set of the completely incomprehensible Harry Stack Sullivan, and a wonderful little book by Gerald Sykes, *The Hidden Remnant,* which I had read from cover to cover when I was twelve, and journals like the *Partisan Review* and *Art News* which were swimming in data on neurotics and neurosis. I read only out of anxious concern that my family unit would explode and I would die. It was always out of context, except for that context which I supplied while being driven by desperation.

I was worried about going to college and that I was always fighting with the Old Man. I told him that I could never really talk to my father and that he seemed to think I was supposed to have raised myself, and that he didn't understand that I had felt stuck in Amagansett School, but that I couldn't have approved being sent somewhere else because it would have meant being a traitor to my friends, but that I now realized I had been deprived of needed extra help. As I warmed up I told him about having been beaten. Then I guessed that was enough.

Wayne said, "Well, I can see that Ray would be a tough guy to be a son of. He's a big guy, quite intimidating. He has a temper. He doesn't seem to be very empathetic toward you kids." Then he talked briefly about his own children. "Now when I talk to my kids, for instance with Leslie, who's still small, I squat down so I'm eyeball to eyeball with her. That helps her to not be afraid, and helps me to see her point of view." Funny, at the time that comment seemed trivial, but I never forgot it. It had strength and relevance. Then, as I remember it, he wrapped my whole life up in a small package, by saying something like the following;

"If you want me to talk to him, I will, but I don't think it would do much good, do you? He's very reticent about talking about himself, except in terms of painting, and even then, he's not terribly verbal. Anyway, as far as what you've missed out on, in terms of education, it's kind of too late. As far as you're concerned, the horse is out of the barn so to speak. You'll just have to make it up, reading on your own, or compensate for what you've missed. Quite a lot of people have had to do that; life is unfair that way. Anyway, your father and I, we're sort of fishing buddies, you know what I mean?"

I wanted to say, "No, he taught you how to fish, you damn fool," but I knew what he meant. He seemed to be saying that I might be facing an ordeal getting out from under my parents and growing up, but that it wasn't impossible. He went on to suggest that once I got away from the family, out from under the Old Man's shadow, out on my own at college, I might feel better. He encouraged me to keep reading and to find out what my own interests were, and said that when I could afford it, I might try analysis. Then we looked at his drip painting and I tried to be encouraging.

I guess I had known that there was no quick fix, though I still had faith in the magic of psychoanalysis, which was part of the air I breathed in those days, on account of Carolyn's influence, and it was a great help for me to be told that analysis wasn't a now or never situation. I could put that procedure off until adulthood.

There were times over the coming decade, while going through long periods of terrible anxiety and despair, when Wayne's homeopathic dose of clarity might have been what tipped the balance and kept me off the ledge. For now I still had my horse, if only for the short time left, and I would take refuge in the love I had for the woods and fields of my town and my competence as a horseman, which had to be good for something.

I hadn't talked to Wayne about girls because my lack of sexual experience was already becoming a source of shame. Those heady, romantic dramas I was weaving in my mind, of being a conquering hero, a lionized artist, and humble champion cowboy, were not the kind of thoughts I could talk to anyone about, except in an expurgated way to my mother, who believed I could step into any role I wanted to at will. That was her fantasy. If I turned to her in a moment of desperation, we could spin great tales of possibilities. As soon as I'd turn to face the world though, her support, thin as it was, would evaporate.

Instead of riding straight home, I rode through some of Hren's Nursery and across an estate hayfield down into the dunes west of Amagansett and then home, with my head clear and a dark cloud gone.

PEORIA

Because of my low grades, the high school Guidance Counselor suggested, sensibly I suppose, that I try getting into a small, midwestern land-grant college. (Ray continued to resent any inference that he should help out in making these life affecting kinds of decisions.) The Guidance Counselor, Charlie Juckett, had a place in mind; Bradley University, in Peoria Illinois. Bradley needed kids for its Air Force ROTC program, which no doubt helped it to finance its winning, though crooked, basketball team. Juckett thought the folks should take me out to Bradley to get a look. Ray begged off, claiming he was too busy. And perhaps he was. The illustration business was in its death throes at that time and since the Old Man had failed to put away anything for a rainy day he was begging for work. And so during spring vacation of my final year in high school, off we went, Ma and me, in the sacred though no longer new Chrysler Windsor. Peoria here we come.

I was ambivalent about traveling with Ma. What I loved was that we could talk. She believed in the importance of my likes and dislikes, my interests, my fear, my self-pity; she found me fascinating. My narcissism was her narcissism. We could analyze each other, and Ray and Elena, even Ray Junior, who had all but disappeared into his electronics designing, group therapy attending, gear-loose oddball West Village Bohemian existence. Junior looked and sounded enough like Ray and butted heads with Ray enough when he did come to visit, that he was further proof of the genetic power of Ray's artistic neurosis.

What I hated about traveling with Ma was the vague sense of emotional incestuousness, what today would be called a boundary issue. When we were in public, an alarm went off in my head that signified fear of exposure. I suppose it was also an acknowledgment of emotional dependence. Psychological stuff does matter, especially when you're in your teens.

Once we were out of the orbit of Bonac though, with its twin authority figures, the Old Man and my still miniscule peer group, we had fun seeing America, both of us traveling somewhere we'd never been, me west of New York, her past Ohio; deep into the heart of the mid-west. We stayed in motels. We shared the driving. Carolyn was reminded of when she was a model, traveling through Pennsylvania and Ohio when she went on a sales tour for Thom McAn Shoes as Little Annie McAn. We had time for extended conversation. We talked about current events and about art and more specifically, the creative process. (At that time she was reading Delacroix's *Journal*.)

At Bradley, all the interviews were brief and cordial. Mid-western civility made registering a breeze. There were no dormitory beds left so, to my delight, I had to rent a room. We found a room only one block off campus in a home belonging to a tiny, shriveled, old Russian Jewish widow named Clara Lipkin. She thought we were Jewish, but we confessed we were not and she took me anyway.

I had grown up in a fishbowl. Our house was at the center of the village and our lives were a source of entertainment for the post office clients, that is, the entire village. We were a house full of screaming egos, of invasive relationships; a violent and needy father, a violent and needy mother, a vulnerable but combative sister, who had a controlling brother. There was no space that was not open to the Old Man's busting in, kicking the door open, the latch rattling, him filling the room with his oversized presence to wake me up from a hangover or threaten me about some smart-assed move I'd just made. Being in Peoria would be like Witness Protection. It might as well have been Timbuktu. It didn't seem that bad.

GRADUATION

From the moment my date jumped into the back seat with me she was completely relaxed and ready to have fun. She caught me off guard and my spine just relaxed into the car seat. My growing pathological fear of girls took a night off. We were in the back seat of Mitch Fulcher's car. It was late May, 1960. Francis Gary Powers had just been shot down. Lucy had just announced that she was divorcing Desi. John Kennedy had just become the presumptive Democratic candidate for President after winning the West Virginia primary. Paul Simon had yet to write that famous line, "When I look back on all the crap I learned in high school, it's a wonder I can think at all!" from the song *Kodachrome*, released thirteen years later.

Like any good 1950s teenager, I had the condom in the wallet. Mine had never been used, but I felt confident I wouldn't be forced to face that first-time impasse that night. The whole purpose of graduation night was to get drunk, and drinking was the one thing I felt good at. Everyone in that crowd was pretty comfortable with it.

Mitch was with Dolly, who had fixed me up with her best friend, Janet. I liked the way she looked. She got past the Carolyn censor that was already lodged in my brain, the critical model-picker. She had a slightly aquiline nose, a toothy smile, short, brunette pageboy hair, a healthy complexion with a typical East End girl ahead-of-summer tan, and a "nice little figure," as they used to say in the illustration business.

There were several parties that we dropped in on, but all I remember is some of what happened when we parked at the various beaches. Because I was so afraid of sex, I celebrated the idea of smoking and drinking as a sex substitute. I had incipient performance anxiety and it was always riding with me. There was an advertising jingle that played all through the Fifties on radio and TV for Bardahl, a gasoline additive. The line I remember is "Is Blackie Carbon riding with you tonight?" It was supposed to instill fear in you about getting carbon on, or in, your car cylinders, something Bardahl could supposedly cure with its metaphorical little man-chemical that would go in and scrub them out good. With me the black carbon was fear of being sexually incompetent, a fear that was not based on any such experience up to that time, but was all too real, for me, anyway.

I had passed on the senior prom, rationalizing that I was too much the James Dean type for that. But graduation night was a more important event and I looked forward to it. As it turned out, it went well. The night was for drinking and we just kept drinking, several cars following each other around, getting drunk as skunks, boys and girls alike pissing at the beach just outside the car, very little puking because we were all by then accomplished beer drinkers; stopping in Montauk so Howie, in another car, could run in and take his insulin shot just before we made it to dawn at the Montauk Lighthouse. We even made out a little. And with that successful mission over, I allowed myself to think, well, I've graduated after all.

During the graduation ceremony on the front steps of the school the previous day I'd stumbled over the gown feeling lame and goofy during the cap and gown ceremony. I remember feeling a great relief that high school was over and saying to myself in all seriousness "Well, nobody's ever going to push ME around again!" What a great sense of freedom I felt! And by that time I'd only had a few cans of beer!

After that night though, I didn't see Janet again, and there was no more socializing with my high school friends. Everyone had summer jobs and on days off everyone had their own beach. I was frightened by their seeming rush toward sex and marriage, which seemed to follow pretty closely with my contemporaries. I wasn't ready for it by a long shot. In that context the next decade would be a series of tactical retreats.

After graduation I was still riding my horse regularly, though my rides were solitary. My riding buddies were distracted by the ordinary romantic pursuits of high school seniors. Usually I rode behind Potter's Farm, through the jump trail and adjoining trails, or in the estate section behind the second dune west of Amagansett. Wherever there was a fence three to four feet high and no people in residence, I would jump. It seemed to me jumping was something Jerry was better than average at. Without much thinking about it, I was preparing him for a new life, where he'd have a marketable skill. I wasn't preparing myself for anything; just counting on a growing ability to be psychically numb and invested in romantic fantasies. Often the intensity of my solitary rides was enhanced by a Rock and Roll sound track that played in my head and that carried me on wild dreams of Elvis-as-cowboy heroism. And when the music wasn't there, there were moody daydreams of alcohol-laced romances which usually took off on fragments of overheard adult gossip.

The problem of what to do with the horse was a serious one; and one which had no resolution that satisfied me deep down. The obvious thing was I had to sell him because I was going to college in the fall. That I wasn't ready for college was not up for discussion; why, I don't know. In retrospect it was an obvious error in somebody's judgment, but not a soul around seemed to have an alternative idea.

Sometime in late June or early July, I asked both Fanny and Roy if they would take Jerry. Fanny wanted no more horses and Roy didn't want Jerry, mostly because he wouldn't fatten up. Fanny said Harry de Leyer, owner of the famous plow horse turned show jumper Snowman,* was looking for a pleasure horse for his wife. I called de Leyer and he asked me if I could meet him at a show "Up Island." So,

Roy trucked us up there (me and Jerry) to Stony Brook that weekend, and Harry jumped him over a practice jump, said he was okay, and peeled off $500 for me. I'm sure I felt sad, but I kept grief stuffed and used the 500 bucks in my pocket as balm. On the way home Roy and I had a conversation about becoming attached to horses and he admitted his attachment to his family of horses that had started with Cappy and Topsy, who had given life to Blackie and Pawnee, and then Blackie's two colts, Chaney and Taffy. It was the closed thing we ever had to a conversation about feelings, and that was fine with me. To be able to keep a stiff upper lip gave me some sort of perverse pleasure. Of course, like my mother, I was covering up tons of hysteria, but by that time I was dependent on periodic drunks to kill those feelings. Roy was a cowboy after all and, when I was with him so was I, and cowboys don't cry. He was an English Yankee from an old Bonac family, and I was half Pierson, something I knew little about then but have added to my life script in recent years.

*See, "Eighty Dollar Champion: Snowman, the Horse That Inspired a Nation," by Elizabeth Letts, 2011, Random House.

Roy's filly Taffy
with my saddle and Navajo blanket

I continued hanging out with Roy and working for him, using it as my last summer job before college, cleaning harness, taking out hayrides and driving other rigs he rented for various occasions. And I broke his two year old mare, Taffy. That is to say, I was the first to ride her after she'd been driven in a three horse hitch and led around for a few minutes with a saddle on. There was never any bucking and she learned without much effort to start, stop, and go left and right. She seemed to be a mare with potential and, as I've said, I sometimes think I should have stayed with her and worked her into a competitive reining horse. She was well formed, though we were slightly disappointed with her Roman nose.

EPILOGUE

The summer went quickly. I was still riding Roy's horse Taffy several times a week, but it was getting closer and closer to the time to go. Right after Labor Day, I said goodbye to Taffy and was driven to the airport by Carolyn. It was the only time I would fly. From then on I would travel back and forth by bus, because it was cheaper. I hadn't saved any of the wads of cash I'd made from working for Roy, I'd spent it all on beer. I flew on a Constellation to Chicago and a DC-4 to Peoria. With my one Samsonite suitcase and $50 of spending money, I settled into my off-campus room. Without savings, the plan was that the parents would send me cash as needed. I didn't expect to need much and I was right about that.

The room I'd rented was nice enough. It was in a small one-story house on North Elmwood St, one block from campus. The houses in the neighborhood were Carpenter Gothic row houses, probably typical for outer reaches of small cities, being built in 1930s, designed by builders to look prosperous and larger than they were.

My landlady was a wizened old woman with a thick Yiddish accent, who was usually sitting in a rocking chair wrapped in a shawl. She had a face not dissimilar to the painting of my Serbian grandmother, hook nosed and bony-browed, but her hair was grayer and I thought she was smaller than my grandmother. The house had that old lady feel, antimacassars and doilies abounded. The dining room table was set with a lace tablecloth and aged and dented plates and silverware. There was of course a grandfather clock which, when everything was quiet, was the only thing you would hear.

Mrs. Lipkin spent almost all her time on the sun porch, often talking to her son, an accountant in Peoria, on the phone, in Yiddish. She had a television. She would sit in front of it with her gnarled little hand to her mouth as if she was contemplating with trepidation the goings on, her face sad and concerned, whether game show or news or whatever was on. It was fall, 1960.

She had only two rooms for rent, mine and one across the hall from me. The other tenant and I shared the bathroom. His name was Johnny Hassenjeager. He was German-American and was from Hinsdale, a suburb of Chicago. His hometown was like nothing I'd ever known, but seemed to be typical of towns throughout Middle America. His high school had fraternities, homecoming queens, and a well-subsidized football team, just like a college. Johnny was a short, well built, button-downed Bob Newhart type, with close-cropped hair like a member of the Kingston Trio.

I was all by myself halfway across the country and I was a kid who had never been alone for more than five minutes. But, the classes were not hard and held my interest. I had never before been so able to stay focused. I was enrolled in an Introduction to Journalism and a course in English, which was actually a beginning writing class, and a fascinating Psychology class that was so big it was taught in an auditorium, something I'd never heard of. The teacher was some sort of star, had longish white hair; wore sandals over knitted socks; was cleaver and witty and made Intro to Psych fascinating, with anecdotes about famous intellectuals he seemed to know, like Aldous Huxley, whom he looked like. Huxley was popular then, almost what you'd call a media star, living in Hollywood and all that.

I was taking a gym class that was obviously for nerds. I could even dribble the ball better than some of the guys. It was gym for dorks. And I took a drawing class. The teacher, right out of Carolyn's playbook, taught the Nicolaides Method! Kimon Nicolaides was a teacher at the Art Students League whom my mother studied with and who wrote a book on drawing called *The Natural Way to Draw*. Although published in 1941, the book along with his method is still in use today. I'd never actually done it, but knew what it was about and picked it up right away and was drawing in no time. One of the models was a jock I'd seen in gym. The teacher was probably gay, but there was no coming on, not even any sexual vibes. During that year I don't remember sexual vibes at all. Just my own well-suppressed lusting after some of the wholesome homecoming queen candidates as they walked across the Quad. It was a perfect small college for me.

I was just getting into the swing of things, very shy but getting along, when it was time for Thanksgiving. I took a Greyhound to New York City and then the Cannonball to Amagansett. There was something wonderful about the Greyhound Bus terminal in downtown Peoria. (Something I'd understand better, years later, after reading Denis Johnson.) I knew, and that was long before I knew what a portal was, that bus depots were the portals to the heart of America. It was near the Y, the inevitable home of whatever perverts hit the circuit, but also to those more romantic people who were just drifters; and it was across the street from a large music store which sold a few pianos and many guitars, from Martins to Les Paul, and which had a great supply of Country and Western sheet music. Upstairs there was a music school where I went for a few guitar lessons before realizing I couldn't afford them. The teacher impressed me enough so that I bought a purple rayon shirt, so that I could look like a Nashville studio musician.

I think the shirt was a bit too much for Hassenjaegger. "Nice shirt," he said. "Goes with your hayseed haircut." Well, that hurt to the quick. After all, I didn't have any friends and his was the only close contact I was having with humanity, the closest thing to intimacy, shall we say. I decided to do something and settled on modifying my haircut, combing it flatter, less Elvis. It was a timid adjustment, mostly a matter of pushing my oiled pompadour down with my hand. This, I felt, made me not a hick, but some kind of half-breed, with the potential, in fact, for some suggestion of intellectualism, something neither Elvis nor Hassenjaeger.

Although this was my first Greyhound trip, I felt right at home. There is something in low self-esteem that finds its own level. A feeling of comfort in being at the bottom of the social ladder. No place to fall. The bus depot; the bus; the next depot; a tavern. It is, after all, a way of seeing the world.

The bus had its one lonely GI with his pint bottle of whiskey, and several unescorted women, one with a snot-nosed brat and one with a crying infant and one that could have been crying inside, dressed in simple country clothes, seeming half-virgin and half potential slut. Was she going to New York to be ground into fodder on 42nd St? I couldn't say, in fact didn't care; I was caught up in my own frightened escape into fantasy about she and I becoming star crossed lovers.

By dawn, I had moved to the front of the two-decker Scenicruiser's second story, with only the road in front of me, and as we swayed two and fro on the two lane country road, it wasn't an express bus, I was thinking we were rolling along just a little too fast in and out of will-o'-the-wisp fog. Then, in front of us popped up a jackknifed tractor trailer, stuck on a rusty old steel bridge. I felt our driver hit the brakes and slide on glare ice in the early morning shade, smack dab into the tail end of the trailer. *Bango.* I was able to brace myself on the dome wall in front of me just in time to see the crash in wonderful slow-mo. Then I remember standing around, smoking and small talking for hours while we waited for a replacement bus. There were back pain complaints, bruises and some bloody foreheads and wailing and crying. An ambulance came and people were bandaged. There was time for the glare-ice to melt and for me to watch the muddy creek below and breathe in the thick air of the inland woods countryside and polish my bullshitting ability with the chain smoking, back-country-worldly bus driver.

Coming home to the house on Main Street, the feeling of being grown up was as uncomfortable as a pair of tight shoes, and my self-consciousness about it contributed to my nearly monomaniacal focus on one effort, that of introducing alcohol into my daily routine in as casually a way as possible. I had, after all, done something deserving; been away at college.

This being the first homecoming of an eventually much traveled Oedipus wreck, there was some intoxication just by virtue of being home. They were in fact glad to see me and the feeling was mutual. One warm bear hug from the Old Man undid all the loneliness of nights alone in my little room. They were as ready as I was to believe that a short trip away from home for a few weeks at an easy college where I could garner some good grades and pick up a few useful facts, were all I needed to be pronounced cured. Cured that is of what pre-Peoria could have been called, "What's-gonna-become-of-that-kid?"

There wasn't much time to do much of anything. There was time to scarf up a bourbon and soda, or two, or three, in an adult manner, without having to beg or cajole. I guess it was their expectation that with this symbolic facing of adulthood, I would now be able to drink like an adult. Those drinks, though, and I remember them all, those drinks my father fixed me, as if they were one, the grace with which he filled the glass with ice cubes, his strong, thick, sensitive fingers fluttering the cubes into the glass, the sound of it, the smell and golden color of the bourbon, it was bourbon still in 1960, later it would be scotch, for the Old Man; the fizz and nose tickle of the club soda which seemed to carry the booze on wings of angels; it did not, though, carry me any place I would have willed to go.

Tommy had gotten married to his girlfriend, Irene. I ran into her on one of my many trips across the street to the post office. (There was something comforting in renewing that ritual, like petting a long-lost dog.) She told me Tommy was tending bar evenings at the Amagansett Inn one hundred yards down the street, and that he'd probably love it if I dropped by.

Though I wouldn't reach legal drinking age for another six weeks, meaning I would no doubt be putting Tommy in jeopardy, that didn't cross my mind, as my overriding concern was that I be permitted to drink, so I made it a point to show up. Tommy was noticeably happy to see me, but also noticeably apprehensive about my being there, knowing, as he well did, that my legal drinking days were more than a month off. I had been one of the few kids in the graduating class not yet eighteen.

Irene is a wonderful optimist who till this day thinks Tommy is a perfect human being and, in fact, through her influence, he did in fact become a successful man and a terrific father. But I'm sure when she said drop in, she didn't mean stay all night and get shit-faced, and I probably didn't intend that either. But that's what happened. I drank a beer with Tommy, toasting to our health and good luck, and then had a second. The owner came in and didn't question my being there, baby faced me who had been seen around Main Street with Tommy since he and I were riding tricycles; so the heat was off, kind of. I might have left then; Tommy might have diplomatically suggested I call it a night; he was savvy and self-protective enough to do that, but with a boisterous entrance, in came a bachelor party of upper classmen I'd ridden to school with on the bus.

Eight or ten guys piled into the corner of the bar where there were three stools, one on each side of me, so tight I could hardly breathe, but I was too buzzed to take the hint and leave them to their reveling. They started talking about the fight. That was November of 1960, so it had to be the Patterson, Ingemar Johansson fight. They were going on, irritating my new found serenity and I popped up with what I thought was a brilliant contrarian crack designed to be annoying, or, as I thought of it, funny. "I'm for Johansson," I said, hearing some grunting approval. Pause. "Because I hate Catholics and Patterson is a Catholic." So ironic. And a parable too, meant to teach fools that prejudice is color-blind. I was just being a drunken smart-ass, no maybes about it. Anyway, this whole crew was Catholic, from the small Amagansett and Montauk churches, all either Italian or Irish with one French Canadian.

As a single mass of young manhood they burst into a rage. Being basically good guys, rather than beat my skinny ass, they began pummeling each other. A stool was broken; a dent was made in the far wall by the kitchen; Tommy ran onto the sun porch, to the old fashioned telephone booth, to call the police, and I faded into a corner and focused on my beer. The fight moved out the front door and then across the street and I could hear loud yelling and the white picket fence in front of the Perkins house began losing pickets. I was drunk. I faded in and out of consciousness, proud of my invisibility, and the next thing I knew all was quiet and I was standing at the curb, trying to make my feet move me off the curb and across the street to my bedroom, when from the east up the slight grade toward the Flag Pole I saw a police car approaching.

I rocked pleasantly on the curb and was still doing that a few seconds later when Sergeant Freddy Notel, Tommy's mentor and friend, pulled up, exited the car quickly and told me to get moving. I looked at him indignantly and said, "Don't rush me, I'll move in a minute." Of course, what I meant was, I'll move as soon as I can get this thing out of neutral, meaning my body, which was hinged at my feet to the curbstone. Freddy was pissed about having to leave his comfortable chair in the kitchen of his father's Inn on the Napeague strip. "You're coming with me then," he said, and threw me into the back seat, calling me a goddamn wise guy and swearing at me half way to the East Hampton jail, about two miles of dark country road to the west; which road was being eaten up quickly in the V-8 Ford.

Soon as I heard those jail doors clang behind me of course I sobered up (using sober in the old fashioned sense of meaning awake) and went into a state of fear, trembling, and self-loathing, the likes of which I hadn't yet experienced. I sat on the wooden bench, first clutching my knees and soon making the fetal position. My hearing became hyper-sharp and I could hear the cops in the next room; a standard Police Station entrance room where the floor behind the long box-like desk is raised two feet to intimidate the presumed guilty. They were talking about me in a nasty loud mouthed bravado, going on and on about my useless wise guy-ness and referring to me as the son of "that artist guy." The talking continued through the night as cops came and went, shifts changed and information was exchanged on the police radio. A moment's sleep brought on a headache which became a dry-heaving hangover which was, thank God, over by around 8am, when my father showed up with a lawyer.

The Old Man was unexpectedly sympathetic. It turned out he was sure it was a plot against him. He'd been talked into running for Town Democratic Committeeman, against Pete Rana the barber. The election, held just three weeks prior, had seen Ray lose by just three votes. My arrest was seen by Ray as an attempt at punishing him for having the audacity to confront the local pols. Well, I pretty much knew that my failure to disperse had been honestly seen as belligerence. How was Freddy supposed to know I was a victim of temporary paralysis? But it was convenient to sell out to Ray's way of thinking, which kept peace in the family against considerable odds.

Back at Bradley after a less eventful Greyhound trip, I continued to experience Peoria as an uncommonly safe space. In art class, which should have been called life drawing, I began to draw well, using the Nicolaides Method. I had been lectured on it by Carolyn throughout my life, without ever feeling the need to practice it myself. I always thought that one needed one's own studio, to draw.

I continued to play doofus basketball with the other nerds and in fact found myself better than some, which wasn't saying much. I wrote sentences and paragraphs which impressed my English Rhetoric teacher with my inventiveness and I found that I was actually turned on by the discovery that in Journalism I was fascinated by something to which I'd never really given much thought. And I also did well in science, which was Botany and Zoology at its most basic level.

Second semester I again did very well. I took swimming, which was the hardest class I had. I felt exhausted at the end of every class; felt like I'd drown, almost unable to lift myself out of the pool. I was too skinny and had no stamina; in the gym I would see guys who were semi-professional athletes (Bradley had one of the country's top basketball teams, though many of its members would later be found to be taking money from numerous sources.) I was grateful that two semesters of nerdball and one of swimming, was the end of athletics for me.

The only friend I made, beside my roommate across the hall, was a guy I met in life drawing, a tall gangly kid with dirty, greasy brown hair. He had a car, a '55 Chevy six-cylinder, and he decided, since we'd been sharing charcoal and had begun to converse, that he'd fix me up with a friend of his girlfriend. We went to a drive-in movie. Greasy haired guy, or I should say the other greasy haired guy, bought a pint of whiskey which we shared in our cokes and which loosened me up rather quickly. I became quite suave and my date, kind of an ordinary looking girl whose petite figure inspired me; was appropriately first-date coy. The date went well and we were well on our way to going steady but on a second date I got too drunk too soon and made our first make-out session into a case study of a fumbling dolt attempting to hide performance fear; too rough and too obviously inexperienced. No sex, just too quick to move from kissing to clumsy groping.

Forget-his-name was disappointed in me, but I retained my friendship with him long enough to get him to buy me a quart of whiskey, which I smuggled into my room and nursed for many nights, pouring a shot into a Coca-Cola for an evening of unwinding; unwinding I must have needed from my earlier, pre-Peoria life, since my life at that time was the least stressful I had ever encountered. Now I was able to experience a nightly buzz, free from the supervision of parents or the local Greek chorus in my mind, an out-of-focus vision of voices from my home town.

But the buzz that the whiskey gave me was short lived and accompanied by fitful sleep, nightmares, and the introduction of surprising repeating dreams of my horse, which dream visits continued for years. In the first dream my horse was in the little barn I had built him. Somehow, he had survived there for all the intervening time from prior to his having been sold until the present; unfed, un-watered, angry and terrified. The reason I knew he was terrified was because he told me. In these dreams he often talked to me. These horse dreams would follow me through life, with the horse aging along with me, growing taller and shorter and fat and fuzzy and on many occasions speaking to me in perfectly good English in a tone sometimes ironic and sometimes judgmental, like a conscience.

The clang of the jail door and the residue of the injection of shame and self-pity from the Thanksgiving arrest haunted me through the following semester, filling me with an ominous dread of future bad luck. With this dread haunting me, I began to gestate and then hatch the truly bad idea of transferring to a school nearer to home, as in New York City. My rationale was that the increasing sophistication of the place would enable me to grow up faster; that the environment would nurture my late blooming brilliance.

On the basis of my good grades at Bradley, two semesters of A's and B's to counteract those grossly bad East Hampton High School numbers, which, as bad as they were, were inflated, and should have been worse, I was able to transfer to New York University. Not, though, without some discouragement from the parents, who appeared uncommonly smart in questioning the leave-taking from Bradley, reasoning along the lines of, if it works why fix it? My grades, though, must have convinced them that I was transformed.

Ray had recently taken over the lease to an apartment on the west side of Manhattan in a building full of artists and photographers. There were two types of apartments in the building, huge ones in the front that included living space and separate studios, and smaller ones in the rear, like the one Ray leased, that had one bedroom and a large studio with a skylight facing north. The studio ceilings were two stories high.

The previous resident, Arthur William Brown, aka Brownie, had recently died. He was a famous illustrator going back to the 1910s and 1920s, a life member of the Society of Illustrators and a role model to the younger illustrators. He was a great lover of women, and in fact had introduced my mother to the world of illustrators when he was a judge at the Miss America contest in which she competed in 1926. It was as a result of his help that she had begun her career as a model and eventually, met Ray.

It seemed like a brilliant idea, getting maximum benefit from a rent controlled, $125 a month apartment. I would go to NYU and live at this fine address, 33 W.67th St. Next door was the Hotel Des Artiste and down from there at #15, lived the poet Robert Lowell and also Stuart Davis, who'd been there for years. My father would be in, on occasion, looking for illustration work, and would be able to do small jobs at "33." Having the studio would make that more feasible. It was becoming a necessity because the illustration business was dying.

A condition of this move was that I get a summer job in the city. Ray arranged for me to work as an office boy for his agent, Lester Rossin. So after a week's vacation at home, Carolyn drove me into the city with some new sheets and arranged my underwear drawer and I moved into 33. It was the summer of 1961, and my life seemed to be on a viable track. I had left childhood behind and entered something which bore a vague semblance to adulthood. Ray would come in, on occasion, and I'd be able to drive home with him. Carolyn too, loving the city as she did, looked forward to coming in. She seemed to like this apartment more than the other apartments Ray had rented for his short hops to the city during the decades of what she thought of as her exile in Amagansett; possibly, I suppose, because this apartment wouldn't be just for him, making it an outpost for a bachelor's life in the city, a place full of possible evidence of his philandering, such as unidentified scarves and lipstick stained cigarette butts.

Across the hall in the other rear, smaller studio, an illustrator named Al Moore would be there if I needed a mature hand. I was living at 33 for about a week when, on a Friday afternoon, Al Moore came by and offered me a bourbon. He was chatty. He revered my Old Man. Al was a burly guy, not much taller than me, a famous illustrator in his own right, having followed a similar career to that of Ray, the same magazines, but with his specialty being women of the pin-up girl type. (Many illustrators were particularly known for their type of woman, from the Gibson Girl to the Coby Whitmore girl.) Al wasn't at all intimidating, in fact he seemed almost meek, a characteristic I would soon connect, at least sub-consciously, to a probable addiction to booze. "That bed in there, Brownie's bed, it's been slept in by some gorgeous women, among them, Kim Novak!" He didn't say Brownie had sex with Kim Novak in that bed, that wasn't the way his generation talked. And he said it with love and admiration, and it was intended, I felt, to enhance my comfort in that bed; it did.

On the ground floor below was a portrait painter named Noel Rockmore Davis, aka Tuffy. Why Tuffy I don't know. Carolyn and Ray had known Tuffy, whose parents were Floyd and Gladys Davis, when he was a baby. The Davis' were both illustrators who had been friends of Ray and Carolyn since the Thirties. Though I never met Tuffy, he seemed to have no male friends, he was something of an inspiration to me in that he seemed to be forever escorting young, lean, pretty, bohemian type girls, ostensibly models, in and out of his place. In the big, front, duplex apartment on our floor was the photographer Phillipe Halsman.

City life was all new to me. I had been in to the city at the most once a year while growing up. I had no memories of living there. Ray told me the proper way to get to work, the IRT to the 42st shuttle, then through the Grand Central Station to the S.E. corner of the Commodore Hotel, where I could exit through the classic luncheonette that was there then, and where I would eventually begin stopping for coffee and a muffin. Also eventually, I would learn about the underground pathway across the street to the building on the S.W. corner of Lexington Avenue which housed a restaurant, a good cheap cafeteria that had stuffed cabbage that I loved.

My new job at Lester Rossin Associates paid less than $100 a week, but I wasn't paying rent, so all I had to worry about was food, transportation and of course, beer. The cost of cigarettes in those days was negligible. Rossin had about a dozen illustrators whom he represented, including my father; a couple of salesmen, a samples storage area where he kept samples of his artist's work, which his salesmen carried around the city to various magazines and advertising agencies, and a bullpen, where several commercial artists on retainer would do jobs too small to assign to the name illustrators. The bullpen artists had specialties, such as lettering, airbrush, and spot drawing, the drawing of small black and white sketches. There was also a production department, which prepared illustrations for shipping to various clients.

Part of my job was to work in the production room, also called the mat room, where mats were made for illustrations and packages were wrapped; and the other half of the job was to make deliveries all around town, usually in the Madison Avenue advertising area. There were two of us shleppers; we were called the mat room boys. Our boss was Charlie Stubbs, chief of production, or head of the Mat Room.

The other boy's name was Freddy. We were the same age, but he had been working at Rossin's for a year, having come straight from a high school in Rockaway. Fred seemed very cool. He knew the ropes, how to make mats and wrap packages; how to get to the various delivery destinations; how to walk there taking shortcuts, rather than take public transportation, so as to pocket some money from petty cash. Freddy could sing and tell jokes and do terrific imitations. Often, while we were talking, he would absentmindedly make sketches on the gray underboard that covered the mat table. Usually, they were portraits of Sinatra. For the moment, I assumed he wanted to be an illustrator, perhaps specializing in album covers.

Freddy was skilled at making friends, something which left me pleasantly surprised. My experience at making friends was limited after all by the sparse kid population in the Amagansett of my youth. It turned out I knew a little about the things that interested him; like art and illustration and drawing and pre-rock n' roll music, like, well, Sinatra. My father's record collection and his ahead-of-its time hi fi had immersed me in a more sophisticated spectrum of musical taste than most kids, hicks or not, would have been privy to.

The job at Rossin's was three-fold. Making mats was done primarily by the straw boss, Charlie Stubbs, but we were supposed to do it when Charlie was busy and we were supposed to learn how anyway as part of our job, wrapping and delivering packages, which were usually illustrations or preliminary sketches going to various magazines and ad agencies.

In the beginning, Freddy was assigned to go with me to show me the fastest routes. This allowed me to learn the proper attitude to adopt when entering various places of business. Freddy was able to throw himself enthusiastically into the pose of smart young sales person, artist or a "somebody," cruising down hallways and giving folks the sure-of-himself wave; he was good at adopting roles that could make an entrance go smoothly. Delivering packages, he was never a delivery boy, more of a baby-faced rep. I was not a natural, but I was a ready and willing student.

About once a month, all he could afford, Fred made the rounds of the lounges in Manhattan, looking for stars in general and Frank Sinatra in particular. He would bring along a demo record of himself singing and telling jokes and doing imitations. I began to go with him; to the Stage Door, the Carnegie Deli, Basin Street East, the Five Spot, the Metropole, and to one of Sinatra's favorite pizzerias, Louis and Gino's on 58th St. I always enjoyed these runs because Freddy took me out of my timidity. He showed me the world of the high-end lounge lizards, which I loved. It was after all 1961, and Sinatra's Rat Pack was the epitome of cool. Freddy, whose last name was Travalena, was, by the end of the Sixties, a successful stand-up comedian, a regular on the *Johnny Carson Show*, and later on in his career, a regular on *Hollywood Squares*.

About every other weekend I would go home to East Hampton. I was tied to the apron strings of my dysfunctional family in a way that was more needy and childlike than I knew, but I'm glad that home was still there, because I wasn't ready for anything else to replace it. I was after all eighteen and still a virgin.

Going home for the weekend I'd pack a flight bag, those were the thing in those days, bring it with me to Rossin's, and after work, take the shuttle and the IRT to Penn Station. I was doing something that seemed adult and interesting and gave me a little buzz that approached a feeling of competence. Right away, I developed the habit of stopping at Nedick's for a hot dog and orange drink. Very tasty.

It took me a few trips to figure out that you were best off waiting for the off-duty cops to get off the train at Patchogue before trying to fight the crowd in the bar car, but after several trips it began to seem like a well-blazed trail, getting to the bar car with its pools of spilt beer and stink of cigarettes and beer, in time to drink two or three beers before getting off in Amagansett.

There was a moment that summer when I looked out on our backyard and saw something that foretold a future. I could see the abandoned Banty chicken coop, the barn red car garage with its striped bass silhouette weathervane, its adjoining woodshed and its attached shed-roofed jeep garage where my empty saddle rack and horse feed bin still crowded the Old Man's fishing stuff. I could see the empty barbed wire paddock where Jerry had been, his former home already full of cobwebs, paint peeling, looking puny now, a year after his departure. Behind the paddock, at the back end of our acre of land, I could see the small orchard of mixed fruit trees, apple, peach and pear, nine dwarf trees in a square, looking crowded in now by the tall privet and arborvitae which hid the new development houses filling up the old potato field. This whole territory, so dense with childhood feeling, was in the process of rapid deconstruction. A new town was growing over the old one, very quickly. And, I felt blinded by a future beyond foretelling. The 60s were just warming up.

THE END

ABOUT THE AUTHOR

From 1997 until 2004, Anton "Tony" Prohaska was Director of The History Project, Inc. The author personally conducted 176 interviews with older residents of the town of East Hampton. The interviews are transcribed and housed in the Long Island Collection of the East Hampton Library, East Hampton, NY, along with over 1,000 archived photographs, donated by the interview subjects. Tony is retired and lives in Delray Beach, Florida with Martha Kalser, his companion of 18 years.

CPSIA information can be obtained at www.ICGtesting.com
Printed in the USA
LVOW12s2152011214

416601LV00002B/315/P